# The Effective Corrections Manager

## Maximizing Staff Performance in Demanding Times

### Richard L. Phillips
Criminal Justice Consultant
Colorado Springs, Colorado

### Charles R. McConnell
Principal
McConnell and Associates
Ontario, New York

AN ASPEN PUBLICATION®
Aspen Publishers, Inc.
Gaithersburg, Maryland
1996

Library of Congress Cataloging-in-Publication Data

Phillips. Richard L.

The effective corrections manager: maximizing staff performance in demanding times/Richard L. Phillips, Charles R. McConnell.

P. cm.

Includes bibliographical references and index.

ISBN 0-8342-0812-1

1. Prison administration—United States. 2. Correctional personnel—United States. 3. Personnel management—United States. I. McConnell, Charles R. II. Title.

HV9469.P47 1996

365′.068′3—dc20

96-3789

CIP

Editorial Services: Ruth Bloom

Library of Congress Catalog Card Number: 96-3789
ISBN: 0-8342-0812-1

*Printed in the United States of America*

1    2    3    4    5

# Table of Contents

# Foreword

In an era of dwindling government resources and a movement to shrink the size of government in the United States, corrections is one of the few areas where growth is the norm. Citizens, social scientists, politicians, and commentators from various disciplines express differing opinions about why this is so. These opinions are inextricably linked to discourse about why our society displays a propensity toward violence, why our citizens (and particularly our young people) turn to drugs, and why our inner cities are breeding grounds for so much dysfunctional behavior. However, these explanations do not erase the sad realities of American life today. More than one and one-half million people are in some form of correctional confinement throughout our country, and the growth trend that has taken our nation to this incarceration level is not likely to change in the foreseeable future. Indeed, the total U.S. correctional population now exceeds 5.1 million, including offenders on probation and parole, or in institutions. This figure represents 2.7 percent of the adult population in our nation.

Accompanying that regrettable trend is the reality that today's prisons are crowded and, in the view of many, far more difficult to manage than even a decade ago. Inmates are serving longer terms and many of them are not eligible for parole. Incentives like good time and some programs are being attacked as contributing to a too-lenient atmosphere of confinement. Many inmates come from a younger, gang- and violence-oriented subculture that does not place a high value on life or authority. Many others have styled their lives around a drug subculture, and have significant emotional and physical after-effects to overcome. Taken together, these factors and the pressures of crowding make prisons in the United States immensely difficult to manage.

These elements make it more important than ever for prisons to be administered in a professional, effective manner. Properly equipping prison managers for this task is critical. *The Effective Corrections Manager* is an outstanding reference work for those involved in either developing their own managerial skills or teaching others how to be effective supervisors in the prison environment.

Corrections is a field that was paid very little attention even a decade ago. Today, effective correctional management is an essential element in the stability and safety of prisons, and thus an important factor in the operation of our nation's criminal justice system. That is why this book is so timely and important. Richard L. Phillips and Charles R. McConnell have identified the central tasks of management at the level of the individual supervisor. They have given not only clear explanations of the dynamics behind those tasks, but also have provided real-to-life examples of how they are encountered in the prison setting. Both are experienced managers who have gathered together their skills into a single work that should be an indispensable guide to supervisors in the correctional setting.

*J. Michael Quinlan, BSS, JD, LLM*
*Director of the Federal Bureau of Prisons, 1987–91*

# Preface

*. . . the quality of prison life depends far more on management practices than on any other single variable.*

—*John DiIulio*

Were it not so vividly and demonstrably true, it might be trite to say that working in the field of corrections is one of the most difficult challenges in our society today. Many other occupations are challenging, and some—police work, for instance—can be dangerous in much the same way. But prisons—long out of sight and out of mind—now are a part of the collective consciousness of the United States. Our nation is experiencing serious public policy questions about how they are managed. As John DiIulio says in addressing this issue:

> Prison administration in a free society poses important questions of political theory and governmental practice. Prison managers govern men who are far from being angels. How ought they to govern? What are the ends of good government in the 'society of captives' and how can they be achieved?[1]

DiIulio, a respected scholar and commentator on corrections and the criminal justice scene, speaks mostly to the macro issues of correctional governance. But his observation about the importance of management practices applies equally well to the individual supervisor and the day-to-day management of prisons at the micro level. Anyone who has worked in a prison for any length of time can find their own examples of how poor management of people or resources at the individual department level has created major organizational problems, and in extreme cases, cost lives.[2]

The singular management challenges of corrections can be distinguished from those of other fields in a number of ways. Prison administrators are asked to protect the public from incarcerated criminals while coping with the problems of institutional crowding in an era of intense fiscal pressures. They must supervise and prevent violence among poorly socialized, aggressive inmates. They are obliged to provide drug treatment and literacy programming to poorly motivated subjects, and to gainfully occupy large numbers of inmates who have minimal or no work experience. They must balance the need to provide a reasonable level of programs and activities for inmates against the public's current sentiment that prisons provide too many amenities and that they are "resorts." No other occupation presents its managers with such a situation on a day-to-day basis.

These factors set corrections aside as a unique field, and many other published works have discussed macrolevel dynamics. Yet at the individual supervisory level, managing in the prison environment has a great number of traits in common with management in other specialties. Prison managers must monitor and control workflow. They must develop and stay within budgets. They must deal with employee performance issues. They must work in an organized labor environment. They must see that supplies are purchased, grounds maintained, plumbing repaired, meals served, hallways cleaned, and laundry processed. In those respects, prison work is not unlike that encountered in other total institutions such as the military, hospitals, and residential mental health facilities. True, in prison many tasks are performed by inmate workers who are not highly motivated and who may not even have the requisite skills for the job to which they are assigned. But to a large degree, prison management at the individual supervisory level has many, if not most, of the same underpinnings of management elsewhere in society.

This book starts from the central premise that many of the insights and skills that have proven so critical to successful management in the private sector and other public organizations are fully applicable to correctional management. Yet, one should bear in mind that supervision in corrections has some very different aspects that require adaptation.

One key difference between prisons and other service organizations and agencies is that the population served by correctional staff is held involuntarily. This produces a work environment that can be hostile and even dangerous at times. It also means that staff at every level must be concerned with security issues that present themselves in very few other occupations. Indeed, this comprehensive overlay of security concerns permeates the prison environment, affects virtually all management issues, and differentiates prison work from all others, save perhaps the high security environment of a locked mental health institution.

Related to this security overhead with which the prison manager must cope is that a prison's population generally has no vested interest in participating in the correctional process. Considering the societal mission of corrections—ensuring public safety and equipping inmates with skills that will reduce future criminality—this lack of inmate interest in supporting prison operations has very clear implications for the staff who try to manage work and other programs in prison.

Paradoxically, it also is true that prisons could not operate in an orderly manner on a day-to-day basis without the compliance of the inmate population. But that compliance is superficial at best. It is grounded in (coerced by, it may be argued) a well-defined security and supervision structure, and backed up by a disciplinary system that can levy considerable punishment against the noncompliant inmate. Every prison staff member is expected to participate in these critical security and control systems. One is hard pressed to find another managerial environment with these overtones, which impact line and supervisory staff equally.

Yet a third difference is that in most prisons the operation of the facility depends on manpower supplied by the inmate population. This bifurcated supervision situation means that a line staff member in the official chain of command also can be a first-line supervisor with respect to inmates working in his or her charge. While this book will not dwell on this aspect of correctional management, it is clear that many of the skills and personal traits that help managers direct staff activities also can apply to directing inmates.

A final difference is that all of the community-like functions of a prison are provided within a security apparatus that can vary from the very low constraints of a minimum-security prison camp to the extreme restrictions of secure penitentiaries. Thus, a manager at a camp will be far less constrained in directing day-to-day operations within the limits imposed by tool control, key control, inmate supervision, and other procedures, than will be the manager in a very secure facility.

These factors are important in understanding how the setting in which prison administrators operate makes their day-to-day management tasks somewhat different from their nonprison counterparts. But they do not mean that fundamental management principles do not apply to prisons, only that in some cases, special approaches are needed for their application. Managing a prison or any other enterprise hinges on effectively recruiting, training, directing, and motivating people, and for that reason at the individual supervisory level, corrections and other professions can draw on the same fundamental management principles.

This book is intended to be read and used by first- and second-line supervisors (including those supervising inmates), middle managers at the institutional and headquarters levels, those with or without formal training in management, and potential supervisors. It can serve as a refresher text for managers at all levels of the correctional organization. It also is pertinent to many upper-level managers—the people who supervise the supervisors of the supervisors—by lending perspective to the top-down view of what happens at lower levels.

Readers can use this book for general information about correctional management. They can use it also as a reference, seeking out specific topics through either the index or the table of contents. They can use it as a textbook for supervisory development classes. This text draws on the excellent material developed by author McConnell for his work, *The Effective Health Care Supervisor,* which is a parallel publication for health care professionals. But it is in every way keyed to the needs of managers in the prison setting, whether at a first-line level or higher in the organization. Most chapters include two or more prison-related case studies or exercises that illustrate or apply the material in the chapter they accompany. These may be used for individual reading and study or informal discussion, and are also intended as activities for supervisory development classes.

Readers will find that there is no required order to reading the material in this book. Although chapters deal with single topics, these topics relate to others discussed throughout the book. The topic of communication is a case in point; it is the primary topic of several chapters, yet the principles of effective communication make their presence felt in a dozen or more other chapters, and indeed this skill is essential for every aspect of management, in or out of the prison environment.

Because of this intertwining of subject material, chapters can be read selectively, but it may be most helpful to begin with the first four chapters for the sake of obtaining an overall perspective. Then read those chapters on topics of specific interest or that touch on a current problem. For instance, if the last meeting you attended was a disaster and you would like to learn about effective meetings, go straight to Chapter 19. Do not worry about skipping chapters that simply do not apply to your situation—just as long as you are certain they do not apply. For example, if you do not have budget responsibility at present, save Chapter 20 until later. Use your valuable reading time for the topics that will do you the most good on the job.

Whether in a prison or some other type of organization, supervision can be a difficult task. One of the conditions making it so is that in many cases there are no clear solutions to problems. If this book were presenting technical task instructions, it would simply say, "Here's how to do it, period." However, the problems of supervision more often than not are commonsense problems of people, most of whom are unpredictably, but quite naturally, different from each other. When presented with a specific problem, the so-called correct answer may be any one of several courses of action, or no action at all, depending on the people involved. The employee involved in technical tasks may spend much of the time in a world where options and choices are clearly delineated, while the supervisor has no such fixed guidelines for his or her actions. Parts of this book are concerned with necessarily gray areas for the correctional manager. The book can guide supervisors in making many decisions; it cannot, however, prescribe solutions to "standard" problems, since few such problems exist in the real world of supervision.

Whatever value this book possesses for corrections professionals lies largely in its potential as a working guide. Use it as your particular questions and needs suggest. If it helps you on the job in any substantial ways, even only now and then, it will have served its intended purpose.

---

## REFERENCES

1. J. DiIulio, *Governing Prisons* (Macmillan Publishing Co., Inc., The Free Press: New York, 1987), 7.

2. The field of corrections includes confinement facilities, probation, parole, and community corrections; the authors draw most of their experiences and examples from the institutional setting, but the management principles and practices described throughout this book are equally applicable to the nonprison segments of the correctional field.

# PART I

# The Setting

## CHAPTER 1

# Corrections: Is It Really Different?

*The end product of all business is people.*

—*Rensis Likert*

*So much of what we call management consists in making it difficult for people to work.*

—*Peter Drucker*

## Chapter Objectives

☛ Examine correctional management versus management in "industry" for similarities and differences.
☛ Provide criteria for typing organizations according to genuine differences rather than by product or process.
☛ Establish an appropriate overall perspective of the organization of the correctional institution.
☛ Identify several key department characteristics that point the way toward the supervisor's appropriate management style.

## PROCESS VERSUS ENVIRONMENT

### The Controversy

In the foreword, we noted a few of the issues that distinguish corrections from other professions, and at both the macro and micro levels, there are valid differences. And yet we presented what is the essential premise of this book—that there are certain core skills and traits that managers can use in all types of organizational settings, including prisons. For the questioning reader, that assertion alone may be insufficient. So we begin by looking at the opposing sides of an age-old argument:

It doesn't matter how well it worked anywhere else, it won't work here—this is a prison.

*versus*

Good management is good management no matter where it's practiced. What worked elsewhere will work in a correctional organization as well.

3

Since we plan to discuss supervision in the correctional setting in detail, it would seem sensible to explain which view governs our approach. Should we focus on the management *process*, thus agreeing that "good management is good management no matter where it's practiced," or should we give the most weight to the *environment*, agreeing that prisons are sufficiently different to warrant a completely different approach to management?

Many correctional managers are undecided on the fundamental issue of process versus environment. Often all organizational considerations are split into these two distinct categories, which are assumed to be mutually exclusive in some way. These considerations are condensed to corrections versus industry, with the latter category including manufacturing, commercial, financial, retail, and all other organizations not specifically devoted to correctional operations. Further, in this simplistic comparison, "industry" frequently becomes something of a dirty word. ("After all, we deal in human life.")

This debate has been refocused to some extent in recent years by the advent of private correctional firms, which manage from the perspective of the business world rather than that of some level of government. Private corrections is not a new phenomenon; for many years private firms have operated community treatment centers housing minimum-security inmates. But the expansion in the last decade of private firms into more traditional confinement facilities for low- and medium-security cases presents a novel situation for public sector correctional managers. For the first time, the precept of uniqueness is being seriously challenged. Privatization of the correctional function, it can be argued, validates at least part of the "process" viewpoint.

## The Nature of the Correctional Organization

That the process versus environment argument exists is not at all surprising when we consider the evolution and character of the traditional correctional organization. Many prisons of the past century provided only custodial care. For all practical purposes, there was only one occupation: the custodial (or security) service. The mission of the organization was security, and the only management activity was the operation of what was in those days called the "guard" force. Although some aspects of prisons involved providing inmate labor to the private sector for agriculture or manufacturing employment—a practice discontinued in light of serious abuses that developed over the years—little thought was given to operating a prison "like a business." In recent years, spurred by federal legislation, there has been a small resurgence in several states in the use of inmate labor in private industrial work projects. But this trend is not widespread.

The modern prison is vastly different from its counterpart of the past century, or even the prison of 30 years ago. The major purpose of a prison used to be custodial confinement with only basic services and very few, if any, self-improvement programs. That is now the primary mission of only a few ultra-maximum-security facilities where a relatively small number of extraordinarily dangerous inmates are held. In the 1990s, the role of the prison has evolved into that of an organization committed to public safety and institutional security, but which also has an obligation to society to offer programs and services that inmates can use, if they so choose, to reach the point where they can live lawfully upon release.

Prisons of the past had a unique mission, which they fulfilled in a simple, one-dimensional manner that had no parallel in other kinds of organizations, perhaps with the exception of the large residential mental health facilities operated by states until the 1970s. Correctional officers supervised even food service, laundry, and other functions, and those support functions were seen as an extension of the custodial function, rather than as separate disciplines. The only similarity with the activities of most other organizations was the direct supervision of the correctional officers who supervised the inmates—the basic process of getting work done through people.

However, the modern prison is far from one-dimensional. A large variety of services and programs are provided that require numerous complex and sophisticated specialized skills. A great many business functions, which are not specifically part of corrections but which are critical to the functioning of a prison, are present in today's prisons. Prison industries certainly provide an excellent example of this new posture, and in many other respects the prison of today resembles a business. Nowhere is this seen to be more true than in the relatively new area of private prisons, to which the management principles of this book are equally applicable. While effective management always was important, it has never been more so, as modern prisons are more crowded, more complex, and more subject than ever before to public and legal scrutiny.

## The Dividing Lines

The argument of corrections versus industry is frequently organized along functional lines. Today, many correctional employees have been originally trained in other kinds of organizations or educated in schools where they were concerned with a specialty field other than the management of prisons. These people, essential to the operation of the prison, include counselors, mental health and medical personnel, accountants, personnel specialists, maintenance staff, food service specialists, and computer specialists. While acquiring their skills in school and perhaps later practicing them in other settings, these individuals may have had no idea of applying these skills in prison. While government employment benefits can tie individual employees to a job, many see their functions as cutting horizontally across organizational lines and applying equally to prisons, hospitals, manufacturing, or any other field. The transition of these specialists into prison management ordinarily requires them to acquire more general knowledge about the field of corrections, in addition to developing specific management skills.

Other corrections professionals, however, do come into the field as a result of a specific, early career choice. College programs in criminal justice, corrections, and sociology often serve to feed entry-level correctional jobs. Courses in management and exposure to correctional management systems through internships may be included in these academic programs. In many correctional agencies, career ladders are established which allow these individuals to build on their academic training. The acquisition of specific, separate management skills that are tailored to the prison environment produces managers who think their field is unique and requires unique skills.

Part of the process versus environment argument seems to stem from the differing background and experience of these two categories of personnel, as well as the vertical versus horizontal view of organizations. Employees whose careers have noncorrectional origins may have applied their education and training in other lines of work; this can reinforce the horizontal view of organizations and encourage the belief that basic skills are transportable across industry lines. For example, a nurse in a community hospital may easily be recruited to work in a prison infirmary, and later move to a position in the private sector working for a managed care organization.

In contrast, staff whose education and training was tailored toward the specifics of the prison environment may have worked in other kinds of organizations, but often in entirely different capacities. Consider, for instance, the person who leaves a job in retail sales to go to college, and obtains a degree in public administration with a concentration in criminal justice. The person eventually takes a position in a prison as a case manager and progresses into middle- and upper-level management.

This path strongly reinforces a vertical view of organizations because the skills involved are specific to that kind of organization and are not readily transportable across industry lines. This individual likely may not view that early job experience in the retail field as part of his or her "real career" in corrections.

Certainly there are some differences between management in correctional organizations and management in other organizations. But once we have looked at the differences, we should concentrate on the validity of applying the same core skills and talents to a variety of organizational environments, including prisons.

## IDENTIFYING THE REAL DIFFERENCES

### A Matter of Need

Organizations come into being to fill certain needs. Business and government organizations of all kinds—including prisons—continue to exist because they provide something that people want or need. This truth is obvious in the business world; food wholesalers and grocery stores exist because people need food. While it may be less obvious, it is no less true that prisons exist because society has a need. It demands that certain types of criminal offenders be separated from other citizens because they are dangerous or because they will not stop committing crimes. Prisons meet that need, and other segments of corrections likewise fill societal needs that have less to do with security than with providing supervision and structure in the community.

> *Government is in business, of course, to serve its citizens, to provide goods and services that elected officials have decided are in the public interest. Citizens want those goods and services to be responsive. . .*[1]

It should follow that if a set of needs can be fulfilled in a number of different ways, the organizations that do the best job of responding to those needs will be the ones most likely to continue to exist. This is especially true in manufacturing, in which competition is keen and the organization that can meet public needs with the best product at the best price will stand the best chance of success. Among correctional organizations the competition to fill needs is less evident, but it is nevertheless there. This is best seen in the development of intermediate sanctions (punishments more stringent than probation and less restrictive than prison). It also is seen in the recent surge of interest in private prison operations, which appear to be able to provide some correctional services at least as well as and at less cost than government agencies.

## "Typing" Organizations

The basic error in considering correctional organizations as different is the classification of organizations by type, that is, by mentally assigning organizations to categories such as prison, manufacturing, retail, commercial, financial, and so on. Such classification is simply not sufficient to allow us to judge the applicability of supervisory practices across organizational lines. Rather, we need to examine organizations for the degree to which certain kinds of activities are present.

Disregarding organizational labels, look at the processes applied within organizations and the kinds of actions required to manage these processes. Look not at what we do but rather at how we do it.

## Two Theoretical Extremes

In his book, *New Patterns of Management,* Rensis Likert developed a view of organizations based on how they do the things they do.[2] He expressed much of his work in the form of a "scale of organizations" running from one extreme type to another. At one end of Likert's scale is a type he called the Job Organization System. This system evolved in industries where repetitive work is dominant, such as manufacturing industries using conveyor belts, assembly lines, and automatic and semiautomatic processes. This system is characterized by an advanced and detailed approach to management. Jobs lend themselves to a high degree of organization, and the entire system can be controlled fairly closely. If you are involved in assembly line manufacturing, it is possible for you to break down most activity into specifically described jobs and to define these jobs in great detail. You can schedule output, deciding to make so many units per day and gearing the input speed of all your resources accordingly. A great amount of structure and control is possible. All this calls for a certain style of supervision.

At the other end of Likert's scale is the Cooperative Motivation System. This system evolved in work environments where variable work dominates most organizational activity. Management itself is considerably less precise in this system. Jobs are not readily definable in detail, and specific controls over organizational activity are not possible to any great extent.

In many respects a prison is better described by the Cooperative Motivation System, despite its apparent regimentation and reliance on policy. Yes, we can make reasonable estimates based on experience—and can even develop post orders for each post that outline the major duties to be performed on that post. But it remains difficult to schedule output. It certainly would be possible to specify some correctional tasks with quantitative measures, such as performing not less than five cell searches each day or writing at least ten classification reports per week, although the mental image of so many inmates per day dropping off the end of a conveyor belt is ridiculous. Overall, close control is a much less prominent feature within the Cooperative Motivation System than in the Job Organization System.

What makes these differing organizational systems work? Likert contends that the Job Organization System depends largely on economic motives to keep the wheels turning. Everything is so controlled that the only remaining requirement is for people to perform the prescribed steps. What keeps the wheels turning are the people who show up for work primarily because they are paid to do so. These people are not expected to exhibit a great deal of judgment; they need only follow instructions.

In the Cooperative Motivation System, however, there are no rigid controls on activities. Jobs cannot be defined down to the last detail, activities and outputs cannot be accurately predicted or scheduled, and the nature of the work coming into the system cannot be depended on to conform to a formula. In the Cooperative Motivation System it is not sufficient that employees simply show up because they are being paid. This system depends to a much larger extent on each individual's effort and motivation to keep the wheels turning. Clearly Cooperative Motivation System is closer to the situation most correctional managers encounter than the Job Organization System.

Examined in their extremes the Job Organization System and the Cooperative Motivation System differ in several important ways. The most important difference lies in the role of the human element—the part that people play in each kind of system. Under the conditions of the Job Organization System, the system controls the people and drags them along; under the Cooperative Motivation System, the people control the system and keep it moving. Certainly this is true in prison, where many staff work in locations some distance from their supervisors and are expected to exercise a certain amount of independent judgment.

Regardless of an organization's unit of output—whether automobiles, toasters, or cell searches—we need to look at the amount of structure that is both required and possible, and at the variability of the

work itself. There are few, if any, pure organizational types. An example of the Job Organization System is the automated manufacturing
plant in which every employee is a servant of a mechanized assembly
line. At the other end of the scale, an example of the Cooperative Motivation System at work is the jack-of-all-trades, odd-job service in which
any type of task may come up at any time. Within corrections, the correctional services department of an institution represents a Cooperative Motivation System situation. There, staff in a variety of posts
throughout the institution deal with inmates with widely varying
needs. They may encounter everything from a drunk inmate to an attempted suicide, an escape attempt, or an inmate assault—each requiring a different response. Even though there are some prescribed tasks
associated with each security post, there is a wide range of discretion in
how they are performed. An even wider range of possible intervening
events occur out of sight of any supervisor and require independent
judgment and action.

### The Real World: Parts of Both Systems

Most organizations possess elements of both the Job Organization
System and the Cooperative Motivation System. In prison, running a
cellhouse is only generally predictable and does not lend itself well to a
rigid routine, while some elements of the booking process certainly are
amenable to an assembly line approach.

While the organization of the modern prison leans toward the description of the Cooperative Motivation System, there are internal exceptions and differences related to size and degree of structure. A small
institution, for instance, may demonstrate many features of the Cooperative Motivation System. On the other hand, while security functions
involve the kind of remote supervision and independent functioning
consistent with in the Cooperative Motivation System, a large facility
will include some departments organized along Job Organization System lines. For example, the records department of a prison entails
many highly procedural functions: there is a specific method prescribed
for calculating the length of an inmate's sentence, and the same people
repeat the same tasks day after day. Food service in a large prison with
many satellite food service locations may include an assembly line process and food delivery by food cart; the principles of this kind of operation are essentially the same as those for product assembly lines in
manufacturing. Laundry will include repetitive tasks that are highly

procedural, and repetitive functions may be found in many other departments as well.

## IMPLICATIONS FOR SUPERVISION

### Environment and Management Style

The concept of Likert's Job Organization System suggests production-centered management; the essential interest is in getting the work done, and the people who do the work are more or less swept along with the system. This system is rigid, and the people who keep the system going need only show up for work. On the other hand, the concept of the Cooperative Motivation System suggests people-centered management. More is required of the employees than simply showing up. They have to take initiative, perhaps make individual decisions and render judgments, and accept a measure of responsibility for keeping the system moving. Nowhere is this more true than in prison, where correctional officers operate semi-independently in supervising large numbers of inmates in housing units or activity areas.

It is perhaps unfortunate that businesses that evolved along the lines of the Job Organization System sometimes tend to overemphasize production while largely ignoring people. Under the Cooperative Motivation System, however, it is not so easy to ignore people—even by default—since the organization may function poorly or not function at all if people are not cooperative. To complicate the situation further, inmates are consummately skilled at exploiting differences among staff for illicit, disruptive, or dangerous purposes. This makes it all the more important that staff work cooperatively and within established policies, however broad or narrow they are.

Decision making can be vastly different for a supervisor in the Job Organization System as opposed to one in the Cooperative Motivation System. In the former, it is more likely to be procedural, with many decisions being made "by the book." In the latter, specific procedures often do not exist (and cannot exist because of the variability of the work), so it becomes necessary to rely heavily on individual judgment. This certainly would be the case for a prison watch commander, who may be responsible for a sprawling institution and the lives of hundreds of staff and thousands of inmates involved in a variety of activities. Policy and procedure may abound on the shelf back in the office, but when confronted with an angry group of inmates in the dining room, individual judgment, leavened by some personal courage, is the operative factor.

## Where Does Your Department Fit?

Decide for yourself what kind of organization you work in. Does it look like a Job Organization System or does it approach the Cooperative Motivation System? How your department measures up in terms of certain essential characteristics will have a strong influence on the style of supervision necessary to assure proper functioning. Examine the following characteristics:

- **Variability of work.** The more the work is varied in terms of the different tasks to be encountered, the length of time they take, and the procedures by which they are performed, the more difficult it is to schedule and control. Tasks that are unvarying and repetitive require supervisory emphasis on scheduling inputs and resources; work that is variable requires supervisory emphasis on controlling the activities of the people who do the work.

- **Mobility of employees.** If all the employees work in the same limited area and usually remain within the supervisor's sight, the supervisor need not be concerned with certain control activities. However, as employees become more mobile and move about in larger areas, there is a need for the supervisor to pay more attention to people who are out of sight much of the time.

- **Degree of professionalism.** There can be a vast difference in supervisory style depending on whether the majority of employees supervised are unskilled, semiskilled, or skilled. Many departments in a prison are staffed with educated professionals who are able, and expected, to exercise independent judgment. Managing the activities of professionals is considerably different from managing the activities of unskilled workers whose primary responsibility lies in following specific instructions.

- **Definability of tasks.** The more structure possible in work roles, the more rigid the style of supervision may be. For instance, the job of a sorter in a large prison laundry may be defined in detail by a few specific steps on a job description. Since the job is completely definable, the supervisor need only assign a well-trained worker and then follow up to see that the work is accomplished. However, the job of a line correctional officer is considerably less definable, because of task variability, the need for independent judgment, and other factors. There is likely to be more need for the supervisor to provide case-by-case guidance when necessary and to rely on the individual officer's independent judgment.

In general, despite the many rules and regulations involved in day-to-day operations, the organization of the modern prison facility leans toward Likert's Cooperative Motivation System, since the activity of a correctional institution is quite variable and centered around people. However, elements of the Job Organization System must be recognized as being present in the institution's policies, procedures, and post orders. This suggests that within any particular institution there may be the need for different supervisory approaches according to the nature of the functions being supervised.

## A Word about Quality

If all organizations exist to serve people's needs, it follows that quality should always be a primary consideration regardless of the form of the organization's output. Businesses basically organized along the lines of the Job Organization System tend to have frequent built-in quality checks at points in the process. As many manufacturers have discovered, however, quality must be built into a product—it cannot be inspected into it. Organizations tending toward the Cooperative Motivation System also have their quality checks, but these are less numerous and less specific. In the kind of organization that relies heavily on individual enthusiasm and motivation, there is considerably more reliance on the individual employee to produce acceptable quality work.

## External Pressure: An Area of Increasing Concern

The "prison-is-different, period" argument generally does not succeed in differentiating correctional management from other supervisory areas. There are nevertheless some legitimate differences in the form of outside pressure that are making themselves increasingly felt in corrections.

This is not to assert that corrections has a monopoly on external pressure. Every work organization that serves people in any way experiences pressure from outside, even if that pressure is as basic as competition from others in the same business. We will not even claim for corrections the burden of maximum external regulation. Other businesses such as hospitals, insurance, banking, and public utilities are highly regulated as well.

But in some cases prisons and entire correctional systems are under strict court supervision which governs many details of facility and agency operations. Growing judicial intervention, increasing financial constraints, and mounting public scrutiny of prison operations are combining to create a unique, frequently high-pressure work environment for the correctional manager. This interventionist environment began to emerge in the mid-1970s and there is every reason it will continue through the decade of the 1990s and into the next century.

Some undeniable forces have entered the field of corrections and are reshaping the way that supervisors do their jobs:

- The cost of sustaining correctional operations continues to rise as the incarcerated population in the U.S. grows. Correctional budgets now compete with education and other vital public services for scarce funds.
- Public expectation for high-quality prison operations and programs (such as drug treatment and literacy training) continues despite constant pressure to contain or reduce costs.
- Many segments of the public are beginning to voice objections to programs that are believed by corrections administrators to be valuable but which the public views as unnecessary or even as "perks."
- Privatization, once confined only to community corrections, is becoming increasingly accepted for higher security inmates. This places a form of competitive pressure on public sector corrections as well as pressure through employee unions that fear a loss of members to these generally non-union organizations.

These and other factors place pressure on the individual supervisor to continually strive to produce more with less. Since the prison organization tends toward Likert's Cooperative Motivation System, with its dependence on individual employees to maintain order and oversee inmate activities, the supervisor also must inspire the employees to willingly work under increasing pressure while conserving scarce resources.

Finally, some have claimed that a preponderance of rules and regulations should make prison management easier; one has only to follow what is prescribed. To the contrary, burgeoning rules and regulations have made some aspects of prison management considerably more difficult and complex. The reality is that the desired outcomes—public safety and humane treatment of inmates—often come only by creatively finding a way through the obstacles.

## Your Supervisory Approach

We should not be misled by what we see as differences between types of organizations. Correctional organizations are indeed unique in terms of the output they produce, but they are not necessarily unique in terms of the management processes employed. Again, examine your own department. How is it put together? How variable is the work? What degree of structure is required? To a large extent, your approach to supervision will be determined not by the idea that "this is a prison, not a factory" but rather by the kinds of employees you supervise and the nature of their job responsibilities.

---

## EXERCISE 1–1: WHERE DOES YOUR DEPARTMENT FIT?

Take a few minutes to rate your department according to the four characteristics discussed in the chapter: (1) variability of work, (2) mobility of employees, (3) degree of professionalism, and (4) definability of tasks. Although this assessment will necessarily be crude, it may suggest where on the "scale of organizations" your department is to be found.

Rate each characteristic on a continuous scale from 0 to 10. The following guides provide the ends and the approximate middle of the scale for each characteristic:

### Variability of Work

    0 = No variability. Work can be scheduled and output predicted with complete accuracy.

    5 = Average condition. Workload predictability is reasonable. Advance task schedules remain at least 50 percent valid.

  10 = Each task is different from all others. Workload is unpredictable, and task scheduling is not possible.

### Mobility of Employees

    0 = No mobility. All employees remain in sight in the same physical area during all hours of work.

    5 = Average condition. Most employees work within or near the same general area or can be located within minutes.

  10 = Full mobility. All employees continually move about the facility as part of normal job performance.

## Degree of Professionalism (by virtue of degree, licensure, certification, or some combination of these)

0 = No professionals are employed in the department.

5 = About half of the employees are professionals.

10 = All the employees are professionals.

## Definability of Tasks

0 = All jobs are completely definable in complete job descriptions and written procedures.

5 = Average condition. There is about 50 percent definability of jobs through job descriptions and procedures.

10 = No specific definability. No task procedures can be provided, and job descriptions must be limited to general statements.

Take the average of your ratings. This may give you a rough idea of whether your department leans toward the Job Organization System (an average below 5) or the Cooperative Motivation System (an average above 5).

## Question

Assuming your ratings of the four characteristics are reasonable indications of the nature of your department, what can you say about your supervisory approach relative to each characteristic?

## Suggestion for Additional Activity

Try this exercise with a small group of supervisors (perhaps three or four) who are familiar with your department's operations. Try to arrive at a group rating for each characteristic.

---

## CASE 1-1: IT ISN'T IN THE JOB DESCRIPTION

George Morton, the prison's maintenance supervisor, felt a growing frustration with general mechanic Jeffrey Thompson. Morton considered Thompson a good mechanic, and this opinion was continually reinforced by the consistently high quality of Thompson's preventive maintenance work, his success in completing difficult repair jobs, and his ability to supervise his inmate work crew.

Morton's frustration arose primarily from Thompson's apparent lack of motivation. Thompson always needed to be told what to move on to after each job was finished. If he were not so instructed, he would take a prolonged coffee break until Morton sought him out and gave him a specific assignment. Sometimes he would even send his inmate crew back to the housing unit in the middle of the day, which created problems for the unit staff.

Morton's frustration peaked one day when a small plumbing problem got out of hand. He knew that Thompson had to have seen the leaking valve because it was beside a pump Thompson and his inmate crew had been rewiring. However, when Morton asked Thompson why he had done nothing about the valve, Thompson said, "Plumbing isn't part of my job."

"You could have at least reported the problem," Morton said.

Thompson shrugged and said, "There's nothing in my job description about reporting anything. I do what I'm paid to do, and I stick to my job description."

"You certainly do," said Morton. "Jeff, you're one of the best mechanics I've ever seen. But you never extend yourself in any way, never reach out and take care of something without being told."

"I'm not paid to reach out or extend myself. You're the boss, and I do what you tell me to do. And I do it right."

"I know you do it right," Morton agreed. "But I also know that you usually stretch out the work, just like I'd expect an inmate to do. I know you're capable of giving a lot more to the job, but for some reason you seem unwilling to work up to your capabilities."

Again Thompson shrugged. "I stick to my job description and I do what I'm told."

## Instructions

1. Consider first the kind of employees Morton supervises and the kind of work Thompson does, and try to apply the scale in Exercise 1–1 to an assessment of Morton's supervision of Thompson (variability, mobility, professionalism, and definability).

2. Must Morton's approach to supervising Thompson be more people centered or production centered? Why?

3. Do you basically agree or disagree with Thompson's literal adherence to the letter of his job description? Why?

4. Put yourself in George Morton's position and consider how you might deal with Thompson. In sets of written steps or guidelines,

describe two ways in which you might go about trying to get this employee to perform more in line with his capabilities.

---

## NOTES

1. J. DiIulio, et al., *Improving Government Performance* (The Brookings Institution, Washington, DC, 1993), 49.
2. R. Likert, *New Patterns of Management* (New York: McGraw-Hill, 1961).

## CHAPTER 2

# Management: Definitions, Titles, and Other Intangibles

*Treat people as adults. Treat them as partners; treat them with dignity; treat them with respect. Treat people—not capital spending and automation—as the primary source of productivity gains. These are fundamental lessons from the excellent companies research.*

*—Tom Peters*

## Chapter Objectives

☛ Provide a working definition of management and establish management as the generic term descriptive of all persons who run organizations or organizational units.

☛ Relate supervisor and manager to each other and to other labels applied to managerial positions.

☛ Clearly identify the supervisor as a manager.

☛ Differentiate between management as a generic term and the various labels used to identify managers in organizations.

## IN SEARCH OF DEFINITIONS

### Management, Manage, Manager

Managing people, in prison or not, is a complex activity. Learning how to "do" management has to begin with knowing what it is. *Webster's New 20th Century Dictionary* (unabridged) defines management as: the act, art, or manner of managing, or handling, controlling, directing, etc.; skill in managing; executive ability; the person or persons managing a business, institution, etc. Synonyms for management include *treatment, conduct, administration, government, superintendence,* and *control.*

Note that management is defined repeatedly in terms of its root word, *manage.* The word *manage* comes from the Latin *manus,* meaning hand. We might feel we are on the right track, since this origin

19

suggests the use of this part of the body in working or doing. However, the original English definition of *manage* is to train a horse in its paces; to cause to do the exercises of the *manege* (defined as the paces and exercises of a trained horse).

The word *manage* developed from the description of a specific kind of work. Yet among the many definitions of manage are the following: to control or guide; to have charge of; to direct; to administer; to succeed in accomplishing; to bring about by contriving; and to get a person to do what one wishes, especially by skill, tact, or flattery. Synonyms for *manage* include *administer, conduct, control, direct, regulate,* and *wield.* These provide little new information about managing or management—either the words or the concept. However, the list of synonyms for *manager* is of interest because it includes the following: *director, leader, overseer, boss,* and *supervisor.*

### Supervisor versus Manager

At least in some uses the term *supervisor* is the same as *manager.* The same dictionary defines supervisor as a person who supervises, a superintendent; a manager; a director. Based on proper use of the English language, then, we can say that supervisor and manager are equal in definition: a manager is a supervisor and a supervisor is a manager.

On a working basis, we will use the terms interchangeably throughout this book. However, the idea of supervisor and manager being equal may not be agreeable to everyone. All of us have ideas of what a supervisor is and what a manager is, and all of our conceptions are not necessarily the same. Our understanding of what these terms mean—the positioning in the organization of persons who may be called managers, supervisors, directors, administrators, or whatever—is largely determined by the use of these words and titles. It is important to realize that our particular definitions of these terms are not absolute. Rather, we and our organizations have artificially created these differences in meaning. The chief correctional supervisor responsible for hundreds of correctional officers may officially be called the Captain, and a case "manager" may supervise only a secretary. A records supervisor, when asked to consider enrolling in a management training program, said, "No. I'm not a manager—I'm just a supervisor." Differences in how we see supervisors and their titles in relation to people who run other organizational units interfere with our complete understanding of what is and is not "management."

## A PRACTICAL DEFINITION

Throughout this book we will be using *management* to mean the effective use of resources to accomplish the goals of the organization. Management can be described as getting things done through people. Regardless of your title, as long as you are responsible for getting work done at least in part by directing the activities of others, you are a manager. This applies to the working chief of a three-member maintenance crew or the working supervisor of a four-person inmate records department as well as to the administrator of a small prison camp, the chief executive officer of a major penitentiary, or even the director of an entire correctional agency. These bottom and top levels both constitute management, just as the people directing the efforts of others at numerous intervening levels also belong to management.

Throughout this book we will speak of management in the broadest generic sense, referring to the processes applied and not to particular job titles. In this context, everyone who directs the activities of others is a manager. By that definition, every employee who supervises inmates—whether the single inmate janitor in a business office or housing unit or hundreds of inmate workers in a prison factory—is a manager.

### Organizational Labels

*Label and Level*

It is easy to guess how so many different organizational labels for manager developed. It was most likely a matter of organizational convenience, initially adopted to differentiate between managers at different levels or in different roles. It could be quite confusing if all three levels in a particular prison's business office carried the title of manager. Rather, it makes considerably more sense to identify them as controller, business office manager, and accounts receivable supervisor.

The use of *manager* and its synonyms as position titles did not develop uniformly in all organizations. We are likely to find that the inmate records departments of four different correctional facilities in different states are run by a records manager, records supervisor, chief of inmate records management services, and records officer, respectively. There is little overall comparability of titles from one organization to another. In one institution, a "supervisor" may be low person on the managerial totem pole and in another may be in the middle or upper part of the hierarchy. The term *manager* also may apply anywhere as a title in the organizational pyramid in almost any institution.

## The Supervisor

Despite this variation in usage, it is probably fair to say that when we hear "supervisor" used to describe a working position, we usually imagine a position in the lower part of the management structure. For this reason we will regularly use the term *first-line supervisor* to describe the lowest level of management in the organization—the lowest level at which persons manage the work of other persons. We will also refer occasionally to the *second-line supervisor,* meaning the second level up—the "supervisor of the supervisor." These title conventions refer to staff supervising staff, although employees in any of these positions could also be first-line supervisors of inmate workers.

## Upper and Middle Management

As the label "top management" suggests, this is the person or people at or near the top of the organization who are responsible for the entire agency or a major prison. Between top management and supervision we may find a number of positions generally referred to as "middle management." Middle management may or may not include many people, depending on the size of the organization.

Organization size may render a large part of the "middle management" discussion irrelevant. In some organizations, such as a small prison camp or halfway house, the first line of supervision is likely the only line. In a small facility the person responsible for maintaining inmate records (and who may be the only employee performing that function) could report directly to the facility administrator, so there is no middle management between the top and bottom levels.

## Line and Staff

It is beneficial to differentiate among managers as to whether the functions for which they are responsible are line or staff: A line function is one that advances the accomplishment of the actual work of the organization; a staff function supports the organization so that it is able to function as intended. For instance, in a prison the departments responsible for security, food service, laundry, educational services, and medical care are among those considered as line activities. The personnel department and the business office are staff activities. The difference between line and staff activities is between doing and supporting.

In terms of formal title, a person can be described as a manager of a line activity or a manager of a staff activity. However, whether the overall function of the department is line or staff, the manager, within the individual department, possesses line authority in the management of the department's employees. Within each function there is a line of authority that extends from the department head down to and including the first-line supervisor. For instance, in the custodial, or security, department of a prison, the line of authority, viewed from the top down, may be: chief of security, captain, lieutenant, sergeant, and correctional officer. Ordinarily, each person at each level directs the activities of those at the next lowest level in a manner that may be felt through the entire line of authority; instructions from the chief of security ultimately result in actions by correctional officers.

In the last sentence above, *ordinarily* acknowledges that in large departments some staff may perform separate support functions for that portion of the organization alone. For instance, within a security department, a lieutenant may be identified as a special investigative officer to handle internal investigations against staff or inmates. He or she would report to the chief of security, and even if a clerk or subordinate investigators were assigned to support this function, the investigative supervisor serves in a staff, rather than line, role in relation to the security department.

The staff of every correctional facility necessarily consists of persons working in both line and staff capacities. Often there is confusion about the degree of authority staff persons are to exercise, and problems sometimes arise from the three-way relationship among a line employee, a staff employee, and the staff employee's line manager.

A great deal of the potential for this problem may be inherent in the way the staff person projects him- or herself into interactions with line employees. The staff employee may appear to be making decisions and following up on them, allocating certain kinds of resources, and even conveying instructions and direction to others. The employee occupied in a pure staff function often appears to be the holder and exerciser of all management prerogatives except the critical one that essentially defines a manager—the authority to direct other people. We might even say that an effective staff person often looks, sounds, and acts like a manager. This frequently causes problems for some line personnel because they perceive that a person lacking proper authority is intruding into another's territory.

Sometimes this misapprehension of authority is because of the place the staff position is in the organization, such as an "executive assistant" to a highly placed executive. Persons in this position have no line authority, but serve in a staff role to their supervisor, the warden, for example. However, to a certain extent the executive assistant carries an aura of authority based on that of the supervisor. Line staff may react to the assistant's comments without regard to their own supervisor. The potential problems of this kind of situation are many.

Often line managers do not know how to make fully effective use of the staff assistance available to them. Some line managers tend to view staff people as regulators or intruders rather than use them as the advisers and helpers they really are. Also, some managers behave as though they believe a request for staff assistance—or even an agreement to accept staff assistance when offered—constitutes a weakness or an admission of inadequacy. In short, the line manager who does not completely understand the role and function of staff personnel often tries to go it alone, attempting to be all things in all situations, operating without the available staff assistance.

The difference between line and staff is the essential difference between doing and supporting. As for nonmanagerial staff, line personnel do, and staff personnel support. But as for managers, all are line managers in the operation of their own departments and in the direction of their own employees. Their functions may be clearly defined as staff functions—like accounting and human resources—but as managers they are by definition line personnel when operating as managers within their own departmental chains of command.

Many correctional organizations are organized along functional lines, giving rise to another way of grouping activities for organizational purposes. We often see prisons structured along a three-way division of functions:

1. custodial (perimeter security, yard patrols, housing unit supervision)
2. program (case management, counselling, religious programs, and others)
3. operations (food service, laundry, business office, payroll, general accounting, maintenance).

Within these three areas, centralized departments are organized along traditional lines of authority.

As a variant on this model, some facilities organize what are identified above as custodial and program staff into what is commonly called "unit management." Under this system, multidisciplinary staff supervised by a unit manager oversee the operation of one or more housing units. Correctional officers, case managers, and education and mental health personnel have varying levels of responsibility to the unit manager, as well as to a supervisor in their specialty discipline. This more decentralized method of delivering services to inmates is considered by many correctional systems to offer considerable communication, supervision, and program delivery advantages, since typically all unit staff have their offices in the housing area.

## A TITLE AS MORE THAN A LABEL

We have been talking about titles of managerial positions and the various uses of such titles to differentiate levels of responsibility, but we should also consider the use of titles as "status points" or as a form of "psychic income." Not long ago most prisons were run by top managers known as wardens. Now, however, we see many chief executive officers, executive directors, superintendents, and similar titles in addition to wardens. The functions and responsibilities of a position may have changed little if at all between the days of warden and superintendent, but the latter title may sound more impressive or professional to a larger number of people than the former title. Differences in title do matter in terms of how some people see themselves and how other persons view the positions of the title holders.

Title differences are significant only to the extent that they may affect your view of your position. Avoid falling victim to the attitude of the person who said, "I'm no manager—I'm just a supervisor." As a supervisor you are in fact a manager, and it is important that you see yourself as a manager and clearly consider yourself to be a member of the collective body known as management.

---

### EXERCISE 2–1: LABELS AND TITLES

Identify and list all the managerial titles used within the entire prison and within the function or department in which you work (for instance, security, personnel, inmate records).

### Questions

1. Which titles do you find most descriptive of the positions to which they apply? Why?
2. What is the line of authority (by position title, from highest to lowest) within your function or department?

3. Is your overall function a line activity or a staff activity? What makes the difference?

---

## CASE 2–1: BALANCING THE FUNCTIONS

Janet Morgan was associate warden at a large medium-security prison. She was an outstanding example of someone who had come up through the ranks; she had been a line correctional officer, sergeant, lieutenant, captain, and chief of security. As her career progressed, she worked her way through college, earning a degree in public administration with a minor in criminal justice.

Because of her broad knowledge gained through experience and academic study, she was seen as a key resource person for assuring that the security functions of the institution were in order. The chief of security, Bill Hallaran, came to rely on her to oversee some of the detailed technical aspects of the institution's security program. She found herself resisting these intrusions on her wider management role. Eventually, her direct involvement in the security program created a problem.

One day the warden asked, "What's wrong between you and Bill Hallaran? He claims that you're not providing him the support he needs on revamping the tool control system and some roster management problems he's been having. He says the roster management committee, in particular, has just about fallen apart because you wouldn't take the chair and see that things got done. Is your work piling up to where you've got too much to do?"

Janet shook her head. "No, my own workload is under control. I know that Bill has needed some help recently because of the state hiring freeze and the fact he hasn't been able to fill those three vacant lieutenant slots. Some of the things he does are hands-on tasks that are pretty technical and detailed, and I always could do that kind of thing easily. Others, like chairing the committee, I can do easily, because everyone defers to me as associate warden, even though that means the committee isn't functioning as the independent body it should be. Actually though, I think the problem really is that I seem to be in a dual role that I'm not comfortable with, and he's become dependent on me to help run his department."

"If that's all there is to the problem, won't it sort itself out when the hiring freeze is lifted and we can promote some people?"

"Yes and no. There's another level to this. Things have reached the point where I don't really know if I'm an administrator, or if I've slipped back to almost being a department head, or neither, or both for that matter. I know how to run that department—you know that very well. But it doesn't—well at least it shouldn't—take a manager at my level to see that tool and key control are running like they should, or that we're getting the most out of staff on the roster. Those things are technical details that are Bill's job, and I can't afford to let my other departments go in order to spend half my time running his. I know that, but I also can see that I'm probably doing even more of Bill's job than I really need to be doing."

Janet continued, "The real problem is that I've always believed that the basic job of a manager was to get things done through people, and I've tried to practice that ever since I entered management. But I slipped back into doing the technical side of Bill's job so easily that I'm worried that maybe taking an associate warden's job was a mistake. I guess I really don't know if I'm supposed to be in upper management or in a more hands-on position that has a technical side."

This case represents a common problem for prison managers as they move up the organizational ladder. They know their former discipline—in this case security—very well. If a lower level manager in that area needs help or is not performing exactly as the supervisor would have in the same situation, then the temptation is great to take over the function. This restores the upper manager's comfort level about that department, but it takes its toll elsewhere in the organization.

### Questions

1. How is Janet functioning at two organizational levels in this situation?
2. Do you agree that Janet's performance of technical work as described could be a sign that "taking an associate warden's job was a mistake," as she fears? Explain your answer.
3. Describe one set of circumstances under which Janet's involvement in the technical tasks described would be fully appropriate.

## CHAPTER 3

# The Nature of Supervision: Prisons and Everywhere

*As we are born to work, so others are born to watch over us while we are working.*

*—Oliver Goldsmith*

### Chapter Objectives

☛ Define the two-sided role of the supervisor as both "functional specialist" (worker) and "management generalist" (manager).

☛ Explore likely reasons for a supervisor's tendency to emphasize one side of the role at the expense of the other.

☛ Introduce the overall responsibilities of correctional management in general.

☛ Establish the nature of correctional management as a strongly people-oriented process unavoidably concerned with day-to-day problems.

## BORN TO WORK OR WATCH?

We often create problems for ourselves by behaving as though Oliver Goldsmith was in fact correct when he made the statement quoted above. Perhaps we can safely assume a bit of cynicism or resignation in Goldsmith's words, but certainly those of us who work for others (as opposed to working for ourselves) are occasionally inclined to agree. We think that people in our organization fall very neatly into preordained managerial and nonmanagerial categories. But regardless of some appearances to the contrary, no one is "born" either to work or to oversee the work of others.

Also, by separating work and watch, Goldsmith's words convey the impression that overseeing is not to be considered work. Unfortunately, many people nurture the feeling that supervision is not real work. We usually find that people who hold this belief are not and have never been supervisors.

Although we cannot say that someone is born to work or born to supervise, we can suggest that supervision is an activity for which a person can exhibit a talent. Many people are called on to become supervisors because they have exhibited talent for certain kinds of work—usually the same kinds of work they are asked to supervise. However, talent for doing manual, technical, or professional work is no guarantee of the presence of talent for supervision. Although the supervisory and nonsupervisory work may both be closely related to the same human activity, doing one well does not guarantee that the other will be done equally well. If you consider the occupations of cook and kitchen supervisor, for instance, you will find that the two are closely related positions, but that it is not necessarily true that the talented cook will automatically be a talented kitchen supervisor.

## THE SUPERVISOR'S TWO HATS

Most first-line supervisors in prisons function in the dual capacities of worker and supervisor. They are constantly required to fill two roles, the functional specialist and the management generalist.

The functional specialist is the worker who is responsible for doing some of the basic work of the department. The correctional officer, the records technician, the telephone switchboard operator, the secretary, the maintenance mechanic, the accountant, and many others are required to perform hands-on tasks involved in actual inmate supervision or supporting the institution's security or program operations. Almost everyone in the organization is or has been a functional specialist of some kind. In any given department, the specialist is ordinarily concerned with some function that is unique or nearly unique to that department.

The management generalist, on the other hand, is concerned with activities that are common to many departments and to most situations in which someone must guide and direct the work of others. Regardless of whether the manager began his or her career as an officer, technician, accountant, maintenance mechanic, or whatever, running a department requires that the manager be concerned with staffing, scheduling, personnel management, budgeting, and other activities that apply to many departments.

The nonsupervisory employee is a pure functional specialist. Only in some instances, however, is the manager a pure management generalist. Certainly there are few if any management generalists among first-line supervisors. Generally, the smaller the organization or department, the more likely is the supervisor to be both worker and manager. The supervisor of a four-person maintenance department will probably be a maintenance mechanic and jack-of-several-trades as well. The manager of a three- or four-person inmate records department will spend considerable time on nonmanagerial tasks. The unit manager in a 30-cell special housing unit may spend more time on hands-on inmate issues than on performing managerial duties. Only in the upper levels of management are we likely to find a few generalists.

The first-line supervisor, then, is both worker and manager and needs to recognize this fact. However, this recognition alone is not enough, for sometimes the wearing of these "two hats" is fully as difficult as wearing two real hats at the same time.

A natural leaning toward one of the supervisor's two roles is created by the nature of management itself. Management is not nearly as well defined in its own right as are many of our working specialties. When we consider specialties such as plumbing, accounting, nursing, or social work, we are able to categorize these according to certain characteristics. We associate each with an expected amount of education and training and perhaps the awarding of a diploma, degree, or license. For instance, a psychologist may be defined as someone who has successfully completed a certain number of years of higher education, received a diploma or degree, perhaps completed a clinical internship, and then passed a licensing examination. Especially among the professions requiring higher education, specialties are well defined in this manner. Even in occupations requiring little or no college level work, we can find a considerable degree of definition through simple instruction, on-the-job training, and experience.

Management as a separate field, however, defies the kind of definition just described. Although a few people trained as so-called management generalists may be identified in the middle and upper levels, in management's lower levels there are no sound criteria for defining "manager" without instantly raising the question: "Manager of what?"

Thus we are not especially well prepared to think of management as a legitimate field in its own right, requiring a certain amount of skill, education, and training. We are not willing to accept management as a profession since it is not readily definable and is not restricted by specific qualifications. Since one requires no particular background to enter the practice of management, many people are left with the feeling that "anyone can do it."

We readily recognize that to be a manager one must manage something. This causes us to consider the individual's functional specialty. It also leads to another consideration: Who is best qualified to supervise the work of the department? Should this be the role of the functional specialist or the management generalist? Is it more important for the supervisor to be knowledgeable of all aspects of the department's work, or should the supervisor's strengths lie in the general functions of management?

After brief consideration, we might reasonably conclude that the first-line supervisor should be proficient in both management and the functional specialty. Indeed, it is usually the individual who becomes well rounded in both areas of activity who makes the more effective supervisor.

## THE PETER PRINCIPLE REVISITED

Almost all first-line supervisors have worked as functional specialists. Although it is true that some people begin their working careers as supervisors, this usually occurs in natural "two hat" situations in which the person enters a small department as both supervisor and worker. Usually, however, a person is offered a supervisory position because of past performance in some specialty. Ordinarily it is the better workers who become supervisors.

However, the fact that one person is a good worker does not guarantee that this same person will be a good supervisor. It is precisely this dilemma that Laurence J. Peter was concerned with in *The Peter Principle*. Peter's tongue-in-cheek but nevertheless serious commentary contains a great deal of truth. In brief, his principle states that "in a hierarchy, every person tends to rise to his level of incompetence."[1] Recognizing that it is the good worker who is singled out for promotion, Peter reasons that the outstanding worker at any level is likely to be promoted to the next level in the hierarchy. This process may continue until the individual reaches a level where performance is mediocre. Here all promotions stop and the person is left, perhaps until retirement, a notch above the level of proven capability for good work.

The best workers do not necessarily become the best supervisors. Although promoting outstanding employees will continue to make more sense than promoting mediocre producers, this practice will never guarantee the presence of effective supervisors.

Much of the problem lies in the individual and organizational attitude toward management of "anyone can do it." Confident individuals step into supervisory positions assuming that all they need to do is begin giving instructions and commands. Likewise, higher managers promote workers and then go about their business as though believing they have created supervisors by simply conferring titles.

The supervisor's hedge against arriving at a level of incompetence is management development. Whether pursued in the institution or outside, through organizational programs or by individual effort, formally or informally, the supervisor must learn much about the second hat before it fits as well as the first hat. Most people enter their functional specialties sufficiently trained to do the jobs for which they have been hired. However, most workers who become supervisors do so with little or no preparation. Management then becomes a sink-or-swim proposition. A few catch on and perform remarkably well after a short period of time. Many generate enough motion to enable them to stay afloat but then continue spending most of their energy simply keeping their heads above water. Some sink quickly, to their detriment and often to that of the organization as well.

The player-to-coach transition in the world of professional sports offers an appropriate analogy to the worker-to-supervisor transition. Most successful coaches gained experience as players at some level in the sports they coach. However, only a few outstanding coaches were star performers in their playing days; most were infrequently noticed, solid, dependable team players. Knowing how to play the game well is not enough. The differences between working and supervising are as fundamental as the differences between doing and teaching and as great as the essential difference between following and leading.

Dan Reeves, while head coach of the Denver Broncos is reported to have said, "I was an assistant coach for many years and made a lot of suggestions. You don't realize until you're a head coach that you have to make decisions, not suggestions." Pope John XXIII once said, "It often happens that I wake at night and begin to think about a serious problem and decide I must tell the Pope about it. Then I wake up completely and remember that I am the Pope."

Reeves' and the Pope's careers, of course, are not an illustration of the Peter Principle—quite the opposite. But these statements suggest yet another part of the problem is making the fundamental shift to full responsibility for a department or function. Not everyone is capable of doing that effectively.

## THE WORKING TRAP

The working trap poses a hazard to every supervisor whose job includes the performance of both managerial and nonmanagerial duties. Much of the reason why any person is titled and paid as a manager is to see that a certain amount of work gets done through the efforts of other people. This requires that the supervisor be primarily a member of management. Any person charged with the responsibility for directing the activities of others is a manager and must firmly believe this is so.

It is all too easy for the supervisor to feel and behave more as a worker than a manager. This is understandable when half or more of the supervisor's duties may be nonmanagerial to begin with. However, this leads to a state of favoring one hat over the other—spending much of the time thinking and doing as a worker rather than behaving as a manager. Falling into the working trap can leave a supervisor's time and energy stretched too thinly over numerous technical tasks while some of the department's pure workers remain underutilized. The case study in Chapter 3 illustrates this point very well.

## NOTHING TO DO?

The following nine points were excerpted from a list of "supervisory activities" that a noncorrectional manager was kind enough to share with an instructor and class in a management development program. Their truth and applicability in the prison environment are poignantly clear.

As everyone knows, the supervisor has practically nothing to do except

1. decide what is to be done and assign the task to someone
2. listen to all the reasons why it should not be done, why it should be done differently, or why someone else should do it
3. follow up to find out whether it has been done, and discover it has not been done
4. listen to excuses from the person who should have done it
5. follow up again to determine if it has been done, only to discover it has been done incorrectly
6. point out how it should have been done and prepare to try again
7. wonder whether it may be time to get rid of a person who cannot do a job correctly; reflect that the employee probably has family responsibilities and that a successor would probably behave the same way anyway
8. consider how much simpler it would have been to do the job oneself in the first place
9. sadly reflect that it could have been done correctly in 20 minutes, but as things turned out it was necessary to spend two days to find out why it took three weeks for someone else to do it wrong

The foregoing is more than just a tongue-in-cheek recounting of some of the frustrations of supervision. Implicit in the nine points are a number of considerations important in the overall supervisory task. For instance, point two suggests that the assignment of work to an employee is more than simply pointing a person at a task and giving the orders. Proper delegation, discussed in Chapter 5, includes thoughtful matching of person and task, thorough instruction, and assurance that the employee understands why the job must be done.

Although follow-up is an extremely important part of all supervisory activity, point three might make us wonder how timely the follow-up was in the situation described, since late follow-up can be as bad as none at all. Point five, again dealing with follow-up, might prompt us to ask if corrective action has been taken and thorough instructions provided, or if once again the employee was simply "told to do it."

Point six states to "point out how it should have been done." If this is the first time instructions were offered or efforts were made to find out if the job was understood, then the supervisor has far more trouble than even these few frustrations suggest.

The musings of point seven are likely to be uncalled for at this stage. The supervisor must do considerable self-assessment before writing off any employee as incapable. Also, if honest evaluation does lead to consideration of firing, the rationalization that a successor would "probably behave the same way" is completely without foundation.

Point eight simply illustrates the thought processes that allow the supervisor to fall into the working trap, and the "sad reflection" of point nine does not carry far enough—it should perhaps go on to include: "Why, then, can't I get an employee to do a simple job like this within a reasonable time?" Otherwise, it suggests that the supervisor has compounded some personal errors and attempted to rationalize them away by tagging the employee with the failure.

## THE RESPONSIBILITIES OF CORRECTIONAL MANAGEMENT

One view of management can take in the entire body of people who are responsible for directing all activities that move employees toward the institution's goals. Consider "management" as a single composite "person" responsible for running the institution. This "person" has several major responsibilities.

First, correctional managers are responsible to the public for safety and cost-effective use of government resources. This includes striving continually to upgrade the capabilities of the correctional system and adapting to the constantly changing fiscal and public environment in which prisons operate. Second, correctional managers are responsible to the staff of the institution for their personal safety and welfare, and for recognizing their reasonable needs for a sense of accomplishment, fair treatment, and fair compensation for their efforts. Finally, correctional managers are responsible to the inmates of the institution for providing them with safe, humane living conditions and programs and services that improve their ability to function lawfully upon release.

Although these responsibilities may be directed toward a common objective—the preservation or restoration of public safety—there is likely to be conflict in their fulfillment. To appreciate the implications of such conflict, felt most severely at management's highest levels, put yourself in the position of our composite "person" and imagine that you must do your job while answering to four or five different bosses. To some extent, correctional managers at all levels find themselves caught in conflict situations, which may involve the needs of the public, employees, or inmates as opposed to the reality of what can be accomplished within the limits of available resources.

## THE NATURE OF SUPERVISION

In Chapter 1 it was established that patterns of supervision may differ from one organization to another according to various characteristics and that such differences may occur among departments in the same organization. Generally, the style of supervision in corrections will be more dependent on people-centered attitudes than on production-centered attitudes, while, paradoxically, also being more regimented than in many other work settings. While predictable on a broad scale, the tasks involved in managing a prison, at the detail level, are more variable than repetitive. Moreover, other than tabulating the raw numbers of inmates coming in and out of an institution, units of input and output at the institution's other systems are difficult to define.

Although a manufacturing supervisor has every need to focus strongly on people, the repetitive-task environment may force concentration on processes and techniques. The necessary orientation for the correctional manager is toward strength in interpersonal skills.

Successful supervision comes only through conscientious effort. A considerable degree of dedication to the job is necessary, but no one should feel it necessary to become a workaholic. The person who gives everything to the job to the exclusion of all else is most likely using the job as an excuse to fill other needs. Rather, the effective correctional manager is a person who has a reasonable liking for the work, who has a sincere interest in delivering quality services to inmates, and who can bring to the job the perspective of a private citizen who evaluates prison operations in terms of decency and humane treatment.

At the end of a management development class in which numerous techniques were discussed, a supervisor said, "I could really get a lot of good work done around here if it weren't for all the problems that pop up every day." When you find yourself feeling that kind of frustration, consider this: the problems—those nagging, unanticipated, annoying difficulties that seem to spring up day after day—are a large part of the reason for your job's existence. If there were fewer problems, fewer supervisors would be needed. To a considerable extent the supervisor is a frustration fighter; if the frustrations did not exist, necessary tasks might well be accomplished without supervisory intervention. The day-to-day problems do exist, and hour-to-hour and moment-to-moment operating decisions have to be made. And the person who must make most of these decisions is the first-line supervisor—the final link between the best intentions of the organization and the actual performance of patient care.

---

## EXERCISE 3–1: YOUR TWO HATS

Divide a sheet of paper into two full-length columns. Label one column "Technical," and label the other column "Managerial." In the "Technical" column, list the tasks you perform either regularly or occasionally in your capacity as a functional specialist. These should be the things you do, not primarily because you are a supervisor, but because you are a specialist in performing certain kinds of tasks. For instance, you may be a lieutenant responsible for the activities of sergeants and correctional officers, but you still work directly with inmates, or you may be the supervisor of a maintenance crew, but you still replace a malfunctioning light switch.

In the "Managerial" column list the tasks you perform as a management generalist. In these tasks you are applying techniques that cut across functional lines (although you are doing them specific to the function you supervise). Such tasks might include departmental budgeting, doing performance appraisals, interviewing prospective employees, and untangling people problems.

You may find it helpful to develop your lists over a period of several days, as you are confronted with a variety of problems and tasks, rather than generating them at a single sitting.

## Questions

1. What do your lists tell you about the "two hat" nature of your job?
2. Can you make reasonable estimates as to how much of your time is spent as a working specialist? As a manager?

## Suggestion for Additional Activity

Compare your lists with those of several other supervisors in a group discussion setting, and develop a composite list that is generally descriptive of the roles of the supervisor. Note that the two sides of the supervisor's job represent two distinctly different roles, either of which must be consciously assumed when the occasion demands.

---

### CASE 3–1: "IF YOU WANT SOMETHING DONE RIGHT. . ."

Samuel Tiggins, food service manager of a sprawling prison farm, dreaded the one day each month he had to spend doing the statistical report for his department. Tiggins was responsible for all meals in the 1,000-bed minimum-security facility, as well as delivery of pre-plated meals to two smaller satellite road camps and a nearby state hospital. At one time the report had been relatively simple, but as Tiggins' scope of responsibility grew and the administration requested more detailed information each month, the report had become more complicated. To adjust to these changes, he had simply modified his method of preparing the report each time a new requirement was placed upon him, so there was no written procedure for the report's preparation.

Faced once again with the time-consuming report—and confronted, as usual, with several problems demanding his immediate attention— Sam decided it was time to delegate the preparation of the report to his assistant, Steve Clark. He called Clark to his office, gave him a copy of the previous month's report and a set of forms, and said, "I'm sure you've seen this. I want you to take care of it from now on. I've been doing it for a long time, but it's getting to be a real pain and I've got more important things to do than to allow myself to be tied up with routine clerical work."

Clark skimmed the report before he said, "I'm sure I can do it if I start on the right foot. How about walking me through it?—doing just this one with me so I can get the hang of it?"

Tiggins said, "Look, my objective in giving you this is to save me some time. If I have to hold your hand, I may as well do it myself." He grinned as he added, "Besides, if I can do it, then anyone with half a brain ought to be able to do it."

Without further comment Clark left the office with the report and the forms. Tiggins went to work on other matters.

Later that day Clark stopped Tiggins in the food prep area and said, "Sam, I'm glad I caught you. I've got three or four questions about how to put together that report, mostly concerning how you come up with the meat and vegetable cost figures for the satellite camps." He started to pull a folded sheet of paper from his back pocket.

Tiggins barely slowed. "Sorry, Steve, but I can't take the time. I'm on my way to a meeting." As he hurried past Clark, he called back over his shoulder, "You'll just have to puzzle it out for yourself. After all, I had to do the same thing."

The following day when the report was due, Tiggins found Clark's work on his desk when he returned from lunch. He flipped through it to assure himself that all the blanks had been filled in, then scrawled his signature in the usual place. However, something caught his eye—a number which appeared to be far out of line with anything he had encountered in previous reports. He took out two earlier reports and began a line-by-line comparison. He quickly discovered that Clark had made a crucial error near the beginning and carried it through successive calculations.

Tiggins was angry with Clark. The day was more than half gone and he would have to drop everything else and spend the rest of the afternoon reworking the figures so the report could be submitted on time.

Tiggins was still working at 4:30 P.M. when Mark Signero, the chief operating engineer in the power plant, appeared in the doorway and said, "I thought we were going to get together this afternoon and talk about getting hot meals for my midnight shift workers instead of those sack lunches. What are you up to, anyway?"

Tiggins threw down his pencil and snapped, "I'm proving an old saying."

"Meaning what?"

"Meaning, if you want something done right, do it yourself."

## Questions

1. In what ways is Sam Tiggins attempting to function as both a worker and a manager? Identify at least one primary activity pertaining to each of Tiggins's "two hats."
2. How—if at all—do you believe Tiggins is emphasizing one side of his role at the expense of the other?
3. What is the apparent "working trap" in Tiggins' case, and why does it appear to you that he has become caught in that trap?

---

**NOTE**

1. L.J. Peter, *The Peter Principle* (New York: William Morrow & Company, 1969), 26.

## CHAPTER 4

# The Basic Management Functions

*You can map out a fight plan or a life plan, but when the action starts, it may not go the way you planned, and you're down to your reflexes—which means your training. That's where your roadwork shows. If you cheated on that in the dark of the morning, well, you're getting found out now under the bright lights.*
*—Joe Frazier, heavyweight boxer*

### Chapter Objectives

☛ Introduce and define the basic essential management functions: planning, organizing, directing, coordinating, and controlling.

☛ Establish the importance of knowledge of each of the basic functions in supervisory practice.

☛ Describe the relative influence of each of the basic management functions on the roles of managers at all organizational levels.

## INTRODUCTION

There are several kinds of basic activities that all correctional managers pursue in fulfilling their responsibilities—activities that are critical to success in the day-to-day management of our organizations. Shirk these fundamentals and, as Joe Frazier intimates, you and your institution suffer.

These key activities, or basic management functions are: (1) planning, (2) organizing, (3) directing, (4) coordinating, and (5) controlling. This five-way breakdown is not an original formulation; rather, it has served for years as a reasonable, if somewhat general, description of what managers do.

In the management literature you may encounter other lists of functions that contain four, five, or even more entries and use labels different from those applied here. One is found in the work of Theo Haimann, who refers to the basic management functions of planning, organizing, staffing, directing, and controlling.[1]

An interesting four-function breakdown appears in a management study guide published in 1985.[2] This division of the management functions at first seems to be only a partial listing of the functions already presented: planning, organizing, directing, and controlling. In this approach, however, directing is subdivided into two categories: goals and directing; and motivation.

Other delineations of the management functions to be found in the management literature include planning, organizing, leading, and controlling; planning, organizing, staffing, motivating, and controlling; and other variations. Even as early as 1916, Henri Fayol, the French industrialist and early management theorist, was basing much of his management approach on the simple four-function breakdown of planning, organizing, leading, and controlling.[3]

It is important to appreciate that none of these lists of functions represents someone's belief that a particular listing is the correct delineation of management functions while the others are lacking. Certainly the various lists of management functions are more similar than dissimilar. Nearly all such lists specifically cite planning, organizing, and controlling, and all such lists begin with planning.

The differences among the lists are simply of semantics and of how one views some of the elements of management. What is directing in one approach may be leading in another; what is organizing and staffing in one approach may simply be organizing in another; what belongs under both coordinating and controlling in one approach (the one used in this chapter) may all be encompassed by controlling in another.

Why all of these differences? Are there not clearly definable management functions that we can keep separate? The truth is that we cannot clearly differentiate among a number of separately defined management functions in a manner that covers all circumstances. In speaking of management we are speaking of a broad pursuit made up of many overlapping and interwoven activities. The management process is a continuum and at the same time is a cycle. All of the business of "defining" management functions is simply a convenience that allows us to examine portions of the management cycle in a way that emphasizes certain kinds of activities.

Regardless of the labels applied, however, it is the concepts that are important. It will be helpful to your understanding of management responsibilities to develop an appreciation of the kinds of activity managers pursue for certain purposes. Later in this chapter we will consider how the emphasis on certain of these basic functions differs according to your position or level in the prison's management structure. Specifically, we will suggest that a manager's organizational position has much to do in determining which management functions are likely to, and perhaps should, consume most of the manager's time and effort.

## MANAGEMENT FUNCTIONS IN BRIEF

Planning is the process of determining what should be done, why it should be done, where it should best be done, by whom it should be done, when it should be done, and how it should be done.

Organizing is the process of structuring the framework within which things get done and determining how best to commit available resources to serve the organization's purposes and to carry out its plans. Our consideration of organizing includes what is often referred to as staffing.

Directing is assigning specific resources or focusing certain efforts to accomplish specific tasks as required. Simply, directing is running an organizational unit on a day-to-day basis. Directing may be considered to include a great deal of leading, yet leading is woven throughout most of the other functions as well. Directing may also include motivating and all it implies in getting things done through the organization's employees, yet motivating is certainly a consideration throughout the other functions as well.

Coordinating consists of integrating activities and balancing tasks so that appropriate actions take place within the proper physical and temporal relationships. Coordinating does not appear by name in a number of other delineations of the management functions, yet in all cases it is directly implied in descriptions of the tasks managers perform.

Controlling is follow-up and correction, looking at what actually happened and making adjustments to encourage outcomes to conform with expected or required results. It is controlling that best illustrates the cyclic nature of management and the inseparability of the basic management functions. Controlling requires directing, coordinating, organizing, and revising plans as they unfold in the real world of the workplace.

## PLANNING

Whenever we try to look ahead and predetermine a possible action sometime in the future, we are planning. This future may be months or years ahead or it may be only minutes away.

Planning can be high level and far reaching, as when the local institution's administration and the agency headquarters staff develop a long-range plan calling for growth and expansion or other major changes. Much planning, however, by working managers, concerns short-term applications.

The development of a five-year plan for a prison is an example of planning, as is the development of a single department's one-year budget. Likewise, if you spend half a day developing the work schedule for your department's employees for the coming month, you are planning. Even if you simply pause at the end of the day to order your thoughts, sort out the notes on your desk, and jot down a list of items you need to take care of in the morning, you are engaged in planning.

## An Imperfect Process

The imperfect nature of planning suggests that plans should be flexible, intended to be changed and updated as the time to which they apply comes closer. Those who have done roster management, for instance, know the prison environment provides interesting diversions from planned courses of action.

It is possible to fall into the habit of overplanning. Indeed, some people spend so much time planning that they rarely have time to do anything. Keep your planning reasonable as to how much you do and how long it takes.

Although much supervisory planning need not be formal or time-consuming, it pays to be sufficiently thorough and organized to commit your plans to writing. Often the simple act of putting your thoughts on paper will serve to crystallize your ideas and help you make decisions.

## The Plan Is Not the Objective

Since we are all aware of what happens to "the best laid plans of mice and men," we might reasonably ask: Why plan at all?

Consider a simple analogy in shooting an arrow toward a target. If the target is simply a blank circle, this whole target is our "mark" and as long as we strike anywhere in the circle, we really do not know much about where we hit relative to where we wanted to hit. However, when we add a bull's-eye and several target rings, we then have a clearer idea of how much we need to adjust our shots to come closer to where we would like to be.

The importance of having well-defined targets in planning must be stressed. When we have a target, even when we miss it, we have learned something. We at least know by how much we missed the mark and perhaps in what direction we were off, and with that information we can assess both our planning processes and our work practices.

Keep in mind, however, that plans may not be realized for any of several reasons. What was once a good plan may no longer be valid in the light of new conditions. Perhaps the plan was inadequate to begin with. Or, perhaps the plan was well conceived and fully adequate, but failed to work because the implementation effort fell short of what was needed. In any case, whether or not our plans work out well, we always learn something from the experience. Even when plans themselves are not particularly worthwhile, the planning process is invaluable. Indeed, what is truly valuable is the cyclic process of examining needs, setting objectives, making plans to reach those objectives, implementing the plans, and following up on the total effort.

Plans should never be regarded as cast in concrete. We sometimes try bending reality to arrive at the results we projected. A certain amount of this kind of effort is called for. Departmental budgets, for instance, should be considered as relatively important targets to be met. However, a plan is first and foremost a guide to action—it is not in itself a predestined action.

As a first-line supervisor you may not feel there is a great deal of planning required of you. However, upon examination you will find that every management position, even one in the lowest levels of management, requires some planning. A certain amount of planning is necessary to help you run your job properly, and if you do not run your job to some extent, there is a good chance that your job will run you.

## ORGANIZING

Sometimes it may seem that organizing, much like planning, is not a particular concern of the first-line supervisor. It is true that much organizing has to do with departmentalization, the process of grouping various activities into separate units to carry out the work of the organization. Much of this takes place at high levels in the organization and may not occur very often. However, as a first-line supervisor you engage in acts of organizing similar to departmentalization whenever you make decisions concerning which people within your department are going to handle certain tasks. Whenever you become involved in making decisions concerning division of labor or separation of skills, you are organizing.

### Unity of Command

One basic principle of organizing with which you should be familiar is unity of command. Unity of command requires you to provide assurance, for all the activities within your responsibility, that in all instances specific employees are responsible for certain specific results on a one-to-one basis. That is, it is inappropriate to assign task responsibilities in such a way that your employees do not know clearly who is ultimately responsible for any given task. Likewise, unity of command suggests that no function within your responsibility should be allowed to "drift" without belonging to some specific person.

### Span of Control

Another important concept within organizing—and one over which the individual supervisor has little influence—is span of control. An individual manager can effectively supervise only a certain number of workers, with this number hazily determined by the manager's knowledge and experience, the amount and nature of the manager's nonsupervisory work, the amount of supervision required by the employees, the variability of the employees' tasks, the overall complexity of the activity, and the physical area over which the employees are distributed.

For instance, the working supervisor of a five-member records department (where all five employees work within the same room) has every opportunity for complete control. The supervisor probably knows all the jobs fairly well, and visual and auditory control of the entire department is relatively easy. On the other hand, a working supervisor in a five-member maintenance department has a limited span of control. This department's employees do many different things and usually do most of their work well beyond the supervisor's visual and auditory control. One supervisor can readily control five employees; the other will have great difficulty controlling five employees. A supervisor can oversee and control more people who do similar work in the same physical area than people who perform variable work scattered over a considerable area.

### Delegation

The most important aspect of organizing to the first-line supervisor is the function known as delegation. Delegation, the process of assuring that the proper people have the responsibility and authority for performing specific tasks, is of sufficient importance to the supervisor to warrant a chapter of its own (see Chapter 5).

## DIRECTING

Directing consists largely of assigning responsibilities on a day-to-day basis, letting your employees know what has to be done, how, and by when. It is the making of all the little but all-important decisions so necessary in the operation of the department. It is the process of steering the department. Although we may occasionally get tired of "team" analogies in management, the example of the football quarterback is appropriate to directing. The quarterback knows the plays and the strategy as a result of prolonged planning sessions; yet when he goes onto the field he does not know the exact conditions he will encounter. It is only when he sees what happens on the field that the quarterback can call on what he has learned and respond to the conditions of the moment. It is in this way that the supervisor must behave, making the day-to-day and sometimes hour-to-hour decisions necessary to run the departmental team.

Under directing you might logically place an entire management library of discussions about management activities. The quarterback example should make clear that people who are most successful at directing are successful at leading. We can direct without leading by simply giving orders; we can fill leadership positions (although perhaps not very well) without being true leaders. However, direction is more successful when we can truly lead.

## COORDINATING

It has been suggested that coordinating, the blending of activities and timing of events, might legitimately be considered a part of the directing function. We are considering it separately out of recognition of its importance to the supervisor.

A dinner of five magnificent courses will not be particularly successful if the courses are scattered over two or three hours, the dessert comes second, and the entree arrives last. Likewise, an essential part of many work activities is not the simple fact of their performance but rather their performance relative to other activities. A large number of tasks require coordination with other tasks.

In day-to-day prison operations, employees, facilities, supplies, and services must work in the right relationship to each other in order for the institution to run smoothly. Activities must be coordinated within and among departments. It would make little sense for the recreation department to schedule a movie for the inmate population if there were no extra correctional officer coverage available for the darkened auditorium, nor would it be wise for the inmate commissary to sell convenience food items packaged in glass containers to inmates in high security housing. Effective coordination is one of the keys to supervisory effectiveness.

## CONTROLLING

Plans rarely come to realization exactly as intended, so many moment-to-moment changes are required in pursuit of departmental objectives. In the controlling function we evaluate progress against objectives and make adjustments or new decisions as we go along. The terms most descriptive of controlling are follow-up and action.

Controlling is often the most neglected of the basic management functions, especially follow-up of earlier decisions. The problem of limited or nonexistent follow-up is examined further under the topics of delegation and supervisory decision making.

## EMPHASIS

The basic management functions of planning, organizing, directing, coordinating, and controlling were presented in a given order for an important reason.

Generally, the first elements of this list should occupy a proportionately larger amount of the time of people in the upper levels of management. Top managers and middle managers are, however, prone to continue behaving in the manner of first-line supervisors; that is, they spend significant amounts of time dealing with day-to-day operating problems. Indeed, managers at all levels in all organizations are prone to "crisis management," expending most of their time and effort in reacting to present events and conditions rather than looking ahead.

The first-line supervisor will concentrate more on activities toward the bottom of the list of basic management functions. It is the lower echelons of management who are rightly more concerned with the problems of the moment. Those at the top of the organization should be more concerned with where the organization is going relative to its long-range goals and should be considering courses of action required to support those goals. The correctional officer in the cellhouse is concerned with bar tapping and counting inmates while the chief of security is planning next year's budget request and developing a new emergency plan for response to a riot. As the case study in Chapter 2 showed, however, even those nearer the top of the organization can fall into the trap of personal involvement in operational details.

As we have seen, planning, organizing, directing, coordinating, and controlling are all part of every manager's job. In a large correctional organization, top management may spend 70 or 80 percent of the time involved in broadbased planning and organizing. In the same organization, except for the regular practice of delegation (a part of organizing), the first-line supervisor may spend 80 or 90 percent of the time on a combination of directing, coordinating, and controlling (Figure 4–1).

How you as an individual manager may see your approach to these basic management functions will be largely influenced by the approach you have taken to the job since becoming a supervisor. Much of what you do has been determined by the concept of management you held before you became a supervisor, and by whether or not you received any solid orientation to supervision.

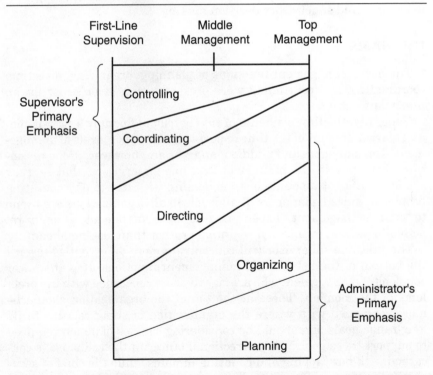

**Figure 4–1** Typical Shift in Emphasis on Basic Management Functions from Lowest to Highest Levels of Management

## PROCESS VERSUS PEOPLE

In discussing the basic management functions we focus on a number of practices that are often described as management processes. In doing so we run the risk of creating an impression that management is strongly process oriented. We might be tempted to believe that to be successful in management we need to learn a number of processes and then apply the appropriate processes to circumstances as they arise.

It is indeed true that planning and organizing are processes. Controlling, delegation, and leading (to name some fairly broad functions) are processes, too, as are absentee control, scheduling, and interviewing (to name some more narrowly delineated functions). And one could name dozens of other so-called functions or techniques that are processes.

With all of this seeming emphasis on functions and processes, it is appropriate to remind ourselves that the central focus of management is people. A person might spend a great deal of time learning management processes—most management education is in fact heavily weighted toward process—and never become a successful supervisor. In the long run, success at any level of management will depend on our ability to work with people.

---

## CASE 4–1: THE MANAGEMENT FUNCTIONS IN ACTION

Marcie Denton is chief of maintenance for a relatively new maximum security prison. Included in her many responsibilities is that of maintaining all electrical and mechanical equipment. Among the prison's equipment are four large air-conditioning units.

When she helped establish the department, Denton designated three men—one of them a working foreman—to handle all electrical and mechanical repairs and maintenance. Agency policy empowered the foreman with the authority to requisition parts and materials through local sources up to a limit of $50 per order.

With the foreman, Denton developed a schedule for preventive maintenance and routine periodic overhaul of the air conditioners. The foreman was to make sure that the schedule was followed.

One warm August day an air conditioner broke down while the foreman and one mechanic were repairing a pump at the power house. The other mechanic was unavailable owing to illness. When word of the breakdown reached Denton, she reassigned the working foreman to the air conditioner and left the mechanic working on the pump.

Since the repair to the air conditioner involved a short interruption of electricity to two departments, Denton arranged for a 15-minute break in electrical service at 2:00 P.M. with the supervisors of those departments, cleared the outage with the chief of security, and notified the associate warden over her department.

The repair to the air conditioner was successful, but unusual wear in the equipment was evident when it was disassembled. To guard against future breakdown, Denton conferred with the manufacturer's local representative and subsequently increased the frequency of scheduled preventive maintenance for this unit. She also decided to check the other units for similar problems.

### Instructions

Analyze the case description paragraph by paragraph and identify the basic management functions which:

- Were apparently performed sometime in the past (for instance, "Included in her many responsibilities is—" implies that organizing has been accomplished).
- Are being actively performed by Denton (for example, "Denton arranged a 15-minute break in electrical service" describes an act of coordinating).

Be especially sensitive to the "management cycle": follow-up and correction (controlling), which frequently involve directing and coordinating, may lead to further planning and organizing.

### CASE 4–2: WHAT A WAY TO START A NEW JOB!*

Randy Parker was appointed to a position as unit manager of a new 180-bed detention unit being built adjacent to a medium-security prison. The unit was intended to serve the needs of the local court, supplementing bedspace available in the local jail. Having served for seven years as a correctional officer and four years as a unit manager in the main institution, Parker was selected 90 days before the unit was scheduled to open. He was to develop a firm budget and staffing plan for the unit.

Parker developed a master staffing plan based on providing each 60-

---

*Based on several actual incidents in the Federal Bureau of Prisons, in which inmates displaced by riot or natural disaster were relocated on short notice to about-to-open housing units.

bed wing of the 3-wing unit with a core staff in line with staffing of special housing units of a similar size in other facilities throughout the agency. A phased activation plan was anticipated, with a new wing being activated and staffed about every 30 days. As is typical for this agency, a small pool of sick and annual relief personnel were included in the roster to cover staff vacancies.

One Tuesday morning, the warden of the main institution received word that a riot was in progress at the State's main penitentiary, and that the institution should be on standby to provide assistance as needed. One of the possibilities mentioned was that the new detention center would be activated to hold inmates moved out of the penitentiary. About the same time, Parker received word that one of his key staff members, the lieutenant with whom he had done a great deal of the planning for the unit's activation—particularly the security procedures—had taken seriously ill during the night.

Parker worked to develop a plan that would allow the detention center to open if that became necessary. With the concurrence of the chief of security, Parker began to locate key staff and position them for new assignments. From available sick and annual staff from the main institution, a group already depleted by vacations and illness in that facility, Parker was able to pull one senior lieutenant. About to be promoted to captain, this man had been a supervisory correctional officer in the county jail some time ago, before becoming a state correctional officer. Parker also located two senior sergeants who had worked the main institution's special housing unit recently and advised them they might be called upon to serve as acting lieutenants in the detention unit. He then made arrangements with the shift captain to cover their regular positions with other sick and annual relief personnel should the move be necessary.

Shift supervisors were needed for the unit, and even though he had identified the two senior sergeants as possibilities for these posts, Parker was tempted to step into the breach himself since he had run a housing unit inside the prison and knew he could run a shift in the new unit. However, he had no idea how long this emergency activation would last and he did not want to spread himself too thin by assuming an additional burden when he might be needed elsewhere. He and the chief of security decided to reassign the three supervisors involved, and to use both sick and annual relief staff and overtime to provide line officer coverage.

The riot was brought under control late that day, and in its aftermath it was determined that one housing unit was too badly damaged to use for at least several months. Parker's warden was advised that

145 inmates would be moved to the detention center the following day. It became necessary to make the changes Parker had planned.

That day, special operations staff from the penitentiary transferred six busloads of inmates to the detention center. These inmates and their personal property were processed and all three wings of the detention unit were activated within an 8-hour span. Asked later if the prison's emergency response plan (a number of elements of which had been put into effect) appeared adequate, Parker was able to suggest that some procedures be strengthened in specific ways.

## Instructions

This case describes the basic management functions of planning, organizing, directing, coordinating, and controlling. Identify as many of these as possible. (Note that a single activity often combines elements of two or more of the basic functions. However, one basic function usually emerges as dominant.)

---

**NOTES**

1. T. Haimann, *Supervisory Management for Hospitals and Related Health Facilities* (St. Louis, Mo.: The Catholic Hospital Association, 1965), 10–12.
2. M.L. Slagle, et al., *Managing* (Study Guide) (Glenview, Ill.: Scott, Foresman & Co., 1985), 27, 41, 57, 72, 87.
3. H. Fayol, *General and Industrial Management* (New York and London: Pittman, 1949).

# PART II

# The Supervisor and Self

## CHAPTER 5

# Delegation: How To Form the Habit

*Surround yourself with the best people you can, delegate authority, and don't interfere as long as the policy you've decided upon is being carried out.*

—*Ronald Reagan*

*One of modern management's most important functions—effective delegation of work—is a subject for plenty of preaching but not enough practice.*

—*Earle Brooks*

## Chapter Objectives

☛ Identify delegation and its practice as a major influence on effective supervisory performance.

☛ Convey the value of proper delegation in the prison environment to supervisor, employees, and organization alike.

☛ Identify the common reasons behind the failure to delegate.

☛ Establish a perspective on delegation that will help the supervisor work under authority of higher management.

☛ Develop a pattern of steps representing a desirable approach to proper delegation.

☛ Encourage the supervisor to build positive delegation habits.

## TAKEN FOR GRANTED

Effective delegation has long been a subject of considerable preaching. It is the basis of numerous workshops, seminars, and other educational programs. One need only review a small sample of current management literature to see how often delegation is discussed in print. Despite its frequent presentation, however, delegation is still a weak link in the chain of correctional management. It often is treated lightly, if at all, even by supervisors who are genuinely interested in becoming better managers.

Although the subject of much good advice, delegation is frequently overlooked when it comes to conscientious practice. All too often we take our ability to delegate for granted, assuming an expertise that is not present.

Many people who are responsible for the work of others tend to take delegation for granted.

- They do not fully understand the true nature of delegation.
- They do not recognize, or fully appreciate, the extent of the power of their own habits to prevent improvement in delegation.
- They have not yet come to view delegation from the perspective of the employee to whom the work is delegated.

## THE NATURE OF DELEGATION

There are some significant problems to be encountered when considering delegation as a management technique. Although most managers believe they should delegate and are convinced they do delegate, these problems exist because much so-called delegation is incomplete and ineffective. Few supervisors believe or will admit that they do not delegate. However, few supervisors delegate significantly beyond simple organizational delegation.

In Chapter 4, delegation was described as part of the basic management function of organizing. Most supervisors are automatically, if passively, involved with organizational delegation. You place a person in a job and give that person a job description or a set of instructions. You have delegated; you have charged an employee with the performance of a number of tasks for which you are ultimately responsible. The job description is the employee's authority to perform certain functions. Any department consisting of more than one person is necessarily subject to organizational delegation because the normal division of activities requires different people to perform various tasks.

Not every task to be accomplished by the department will appear on someone's job description. Indeed, many of the department's activities fall between the lines of the job descriptions or are not listed at all. You will usually find that the job description for a supervisor, as well as the job description for a partially self-directing professional such as a case manager, will include a catch-all statement such as: "perform all other duties as required by supervision." The responsibilities of each department include many tasks not specifically mentioned in the job descriptions. These tasks may be found at various levels within the department, but invariably the supervisor is responsible for ensuring that someone does them.

A supervisor's job description may also contain many tasks that rightly belong there but that need not necessarily be done by the supervisor in their entirety. There are probably a number of tasks within your area of responsibility that can be accomplished by you or by someone who works for you. Much of a supervisor's effectiveness is determined by how well he or she uses the capabilities of employees to accomplish properly many such tasks.

Delegation is both a process and a condition. It is, in part, the process of assigning work to an employee, a process that generally is well understood. But much consideration of delegation stops at this point. The condition of delegation exists when there is thorough, mutual understanding by supervisor and employee of what specific results are expected and how these results may be achieved. Too often delegation is treated as a simple process and no further steps are taken to attain the true condition of delegation.

The hows and whys of the delegation process are relatively simple, and it is by understanding and pursuing them that we approach the condition of true delegation. The all-important consideration in effective delegation is practice; like any desirable activity, effective delegation must be pursued conscientiously and intentionally, perhaps for a considerable time, before it becomes a habit. We also must first break some old habits. Unfortunately, most of us are much more accustomed to doing than to having others do.

## WHAT ABOUT EMPOWERMENT?

The concept of empowerment rose to prominence in the latter 1980s and early 1990s, partly in conjunction with the total quality management (TQM) movement. It has become a latter-day buzzword. Business proposes that empowerment is "the thing to do" with employees to enable them to make their best possible contributions to organizational success.

Although it is described in a variety of ways, empowerment in work organizations means letting the employees solve their own problems and implement their own solutions.

What is the difference between empowerment and delegation? Absolutely nothing. That is, there is no difference between empowerment and proper delegation. *Roget's International Thesaurus* (5th edition, 1992) lists *empowerment* and *delegation* as synonyms along with *commission, assignment, deputation,* and a number of other words.[1]

Although, as words, *delegation* and *empowerment* mean exactly the same thing, they are being regarded quite differently in practice. Empowerment is "in," and a great many people are behaving as though this concept is a vast improvement on mere "delegation." But if the concepts are really one and the same, what happened to delegation?

Over decades of misuse delegation came to be regarded as meaning no more than giving someone a task to complete or giving someone an order. Proper delegation, however, has always consisted of giving someone the responsibility for task completion and also giving that person the authority required to complete the task. True empowerment is identical to proper delegation: one gives an employee a problem to solve or a condition to correct, specifies the desired outcome or acceptable range of results, and provides the employee with the authority or whatever resources are necessary.

The problem at the heart of most difficulties with delegation is a problem of management style and approach by the delegating manager, and is a control issue with many higher managers. These managers cannot let go sufficiently to allow delegation or empowerment to work. Their still-authoritarian management styles send one clear message to the employees: You are free to make whatever decisions you want, as long as they are the same decisions we would make ourselves.

The prison environment has a particular claim on this problem, partly because of the high degree of public sensitivity to prison riots and escapes. Correctional administrators often believe they must keep a personal hand in lower-level decision-making in order to prevent such problems from arising. Proper delegation or empowerment will work as intended only if the manager—the person who does the delegating or empowering—is committed in advance to accepting the decisions of the employees. And for many prison administrators, that is a difficult and sometimes risky thing to contemplate.

## WHY DELEGATE?

### For Yourself

The old adage, "If you want a thing done well, do it yourself," is largely a fallacy as far as management is concerned. One person, no matter how competent, can do only so much and still continue to do things well. We frequently see supervisors who try to handle so many activities that they are able to hold things together only loosely at best. You may believe that because you work long hours, take extra work home, and generally try to fill every request that comes along and solve every problem that arises that you are a dedicated, effective, hard-working manager. You may be dedicated and hard-working, but if this is the way you approach your job, chances are you are not effective.

Failure to delegate effectively is one of the principal causes of managerial failure and is a leading reason why many people in management do not get promoted to more responsible positions. Failure to delegate effectively will not necessarily halt a management career at the first level; many persons, by dedication and workaholism, manage to rise several levels through sheer energy and activity. However, even the workaholic—the manager who continues to do as much as possible alone—will eventually reach a level where the job is too big to handle. Failure to delegate effectively is an even greater hazard for higher-level managers than for first- and second-line supervisors. In fact, delegation failure at all levels of management is damaging.

You owe it to yourself to delegate, to assure that some of your employees are capable of taking care of some of the tasks, problems, and requests that you usually have to handle. You can achieve a measure of peace of mind by knowing that one or more persons can capably act on your behalf when you are ill, on vacation, or busy elsewhere. Delegation can build your image as a leader with your employees and will likely improve your standing with higher management, since as a supervisor you are properly judged not by what you do, but rather by what your department does.

Delegating certain tasks can give you more time to concentrate on true supervisory activities. Rarely is there enough time in the supervisor's day for all the thinking, planning, and communicating needed to maintain and improve a department's effectiveness. Generally, a supervisor who delegates effectively gains a greater degree of freedom from technical tasks and is able to function as more of a manager more of the time. This could also include sufficient freedom to enable you to assume greater responsibility by taking on functions delegated by your immediate manager.

## For Your Employees

You owe it to your employees to delegate. As their supervisor you should be seeking to help them learn and grow, rather than acting in a manner that holds them back. You build a department by building individuals.

In the same way that much of your fate is determined by your immediate supervisor, so the fate of your employees is largely in your hands. You can guide your employees upward in terms of growth and development, or you can hold them back. You can challenge and interest them by giving them responsibility and opportunity, or you can lock them into routine and boredom.

Most employees would rather be stimulated and interested than unchallenged and bored. Most would rather learn and grow than stagnate. Most would rather be serving useful purposes than doing unimportant or inconsequential work. And most would rather work—because they enjoy work or because they wish to pass the time more quickly—than be idle. When you delegate, your employees get a taste of greater responsibility and perhaps some decision-making experience. They are likely to take more pride in what they do, reflect higher morale, both individually and as a department, and exercise more individual initiative.

Effective delegation within a department represents opportunity to the employees. All employees will not react the same way to the chance to assume greater responsibility or do different work; some people do not wish to go in those directions. However, the simple presence of the opportunity is a tonic to all employees whether they avail themselves of that opportunity or not.

## FAILURE TO DELEGATE

Managers fail to delegate for a number of reasons. Some of these reasons are complex and involve fear of competition from employees or the loss of recognition for task accomplishment, factors about which the supervisor may be only dimly aware. It is often difficult to avoid thinking of yourself as being in competition with your employees, since some employees seem to foster such competition as they attempt to grow in the organization. However, the effective supervisor encourages growth, and a legitimate challenge taken up by an employee can look much like direct competition. The fear of competition from subordinates often goes hand in hand with a degree of insecurity, but the presence of two or three eager promotion-oriented employees with their sights set on the supervisor's job can be a stimulus that keeps the supervisor in a heads-up and growing attitude.

Although all employees are legitimately concerned to some extent with how they may be doing in the boss's eyes, as a supervisor your first concern should not be, "Does my boss think I'm doing a good job?" Rather, your concern should be, "Is this department seen as doing a good job?" When your employees perform well, the credit is yours as well as theirs. As the department is recognized, so is the supervisor recognized.

Old habits are a major reason for failure to delegate. Our earliest working years were devoted to the hands-on doing of work, and we often fail to de-emphasize that habit even though we may have spent more recent years supposedly directing the doing of work.

A great deal of sound advice is available concerning delegation. That is, it is sound advice if it is followed, but most of the time the advice offered in step-by-step approaches to delegation is either not followed or, if followed at all, not conscientiously pursued for a sufficient amount of time to become ingrained in the supervisor's habit pattern.

One of the most significant barriers to effective delegation is habit. If we are to try to adopt a new approach to delegation, we must change our ways of doing things. Such change means altering habit patterns, shedding old habits and replacing them with new ones. Like the former chief of security who, after being promoted to warden, cannot stop hanging around the shift supervisor's office offering advice, many a technical specialist who has excelled to the point of being recognized and promoted to upper management is more comfortable reverting to old tasks than in learning and exercising new management duties.

Anyone who has put forth a conscious effort to change a deeply ingrained habit should fully appreciate how difficult it can be. It certainly can be done, depending on how much effort is applied, how long this effort is sustained, and how deeply ingrained the old habit is. Attempts to improve the way we delegate frequently go the same way as attempts to apply what we learn at a time management seminar about improving effectiveness: a flurry of initial activity is followed by stops and starts that diminish and eventually vanish as old ways take over again. This ordinarily occurs because we are barely aware of, or perhaps have not thought at all about, the immense barrier presented by habits so deeply ingrained through years of practice that they are now second nature.

The key to improving your skill at delegation lies in the constant awareness of the need to overcome old habits. It is necessary to start on a modest scale, conscientiously applying the new process to one well-defined task or project at a time and doing so over and over until the new way becomes a habit that is strong enough to keep the old habit from returning.

Another common reason for the failure to delegate, one that many supervisors may readily recognize and admit, is the feeling that available employees simply cannot handle greater responsibility. This is a classic situation: you hesitate to try someone with more responsibility because you do not know if they can handle it; yet the only way you will find out if they can handle it is to try them. If you find yourself feeling that you do not delegate because you have no one who can handle additional responsibility, ask yourself if you have seriously tried to prepare someone to assume more responsibility. The prison environment is prone to foster this kind of problem; the consequences of internal prison management problems can reach life-threatening levels and many managers place themselves under pressure to personally be sure the institution is running properly.

The most prevalent reason for failure to delegate is also the most obvious reason: lack of time. Here we find ourselves caught in a basic contradiction—we tend to think most seriously about the need to delegate only when the pressure is most intense. The in-baskets are overflowing, problems are coming from all directions, and we realize we need to delegate to improve our effectiveness—or simply to help us get caught up. However, delegation takes time—time to pick people and prepare them, time to prepare the work, time to do several other things—and when the workload is heavy, we simply do not have that kind of time. We may promise ourselves to do some serious delegating "as soon as the rush is over." However, when the rush finally goes away so does the feeling of urgency that came with it: "Delegate? The workload is under control, so where's the need?"

The time required to accomplish proper delegation is an investment, an investment that must often be made when there is precious little time available. The returns of delegation are not immediate; it is often necessary to expend an additional amount of time and get even further behind for the sake of improvements that will not appear as real time savings until weeks or perhaps months have passed. However, this hurdle—the time trap—must be overcome before improved efficiency through delegation can become a reality.

Consider the case of the prison education department supervisor who was required to submit a detailed statistical report of the department's classroom and vocational training operations each month. Each time the manager faced the report, which required about four uninterrupted hours to complete, this person considered delegating this task to a certain employee who could handle it with proper training. However, the supervisor estimated it would take eight to ten hours to go through the report point by point with the employee, so the employee's training was put off until a so-called convenient time between reports. However, the convenient time never came, and soon it was time to submit the next report and the pressure was on again.

After rationalizing the way through this time trap several times, the supervisor finally recognized the need to invest extra time and effort. When the time came to do the next report, the supervisor and the designated employee closeted themselves and went through the report number by number and line by line. It took an entire day. The next month's report took the two of them nearly six hours, still longer than it had taken the supervisor alone. The third report was done in the same way in about four hours.

The fourth month's report consumed about six hours. However, this consisted of five hours of the employee's time, working alone, and an hour of the supervisor's time to audit some important statistics. By the sixth month of the new arrangement, the employee was doing the report in four hours and the supervisor was spending perhaps five to ten minutes to review and approve the report. Improvement took a long time, but the early investment of time and effort paid off in later returns.

A failure to delegate can be felt well beyond the nondelegating supervisor. Consider the case of the business office manager in a correctional agency's headquarters who was not promoted to assistant comptroller primarily because of delegation weaknesses: neither of the two assistant business managers in the office had been tested with responsibility and the department was without a potential successor to the manager. The business office manager had been the only possible in-house candidate, so the agency was forced to search elsewhere for a new assistant comptroller. Because the manager lost out on a promotion, one of the two assistants also lost the chance to become business office manager. In addition, two lower-level jobs that could have been opened up by this promotional chain reaction remained closed. Thus, four people missed out on possible promotions simply because one of them had not practiced effective delegation.

The department of a nondelegating supervisor suffers in a number of ways. Unchallenged people with time on their hands usually do not exhibit high morale. As morale goes down, productivity and quality suffer. A department so afflicted can acquire a reputation for discontent and unreliability, and, once acquired, such a reputation is not easily shed. In the extreme case, such a department will begin to lose its better people as they go elsewhere in search of work environments where there is opportunity for growth and advancement. Employees who do not consider job interest and challenge as particularly important will remain to drift—and complain.

We have repeatedly referred to management as "getting things done through people." This is accomplished through delegation. As a supervisor you obtain your own authority through delegation. It is up to you to learn how to use that authority, including how to redelegate part of it when doing so is in the best interest of the organization.

## LOOKING UPWARD AS WELL AS DOWNWARD: THE PERSONAL APPROACH TO DELEGATION

The supervisor who sincerely wants to improve at delegation should look both downward and upward: downward toward the employees to whom he or she will delegate and upward toward the higher manager from whom delegated tasks are received. Look upward at your superior and consider how he or she delegates to you. It helps to look toward your boss regarding delegation because your employees similarly look toward you.

Although the motivational forces that cause people to work exist in a complex mix that may vary dramatically from person to person, the net effect of these motivating forces is often not all that different between you and most of your employees. For the most part the majority of your employees will want many of the same things that you want; many of them will perhaps aspire to supervision, wishing to rise from the ranks of the work group as perhaps you did.

Not all of your employees are likely to aspire to management, and not all of them will seek challenge in their work as perhaps you do. Generally, however, their motives will parallel yours so that you can deal with them in a manner similar to the way you would like your boss to deal with you.

You are therefore on a reasonable course if you try to pattern some elements of your relationship with each individual employee after an idealized working relationship with your boss. Attempting to do so will put you in a position of being able to work on improving delegation both upward and downward—that is, while you strive to become better at delegating, you can work to achieve a more appropriate delegation relationship with your superior. This is a highly personal approach, because it finds you looking out for your own best interests—as well as the best interests of your employees and the organization—by improving the effectiveness with which you delegate and simultaneously improving your communicating relationship with your superior.

## Ideal versus Real

In an ideal relationship with your boss, you and that higher manager would both know where you stand with each other at all times and on all matters. In the real world, of course, this relationship may be somewhat less—perhaps even significantly less—than the ideal. However, it is possible to use your knowledge of your needs as a supervisor and your concept of an ideal relationship with your boss to:

- reshape and generally improve your relationship with your boss, actually guiding your boss along the path toward a more effective delegation relationship with you.
- establish a new and more effective pattern for how you delegate to your employees.

It is necessary to determine initially how you want to be treated by your immediate superior concerning delegation. This usually means deciding how, as realistically as possible, you need to be treated so that you can fully meet the requirements of your job. What follows after your needs have been defined is the application of the same line of thought to your relationship with each employee in your work group. Constantly envisioning yourself as "in the middle," you can apply a number of considerations to delegation both upward and downward.

## Differing Perspectives

The upward view between adjacent points in the chain of command is not the same as the downward view between those same two points. Looking upward, you are likely to see your superior as a single point of information, advice, and assistance; looking upward, your employees probably see you in the same way. The upward view between adjacent points in the chain of command focuses on a single person, and more often than not that person, an organizational superior, is seen as a source of support. However, the downward view is quite different.

The superior, whether it is you looking downward at your employees or your manager looking downward at you and your peers, sees not one point of contact but several. Furthermore, the superior frequently sees these several points of contact as sources of problems and grief. Every person in the chain of command has one primary upward channel of communication; however, every managerial person in the chain of command has as many primary downward channels as he or she has direct reporting employees.

As the person in the middle of three consecutive points in the chain of command, the supervisor needs to appreciate the differences between the upward perspective and the downward perspective. Therefore, the most constructive view to take when looking up the chain of command is: I am but one of a number of people reporting to this superior, so I need to make it as easy as possible for my superior to communicate with me. Conversely, the downward view suggests: Each of these people who reports to me is looking to me for guidance, so I must show him or her how to relate to me so that I can meet his or her needs as well as possible.

### Not Just Problems, But Solutions

A large part of becoming an effective delegator consists of teaching employees to do their homework before bringing problems and concerns up the chain of command. However, the business of homework, or thorough staff work, as it might be called, can be dealt with both upward and downward by the individual supervisor. The reaction of many employees to the presence of a problem is to take that problem to the boss and ask for advice and assistance. The boss, however, whether it is you or your immediate superior, does not need problems. Rather, the boss needs solutions.

The way to communicate with one's superior is not to say, "I have a problem and I need your help." Rather, it is necessary to do some homework first: Analyze and isolate the problem, identify causes if possible, develop alternative solutions, and identify specifically what is needed from the boss. Then go to the boss and say, "Here's a problem. This is why I think it's a problem and what probably caused it. Here are two or three possible solutions, and here's the solution I like best and why. This is what I think I need from you in order to proceed. What is your advice?"

Now the boss need only answer "yes," "no," "do this," or "do that." Just as often the problem will be nearly self-solving once you have subjected it to analysis. In any case, you will have made it as easy as possible for the boss to communicate with you, without intruding on the boss' time to analyze the problem and without transferring ownership of the problem to your superior.

In parallel fashion the supervisor should encourage individual employees to do the same kind of homework to the fullest extent of their abilities. Whether dealing with a specifically delegated task or a problem encountered directly by the employee, the supervisor should instruct the employee in techniques of analyzing and refining everyday problems, of offering alternative solutions, and of making recommendations. The employee who does the necessary homework does not always relieve the supervisor of involvement; the supervisor may have input to offer beyond the reach of the employee. However, the employee who does the necessary homework has accepted partial ownership of the problem and has focused the problem so that it can be dealt with more efficiently. At the heart of effective delegation is the need to teach the employees to do as much as possible on their own before calling for help. One highly successful supervisor expressed management's needs well by saying, "Don't bring me more problems, bring me solutions."

## Reasonable Deadlines and Follow-Up

Although your superior may be lax with you regarding deadlines and follow-up—no level of management is exempt from such weaknesses—there is no need to be similarly lax with your subordinates. This is another area of supervisory behavior in which you can do much for yourself to improve how you work both upward and downward.

The supervisor who is lax concerning deadlines and follow-up shapes subordinates' expectations accordingly. If the boss says simply, "Take care of this when you can," the subordinate may respond immediately, within days or weeks, or never. And if the superior says, "Let me have this by Friday," but the subordinate knows through past practice that the boss is not likely to mention it again for two weeks, it will probably be two weeks before the work gets done. Such managers have, through their actions over time, conditioned their employees to expect this kind of behavior. Add to this conditioning the fact that some time-related instructions—"When you get a minute," "Whenever you can," "Sometime soon"—can mean anything from right this minute to never, depending on the employee's interpretation.

No matter how non-urgent or unimportant it may be, any task that is worth assigning is worth assigning a reasonable deadline. Once a deadline is assigned, regardless of the task's significance, that deadline should never be allowed to pass without some kind of closure taking place. If closure does not occur in the form of delivered results, then the manager who assigned the task and set the deadline should immediately follow up with the employee.

If your manager does not set deadlines for you, set them for yourself. Commit yourself to such deadlines, if possible, by promising results to the boss by some given day and time. Do not be too tough on yourself by promising immediate results. (If your boss is at all fair and effective, he or she will immediately tell you that you are allowing yourself too much or too little time.) If you are unable to deliver when you promised because of circumstances beyond your control, do not wait for the boss to follow up; rather, inform the boss of the delay and its causes.

This notion of applying reasonable deadlines and faithful follow-up is even more important in the supervisor's relationship with the employees in the work group. These are also the steps that ensure the thoroughness and effectiveness of proper delegation. One can assign a thoroughly defined task to a well-instructed employee and still get nothing if there is no specific requirement for completion or follow-up. The supervisor who assigns no deadlines projects a casual attitude toward timely accomplishment of work that can permeate the group. Worse still, if the supervisor usually assigns deadlines but lets them slide by without saying anything, the employees will come to see the supervisor as lax, disorganized, and possibly uncaring. It is this latter condition that is most likely to occur. Apparently, it is easy to assign a deadline when a task is assigned, but it is not quite as easy to remember to follow up on that deadline. Many supervisors fail to follow up on the deadlines they set, and in doing so they create credibility problems and other difficulties for themselves.

Assigning reasonable deadlines and following up on them represents the one area of performance in which a supervisor can considerably improve his or her managerial effectiveness the most with the least amount of effort. The supervisor can simply set reasonable deadlines for every task that is delegated and faithfully follow up every time a deadline is missed.

## THE PATTERN: THE NUTS AND BOLTS OF DELEGATION

### Select and Organize the Task

As discussed in Chapter 3, your work as a supervisor lends itself to separation into two general categories: technical tasks and managerial tasks. For instance, the records office supervisor still must have technical knowledge about sentence computation to be sure the department's employees are doing their jobs properly, but the supervisor also must tend to purely managerial tasks like budgeting and scheduling coverage. Most of your technical tasks are likely to be subjects for delegation, although there may be a few you should continue to control personally, either because they are of sufficient importance to warrant your personal attention or because they occur so infrequently that any training time you invest would never be paid back. Of your true managerial tasks, however, few if any can be delegated in their entirety.

Most of your pure managerial tasks cannot be delegated; they are among the reasons why you were entrusted with supervisory authority in the first place. For instance, the general personnel management tasks of hiring, firing, promotion, demotion, criticism, discipline, and performance appraisal cannot be delegated. Other managerial activities may lend themselves to partial delegation. For instance, you may obtain staff input and assistance in planning, scheduling, budgeting, purchasing, and other such activities, but the authority to approve, recommend, or implement still calls for the exercise of your supervisory authority.

Take the time to make a list of duties you perform that could reasonably be delegated to an employee. If you consider each workday for a period of weeks, writing down each such task whenever one occurs, you may be surprised at the significant amount of work falling into the category of tasks that can be delegated. Preparing routine reports, answering routine correspondence, preparing service schedules, ordering supplies, serving on certain committees, performing actual patient care or other technical tasks, and many other activities may present themselves as candidates for delegation. List them all, and rank them according to two criteria: the amount of your time they require and their importance to the institution. Establish a priority order of tasks for delegation.

Do not, however, attempt to delegate all these nonmanagerial duties at once. Do not even consider working with just two or three of them at the beginning. We are interested in establishing delegation as a habit, and new habits are tough to form.

Pick one task to begin with, preferably that which is either of most importance to the institution or takes the largest part of your time or both. You should plan on delegating a single function, or as much of one as possible, to a single person and thus avoid the situation in which a function is so broken up that no one person is able to develop a sense of the whole job. Also, in considering activities to delegate, concentrate on ongoing functions, on jobs that regularly recur. There is little to be gained by delegating a one-shot activity if you can do it faster and better by yourself.

Determine the specific authority you will have to give the person to whom you delegate an activity. Plan also on defining the limits of that authority. As suggested earlier, operating instructions themselves are often the full "authority" needed to perform a task. However, there are instances in which the person must be able to call on certain resources necessary to do the job. In all cases the authority given should be consistent with the responsibility assigned. For instance, if you make an employee responsible for ordering office supplies, you should also be sure that agency policy gives that person authority to sign the necessary purchase requisitions.

You should consider delegating as much of your technical task authority as possible, within policy. Even some of the routine portions of a few of your managerial tasks can be delegated. For example, you can delegate much of the numerical work involved in preparing your departmental budget as long as you maintain final decision-making authority over the complete budget.

### Select the Appropriate Person

To emphasize a widely-violated precept, if you happen to be at the second line of management (you supervise one lower level of supervision), keep in mind that when you delegate it should always be to an immediate subordinate. The chief of security should not be issuing orders to line correctional officers without going through the shift commander. To bypass that intervening level and delegate directly to an employee two levels below is to undermine the authority of the first-line supervisor. First-line supervisors, however, will not have this problem since all of their employees report directly to them.

Pick the employee you will delegate to by matching the qualifications of available employees with the requirements of the task to be delegated. How well you can do this will depend to a great extent on how well you know your employees' strengths and weaknesses and attitudes and capabilities. For instance, if the task you want to delegate consists of guiding new employees through a department orientation, you should be looking for an employee who knows the rest of the employees well enough to introduce new people to them, knows the department's work well enough to describe it to a newcomer, and is reasonably friendly and adept at conversing with new people. If you wish to delegate a portion of your budget preparation, you should be looking for an employee who appears to have the aptitude for numerical work.

However, it is not enough to simply make a judgmental match between the requirements of the task and what you perceive to be the abilities of the person. In addition to your assessment of untested skills, you need to consider who is probably ready to assume additional responsibility. You need to concentrate on those people you think are sufficiently mature and reliable to give the assignment an honest try.

Beware of either overdelegating or underdelegating. When you overdelegate, the employee to whom you give a task is clearly not ready to handle it. While a modest amount of challenge is certainly desirable, too much challenge can be overwhelming to the employee. Overdelegation frequently leads to an employee's failure in a first attempt at handling increased responsibility, a harsh beginning that is not easily overcome. On the other hand, underdelegation—assigning a task to an employee who is overqualified and can obviously handle it with the greatest of ease—can be fully as damaging. Underdelegation is a waste of an employee's capabilities and often results in that employee's boredom and stagnation. Ideally, delegation should provide a modest amount of challenge with a recognizable opportunity for growth, and the opportunity for diversification and expanded usefulness. Also, the employee must be able to see the importance of the delegated task.

You must also be reasonably convinced that the employee you have in mind has the time available to handle the delegated task. Even if person and task are properly matched you can create a hardship by assigning more work to someone who is already fully occupied. As a final caution, a supervisor who regularly gives the toughest jobs to one person—even if that worker is the best person for the job—runs the risk of burning out that individual.

### Instruct and Motivate the Person

One of the most common errors in delegation is turning an employee loose on a task with inadequate preparation; another look at the case study in Chapter 3 is instructive here. It is at this point that the pressure of time can set the stage for delegation failure. If the task you are delegating is one you have previously done yourself, and very often this is the case, there may be few instructions, procedures, or guidelines existing in writing. It may be that the only available instructions are those in your mind. In gathering the information you need to turn over a job, it may be necessary for you to put those instructions in writing as well as prepare to teach the employee how to do the job.

When you are completely ready to turn a task over to an employee, you should be able to provide satisfactory answers to the following questions:

1. Am I prepared to give the reasons for the task, fully explaining why it is important and why it must be done?
2. Am I giving the employee sufficient authority to accomplish the results I require?
3. Are all the details of the assignment completely clear in my mind?
4. If necessary, can I adapt all the instructions and procedural details to the level of the employee's knowledge and understanding?
5. Does the assignment include sufficient growth opportunity to motivate the employee appropriately?
6. Does the employee have the training, experience, and skills necessary to accomplish the task?
7. Are the instructions or procedures sufficiently involved that they should be put in writing?

Assuming you can answer these questions satisfactorily, turning a task over to an employee becomes a critical exercise in two-way communication. When meeting to make the actual assignment, encourage the employee to ask questions. If questions are not readily forthcoming, ask the employee to restate your instructions. Whenever possible, demonstrate those parts of the activity that lend themselves to demonstration and have the employee perform those operations to your satisfaction. Throughout the entire process, emphasize two-way communication.

Last in the process of turning over a task, but extremely important, is the necessity for you and the employee to achieve agreement on the results you expect. The precise methods by which those results are achieved may not be particularly important—several people may do the same task slightly differently—but the anticipated output must be known and agreed upon.

## Maintain Reasonable Control

Control of delegation is largely a matter of communication between supervisor and employee. The frequency and intensity of this communication will depend significantly on your assessment of the individual. You should know your employees well enough to be able to judge who needs what degree of control and assistance. Your people are bound to be different from each other. Some you may need to check with frequently and to monitor their activities with reasonable closeness; with others you may be quite comfortable simply touching base every few days.

Since the degree of control necessary will vary from employee to employee, the hazards of overcontrol or undercontrol are always present. Overcontrol can destroy the effects of delegation. The employee will not develop a sense of responsibility, and you may remain as actively concerned with the task as though you had never delegated it at all. Undercontrol is also hazardous in that the employee may drift significantly in unproductive directions or perhaps make costly or time-consuming errors that you could have helped to avoid.

Having decided the approximate extent of control the individual needs, proceed to set reasonable deadlines for task completion, or for the completion of portions of the task, and prepare to follow up as those deadlines arrive. Two points to be stressed at this stage are (1) the reasonableness of the deadlines and (2) the timeliness of follow-up. Give the employee plenty of time to do the job, including, if possible, extra time for contingencies. However, when a deadline arrives and you have not been presented with results, take the initiative and go to the employee. You have few, if any, valid reasons for letting a deadline you have set slide quietly past without asking for the results you expected.

Laziness in enforcing deadlines will cause you far more grief than just weakening the effects of delegation. Even if you let only a few deadlines slide by unmentioned, some employees will automatically adapt to this pattern of behavior and assume that the deadlines you impose are unimportant. On the other hand, if you make it a habit always to follow up on deadlines, your employees will pick up on this pattern and expect you to look for timely results.

Throughout the entire delegation process, try to avoid being a crutch for the employee. Regardless of how much guidance and assistance you are called on to provide, try to avoid solving problems for your employees. Rather, focus on showing your employees how to solve their own problems.

In most instances of delegation failure, the responsibility rests with the supervisor, not with the employee. Some failures are to be expected; delegation is an imperfect, sometimes highly subjective process. However, to keep failures to a minimum you should regularly assess your performance with the following questions:

1. Did I assign a task only to take it away before the employee could truly demonstrate any competence at the task?

2. Did I maintain too much or too little control?
3. Did I really provide the employee with authority commensurate with the responsibility I delegated?
4. Did I split up an activity such that no single person with some authority could develop a sense for the whole?
5. Was I overly severe with an employee who made a mistake?
6. Am I giving proper credit to the employee for getting the job done?
7. Am I keeping the more interesting tasks for myself, delegating only the mundane or unchallenging activities?
8. Have I slacked off in my own work as I delegated certain activities away, or have I used the time saved to increase my emphasis on managerial activities?

## AUTHORITY AND RESPONSIBILITY

From time to time you are likely to encounter some differences of opinion as to which is truly delegated: authority or responsibility. In some contexts it is correct to speak of delegation of responsibility, authority, or both. To be strictly correct, however, when you speak of delegation—the assignment of work to an employee—you are talking exclusively about the delegation of authority.

Think of the authority of your position as a physical object that can be cut up and distributed. Your authority is like a pie; you cut out a piece and give it to someone. The chunk of authority necessary to perform that work used to be yours; now it belongs to someone else. This is delegated authority.

Responsibility, however, is quite another matter. The analogy of the pie does not apply to responsibility. The only workable analogy that comes to mind is in the character of the one-celled creature, the amoeba. When the amoeba subdivides it becomes two one-celled creatures each equivalent to the other. In delegating the authority to perform a task you make the employee responsible for task completion. However, you remain responsible to your supervisor for the completion of that task. Thus authority is actually delegated, but responsibility is simply duplicated at a lower organizational level.

## FREEDOM TO FAIL

General Colin Powell, U.S. Army (Retired), said on the subject of failure, "The same day I have a disappointment, I try to reflect on it and say, 'What did I do wrong?' I never look for scapegoats. Once you have experienced a failure or disappointment, once you've analyzed it and gotten the lessons out of it—dump it."

Would that we all could have that attitude, even in circumstances where we live with the concrete results of our mistakes and those of our subordinates. Would that we could instill that in our subordinates.

When an employee fails in the performance of a delegated task, the failure is often shared. Sometimes the failure is largely the employee's for doing something incorrectly or for not following instructions, but many times the fault lies with the supervisor for bringing task and person together but not providing direction and support. Since failures at delegation must be shared, and since we all learn from our failures far more often than we learn from our successes, punishing or overcorrecting an employee who makes a mistake makes little sense. Criticism should, of course, be delivered when deserved, but it should always be constructive and include the means for correcting the errant behavior and avoiding a repetition of the problem.

In many prison situations, there is no room for error without grave consequences; a warden simply cannot afford to allow a death row inmate to escape without paying a significant price in career status and perhaps even in human life. Thus, there is little, if any, room for the tolerance of mistakes. However, in headquarters functions and in many support and administrative activities in the institution itself there is indeed room for errors, and they occur frequently. A tabulation error in a monthly report on consumption of dairy products may cause a budget problem next quarter, but this kind of problem has much less impact than a riot caused by a lieutenant misjudging how to break up an unauthorized inmate group.

The employee who is soundly taken to task for making a mistake while exercising reasonable individual initiative will likely shy away from exercising further initiative for fear of punishment. While the stakes can be higher in prison, as noted above, errors are a natural part of career growth, and we might say that the employee who never makes a mistake is not growing much.

A decision to delegate is a calculated risk. You should be willing to take that risk. After all, you do not know for certain about an employee's capability until you have given that person a chance with an actual assignment.

You should feel a strong incentive to practice delegation. You cannot always expect to do everything of importance yourself. However, you should also feel the incentive to exercise reasonable control over the delegation process. Since you cannot shed final responsibility for task performance, you will be held responsible for any serious mistakes the employee may make. Your knowledge of this retained responsibility can be frightening at times, but to function as an effective supervisor you need to recognize the necessity to delegate to get things done through people.

## BUILDING THE HABIT

You begin to build the delegation habit by concentrating on a single activity at a time, working with one employee until that activity has been completely incorporated as a part of the person's job. Proceeding in this fashion, one activity at a time, it may take you a long time to make significant progress with the list of activities you decided you could delegate. However, this methodical approach, conscientiously pursued, is the surest way to learn delegation as a true habit.

Incomplete or improper delegation is an undesirable habit and as such can be difficult to alter. However, the practice of proper delegation, once substituted for your old habits, is itself a strong, useful habit that will serve you well throughout your management career.

---

### EXERCISE 5–1: TO WHOM SHOULD YOU DELEGATE?

You are the controller in the headquarters office of a state correctional agency. Eight of your staff members are briefly described as follows:

1. Frank is technically competent, seems to communicate clearly, especially in writing, and pays attention to details.

2. Marsha has consistently shown good judgment in matters of finance, particularly in analyzing reports and statements for financial implications.

3. Barbara is a dependable employee. Young and fairly new to the institution, she nevertheless appears ready to handle increased responsibility.

4. By both credentials and experience, Tom is your most technically qualified employee.

5. Carlos is low key, polite, and a diplomatic "people person." He is clearly your best letter writer.

6. Paula is an empathic individual. People are generally comfortable with her and inclined to speak freely.

7. Sam has displayed both technical and managerial skills. He has successfully run several special projects.

8. Maria is an organizer. Few if any details of arranging a gathering of people escape her attention.

**The functions you can delegate to your employees include the following:**

a. Provide technical support on a special system-wide study of the operation of the inmate commissaries in all of your agency's institutions.

b. Manage the study, including responsibility for technical content.

c. Schedule and organize periodic project review meetings.

d. Review and approve all correspondence relating to the study.

e. Analyze and approve all expense reports relating to the study.

f. Write monthly status and progress reports for the study.

g. Answer all inquiries concerning certain activities of your department and the agency itself, with respect to fiscal matters.

h. Locate and screen applicants for potential employment in the department.

i. Requisition standard supplies for the office and assure that the supply room is adequately stocked.

## Instructions

Create a possible pattern of delegation by matching employees and assignments in a manner that appears to make best use of each person's capabilities. Note that there are more assignments than people and that any one person may be capable of taking on more than one of the assignments. (Caution: avoid overdelegation—assigning an employee a job for which he or she is probably not qualified.)

| _____1. Frank | _____5. Carlos |
|---|---|
| _____2. Marsha | _____6. Paula |
| _____3. Barbara | _____7. Sam |
| _____4. Tom | _____8. Maria |

## CASE 5–1: A DELEGATION KEY

The following paragraph is drawn from Case 4–1 concerning Marcie Denton, chief of maintenance:

> When she helped establish the department, Marcie Denton designated three men—one of them a working foreman—to handle all electrical and mechanical repairs and maintenance. She empowered the foreman with the authority to requisition parts and materials up to a limit of $50 per order.

### Questions

1. Since Denton has already made the foreman responsible for maintenance and repairs, why would she then find it necessary to take specific steps to give the foreman "authority to requisition parts and materials up to a limit of $50 per order"?
2. What does this illustration tell you about responsibility and authority in proper delegation?

## CASE 5–2: WHAT—ME WORRY?

Juan Ramirez, manager of the inmate-operated print plant at a large medium-security prison, was about to retire in six months. Ramirez was responsible for production of all printed forms for state agencies, as well as overseeing the operation of two warehouse facilities staffed by minimum-security inmates from adjacent prison camps. Over time, it had become obvious that the workload for the plant was going to grow to the point where new facilities would be needed. Juan had done little planning for the future because he knew he wouldn't have to deal with the consequences of his delay.

Finally, pressure from the warden forced Ramirez to face the daunting task of preparing a proposal for a new, larger plant, with more modern equipment, including an elaborate climate control system that would keep humidity and heat from affecting the print process. The lead time for the entire process would be at least 18 months and the inmate population was going to be a critical factor in about two years. To make matters worse, there were only ten weeks until final budget submissions were due in the legislature.

Ramirez decided he was going to delegate the preparation of the plant proposal to his assistant, Frank Santarelli. He called Santarelli to his office, and said, "Frank, we've got a problem. We need to get a plan together for the legislature to design, spec out, and fund a print plant that will employ twice as many inmates as we're working now. The population is going to be going up so fast with this new 'three strikes legislation' that we are going to be in big trouble if we don't have those new jobs on line within two years. This is your baby. Run with it. And by the way, you only have ten weeks to get it done!"

Santarelli wasted no time in voicing his concerns. "Juan, I'm sure I can do this, but I've never been involved in construction planning, budgeting on this scale, or for that matter, writing anything that is going to go before the legislature. How about let's work on this together, at least at the start until I can see how you want me to do it?"

Ramirez said, "Look, the reason I'm giving you this is because I'm not going to have to live with this new factory—you are. Besides, if you don't have any more initiative than that, I may as well do it myself." He grinned as he added, "Actually, if you really want that promotion to factory manager at the penitentiary, this could be your ticket out!"

About three weeks later—after hearing nothing back from his boss— Santarelli stopped Ramirez on the plant floor as the latter was making an impromptu inspection of a big forms job for the Department of Social Services. He said, "Juan, I need to talk to you. There is no way I can pull this all together in the next two weeks."

Ramirez replied, "What do you mean two weeks? You should have seven weeks to go."

Santarelli responded with, "What you didn't know was that the warden needs a week to review it and then headquarters wants three weeks to give it a once-over before it goes to the legislative budget committee. And it has to be to the committee a week sooner than you thought so their analysts can figure out where to get the money. I just found all this out today. We're in big trouble here."

## Instructions

1. Ramirez committed several significant errors in "delegating" the preparation of this proposal to Santarelli. Identify at least three such errors in the case description.

2. Using as many steps as you believe necessary, describe how this instance of delegation might have been properly accomplished.

## CHAPTER 6

# Time Management: Expanding the Day without Stretching the Clock

*Time is fixed income and, as with any income, the real problem facing most of us is how to live successfully within our daily allotment.*

—*Margaret B. Johnstone*

*Whether these are the best of times or the worst of times, it's the only time we've got.*

—*Art Buchwald*

### Chapter Objectives

☛ Place "time" in perspective as an unrenewable resource that influences all managerial activity.

☛ Identify the common time-wasting practices encountered in organized work activity.

☛ Identify delegation and planning as key considerations in the manager's effective use of time.

☛ Offer practical suggestions to improve one's effective use of available time.

☛ Isolate the sources of time-wasting pressure inherent in the organizational environment and suggest the manager's appropriate response to these pressures.

## TIME AND TIME AGAIN

Time is, for all of us, a resource of considerable value. Moreover, time is always moving, always going forward regardless of whether we are putting it to some specific use. Dream though we may, we cannot call back a single minute that has gone by.

Time is a resource that is fixed in amount, but for all practical purposes the demands on our time are unlimited. Effective time management is critical to being a good manager.

We have heard all our lives that "time is money." To many people in business, time well spent is the difference between loss and profit. But to providers of all kinds of services, including corrections, wasted time represents wasted cash resources, since salaries and expenses go on

80

even when service is not being rendered. To the corrections professional, time is not only a measure that inmates mark very carefully, it
often is a critical factor in fulfilling the agency's or institution's objectives to ensure public safety and provide humane conditions of confinement for inmates. The need to quickly and effectively respond to a plot
or escape plot are obvious examples, but there are many other less dramatic instances where time-bound decisions are a factor in day-to-day
prison activities—counts being the most obvious.

In this chapter we will begin with the assumption that few of us, no
matter how organized and efficient we may be, could not improve our
use of some of the working time available to us.

Managers are often ruled by the demands of the job. It may seem as
though the work and the hours rarely come out even, there being considerably more of the former than the latter. Managers react to this
disparity in various ways. At one extreme is the supervisor who continually stays late in an effort to get "caught up," a state that seems
never to arrive. This approach is not the answer, and neither is the
answer found in the other extreme—walking out the door at quitting
time although many problems remain to be solved. Certainly there are
days when extra time and effort are the only answer, but when this is
relied on as a regular solution, it simply turns a full-time job into a full-
and-a-half-time job without truly improving the way the department
runs.

With exceptions, the place to begin improving performance is in the
use of our regularly scheduled job time. We owe it to ourselves, and
certainly to our agency, to get more out of each day by putting more of
the proper effort into each day.

Task performance aside, consider where much of the working time
goes for many people. Late starts, slow starts, long breaks, long
lunches, meetings of questionable value, and especially periods of social conversation, are part of many people's working style and can
drain supervisory and nonsupervisory productivity. Although personal
considerations and social relationships are important in a work environment, few people realize the extent to which these things cut into
the time for which they are being paid to perform certain duties. Many
a manager has stretched a coffee break into a half hour while complaining of how much work there was to be done.

Aside from out-and-out nonproductive activity, however, a great deal
of time is wasted in the ways we approach supposedly legitimate tasks.
We will briefly highlight the readily identifiable time wasters, then offer suggestions for incorporating time savers into our behavior.

## THE TIME WASTERS

### Failure To Delegate

Failure to delegate thoroughly and effectively is one of the greatest time wasters to which a supervisor can fall victim. We will not repeat the cautions of Chapter 5 but will simply remind you of the importance of remaining open to delegation possibilities.

### Failure To Plan and Establish Priorities

A 1959 Walt Kelly "Pogo" cartoon shows two characters leaning against each other. One says, "MAN! You know, it ain't the work so much what tires you, it's the planning." The other character responds with, "WHOO! If you got the strength you can say that again."

Planning takes effort. And often it is an unwillingness to put effort into planning that catches up with a manager. You may have heard the term *traffic-cop management* or perhaps *firefighting management*. These describe an all too common approach to supervision: very little looking ahead and not much consideration given to deciding which of a number of tasks is most important. It is usually the problem of the moment that gets the attention or the people making the most noise who get heard.

Prisons are a very fertile environment for this management style, with their never-ending series of minor crises and the occasional major crisis. Each emerging situation is the perfect rationale for abandoning structured management activities. A manager can be extremely busy practicing this form of management but can nevertheless be wasting significant amounts of time. Without some rationale for approaching work in a manner consistent with its necessity, and for dealing on an ad hoc basis with only real crises, tasks of lesser importance consume disproportionate amounts of time and not enough time is devoted to more important, but non-emergency situations.

### Overplanning and Overorganizing

Overplanning and overorganizing are two common traps that many people fall into when making what they believe are conscientious efforts to improve their use of time. Because they hear so much about the necessity of planning and the importance of being organized, some supervisors tend to overcompensate for their self-perceived weaknesses by going overboard with plans, task lists, schemes of objectives and subobjectives, and open files, active files, tickler files, and dead files.

We could insert here a psychological treatise exploring the possible reasons behind the tendency to overplan and overorganize. These reasons would probably include avoidance of unpleasant tasks (planning is "good," and while one is busy planning one does not have to be doing), a sense of insecurity, uncertainty concerning how superiors will deal with mistakes, and a fear of failure. Whatever the reasons, a manager's personal planning and organizing become time wasters when they occur to excess.

What is excess planning and organizing? Only you know for certain how much is adequate for you and when you are overplanning and overorganizing. But a few examples are clear. Consider the manager who maintained his calendar in duplicate—one a full-size loose-leaf binder and one a version that would fit into a pocket. When asked bluntly by another manager why he maintained duplicate calendars, he could say only that he especially liked the features of the desktop book but that it was too large to carry around conveniently. Thus nudged into thinking about what he had been doing, the manager realized that the time and effort of maintaining duplicate calendars was not worth the minimal benefit gained.

Many managers engage in many activities that are not worth the benefit or convenience gained. If we update a "To Do" list daily, fine; but if every day sees the To Do lists—plural, because there are lists A, B, C or 1, 2, 3—revamped, reworked, and reordered, then time is being wasted. And if we are "organized" to the extent that a task is pulled from the To Do folder, stuck in the Active or Open file, and advanced through three or four other stages, each with its own name and filing system, then organizing has become overorganizing.

Planning and personal organizing are surely important. However, both of these virtues can become excesses. Quite simply, even the noble pursuit of planning should be kept consistent with the expected results. That is, never pour a dollar's worth of effort into assuring a two-bit payback.

### Face-to-Face Contacts

Face-to-face contacts represent the essence of a supervisor's job. However, one-on-one situations readily get out of hand and waste our time. Aside from social conversation, which you should be able to control within reason, you will experience numerous interruptions during your workday. How you handle these interruptions will influence the degree of effectiveness with which you use your available time. For instance, the last time a vendor or your counterpart in another agency called to say he or she "was in the neighborhood" and wanted to see you, did you drop something else in your schedule to see that person? Or the last time you were talking business with one of your employees, did you allow another employee or fellow manager who wanted your attention for a moment to interrupt? In short, do you usually give in to the pressures of interruptions and unexpected visits? Other people will readily waste your time if you allow them to do so.

## The Telephone

One of the most useful communication facilitators ever devised, the telephone, can also be one of the greatest time wasters. The telephone can be of considerable value when effectively controlled, but often we allow it to control us. Modern phone messaging systems or E-mail may help in this regard. These systems can help cut back on "telephone tag" by enabling callers to relate complete thoughts on a subject, and to receive feedback on that issue via the same technology. Whether these systems are a real aid to managers depends on how the organization structures them, as well as the expectations the agency sets for managers to use them.

## Meetings

Like the telephone, the meeting is another means of communication that is misused and abused, to the extent that its effects are often the reverse of what was intended.

Sometimes it seems as though the modern prison runs on meetings, and this appearance might seem to justify the need for more and longer meetings in which to conduct business. However, close analysis of our meetings will reveal significant wasted time in many cases. We do not claim that most meetings are unnecessary, although some certainly are, but rather that the majority of meetings are too long relative to the results they produce and too loosely managed to be truly effective.

## Paperwork

Today, many prison managers say that their institutions seem to run on paper. Many must feel as though the in-basket is like the magic pitcher in the children's story of many years ago—no matter how much you took from it, it was always full. We seem never to be caught up on paperwork, and the supervisor who conscientiously tries to keep the in-basket current usually discovers this cuts into time needed for more important tasks.

Like many other activities, paperwork can be essential as well as wasteful. It becomes a time waster when some things get done at the expense of others, items of minor consequence get attention while important items remain in the stack, and items that should be ignored receive attention simply because they are there.

### Personal Habits

Whether or not you waste significant amounts of time on the activities mentioned above will depend largely on the habits you have formed regarding these activities. You can, for instance, allow your meetings to be loose and rambling simply out of habit—you may have always worked that way, following the path of least resistance.

Beyond your personal approach to specific activities, however, there is your overall pattern of behavior to consider. Are you perhaps a slow starter, entering the day with an hour's worth of coffee and procrastination until you take hold and begin to produce? Are you in the habit of jumping from task to task, starting many jobs but completing few? When you reach a point in a task when you need information and assistance from others, do you simply stop and wait for them rather than fill your waiting time with productive effort?

For good or for ill, unless you exercise conscious control, your approach to your daily duties will be governed largely by your personal habits.

### THE TIME SAVERS

### Plans and Priorities

To get control of your time you must first determine what must be done and in what order things should be accomplished. The process of planning and setting priorities, along with the practice of proper delegation, is a major force in the productive use of time. Volumes have been written about planning, but for our purposes some simple suggestions will provide an effective basis for a solid start in managerial planning.

### Determine How You Really Spend Your Time

Make the decision to analyze critically your use of time to determine if you are really using most of your time wisely. To perform this analysis honestly, a degree of commitment is necessary, and it may also be necessary to accept the likelihood of sacrificing some old habits for the sake of self-improvement.

Check up on yourself. For some period of time (at least two weeks but preferably three or four weeks) keep a record of how you spend your time. This need not be an elaborate scheme in which you write down every 30-second task or record your activities down to the minute. Rather, reasonable entries might look like: "weekly staff meeting—90 minutes"; "interview prospective employee—one-half hour"; and "prepare monthly statistical report—three hours."

When you have sufficient information to work with, sort the results and determine the approximate portion of your time spent on routine tasks, unscheduled tasks, and tasks that could be considered emergencies. Routine tasks are those you do on a regular basis (for instance, daily, weekly, or monthly staff meetings). They are routine in that you know what they are and approximately when they occur. An unscheduled task is one for which you know the what but not the when. For instance, you may know there will be times when you have to write a report because of an inmate-related incident or other unusual event, but you have no way of knowing when this will occur. An emergency task is one for which you know neither what nor when; you simply know that unplanned events occur and you must respond. Responding to an escape plot or an assault would fall into this category

When you have finished analyzing your time record, you should know most of the things you do and the approximate portion of your time spent on routine, unscheduled, and emergency tasks. Further, you should be able to tell which of your tasks are likely candidates for delegation.

One of the first useful pieces of information gained from this process is an appreciation of how much of your time on average goes to what you categorize as emergencies—tasks for which you are aware of neither the "what" nor the "when" in advance. Prison life is full of such episodes, and the average supervisor (if there is indeed such a person) will find a surprisingly high percentage of time consumed by "emergency" tasks. Of course, in making your analysis, you also should be sure that all of the incidents categorized as emergencies really are, or whether there are some categories of incidents that really do not demand your attention. Although you cannot ordinarily avoid genuine emergencies, especially those falling clearly within your responsibility, you can learn enough to enable you to allow for them in your planning. For example, if your three-way analysis of several weeks' activity suggests that you spend an average of 35 percent of your time on so-called emergency tasks, then on average you should leave that much of your time flexible to meet emergencies rather than scheduling yourself to the hilt with known work. Although you cannot do much about emergency tasks, you can maintain flexibility in your scheduling and whenever possible allow extra time for the unexpected.

When you have eliminated from consideration those tasks you can delegate, you are left with a number of activities—routine tasks as well as unscheduled tasks—that you must do. The next stage of your planning involves determining how you will approach them.

## A Personal Planning Gimmick

You may have heard the following suggestion before, but its enduring applicability makes it worth repeating here.

Of the tasks you must personally perform within the coming few days, write down in list form the four or five you consider most important. Then spend a few minutes putting these tasks into their order of importance; that is, task number one should be the first task you must accomplish. The result should be a list of the several most important jobs you must do and the order in which they must be done.

The approach is simple: go to work on number one and stay on it until it is done. Granted you may be pulled away for an emergency; however, when the emergency is over, get immediately back to task number one. Turn away all other interruptions, and do not allow your efforts to be diverted. When task number one is completed, move on to task number two and tackle it the same way.

These need not be only desk-bound activities. If, for instance, you are factory manager of a prison industries operation, it would not just be desirable, but critical, that you allocate a significant amount of time out to being on the production floor, talking with civilian and inmate workers.

You may not get through your entire list as quickly as you would like, but rest assured you will have accomplished more than if you had attacked these several tasks in any other manner. Also, when working this way you are always at work on the most important task of the moment.

Do not forget to allow yourself some planning time. The planning process is essential, urging you to think ahead and establish priorities and determine direction before proceeding. A "plan" as such need not be elaborate—perhaps a list on your calendar of four or five items to tackle tomorrow. However, the time you devote to planning will ordinarily pay itself back in improved efficiency several times over.

### Set Objectives and Work to Deadlines

It always pays to be working toward a specific objective, whether that objective is the completion of your most important open task or simply the completion of a particular part of a larger task.

Any objective, whether organizational, departmental, or personal, should consist of what is to be done, how much is to be accomplished, and when it should be completed. For a unit manager of a housing area, one objective may be to complete the performance appraisals (what) for all five counselors in the unit (how much) by the end of Wednesday (when). In the case of the prison industries manager, objectives can be quite clear—the production of a certain number of desks or brooms every month at a certain cost. For the chief of classification, the objective may be to assure that no more than 35 unclassified inmates remain in the orientation unit by Friday afternoon, without resorting to overtime on the part of the classification department. For the business manager, it may be that all financial statements must be completed and reconciled with headquarters records within five working days after the end of the month.

Related to the "when" portion of any objective, the time boundaries of the task may be externally imposed, as in some statutory reporting requirement. They may relate to internal institutional needs, like the goal to keep fewer than 35 inmates in the orientation unit over the weekend, which is rooted in a need for another department (security) to keep a low level of staff in that unit. But even if there are no outside time limits, be sure to set a deadline for yourself.

### Write It Down—and Change It

Even if you are used to doing your day-to-day task planning in your head, commit your plans to paper. Your plan may, and usually should, be extremely simple: a few lines on a desk pad, perhaps a few entries in a pocket notebook. Make sure that your tasks, priorities, objectives, and deadlines exist in writing in a place where you will see them frequently.

However, simply noting two or three days' planned activity in writing does not guarantee that you will be able to follow the plan as written. Each time some unforeseen event intrudes on your activity and upsets your plan, take the new requirement into account and revise your written plan. Get in the habit of spending a few minutes at the end of each day planning for the following day; at that time you can revise your plan to reflect current needs. Many managers who have access to a computer find that keeping these lists in an automated form enables quick updates on these planning documents. A few minutes at the end of each day making necessary changes yields a fresh list, and also can allow old list items to form the basis for a record of past activities.

*Face-to-Face Contacts*

Face-to-face contacts need not be significant time wasters if approached properly.

The biggest waste of time in face-to-face contacts is the tendency to engage in excessive small talk and social conversation when we should be dealing with business. The images of the crowd around the coffee pot or a group of correctional officers hanging around the yard shack are based in reality, and managers are prone to the same kind of socializing on the job as line staff. We are not suggesting that social conversation should be taboo; a certain amount is essential to morale and good interpersonal relations. However, business can also be conducted on a friendly level, and beyond minor social pleasantries, you should make an effort to stay on business in contacts with employees and co-workers.

Much of the manager's most important work takes place within the context of the one-to-one relationship with each employee, and developing that relationship with each employee is recognized as one of the supervisor's most important tasks. It is not at all suggested that supervisors minimize contacts with employees or that each contact necessarily advances the business of the department. Listening to a troubled employee may take an hour without apparently advancing the work of the department at all, but the time is well spent if it results in upholding the morale and productivity of the employee. However, talking about fishing for an hour with an employee who happens to be an enthusiastic angler and who brings up the topic at every turn is a clear waste of time.

While you should not allow employees to waste your time, neither should you waste their time by delaying them for irrelevancies and nonessentials simply because you happen to be the boss. One of your primary functions is to enhance your employees' ability to accomplish their assigned tasks, and you are not doing this if you are wasting their time.

Visitors from outside the institution are another form of face-to-face contact that frequently wastes time. The supervisor of education may be approached on a regular basis by textbook vendors or persons who want to demonstrate the latest in programmed-learning computer software. The hospital administrator may be besieged with calls from salespersons seeking to come in to promote new pharmaceutical products. The chief of maintenance and business manager probably have more than their fair share of inquiries about how to get on the institution's procurement list, with offers to demonstrate their products' superiority.

If you are involved in a significant number of such distracting contacts from outside the institution, your productivity will suffer. Salespeople, especially, will tend to adopt the practice of calling to see if they can "just drop by" once they have discovered that you will stop what you are doing to meet with them. It takes little effort to refuse politely to meet with these visitors on short notice. Once you begin to signal to these inquirers that you are available on your terms, not theirs, these visits are likely to decrease or cease entirely.

## The Telephone

How we make or take telephone calls will determine the extent to which the telephone rules our activities and consumes excessive amounts of time. Granted, there are many times when you cannot avoid a telephone interruption. But many calls can be controlled with a little effort.

When interruptions would be harmful to what you are trying to accomplish, have incoming telephone calls held. This is especially important if you are already speaking with someone; when you stop to answer the telephone, you are wasting someone else's time as well as possibly your own. If possible, have your calls screened with messages taken for you to act on later. Only genuinely urgent calls should reach you. As a general rule, if there is not a staff member to perform this screening function, do not use an inmate. (Those instances where an inmate may be used to answer a phone should be very carefully controlled and limited to phones that do not connect to an outside line).

Likewise, do not interrupt something important you may be doing to make or return a call simply because you happen to remember it just then. Note a reminder of the necessary call and take care of it later.

When you make telephone calls, for all but the simplest messages, it is helpful to spend a few seconds organizing your thoughts before you dial. Jot down the points you need to cover. Have necessary references and notetaking materials handy. Otherwise, you are likely to prolong a call unnecessarily only to remember that there was something else that you should have mentioned.

As you return to your desk during the day and find calls you have to return, do not always feel it is necessary to return every call then and there. Urgent calls, of course, should be returned at once. Routine call-backs are most appropriately handled if you pick one particular time of day to do most of your telephoning and go through all possible calls at a single sitting. For someone who works the day shift, for instance, the best time is usually from early or mid afternoon until the end of the workday. This time may be more restricted for some staff (such as shift supervisors) since many supervisory posts have a log, shift report, or other paperwork to contend with as the shift ends. The noon hour is probably the worst time to return telephone calls because people are often away from their desks.

Use the telephone wisely and it can be one of the best time savers available to you. However, let the telephone use you and you will suffer through lost efficiency and reduced effectiveness.

Some agencies are using phone messaging services and E-mail technology to facilitate contacts that otherwise would be handled by telephone. This approach works particularly well for noninteractive messages, such as daily updates throughout a large organization and for disseminating bulletins, such as changes in routine or scheduled activities. Phone messaging can be quite usable for transacting a great deal of business that otherwise would be slowed down by managers playing "phone tag." However, these communication methods do not allow a fully efficient, free flow of interaction between two parties on a complex subject or range of subjects; successive computer-recorded or E-mail messages to cover the same material take more time than a personal call covering those topics. While these technologies cannot substitute completely for personal phone contacts, they can be used to good effect to supplement normal channels of communication.

### Meetings

The subject of meetings is of sufficient importance to warrant a chapter of its own (see Chapter 19). Meetings should be held only when necessary; planned and organized with specific purposes in mind; started on time; kept to the subject; and consume only the amount of time required to accomplish their specific objectives.

## Paperwork

We suggested earlier that it was all too easy to allow the in-basket to control much of our time. Although we all receive much material deserving attention and action, not everything that comes in is of equal importance.

When you are faced with one or two days' accumulation of incoming material—and for some managers this can be a significant amount of paper—rather than simply working on the basket from the top down (or bottom up, for that matter), first sort all the paper into three categories.

Your first category should consist of those few items that genuinely deserve your immediate attention and those that can be disposed of by noting a quick word in response, such as memos from the associate warden on current issues and routine approvals that require no research or consideration.

Your second category should include those items that will take you some time to resolve because they require research or more extended effort, and noncritical items that you can afford to resolve at your leisure. They might include policies to review, memos from subordinates, proposed activities requiring coordination with other departments, and similar items. Some of the items you put in this category may become part of your workload of routine or unscheduled tasks and should be worked into your priority planning. Also, a few items in this pile may be clear candidates for delegation. As you come across these, you should be making some tentative decision as to who might be able to handle them.

The third category of incoming material, and often the largest stack, consists of items you can safely discard. Resist the temptation to file every information memo or advertising brochure that comes in; this kind of material, especially information on routine inmate programs or vendor brochures, rapidly becomes out-of-date. In most instances, when you later wish to find out about a specific inmate program or investigate a certain line of supplies or equipment, the institution department with the primary interest in that item of information (the education supervisor's office or purchasing agent, in this example) should be able to come up with current information. Simply screen all this material for topics of special interest, pass along things you think may be of interest to someone else, and throw away the rest. Rest assured; it is more than 99.9 percent certain that the memo or brochure in today's mail will never be more than office clutter or file cabinet filler should you keep it.

## TIME-WASTING PRESSURES AND THE MANAGER'S RESPONSE

Time-wasting pressures come toward the manager from every direction. Your choice is simple: give with pressures and bend in the direction they take you, or, become a positive force, refusing to bend, and influence others in productive directions. Time-wasting pressures are likely to come from the following sources.

### Your Boss

At times it seems as though higher management is insensitive to the demands on your time. There is no end to the reports you are expected to produce and the meetings that you must attend. It seems this way especially when you already feel overloaded and the boss comes along with something else for you to do. However, the manager who places more work with an already overburdened supervisor is not necessarily being insensitive—remember, your boss sits at a different organizational level and does not have full knowledge of everything you have to do. You are the only one who can truly say if the new assignment you were just handed is too much. Depending on your relationship with your immediate superior, perhaps you need not simply accept that new assignment when you are short of time to begin with. Speak up. Let the boss know where you stand in terms of workload and that you do not have time to do it properly. Talk it over; your boss needs two-way communication with you as surely as you need it with your employees. Chances are you will be able to work out something—a compromise, perhaps, or a reordering of priorities that will serve both the manager's purposes and yours. There may be many times when the boss will not really know how much you have to do unless you say so.

### The System

Inefficient practices prevail to some extent in most workplaces, and government organizations and correctional agencies are no exception. If it seems you are surrounded by people who are disorganized, careless, and always late—and if your organization tolerates or even fosters that behavior—you will be under pressure to behave in the same manner.

However, no organizational system was ever made better without someone taking the initiative to start improving one small section first. And today few, if any, organizations will resist well-reasoned initiatives for improving operations. More than ever in this day of citizen concern over government activities and the resources devoted to sustaining them, bureaucrats and politicians see the rationale of facilitating changes that benefit the public through cost-effectiveness and increased productivity. A few managers who are determined not to give in to the time-wasting pressure of the system can begin to apply positive pressure that will eventually be felt beyond their own departments.

### Your Employees

Time-wasting pressure will frequently come from your employees, especially those who may be insensitive to the true requirements of your position. It is true you are there to help your employees and run interference for them. You may have many employees, but some of them may see you only in terms of their individual needs. Some supervisors have found they could spend most of their time in unnecessary handholding if they gave way to the pressure. (However, in all fairness to the employees who seem to require handholding, if this pressure is widespread in your department, many elements of your approach to supervision need examination.)

### Yourself

This area is, of course, largely what we have been talking about in this chapter. Inefficient planning, poor approaches to delegation, and poor personal work habits can produce the subtlest and yet the most wasteful pressures of all because they originate with you. Only you can eliminate them.

### THE UNRENEWABLE RESOURCE

Time is a resource you cannot replace. Once an amount of time is used, it is gone forever; if it is not used, it is still gone. As a manager, when you do not spend your time effectively you are not simply wasting your own time. In most instances you are also wasting the time of your employees. Conversely, any time you save may also save time for some or all of the employees in your department.

In managing your time, you should most certainly be interested in doing a sufficient amount of planning to assure that you and your employees do things right. However, even more important is your constant awareness of priorities; you must strive for assurance that you and your employees are doing the right things as well as doing things right.

---

### EXERCISE 6–1: THE TIME-USE TEST

This exercise may provide you with useful information about the way you use your time. Time yourself to determine how long it takes you to complete the exercise.

1. Read everything before doing anything.
2. Write your name in the upper right hand corner of this page.
3. Circle the word upper in instruction 2.
4. Draw four small squares in the upper left corner of this page.
5. Mark an X in each square.
6. Draw a circle around each square.
7. Sign your name immediately below the title.
8. To the right of the title write "Yes, Yes, Yes!"
9. Circle each word in instruction 6.
10. Mark a large X in the lower left hand corner of this page.
11. Draw a triangle around the X you just marked.
12. Somewhere in the margin, multiply 7,125 by 306.
13. Draw a box around the word page in instruction 4.
14. Speak your first name out loud.
15. If you have followed instructions to this point, say "I have."
16. Add 7,840 and 8,740.
17. Draw a circle around the answer to 16.
18. Draw a square around the circle you just drew.
19. In your normal voice, count out loud backward from ten to one.
20. Now that you have finished reading carefully, do only steps 1 and 2.

### EXERCISE 6–2: THE TIME-WASTING PRESSURES

For a period of at least one full work week, keep track of the occasions when you felt your time was wasted. Make a note briefly describing each such occasion and also note the approximate amount of time involved. When you have a week's worth of notes, review them and attempt to relate each occasion to a source of time-wasting pressure. The sources of time-wasting pressure are your boss, the "system," your employees, and yourself.

Considering your position relative to the sources you noted, next arrange your occurrences of wasted time into three categories according to how much or how little control you can exercise in such situations. Use (1) full control, (2) partial control, and (3) little or no control.

If you have made realistic, objective assessments throughout the exercise, the resulting category listings should suggest several areas where you can apply concentrated effort to improve your use of time.

---

### CASE 6–1: TEN MINUTES TO SPARE?

You are a unit manager at a medium-security prison.

This morning you return to work following a week of annual leave to find your in-basket overloaded and your desk littered with telephone message slips. You are greeted by your secretary, who informs you that you are expected to substitute for your boss, the associate warden, at an outside meeting today. You have to leave no later than 9:30 A.M. to make the meeting on time, and you know you can plan on being gone the rest of the day.

You are left with one hour in which to begin making order out of the chaos on your desk before leaving for the meeting. True to your usual pattern, you set about reviewing all the items on your desk—telephone slips as well as in-basket items—and sorting them into stacks according to their apparent order of importance. You feel that perhaps you can at least get sufficiently organized to be able to begin work the following day with emphasis on your most important unfinished tasks.

About halfway through your hour of organizing your secretary enters to say, "Mr. Wade (the business manager) is here asking to see you. He says he wants ten minutes of your time to discuss a minor problem with our fourth quarter budget request. Shall I tell him you'll call him about it? Or that maybe he should send you a memo?"

You cannot help feeling that the last thing you need during this hour is an interruption, especially for a nonurgent reason. It occurs to you that your secretary has briefly suggested two alternatives; to these you add a possibility of your own so that you see three choices:

1. Say that you cannot see Wade right now but that you will call him the following day.
2. Ask for a memo detailing the problem so you can look into it at your convenience.
3. Agree to the request for a meeting then and there, and try to limit the discussion to five to ten minutes.

## Instructions

1. Enumerate the advantages and disadvantages of each of the fore-going three alternatives.
2. Indicate which alternative you would most likely choose, and fully explain the reasons for your decision.

---

## CASE 6–2: THE VISITOR

As the door closed behind her departing visitor, shift supervisor Janet Mills glumly reflected that she had just lost an hour that she could ill afford to lose. To complete the roster she was working on, she was either going to be late for an upcoming labor-management meeting or have to work late.

It had been a busy day anyway, and the hour had been lost because of a visit from a pleasant, but overly talkative, state police investigator. It seems he was more interested in trading "war stories" about prison cases he had investigated when he was assigned as investigative liai-son officer to the state's main penitentiary than he was in discussing current cases. As was her practice, Janet consented to see him when he stopped by her office to discuss a recent stabbing, although she re-sented the intrusion. As the hour went on, she knew she was losing time, but didn't want to alienate the investigator, since she knew she would be working with him on other cases in the future.

This incident, occurring on a Friday, made Janet realize that she had lost time to four such drop-in visits this week alone. Even though this was the only nonprison staff member who intruded on her workday routine to this extent, she generally did not like the idea of simply saying no or otherwise trying to avoid people who wanted to see her. This episode made her more aware that her work was beginning to suffer because of such demands on her time.

## Instructions

Develop some guidelines that might help Janet and other supervisors deal with the problem of drop-in visitors.

## CHAPTER 7

# Self-Management and Personal Supervisory Effectiveness

*Technical training is important but it accounts for less than 20 percent of one's success. More than 80 percent is due to the development of one's personal qualities, such as initiative, thoroughness, concentration, decision, adaptability, organizing ability, observation, industry, and leadership.*

*—G. P. Koch*

### Chapter Objectives

☞ Round out the review of "The Supervisor and Self" by supplementing delegation and time management with important personal considerations.

☞ Highlight the key influence of individual initiative on supervisory effectiveness.

☞ Review the principal barriers to effective performance.

☞ Discuss the relationship of stress to personal supervisory effectiveness.

☞ Provide suggestions and guidance for organizing for effective performance.

☞ Provide guidelines for assessing one's suitability for a supervisory role, with implications for successful self-management.

## IT STARTS WITH YOU

If you would like to gain true control of the practice of management, do not look to sophisticated management theories or techniques and do not rely on gimmicks. Also, do not expect higher management to wind you up and point you in productive directions. The unfortunate reality of corrections, like many other professions, is that although a certain amount of management direction is essential, it will not always be there when you believe it should be and it will not always take the form you would like it to take.

For a solid foundation on which to base your development as a supervisor, begin with yourself. Do not presume to manage anything else until you have captured and controlled the essentials of managing yourself.

Every employee is a manager of sorts. Even the worker with a few simple tasks and no subordinates is partly a manager of time, methods, and supplies. Since all resources apply together to influence output, the individual worker has at least a limited amount of flexibility in managing output. For supervisory personnel this flexibility is much greater. Performance expected of managers is more results oriented and less methods oriented than what is expected of nonsupervisory personnel, so for many managerial tasks any of several approaches can be taken as long as desired results occur.

Conscientious self-improvement in the use of your personal resources will improve the effectiveness with which you manage yourself. It also will enable you to manage the efforts of others more effectively, whether the staff involved are correctional officers in a cellhouse, a plumber supervising an inmate work detail, or an accountant working independently in the business office. These personal resources include initiative, organization, and time.

The effective use of time was covered in Chapter 6 and many of the implications of organization were discussed under delegation in Chapter 5. A few pertinent remarks will round out our consideration of "The Supervisor and Self."

## INITIATIVE

In his film about self-motivation titled, "You, Yourself, Inc.," J. Lewis Powell referred to a junior manager preparing to take a course using a text called *How to Develop Initiative*. The young man was ready—he was waiting for his boss to order him to begin. This is what Powell referred to as the "wheelbarrow personality"—useless unless someone else does the pushing.

As supervisors we should recognize that we cannot always be exercising initiative in all directions, because of limits on our authority. However, when it comes to self-improvement the only constraints on our initiative are those we place there ourselves. Even in the area of task performance closely circumscribed by institution or agency policy, a great amount of initiative can be possible.

Some first-line supervisors may counter this claim by pointing out that their managers do not seem to encourage initiative but seem content to function as "wheelbarrow pushers" rather than as true leaders. This may be a fact of life at times, but the higher manager who is operating as a wheelbarrow pusher is guilty of misguided performance. What do you suppose will happen when the administration decides to eliminate a wheelbarrow pusher (or that person retires) and you suddenly find yourself reporting to a manager who expects you to be self-propelled?

Your ability to exercise initiative in self-improvement will depend largely on one critical question: how well do you like your job? There are probably not many supervisors who truly enjoy every minute of every day; our jobs are mixtures of things we like and things we do not like, and we can only hope that the former usually outweigh the latter.

If you honestly dislike most of your job most of the time, there is little to be done for you. Dislike of one's job is usually reflected in a poor attitude and, in turn, by the absence of initiative. It also has the effect of hurting both the individual and the organization. After all, you can put a square peg in a round hole if you pound hard enough, but in the process, both the peg and the hole will be damaged. We hope supervisors who find themselves in a job that is a bad fit will see the problem (if their supervisor doesn't see it already and act on it) and find a new job or a different niche in the organization.

You will never improve as a supervisor unless you get moving, driven by the determination to do it yourself. The occasional swift kick administered by higher management has only a temporary effect and usually generates resentment and resistance. You have the source of all learning and growth buried within you; no one but you can tap this source.

We are all occasionally haunted by the realization of the need to do more useful things and do a better job with the tasks we now perform. However, we are always waiting for the "right" opportunity. You have heard a thousand declarations of what will be done "when next year's budget kicks in," "as soon as count goes back down," "when I get more staff," or "after the first of the year." However, true initiative says the time is now, not later, and the first places to go to work making initiative count are personal organization and the use of time.

## BARRIERS TO EFFECTIVENESS

Before any further discussion of personal organization, we must examine some of the traditional barriers to effectiveness (other than those presented by the poor use of time) that can have a bearing on how we approach our work. A few of these may be reflections of our personalities. Some, perhaps, are so deeply ingrained that we may never be able to alter them completely. However, the mere awareness of the presence of these barriers can be valuable in helping us understand our behavior. This understanding can, in turn, lead us to ways of compensating for what we may see as shortcomings in ourselves.

## Fear of Failure

One major barrier to effectiveness is the fear of failure. Perhaps we shy away from taking calculated risks or making certain decisions because we are afraid of losing or simply afraid of being wrong. This certainly is a prominent factor in prison management because the human stakes for error can be so high. However, fear of failure generally leads to procrastination and inaction, which in turn lead to ineffectiveness. We need to recognize that there is considerable risk and uncertainty involved in management at all levels. Were this not so, far fewer managers would be needed.

## The Search for Perfection

Another occasionally encountered barrier to personal effectiveness is the search for perfection. This can show up as excess time and energy poured into an undertaking or as the drive to continue seeking the "ultimate solution" rather than solving one problem and moving on to the next. Although we should always strive to do the best job possible under the circumstances, the person who is lured by the prospect of perfection (or driven to it by a perfectionist supervisor) is bound to discover that perfection is rarely attainable.

## Temper

Another common barrier to supervisory effectiveness in day-to-day working situations is temper. Almost without fail, interpersonal communication is impaired by the intrusion of temper. Generally, as temper increases, true communication decreases, and personal effectiveness suffers.

\* \* \*

The foregoing barriers to effectiveness were discussed after the section on initiative for a particular reason. The degree to which we encounter these barriers may be largely a reflection of our personalities— of who and what each of us happens to be. However, the awareness of these barriers is what often opens the door to possible change. And this change cannot come from outside; it must be self-inspired.

## ORGANIZATION

For many years a popular cartoon has hung on countless office walls. It pictures two little men facing each other across a table. Both are leaning back in swivel chairs and both have their feet on the table. The area around them is in general disarray. The caption is, "Next week we've got to get organized." The cartoon touches on the biggest problem in the business of personal organization: although it is frequently thought about, it is usually put off until some more convenient time.

Of course you know that organizing is one of the basic management functions, the process of building the framework needed to accommodate the work your department is expected to do. Thinking for the moment of managing yourself, you should be organizing those things around you that have a bearing on the way you work.

People vary greatly in how they relate to some degree of order—or lack of order—in their surroundings. Some people are meticulously organized, and others seem to function well in the midst of clutter. However, just about everyone can reach a point beyond which clutter becomes confusion.

Not everyone can be like a certain institution's records manager who never used desk drawers or file cabinets. Most flat surfaces in his office were piled high with ragged towers of unsorted documents ranging from one-page letters and thick pre-sentence reports to court documents and memos. However, this individual seemed to have the uncanny knack of being able to reach into a stack at the right place and pull out the necessary document. This practice worked well for many years, at least when he was there, but when he was on leave or sick, it was virtually impossible for his subordinates to find anything. He also failed to realize that the visual effect of the turmoil in his office was to reduce staff confidence that things were under control in the records department. Eventually, events overtook the nonsystem. The institution was expanded to include four new large housing units, the scope of responsibility of the records department increased, the amount of paper in the office expanded accordingly, and the disordered stacks became overwhelming. Things got lost and stayed lost. As this happened, the manager at last felt compelled to put things in order. His staff rejoiced, efficiency in the department increased, and confidence in his effectiveness rose as well.

It is not only the material lying about in the open that cuts into your effectiveness. A great many things out of sight in desk drawers and file cabinets also can breed confusion and delay. Someone once referred to a refrigerator as a place to keep leftovers until they are old enough to qualify as garbage. Desk and file drawers often are used much the same way.

Let's look at one proven method for restoring control to office paperwork. Go through your desk drawers and file cabinets and clean house thoroughly. Keep as few files as necessary, and consider arranging these according to their importance. First and most accessible should be those things you are currently working on, perhaps a number of one- or two-page items in an "open items" file backed up with a few folders for open tasks of greater size. Next keep a few folders devoted to items pending, on hold, or likely to become active in the near future.

A third personal file section would reasonably consist of some limited files of a general nature. Here you would probably want to keep job-related correspondence that may be in your best interest to retain, and frequently used reference material.

Least important in your personal filing system are those things you believe you may find useful or helpful someday. These are the items you refer to seldom if ever, and they are the things that create most office clutter.

Many supervisors suffer from the pack rat syndrome, something that is reinforced by the way a bureaucracy encourages staff to retain documentation in order to "CYA." They hesitate to discard anything because they feel it may be needed some day. They are likely to keep outdated computer printouts, notes of meetings and incidents long past, old magazines and professional journals, and suppliers' catalogues, brochures, and price lists.

If you are inclined to be a "collector," consider this: most of what you have saved will never again fill a real need as long as you work for the institution. The problem, of course, is guessing which things are likely to be important so the unimportant ones can be thrown away. Since there is no sure solution to this problem we tend to save everything.

Overcoming this begins with an honest effort to clean out your office. Go through the clutter and throw out or shred everything you have not referred to in the past two years and are not likely to use in the foreseeable future. Be mindful of any regulations your agency has about preserving key records, and be sure to retain any material that may have a bearing on any litigation in which you or your agency are involved. For most people, this can be a productive exercise. Certainly you are going to toss a few things that might have been helpful some day, but what of it? You cannot possibly cover all anticipated information needs with your own resources. Your best bet lies in knowing where to go for information when a specific need arises.

Go through your office at least twice each year, purging material and condensing files, being mindful of litigation and other regulatory concerns. You will gain two distinct advantages: you will limit the amount of material you keep, and in the process you will be reminded of what you are retaining and where it is kept.

Do not allow material to pile up on your desk, table, or any other surface in your office. Some managers strive to keep the material on their desk limited to an amount that can be put into a drawer at the end of each day. If this isn't possible or doesn't fit your style, at least once a week review the things that have accumulated and either file them in appropriate places or get rid of them. Keep the reference material you use most often nearest your usual work place, and consider using a desktop organizer to keep things straight.

Do your best to avoid becoming a generator of the worst kind of clutter—unsorted and undated notes. Some supervisors generate many pages of handwritten notes each week. This practice is itself no problem, and often it is better to err on the side of too much documentation than too little. However, this applies only when the problem or activity is current or the nature of the subject suggests that all documentation should be preserved. When the immediate need has passed, your notes should be sorted down to essentials, assembled in order, properly identified, and filed.

As far as note writing is concerned, there is one small rule you can follow to vastly improve the usefulness of your informal documentation: whenever you put pen or pencil to paper, first put the date on the page.

## STRESS AND THE SUPERVISOR

The classic definition of stress, attributed to Dr. Hans Selye, a leading authority on the subject, is the nonspecific response of the body to any demand made on it. In 1914, years before Selye's work, Dr. Walter B. Cannon defined stress as the body's ability to prepare itself instantaneously to respond to physical threat. The latter definition describes the "fight-or-flight" response.

We now know, of course, that the threat Cannon referred to can be emotional as well as physical. Indeed, the demand that triggers stress in the body can be purely physical, purely emotional, or a combination of the two. And we should all be more than passingly familiar with the fight-or-flight response—increased heart rate, faster breathing, tensed muscles, flowing adrenaline, and other signs that the body is ready for action.

The prison environment provides more than enough stimulus for this phenomenon. But even in the normal ebb and flow of life, we cannot avoid experiencing a certain amount of stress. It is inextricably related to change. Stress is largely the way we respond to change, not through our conscious actions but involuntarily, both physically and emotionally.

Often, stress originates in a feeling of loss of control. When some outside influence—some change—disturbs our equilibrium, we react involuntarily in ways that suggest we no longer have the measure of control we need over events and circumstances.

Stress can be both positive and negative. It is positive when you are up for something, prepared and alert and determined to regain control. People who seem to perform at their best when under pressure usually do so out of response to positive stress. Consider, for example, a key presentation you are required to make to top management. The future of your department, as well as your career prospects, may depend on how well you do. You feel up for the occasion—tense, perhaps anxious, experiencing butterflies in the stomach. Knowing how much is riding on your presentation, you are thoroughly prepared (or one would hope you are) and determined to do a good job. You are taking control, reacting to positive stress.

A great deal of stress, however, can be negative. And no one can say with any certainty which events constitute positive stress and which constitute negative stress. People vary greatly in their ability to cope with stress in general and to perform well under pressure in a job situation. Whether stress is positive or negative depends largely on how you react after the stressful event has passed. Positive stress, or "good" stress, is invariably followed by relaxation. Negative, or harmful, stress is not followed by relaxation, and you continue to experience tension, anxiety, and the like.

### Sources of Stress

Stress emanates from three general sources: your personal life (life outside work), the job environment, and yourself—your personality, inherent capabilities, and approach to daily living whether at work or away from work.

We have all known people who seem incapable of leaving the problems of the job at work, instead carrying their frustrations home and allowing them to affect their personal lives. Corrections, and law enforcement in general, is known for high rates of divorce, alcoholism, and other dysfunctional employee behaviors, many of which are thought to be related to job stress. And we have certainly known employees who regularly bring their personal problems to work and allow them to affect their performance. Some of the most frequently encountered employee problems a supervisor faces arise with employees whose performance and interpersonal relations are adversely affected by personal difficulties.

We need to recognize that it is not possible to separate the person on the job completely from the person off the job. People vary greatly in their ability to keep the work and nonwork sides of life separate. To some people home is a welcome respite from the problems of the job; they can leave their worries on the doorstep. To others, work is a refuge, an escape from a chaotic personal life. To a great many people, however, trouble at work usually means trouble at home, and trouble at home usually spills over into their employment.

The job environment can induce stress in a number of ways. Inmate contacts and confrontations, of course, are prominent factors. But things as simple as physical working conditions—heating, lighting, furnishings, space, and noise—can create stress as can organizational policies and practices that are inconsistent or unpredictable. These are common sources of stress for supervisors and line employees alike.

A supervisor's feeling of having less than total control over the work situation can induce stress, especially when the supervisor has full responsibility for a given situation without having full authority over all the elements that must be brought to bear to address the situation. It is common among supervisors to find that they have responsibility—at least implied responsibility—but that they have not been given authority consistent with that responsibility.

A great deal of supervisory stress comes from negative practices of higher management. "Bossism," management that pushes rather than leads, and management that is authoritarian, unreasonably demanding, or fault finding create supervisory stress. And although not necessarily negative itself, a change in management that leaves a supervisor reporting to a new superior can be a stress producer. Frequent changes in the chain of command or organizational structure that leave the supervisor reporting to a new manager every few months are virtually guaranteed to produce considerable supervisory stress.

Finally, a major potential stress producer for supervisors is work overload—having too much to do, not enough time to do it, and not enough resources for its accomplishment. Today's crowded prisons are a classic example of this situation. Many supervisors have learned the hard way that they cannot be all things to all people in a finite amount of time.

As functions of personality, capabilities, and approach, the stress producers that can be at work within ourselves include:

- self-doubts; a lack of confidence in our own abilities
- lack of personal organization
- inability to plan out our work and to establish priorities and address them appropriately
- perfectionism; placing excessive and unrealistic demands on ourselves
- the inability to say no to any request or demand
- the tendencies to take all problems as indications of your own shortcomings and to take all criticism personally

If you are never stressed on the job, you may have too little to do and little or no true responsibility. Also, if you are never stressed by the demands of the job, you are probably falling short of doing your best work. Positive stress, by urging you to perform under pressure, produces learning and growth.

Stress goes with the supervisory territory. But if you are always stressed, if you are chronically on the verge of anxiety, depression, or panic, this stress can lead to personal ineffectiveness and ultimately to physical or emotional illness.

## Coping with Supervisory Stress

To succeed on the job over the long run, supervisors must gain as much control over both themselves and the work environment as possible. To combat stress, the supervisor may want to consider these approaches.

- **Learn to say no, or at least to speak up, when that last request or demand finally adds up to too much.** Your boss is only human and is likely to be as stressed as you are, if not more so. Most bosses will understand, especially if you can suggest alternatives or offer to reorder priorities to serve a pressing need.
- **Do not let your pile of accumulated work grow until it becomes totally uncontrollable.** Take time to plan. Establish priorities. As suggested in earlier sections of this chapter, tackle one important task at a time and do it completely. Avoid piecemeal tasks, intermittently doing a little on each of several items because "they're all important."
- **Delegate.** Take Chapter 5, "Delegation: How To Form the Habit," seriously. And delegate in anticipation of stressful times to come.

Do not wait until the pile is so high that you can no longer see over it to think about the need to train others to do some of the work.

- **Vary your pace.** Intersperse short, quiet tasks among the more hectic, tension-producing contacts required of you. If you have been in staff meetings all morning, try to allow yourself an hour or two of solitary work in the afternoon. Once in a while reward yourself by working on something that you especially like to do.
- **When the going gets rough, take a few minutes to relax.** Stretch. Breathe deeply. Take a few minutes to walk to a fellow manager's office instead of calling on the phone. Go out on the yard and talk to the staff or inmates there. A few minutes spent clearing your head by doing something different will pay themselves back in efficiency many times over.

As for managing stress outside of work, there is still no advice better than what we have heard time and again: proper nutrition, proper rest, and regular exercise.

Accept stress as part of the supervisory job. Recognize stress when it strikes. By taking control of your situation and consciously managing the stresses that otherwise threaten to overtake you, you will accomplish more in terms of both quantity and quality, take more enjoyment from your work, and reduce your potential for stress-related illness.

## EFFECTIVE USE OF TIME

The local chief of police once dropped into the office of a prison warden, to discuss joint emergency preparedness planning. The warden was talking on the telephone; he motioned his visitor to a chair at a conference table. The table was covered by a disarrayed pile of policies, memos, and other clutter, among which the chief spied a book entitled *How to Manage Your Time Effectively*.

When the warden hung up the phone, the visitor held up the book and said, "I was thinking of buying this myself. Is it any good?"

The response was, "I really don't know. I got it three or four months ago, but I haven't had time to read it yet."

The warden said something we have probably all said to ourselves about learning how to make better use of time: we want to do it, but we do not have the time to learn how. We might just as readily admit that we are too busy doing things inefficiently to learn how to do them more efficiently.

## HOW WELL ARE YOU SUITED TO THE SUPERVISORY ROLE?

Not all persons who work in supervision are equally effective at all parts of the job, nor do they enjoy all parts equally. The relative effectiveness of many supervisors in the work force can be directly related to how well, personally and temperamentally, they may be suited to the role of supervisor.

How well does any supervisor fit into the supervisory role? Examine a few facts and conclusions about yourself and look at the way you relate to the job so you can decide: How well do I fit the supervisory role? and, What can I work on to improve the way I fit this role? This can be accomplished through a thoughtful examination of both your personal orientation and your performance orientation.

### Personal Orientation

To a considerable extent you will unconsciously approach your everyday job activities in the same manner you approach tasks and activities in your personal life. You are the same person whether on or off the job, and unless you make a conscious effort to behave differently in one or another area of your life you are likely to be governed by the same tendencies in all that you do.

Personal orientation can be illustrated in simplified form as a graph with axes representing ranges of capabilities or tendencies (see Figure 7–1).

The vertical axis of personal orientation is focus, ranging from totally internal at the bottom of the graph to totally external at the top. Focus represents the extent to which one is affected by or actively, emotionally involved in activities or events. External focus is typified by detachment; internal focus is represented by involvement.

As with any rendering of human tendencies or characteristics, this focus axis, as well as other supposed scales discussed here, represents a range with an infinite number of gradations possible between extremes. Rarely do the extremes apply in full. Rather, we can say only that any of us might show a tendency toward one end of the scale or the other.

The individual with an external focus is not personally affected by matters in which he or she is involved, is witness to, or is otherwise party to. An external focus suggests the ability to not take things per-

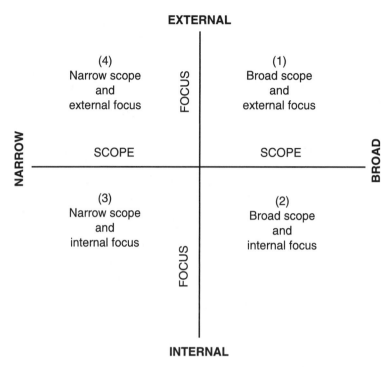

**Figure 7–1** Personal Orientation

sonally, and it also suggests the ability to better cope with events and demands that are stressful in some way.

Internal focus is of course the opposite. The person who is internally focused is personally affected by most of what goes on. All events that the individual is party to are internalized, and the individual finds it difficult if not impossible to remain unaffected or unchanged by events.

We may appear to be assessing sensitivity, sympathy, or empathy, but this is not the case. It is possible to be extremely sensitive to another's problem, for example, and to engage in sympathetic involvement, without taking on the full measure of the other's pain. For the externally focused person, that which happens occurs in the world around the self and is to be dealt with and coped with as necessary while remaining at a safe emotional distance. For the internally focused person, the self is inevitably affected by events and cannot deal or cope with others' distress without experiencing it internally.

As far as the role of the supervisor is concerned, an individual who is totally externally focused may be able to cope rationally with a great many difficult matters, but the result may be a "supervision machine"—a decisionmaker operating on logic and fact to the exclusion of intuition and all other human consideration. At the other extreme, a supervisor who is totally internally focused probably will not survive for any appreciable time. Considering all of the difficulties that arise in managing people, and recognizing the prison environment as one that presents particular difficulties, it is easy to recognize the internally focused supervisor as a likely candidate for early burnout.

The most desirable focus orientation for the supervisor lies above the origin of the graph. A tendency toward an external focus reflects the ability to deal with the various events, problems, and unpleasant situations that come with the supervisory task.

The horizontal axis of personal orientation is scope. Scope refers to the kind of activity that an individual can best handle according to temperament or individual ability. The person with a broad scope can "juggle," coping with a variety of tasks in bits and pieces, moving from task to task and back again, and solving unanticipated problems as they arise. The broad-scope individual can function in firefighting style without experiencing undue stress and without becoming overwhelmed by a seemingly unending stream of problems or by the inability to truly "finish" much of what is started.

At the opposite end of the horizontal axis are persons of narrow scope, those who cannot readily function in the scattergun fashion of the broad-scope person but whose talents are most comfortably applied to one specific task at a time.

The chances of long-run success in the supervisory role are enhanced if one is possessed of a broad scope and is generally able to frequently reorder priorities and cope with a continuous series of unanticipated demands. Combining the two axes that have been used to describe personal orientation, we can reasonably suggest that one is best suited to the supervisory role if one's personal orientation lies somewhere in the upper right hand quadrant of Figure 7–1. This person will be externally focused, dealing with most matters at a reasonable emotional distance, and will be of broad scope, taking what comes as it comes. The supervisor who may be placed by personal orientation in any of the other three quadrants of Figure 7–1 may experience problems of orientation ranging from mild, such as staying too long on a pet project, to severe, such as a stress reaction to the internalized pain of others.

## Performance Orientation

Performance orientation can also be described by a pair of perpendicular axes along each of which there can be an infinite number of gradations (see Figure 7–2).

The vertical axis of Figure 7–2 represents a continuum from totally personal at the bottom to totally functional at the top of the graph. The higher the degree of functional emphasis evident in a supervisor's performance, the more visible will be that supervisor's degree of attention to activities of highest priority. The supervisor having a strong functional emphasis will ordinarily be attending to the most important task at any given time. On the other hand, the more personal a supervisor's emphasis becomes, the more likely that supervisor is to be giving attention primarily to those tasks or concerns that he or she prefers or enjoys. This may be all well and good when it happens that what the

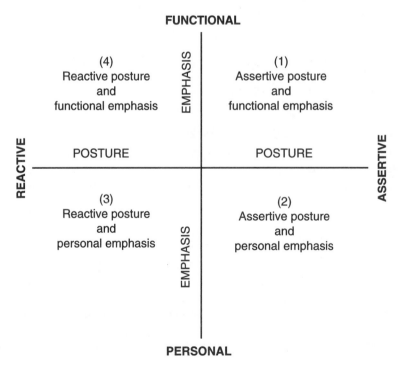

**Figure 7–2** Performance Orientation

supervisor likes to do and what most needs to be done coincide. However, most of the time the tasks the supervisor favors and the tasks that most need to be done are not the same.

The horizontal axis of Figure 7–2 represents posture along a continuum ranging from completely reactive to fully assertive. The supervisor who tends toward the assertive end of the scale ordinarily initiates action, advances ideas or solutions, and moves to resolve difficulties in their early stages and to head off problems before they occur. The supervisor who tends toward the reactive end of the scale ordinarily waits to be told what to do, procrastinates on important decisions until there is no more room for delay, and waits until a problem can no longer be denied before attempting a solution. The assertive supervisor deals in innovation and prevention; the reactive supervisor simply responds when pushed by circumstances.

The effective supervisor tends more toward functional than personal in emphasis and more toward assertive than reactive in posture. However, emphasis and posture cannot be considered separate from each other; together they exert combined effects that can be described through association with each other in the four quadrants of Figure 7–2.

In the first quadrant (upper right), tendencies toward functional emphasis and assertive posture describe a supervisor who is generally in control of the job and who operates with a noticeable degree of autonomy. In this, the "best" of the four quadrants, the supervisor:

- concentrates on high priority tasks most of the time
- tackles the important problems in timely fashion even though they may be difficult or unpleasant
- experiences job satisfaction from accomplishment and achievement
- is meeting the needs of the organization in doing what he or she is expected to do as a member of management

A supervisor functioning in the first quadrant is applying the right approach (assertive posture) to the right tasks (functional emphasis), moving in the right direction without being told.

The second quadrant (lower right) suggests the combined effects of a tendency toward an assertive posture and a tendency toward a personal emphasis. A supervisor functioning in this quadrant may frequently be described as pursuing personal preferences or being out of step with reality. In this quadrant the supervisor may:

- be unwilling to delegate, personally monopolizing preferred activities, or unable to delegate out of a sense of insecurity
- take frequent refuge in preferred tasks of low priority as relaxation, self-satisfaction, or escape
- experience goal displacement, being unable to reconcile organizational goals with personal goals
- have little appreciation of job purpose, failing to see how this specific supervisory position is supposed to mesh with others as part of the organizational whole

A supervisor functioning in the second quadrant is generally applying the right approach to the wrong tasks (personal emphasis), moving without being told but going in the wrong direction.

The third quadrant (lower left) is readily describable as the "worst" of the four general situations. The supervisor functioning in the third quadrant may:

- appear to be running fast and working hard while going nowhere and accomplishing little
- exhibit an inability to control interruptions
- be unwilling or unable to say no to any request that comes along, no matter how unreasonable or intrusive it may be
- avoid that which is difficult, complicated, unpleasant, or potentially stressful whenever possible, taking the easiest route through most problems
- become disillusioned with the job and the organization

A supervisor functioning in the third quadrant is ordinarily taking the wrong approach (reactive emphasis) to the wrong tasks (personal emphasis), moving only when pushed and then going in the wrong direction.

Because a person falling into the fourth quadrant (upper left) will usually be doing most of the right things, the combination of emphasis and posture evident in this quadrant might present no problems at all if this discussion concerned people employed in any number of nonsupervisory capacities. However, the supervisor falling into the fourth quadrant may:

- experience considerable frustration with a nearly complete lack of autonomy
- feel "out of control," reacting to the seemingly unending and unpredictable stream of demands made by others

- use time ineffectively, moving from task to task and crisis to crisis as directed, having no time left to plan and organize

A supervisor functioning in the fourth quadrant has the proper functional emphasis but is applying an improper, reactive approach. This may be acceptable in some nonsupervisory employees; although assertiveness is to be desired in many employees, supervisory or otherwise, there are still many jobs in which an employee may best serve by performing as directed. Whereas a reactive posture may be appropriate—or at least tolerable—in many nonsupervisory employees, it is contrary to what is expected of an effective supervisor.

## How Well Do You Fit?

Many people who did not fit well into a supervisory role have either voluntarily abandoned supervision or have failed as supervisors. Many others who also do not fit especially well into a supervisory role have nevertheless remained supervisors, with widely varying degrees of success. It is highly likely that absolutely "perfect fit" supervisors are a minority of the supervisory population of any organization. It is just as likely that most supervisors have weaknesses that can potentially affect their performance and determine whether they succeed or fail in the long run.

Simply identifying one's own weaknesses is a large part of the struggle for improved personal effectiveness. Once these weaknesses are identified, the next essential process is recognizing the difference between those things about one's self that one can actively change and those things about one's self that one cannot readily change but must compensate for or otherwise work around. The final step in the process is acting to remove or guard against one's own weaknesses.

Consider how you believe you must place yourself in regard to personal orientation. You might find, as would most people, that you have more control over your scope than you do over your focus. Although both scope and focus are rooted in personality, focus is much more emotionally based and is therefore much more difficult to alter artificially. If you are strongly internally focused and sensitive to the point of creating intolerable stress within yourself when having to apply firm disciplinary action, you are more prone to minimize this aspect of the supervisory role and thus impair your effectiveness in handling problem employees. Since your focus is emotionally based, unless you are sufficiently near the middle of the graph to allow you to accommodate the occasional emotional stresses of the job, you may be consigning yourself to a working life of strain and unhappiness by remaining in supervision.

Since scope is less emotionally tied than focus, we can all do more to control this dimension of personal orientation. Broad-scope people are team members; narrow-scope people prefer to function as loners. The supervisor needs to be a team member. However, it is acceptable to give in to a tendency to enjoy working as a loner once in a while—as long as one is conscious of the need to be a team member and to willfully function as a team member whenever circumstances demand (which, for the typical supervisor, is most of the time).

Aspects of personality ordinarily have a great deal of influence on both major dimensions of one's performance orientation. Of the two, posture is probably more deeply rooted in personality than is emphasis. Surely there are some whose posture is essentially reactive because they are self-doubting and insecure. Just as surely, however, there are some who are reactive because they lack goal orientation or because they have never been given any clear idea of what is expected of them. Perhaps one's insecurities can be overcome with a great deal of effort and the right kind of assistance and support. However, not nearly so difficult as overcoming insecurity is the deliberate development of goal orientation—which can surely be done if someone wants success strongly enough—and one can pointedly ask for higher management's expectations.

Although unavoidably influenced by aspects of personality, emphasis is more readily altered by the individual than is posture. The key to emphasis is self-discipline, the ability to make oneself give the most attention to the highest priority tasks at hand. The supervisor who can enter each work day by asking, "What is the single most important task I need to accomplish today?," and plan to get that task done and proceed to do it, is on the path of effectiveness. Even the supervisor whose workload may loom as overwhelming is making progress if he or she is always at work on the highest priority task of the moment. To self-discipline one need only add consideration of the need to plan and organize, and to control interruptions while concentrating on priorities, in order to develop a true functional emphasis.

Self-discipline is crucial to the improvement of one's personal orientation and performance orientation. To develop an improved personal orientation and to adopt a more appropriate performance orientation is to become a more effective supervisor. Self-discipline as applied by the effective supervisor is self-management, and self-management comes before the management of others. The person who would aspire to manage others must first become proficient at self-management.

---

### EXERCISE 7–1: THE EFFECTIVENESS CHECKLIST

Provide honest, self-searching responses to the statements listed below, using these responses:

**U** = usually (or always)
**S** = sometimes
**R** = rarely (or never)

(Be candid. No one needs to see your answers unless you choose to share them.)

_____ 1. I put my objectives—and plans for reaching them—on paper.

_____ 2. My objectives are expressed in specifics: what, how much, and when.

_____ 3. For sizable tasks, I use checkpoints or sub-objectives so I can assess progress along the way.

_____ 4. I break large jobs into smaller, more manageable pieces.

_____ 5. I set deadlines for myself and hold myself to them.

_____ 6. I use written reminders of what must be done today or tomorrow.

_____ 7. I avoid thoughts or circumstances that might sidetrack my efforts.

_____ 8. I know my limitations; I do not set objectives I know I cannot achieve or make promises I know I cannot keep.

_____ 9. I use positive motivation by reminding myself of the benefits I expect from the completion of a task.

_____ 10. When facing a disagreeable or difficult task, I am able to distinguish between "I can't" and "I don't want to."

_____ 11. I am willing to take risks, to try new ways of doing things.

_____ 12. I allow myself the freedom to fail, to make mistakes and learn from them.

_____ 13. I keep my personal work area organized and under control.

_____ 14. I recognize conflicts for what they are and do not back away from making decisions.

_____ 15. I have a sense of priority that allows me to distinguish between what must be done and what I would like to do.

If you gave yourself **U** on all 15 statements perhaps you had better go through the list again. There are few managers who do not rate **S** on at least a few items. Each **S** or **R** represents a clear opportunity for self-improvement.

---

### CASE 7–1: "WHERE DOES THE TIME GO?"

Bill Martinez, supervisor of education, decided he had to get organized. Recently his work days had been running well beyond quitting time, cutting noticeably into time with his family; but instead of going down, the backlog of work was growing.

Inspired by an article he had read about planning and setting priorities, Bill decided to try to plan each day's activities at the end of the previous day. Monday, he came to the office with his day planned out to the last minute. During the morning he had to complete a report on a recent learning-needs analysis, write the performance appraisals of two part-time instructors, and assemble the balance of materials for a two-hour in-service training session he was scheduled to conduct that afternoon. After lunch he had to conduct the class, complete the schedule of the next three months' training activities (now ten days overdue), and prepare memos—which should be posted that day—for two upcoming inmate classes.

Bill got off to a good start; he finished the report before 10:00 A.M. and turned his attention to the performance evaluations. However, at that time the interruptions began. In the next two hours he was interrupted six times—three telephone calls and three visitors. The calls were all business calls. Two of the visitors had legitimate problems, one of them taking half an hour to resolve. The other visitor was a fellow supervisor simply passing the time of day. Neither performance evaluation was completed, and the training materials were assembled in time only because Bill put them together during lunch while wolfing down a sandwich at his desk.

Bill's afternoon class ran 20 minutes overtime because of questions and discussion. When he returned to the office, he discovered he had a visitor, an investigative supervisor who stayed for almost an hour talking about several inmates who were in educational classes but who were also under suspicion of involvement in an escape plot. This interview was time-consuming but necessary, since the inmates might have tried to escape during an evening school session.

After the investigator left, Bill spent several minutes wondering what to do next. The performance appraisals, the three-month schedule, the class notices—all were overdue. Deciding on the class notices because they were the briefest task before him, he dashed off both notices in longhand and asked the department secretary to type them, run them off, and post them immediately. He then tackled the training schedule.

When Bill again looked up from his work, it was nearly an hour past quitting time. He still had a long way to go on the schedule and had not yet gotten started on the two performance appraisals. As he swept his work aside for the day he sadly reflected that he had not accomplished two-thirds of what he intended to do that day in spite of all his planning. He decided, however, to try again; when he could get a few minutes of quiet time late in the evening, he would plan his next day's activity.

On his way out of the education building, he happened to glance at the main bulletin board. The small satisfaction he felt when he saw the posted class notices vanished instantly when he discovered that both were incorrect—the dates and times of the two classes had been interchanged.

## Questions

1. What errors did Bill commit in his approach to planning and the establishment of priorities?
2. In what respects could Bill have improved his use of time on the "blue Monday" described in the case?

# PART III

# The Supervisor and the Employee

## CHAPTER 8

# Interviewing: The Hazardous Hiring Process

*The best man for the job often is a woman.*

—*Anonymous*

### Chapter Objectives

☛ Stress the importance of supervisory involvement in the hiring process.

☛ Offer advice on how to prepare for an employee selection interview.

☛ Present guidelines for interview questioning, specifically identifying kinds of questions that should be avoided and suggesting appropriate lines of questioning.

☛ Describe a recommended general approach to the supervisor's conduct of the actual employee selection interview.

☛ Describe desirable follow-up action to conclude the interview cycle effectively.

## THE SUPERVISOR AND THE INTERVIEW

There is an immense irony to contemporary hiring practices, in that the personal interview—usually the heart of the process—often is not a particularly reliable means of finding good employees. Even though many correctional and other government agencies have specific interview procedures, there is no guarantee that the process will always generate positive results. No matter how good we become at interviewing or how much we know about the jobs we are attempting to fill, it frequently remains impossible to separate true ability in a job candidate from the ability simply to "talk a good job." However, in spite of its shortcomings and weaknesses, the face-to-face employee selection interview for locating new employees is the only practical means available for approaching the task.

Institutions may vary considerably in the extent to which supervisors become involved in the hiring process. In some correctional agencies, major departments or divisions recruit and screen their own job applicants, usually through some specifically delegated authority from the state's personnel department. In most agencies and prisons, however, the employment needs of all departments are served to a more or less equal extent by the personnel department.

Make it a point to know specifically how much of the employment process is yours and how much is done by personnel. Ordinarily you can expect to look to the personnel department for locating a number of candidates who generally fit the requirements of the open position; that is, the personnel staff find people who have the appropriate academic or other credentials, minimum required experience, and who otherwise fit the hiring criteria you establish or which are established by agency policy. In most cases the personnel staff will screen applicants to locate generally qualified candidates and will arrange personal interviews for you.

A very few organizations still may follow the age-old and highly undesirable practice of having a very few people, perhaps only one or two, doing all of the actual employee selection for the entire organization. This outmoded practice is contrary to the fundamentals of supervisory responsibility; we cannot simply "give" an already-chosen employee to a supervisor and expect that a proper employee-supervisor relationship will be established. If the supervisor is to be responsible for an employee's output, then the supervisor must be allowed a consistent amount of authority in selecting that employee. The supervisory role should include, subject to carefully drawn ground rules, the authority to hire and fire. In the past, the authority to hire sometimes was retained by "higher ups" (although the supervisor may have been left to do the firing when things did not work out). As supervisors, however, we need to recognize that although hiring is a sometimes difficult and time-consuming process, it is nevertheless an essential part of the job. To be blunt, if we are not capable of hiring people then we should not be supervisors.

## CANDIDATES: OUTSIDE AND INSIDE

Job applicants often come to your organization in response to employment advertising specific to certain personnel needs. Many also come, not in response to specific recruiting efforts, but unsolicited; they fill out employment applications in the hope of finding work. Both solicited and unsolicited applicants reach the attention of the interviewing supervisor after screening interviews in which the personnel department determines that the applicants are qualified to fill some specific need. This determination is most often made in accord with broad qualifications established by the state's or agency's personnel department.

Most correctional agencies operate job-posting systems and have policies governing employee transfers, so a number of candidates for any particular position may also come from within the present work force. Although upward mobility from the correctional workforce is a priority for many agencies, the more specialized a need, the more likely the supervisor is to see a preponderance of external candidates (electrician, pharmacist, powerplant engineer, and so on). The more generalized a need, the more likely the supervisor is to see a preponderance of internal candidates (case manager, records technician, and so on). For many positions, you will be able to choose from among a pool that includes both external and internal candidates.

Most organizations espouse a philosophy of development from within the organization by way of either lateral or promotional transfers. The employee selected from within the agency brings to the job a fund of essential knowledge about the prison and the agency in general that would require a great deal of time to instill in an outside candidate—time that is taken from productivity on the job. It should be stressed that in some agencies this notion of development from within is more likely to be philosophy than policy. No astute top management official will absolutely require the supervisor to select an internal candidate over an outside applicant in any particular situation. To do so would place the supervisor in a position of having sometimes to select a candidate who is less qualified than the one who appears to be the best available. But even though the notion of development from within may not be inviolable policy, you should nevertheless incorporate it into practice whenever reasonably possible, for both organizational and practical reasons.

As supervisor, you will undoubtedly make most of your hiring decisions with your immediate departmental needs in mind. However, you should also hire in consideration of the long-range needs of the organization and its employees. These needs suggest that certain positions should be filled from within the organization. Neither "always outside" nor "always inside" is appropriate. However, when presented with two or more equally qualified candidates for a given position, there is every good reason for giving preference to the internal candidate.

In-house opportunities for varied work experience, promotion, and professional growth will foster employee retention. If lower-level employees continually see all the "better" positions—primarily the promotional opportunities—going to external candidates, the organization will gradually lose those lower-level employees who are capable of growing and who are interested in promotion.

## PREPARING FOR THE INTERVIEW

Presuming the skills and knowledge called for have already been identified, your first step in preparing for a selection interview should consist of careful review of the individual's employment application. Standard agency information will be on the application form, which will facilitate comparison of qualifications of candidates. If only a resume is used, you may need to be ready to ask additional questions to elicit sufficient detail about the candidate.

You should have the application materials in advance of the interview. Do not allow yourself to be put in a position in which you must read the application for the first time while the applicant sits before you. Do what you can to discourage the personnel department or other referring office from sending you applicants with applications in hand. You need at least a few minutes to familiarize yourself with information about the job applicant. Otherwise you may make the applicant uncomfortable by reading when you should be speaking or listening, or you may miss something important and ask questions that have already been answered on paper.

In reviewing this information, remember that regardless of whether a standard application or resume is used, there is a great deal the employment application will not tell you. Employment applications of years past called for much information that now cannot be legally requested. Assuming that you are likely to have no control over what is asked on the application, we will not go into detail concerning what can or cannot be requested on an employment application. However, we will shortly discuss some kinds of questions you cannot or should not ask during an interview, and it should go without saying that these same questions cannot be asked on an application. Many of today's employment applications are necessarily sketchy compared with those of years ago. In fact, chances are that if you have worked for your present employer for as few as 2 or 3 years, the application you originally completed might today be considered illegal or at least questionable in some small way. If you have worked at the same place since 1980 or earlier, information requested on the application you originally submitted would today almost certainly be illegal in a number of respects.

After reviewing the written material about the candidate, have a definite plan in mind when you approach the interview. Know all you can about the job you are trying to fill, and back up this knowledge with a copy of the job description or at least with a fairly complete list of the duties of the job. Be especially aware of any unique aspects of the job or any unusual requirements the applicant should be made aware of. Be prepared to tell the applicant precisely where the job fits in the total operation of the department and the overall role he or she would play within the prison.

It may also be useful to have a few sample questions prepared in advance of the interview. You are likely to discover that the most valuable questions emerge while you are in conversation with the applicant, but you may well need some starter questions to enable you to get the conversation going. Prepare yourself to guide the applicant and listen, never losing sight of your basic purpose: to learn as much as possible about the applicant.

Make sure the interview takes place in private and in relatively comfortable surroundings. If you have a private office, use it unless you are sure to experience constant interruptions. If necessary, borrow someone else's office, make use of an open conference room or other available space, or use interview space in the personnel department. Your ability to learn about the applicant is severely impaired by interruptions, and interruptions can be unsettling to the applicant.

Be aware of the likely state of mind of the job applicant. Even though the person is not yet and may in fact never become an employee, you are already in a position of authority relative to the person looking for a job. To a potential employee you are an employer; you enter the interview situation at a definite psychological advantage.

Look at the interview situation from the applicant's point of view. You automatically have the upper hand; the applicant has far more at stake than you have. The applicant is looking for a job; you not only have a job, but you are an authority figure as well. Often the applicant, if truly serious about finding work, will be determined to make a good impression and may be nervous.

Be familiar with affirmative action, equal employment, and other legal considerations (see Chapter 24) that apply to your agency. Use this familiarity to guide your interview behavior, but resist the temptation to "play lawyer" and render your own interpretations in questionable areas. When you are able to do so, get advice from the personnel department and other knowledgeable people in the organization. If you follow the questioning guidelines offered in this chapter, you should encounter few difficulties. However, if you find you have serious doubts about a particular question that occurs to you, do not ask it.

## GUIDELINES FOR QUESTIONING

Although common courtesy should prevail in your interview behavior at all times, courtesy itself is not enough. You must be constantly aware of questions or comments that could be taken as discriminatory in some way although not intended as such. An applicant may volunteer information related to the following areas, but you may not ask for it.

### Questions To Avoid

You may not ask any question that requires the applicant to reveal race, religion, or national origin. Direct questions on these subjects should be easy to avoid. Watch out, however, for indirect questions through which a person can claim you were "fishing" for specific information. For instance, a question that is not allowed is one such as: "I'd say you were from [name of neighborhood with a population predominantly of one ethnic group], perhaps?"

*Age*

Age considerations present an interesting situation. Some correctional agencies are subject to statutory limitations on the age at which their employees must retire. Ordinarily, this means that to qualify for a pension, new employees must not have attained a certain age before being hired. In those cases, questions about age are permitted. However, even in those agencies, all positions may not be subject to those statutory provisions, and thus the following discussion is important to bear in mind.

The matter of age has become a particularly sensitive area in recent years, calling for heightened awareness on the part of the supervisor. Although the Age Discrimination in Employment Act (ADEA) has been in place since 1967 (see Chapter 24), it was given added scope and influence by the Age Discrimination in Employment Amendments Act of 1986, effective January 1, 1987. Although mostly the concern of the personnel department, this law nevertheless has implications for the supervisor.

The 1986 act prohibits mandatory retirement for most employees and removes the age 70 limit on ADEA protection. Therefore, stay away from all questions related to an applicant's long-term intentions, such as, "How long would you plan on working before thinking about retirement?" because of the age-related inferences that one might draw.

Except where age-related issues are permissible under statute, you may not ask any obviously older applicants if they are receiving Social Security benefits. There have been cases of older persons applying for part-time work, with some employers discriminating in favor of applicants receiving Social Security payments. Their rationale apparently was that a person receiving a combined income may be more likely to remain on the job longer than one to whom the part-time job is the sole means of support.

Except as noted above, there are no safe questions (direct or indirect) that a supervisor can ask about age, except perhaps to inquire whether an apparently young person is of legal age to enter full-time employment under the circumstances required of the job in question. (This would be particularly true in the case of a position involving the use of firearms or deadly force, for which there may be statutory age restrictions.)

Also, you need to assure yourself that all the qualifications you are seeking are truly related to the job. Evaluate individual applicants on their individual capabilities and qualifications, not on your general beliefs or personal preferences. ("An older person just couldn't keep up," or "Someone her age would resist new technology," or "I want someone who's more likely to stay 10 or 20 years.")

*Disability*

There are few if any safe questions the supervisor can ask about disability, whether or not a job candidate's disability is evident. The Americans with Disabilities Act of 1990 (ADA) provides a national mandate barring bias against persons with disabilities. This act calls for supportive and accommodating behavior by employers in maintaining disabled persons in the work force. There still is a great deal of litigation on the issue of how this recent legislation applies in certain work settings. However, it is likely that an agency could establish bona fide occupational qualifications (BFOQ) for a correctional officer that would preclude hiring a wheelchair-bound individual for such a position.

However, sometimes apparent disabilities are not a real bar from employment. Early in his career, one of the authors had a secretary who was totally blind, and yet who did a fine job. Her hard-working, cheerful attitude, and solid skills more than made up for the occasional problems her blindness created.

On another occasion, when interviewing correctional officers for a new institution, an applicant with rather prominent movement limitations in one leg (the aftermath of childhood polio) was being closely considered over the objections of other managers involved in the hiring process. They believed that the leg problem would predispose the candidate to linger on the main floor of the four-level housing areas, rather than circulate throughout the units. Noting the fact the applicant had engaged in many athletic endeavors over the years and his aggressive, no-nonsense approach to questions on this issue, he was hired. He was one of the most effective, active officers that institution had. These examples do not mean that every person with a disability can work in the correctional setting, but they do illustrate why a manager must give full consideration to such individuals.

Concerning the employment selection interview and the disabled person, the supervisor should ask questions about the applicant's qualifications and experience that focus strictly on the essential functions of the job. The job's peripheral activities that have no bearing on its essential functions—for example, occasional filing or report delivery related to the position of a billing clerk—are subject to "reasonable accommodation" by the organization and have no bearing on the person's capabilities as a billing clerk. (See more about the ADA in Chapter 24.)

### Recommendation

You may not ask if the applicant has a recommendation from a present employer. This may be taken as discriminatory, since it may be difficult for the applicant to secure such a recommendation because of reasons other than job performance (e.g., race, religion, political affiliation).

### Relatives

You can no longer ask the identity of the person's nearest relative or "next of kin," even for the simple purpose of having someone to contact in case of illness or accident. This can be taken as probing into the existence of spouse or family, which you cannot do. Even asking about "the person to be notified in case of illness or accident" is risky until the applicant is actually employed.

### Immigrants

It is generally permissible to ask if an applicant is a U.S. citizen or is legally eligible for employment. However, this should not be an active concern of the supervisor if the personnel department is fulfilling its proper role in complying with the Immigration Reform and Control Act of 1986 (IRCA). This law requires employers to hire only U.S. citizens and lawfully authorized alien workers, and provides penalties and sanctions for employers who knowingly hire or continue to employ illegal aliens or who fail to verify legal eligibility for employment (see Chapter 24). Also, most states have statutory requirements in this area, which also should be part of the screening process conducted by the personnel department.

In compliance with IRCA, the personnel department must require an applicant to produce certain proofs of identity and employment eligibility within three working days after an offer of employment is made. For your part in helping the organization comply with IRCA, you should resist the temptation to prevail on the personnel department to allow a much-needed new employee to begin work before the necessary proofs are produced.

Immigration reform has presented employers with a set of risks and pitfalls of a kind never previously experienced. The supervisor who might seek to avoid IRCA problems by not considering an applicant because of foreign appearance or language can face discrimination charges as defined by other laws.

### Military Service

In asking about the applicant's military service, you may inquire only into general training and experience. Depending on state regulations, you may not be able to ask the nature of the person's discharge or separation; whether the discharge was honorable, dishonorable, general, or otherwise may be privileged information, which the applicant may reveal voluntarily but which you may not request.

### Marital Status

You may not ask the marital status of the applicant at the time of the interview. Particular sensitivity has developed along these lines in recent years. Many women have been able to claim, with considerable success, that they were denied employment because of marital status. Employers often proceeded on the assumptions that:

- Youngz women recently engaged often quit shortly after they get married
- Young, recently married women may leave after a year or two to begin families
- Unmarried women with small children tend on the average to have poorer attendance records than other workers

Even if an applicant, male or female, has willingly revealed marriage on a resume, you are not permitted to ask what the spouse does for a living. In the case of a married female applicant, you are also forbidden to ask her maiden name because this question can be interpreted as probing for clues to national origin.

### Financial Information

In general, you may not ask if the applicant's wages were ever attached or garnished. Credit information ordinarily is privileged information; in most situations it may be volunteered by the applicant but not requested by the prospective employer. In some agencies, however, "integrity interview" procedures do include developing information on applicant financial status in order to determine whether that person is susceptible to corruption by inmates by reason of excessive personal debt or demonstrated poor financial responsibility.

You may not ask if the applicant owns a home or a car. This may be interpreted as seeking to test affluence, which may in turn be taken as discriminatory against certain minorities. You may, however, ask if the applicant has a driver's license—if driving is a BFOQ. Generally, you are on your soundest footing when all questions of a personal nature relate to BFOQs.

### Physical Features

You may not directly ask any applicant's height or weight. Neither of these factors should have a bearing on the applicant's suitability for the job unless there is a specific BFOQ on these criteria that is uniformly applied to all applicants for that job category. In most such cases, there is a performance-based criteria (be able to run one mile in eight minutes) against which all applicants are judged at some point, usually during training.

### Testing

Beware of requesting that an applicant take qualification tests not approved at the agency personnel department level. Pre-employment tests have long been under fire as discriminatory in matters of age, race, and economic background. Pre-employment testing is best left to professionals who design tests that are specifically related to the requirements of the job, statistically validated as nondiscriminatory, administered consistently and in good faith, and evaluated impartially. If your agency has such a test, in all likelihood it has been validated statistically and may even have been subject to review through the labor-management structure of which the organization is a part. In any case, ad hoc or locally developed tests would be subject to question and should not be used.

## Education

There are also pitfalls in asking an applicant's educational level, such as completion of high school or possession of a college degree. An employer may require specific educational levels when these are BFOQs directly related to job performance. Otherwise, it may be possible to show a pattern of employment discrimination. You can require, for instance, a social worker to possess a diploma or degree and a state license since these are essential to the performance of the job as it is structured. However, you cannot require a food service foreperson or plumber to have a high school diploma since it is possible to demonstrate that people in these job categories may perform equally well with or without the diploma. Effective personnel department procedures should take most of the burden off the interviewer in this matter.

## Union Activities

You may not ask whether an applicant is or has been a member of a union or has been involved in organizing or other union activities.

\* \* \*

There is a final, ironic note to this subject. A great deal of the information not available to the interviewer may ultimately come to light in the process of background investigations performed by many law enforcement agencies.

## Questions To Ask

The questions you are permitted to ask are broad and in many instances open-ended. This is as it should be; remember, you are interested in learning as much as you can about the applicant in a limited amount of time and the way to do this is to listen to the person talk. Try these in conversation with the applicant.

- What are your career goals? What would you like to be doing five or ten years from now? How would you like to spend the rest of your career?
- Who have been your prior employers, and why did you leave your previous positions?

- What did you like or dislike about the work in your previous positions?
- Who recommended you to our institution? How did you hear about this job opening?
- What is your educational background? What lines of study did you pursue? (Be careful, however, of attempting to delve into specifics as cautioned in the list of questions to avoid.)
- What do you believe are your strong points? What do you see as your weaknesses?
- Have you granted permission for us to check references with former employers? (See following section).

If the personnel department has not already done so, ask the applicant to explain any gaps of more than a few weeks duration that appear in the resume or application. Some applicants will omit mention of unsuccessful job experiences or other involvements that they believe might reflect negatively on their chances of being hired. As the hiring manager, you should be in a position to make a fully informed decision based on more than just selected pieces of a candidate's background. Also, you share a responsibility for ensuring that the organization is protected from possible negligent hiring charges should an employee who was hired without reasonable background verification cause harm.

### Employment References

The whole topic of employment references represents a quagmire of potential legal traps for both the supervisor and the personnel department. Regulations vary greatly from one jurisdiction to another. Ideally, the personnel department should have secured the applicant's signed permission to check references as part of personnel's screening interview, calling for a specific signed release for each former employer. For good reasons, many applicants indicate that their present employers not be approached for reference information in the preliminary stages of the application process, but they ordinarily grant permission to check with most, but not always with all previous employers. No reference checks should be performed by anyone in the absence of an applicant's signed authorization to do so. Even if a signed release is presented, reference checking should be left to the personnel department. Unless specified in agency policy, interviewing supervisors should not endeavor to check an applicant's references personally.

References must be checked systematically in accordance with strict guidelines governing the kinds of information requested and the kinds of responses to expect. In these litigious times, many unsuccessful applicants are quick to charge that they were not hired because of defamatory information acquired from previous employers. It is therefore important for all references to be checked by persons who do so regularly enough to be sensitive to the legal pitfalls that can be encountered. For example, an applicant might claim to have been defamed in being labeled on a reference check as "uncooperative and unreliable"— and can succeed in pursuing such a claim if there is insufficient information in the individual's past employment record to support such contentions.

Reference information used in making a decision not to hire needs to be substantiated in the past employment record. For instance, to stand up as valid if challenged, a reference of "poor attendance" should be backed up (in the personnel file maintained by the employer supplying the reference) with attendance records or with records of disciplinary actions dealing with attendance.

You might be tempted to use personal contacts such as your counterparts at other institutions to check on potential new employees applying from those locations. However, this information is not considered valid in making an employment decision, and it should not be used in the selection process.

## THE ACTUAL INTERVIEW

Assume you have reached the point where you are well aware of questions you should avoid and well advised of the kinds of questions you should ask. You and an applicant are now face-to-face in private and that you are mindful of the edge you hold in this interchange and of the possibly uncomfortable position of the applicant. Proceed according to these guidelines.

### Put the Applicant at Ease

At the beginning of the conversation you need to put the individual at ease and instill a degree of confidence. You might want to try several different topics at the start of the interview—for instance, the weather, the ease with which the person may have found your office, or an invitation to enjoy a cup of coffee—to get the person talking and take you a step toward conversational rapport. Whatever opener you employ—

and usually it need be only brief—it will get you off to a far better start than the shock of something like: "Good morning. Why do you want to work in a prison?"

During these first few critical minutes try to avoid making judgments and freezing a picture of the applicant in your mind. First impressions are often difficult to shed, and when formed while the person is not yet at ease they can be unfair.

### Avoid Short-Answer Questions

Avoid asking questions in such a way that they can be answered in one or two words, and especially avoid questions that can be answered simply "yes" or "no." For instance, a question such as: "How long did you work for the sheriff's department?" might simply be answered: "Three years." This gives you very little information. Rather, a request on the order of: "Please tell me about the work you did at the sheriff's department," requires the person to use more than just a couple of words in response. Your purpose is to learn about the applicant, and you can do so only by getting the person to talk.

However, you should avoid permitting the applicant to wander off the subject for minutes at a time. When this occurs, interrupt (as politely as possible) with another question or a request for clarification intended to draw the conversation back to the focus of the interview.

### Avoid Leading or "Loaded" Questions

Avoid questions that lead the applicant toward some predetermined response. For instance, if you ask: "You left the sheriff's department because the pay raises weren't coming along, is that right?" you are channeling the applicant toward a response that you may have already decided is correct. It is far better to ask, "Why did you leave the sheriff's department?"

Leading questions can be a particular hazard when you are talking with someone who is shaping up favorably in your eyes. In the process of unconsciously deciding you like this person, you may begin to bend the rest of your questions in a fashion that calls for the answers you would like to hear. Most people are sensitive to leading questions and, depending on the nature of the questions, will feel either forced or encouraged to deliver the answers that seem to be wanted.

## Ask One Question at a Time

Avoid hitting the applicant with something like: "What kind of work did you do there and why did you leave?" This is in fact two questions, and although they may well be properly asked one after the other, the person should be given the opportunity to deal with them individually. Combining or pyramiding questions tends to throw some people off balance; a person prepared to deal with a single question is suddenly confronted with two or three at once. It is always preferable to limit your questioning to one clear, concise question at a time.

## Keep Your Writing to a Minimum

Unless the agency has certain forms that must be filled out during the interview, try not to take extensive notes while the prospective employee is talking. This can be disconcerting to the individual, as note-taking creates the impression that everything that is said is being taken down in writing. Also, it is distracting to you. Writing and listening are both communication skills subject to their own particular ground rules and neither can be done with maximum effectiveness if you are trying to do both at the same time. The more writing you attempt, the more it detracts from your listening capacity. Take down a few key words if you must, but focus most of your attention on listening to the applicant. If you need or desire a written report of the interview, generate this report immediately after the applicant leaves and the conversation is still fresh in your mind.

## Use Appropriate Language

At all times deliver your questions and comments in language appropriate to the apparent level of education, knowledge, and understanding of the prospective employee. If you are a chief psychologist interviewing an applicant for a psychology position, you will likely talk on a level at which you would ordinarily expect to communicate with another mental health professional. However, if you happen to be interviewing for the position of unit secretary and are talking with a person who has never worked in a prison, you should alter your language accordingly. Always assume a reasonable degree of intelligence—you wish to avoid talking down to the person—but do not dazzle or confuse the applicant with unfamiliar terminology.

## Do More Listening Than Talking

Throughout the interview be interested and attentive, never impatient or critical. Avoid talking too much about yourself or the institution. Remember, you are not selling yourself to the applicant—it is supposed to be the other way around. Also, you are not selling the institution or the job to the applicant, although if the interview moves far enough in constructive directions, you may wish to answer the applicant's questions about the prison work in general or the duties at this location in particular.

However, even on this score there are precautions to note. Specifics of certain features of employment like insurance, retirement, and other benefits for which you may not have all the details should be left to the personnel department. You should not mention them until you are ready to extend an offer of employment and the individual needs this information to aid in making the decision.

## Indicate Some Type of Follow-up

Conclude the interview with a reasonable statement of what the applicant may expect to happen next. It is true you generally cannot (and probably should not) make a definite statement at this time, but you should suggest what may be expected and when it might occur. For instance, you can always say something like: "We'll let you know our decision after we've finished all scheduled interviews, say within a week or 10 days," or "You should be getting a letter from us next week," or perhaps simply "We'll call you by next Friday." In any case, conclude the interview with some simple indication of impending follow-up. Never let the applicant go away with the feeling of "Don't call us—we'll call you."

## FOLLOW-UP

Follow-up is no problem when you decide to extend a job offer to an applicant. You will extend the offer and the person will either accept or decline the job. In either case the interview process has been taken full circle.

When you do not wish to extend a job offer, you should follow up and complete the interview cycle. Follow-up by the institution is a simple but deserved courtesy. Although the applicant was looking for a job, you were also looking for an employee, and this particular individual traveled to meet you and gave you a certain amount of time.

Appropriate follow-up takes very little time. Once you have decided you do not wish to extend a job offer, a short, polite letter to that effect is appropriate. Also, you can use this same approach to let individuals know that although you cannot extend a job offer at the present time, you would like to keep their applications on file for future consideration, or that they may wish to apply at another institution. Depending on your agency's employment system, these letters might originate with you or they might go out from the personnel department.

In most organizations the personnel department will take care of applicant communication, but you can follow up with personnel to make sure this has occurred. In any case, and even for the most clearly unqualified of applicants, you should conclude the interview process with an answer. It is a courtesy due the applicant, and it serves to protect the prison's image as an employer in the community.

The employee selection interview can be a hazardous process filled with opportunities for miscalculation and misjudgment. It offers no guarantees that you will always locate the right person for the job. However, despite its flaws and pitfalls, the interview is still a key method for gaining information about prospective new employees. It remains one of the most important kinds of personal contact for the supervisor.

---

### EXERCISE 8-1: PRE-EMPLOYMENT INQUIRIES

Indicate whether each of the following questions is lawful (**L**) or unlawful (**U**) for you to ask an applicant in an interview situation:

1. Have you previously been employed under a different name?
2. What was your name before you married?
3. Where were you born?
4. Have you any condition that would prevent you from adequately performing in the position for which you are applying?
5. What was your title in your last employment, and who was your supervisor?
6. Do you have any handicaps?
7. In what country do you hold citizenship?
8. Who is the relative you would designate to be notified in case of emergency?

9. What foreign languages do you read, write, or speak fluently?
10. What other countries have you visited?
11. How did you acquire your foreign language abilities?
12. At what schools did you receive your academic, vocational, or professional education?
13. What major credit cards do you hold?
14. Have you ever filed for bankruptcy?
15. Who would be willing to provide you with a professional reference for the position for which you are applying?
16. Are you a single parent?
17. Have you any commitments or responsibilities that may interfere with meeting work attendance requirements?
18. What relatives of yours, if any, are already employed here?
19. Did you receive an honorable discharge from the military?
20. Why do you want to work here?
21. Where did you live before moving to your present address?
22. Do you own or rent your home?
23. What experiences, skills, or other qualifications do you feel make you appropriate for the position under consideration?
24. Why did you leave your last employer?
25. What organizations, clubs, and societies do you belong to?

**Answer Key:**

(L)awful: 1, 4, 5, 9, 10, 12, 15, 17, 18, 20, 23, 24
(U)nlawful: 2, 3, 6, 7, 8, 11, 13, 14, 16, 19, 21, 22, 25

---

### ROLE-PLAY 8–1: WOULD YOU HIRE THIS PERSON?

**Interviewer: Business Manager**

You are the business manager for a small state prison. You are interviewing applicants for a junior accountant vacancy. In your department you have: two accountants, both qualified, reasonably effective individuals; one junior accountant; one open position for a junior accountant; and two clerks.

The personnel office is sending you the second and third job candidates to interview. The first you rejected as overqualified and looking for more money than the junior position would warrant. It is your understanding that the stream of job applicants dried up after candidates two and three submitted their applications. You feel strongly about the necessity to fill this position in the near future and will have this foremost in mind when you interview candidates two and three. You do, however, have an alternative—you can hold the job open for a longer time and wait for the ideal candidate to appear.

After the initial review of applications, you contacted some people you know to get an idea of the character of candidate three. You learned that he has been with his present employer only four months but has not missed a day's work nor come in late. You did not check on applicant two because his application indicated he preferred you not contact his present employer.

## Candidate Two

You are 42 years old and you have approximately 15 years of routine bookkeeping experience in a large commercial organization. You believe you are probably older than most persons who would be expected to apply for this position, and you have done approximately the same level of work for about ten years.

You are still employed but you are not especially happy with your job. You have realized that you will probably go no higher in the organization, so you decided to look for something better.

## Candidate Three

You are a 23-year-old high school graduate from another state. You did factory work for a year before taking one year of liberal arts courses at a community college. You then spent three years in the military service and after being discharged settled in this area, married, and took a laborer's job in a local cotton mill.

You are not hesitant to reveal that you have been looking for a new job since the day you were hired at the mill. You generally agree that your background seems not to qualify you for accounting work but you have started a crash program of learning basic accounting on your own, primarily by acquiring books and practice sets and getting assistance from an acquaintance who is an accountant.

## Instructions

This is a group exercise appropriate for groups of six or more people.

Divide all participants into three smaller groups of approximately equal size. Assign one of the three roles to each group. Each small group should designate a spokesperson to play the role assigned to the group.

The business manager group should prepare its "interviewer" by developing a tentative line of questioning for the interviews. It should be this group's intention to learn as much as possible about each candidate—following acceptable lines of questioning—in a brief simulated interview.

The groups representing candidates two and three should prepare their spokespersons by considering the kinds of questions they might expect to be asked. It is up to the "candidates" to respond to questioning, making reasonable assumptions as necessary, and "sell themselves" to the "interviewer."

Devote approximately ten minutes to group preparation; then allow about five to seven minutes for each interview. Those participants not involved in the exercise as spokespersons should critique the interviews according to the interviewing guidelines provided in the chapter.

Discuss the conduct of the interviews.

## CHAPTER 9

# The One-to-One Relationship

*I know that you believe you understand what you think I said, but I am not sure you realize that what you heard is not what I meant.*

*—Anonymous*

*I wish I had done a better job of communicating with my people. If people understand the why, they will work for it. I never got that across.*
*—Roger Smith, former chairman of General Motors*

## Chapter Objectives

☛ Emphasize the importance of establishing an effective one-to-one communicating relationship with each employee.

☛ Stress the essential two-way character of interpersonal communication.

☛ Highlight the common barriers to effective communication and suggest how they can be avoided or overcome.

☛ Offer guidelines for improving your listening capacity.

☛ Suggest guidelines for effective interpersonal communication in the supervisor-employee relationship.

## THE TRANSFER OF MEANING

Communication is critical in the prison environment. On any given day the largest part of a correctional manager's job is likely to consist of interpersonal contact with other employees of the institution (and to a lesser extent with inmates); these employees are primarily those who report directly to the supervisor. In recognition of the supervisor's constant contact with employees to get things accomplished through them, we will concentrate in this chapter on face-to-face communication specifically within the context of the supervisor-employee relationship.

A simple beginning for a complex subject that goes far beyond the limits of this chapter might be to describe communication as "the transfer of meaning." In an organization, communication involves the transmission of information and instructions from person to person to accomplish understanding shared by the sender and the receiver of every message. The goal of communication is always a complete and accurate transfer of meaning resulting in assurance that the understanding of the person who received the message is identical to that of the person who originated the message.

Regarding the supervisor-employee relationship, we can say at the outset of this discussion that there is no single absolutely "correct" way of dealing with employees. All of your employees are different from each other, and they are all different from you. What works well in your relationship with employee A may not work at all in your relationship with employee B, and vice versa. We can go so far as to say that in your relations with your employees there may be fully as many "correct" ways of dealing with employees as you have employees.

An effective relationship with each employee is not something that can simply be established and assumed to exist forever. No such relationship between two people is ever completely "established," and the relationship must be constantly nurtured and conscientiously maintained if it is to serve appropriately the needs of the people involved and of the organization.

Although interpersonal relations constitute a large part of the supervisor's job, it is not always easy to concentrate on people and their problems and needs. There are hidden pressures that encourage us to focus on things rather than people. After all, things cannot hurt, disappoint, frustrate, influence, disagree, or misunderstand. There is a measure of safety and security in things. However, the supervisor must learn to overcome the tendency to seek reduced vulnerability and to look in the direction of the job's true demands.

The effective manager is called on to acquire and practice empathy—the capacity to put oneself in another's place and respond accordingly. Not many people are naturally attuned to the feelings and needs of those about them, but empathic sensitivity can be developed through conscious effort. Although we tend to take our communication capacity for granted, we are not really very good communicators by nature. We can, however, learn to communicate effectively. To do so we first need to appreciate the difficulties inherent in human communication, and we need to recognize one critical tendency in ourselves: the tendency to believe that we are better communicators than we in fact really are.

We use our primary tools of communication, words, to express meaning. Yet a tremendous gap exists between the thought or feeling we experience inside and the words we use to direct this toward another person. Likewise, a large gap exists between the words taken in by the other person and the thought or feeling experienced as a result of those words. It is possible only rarely, except in the most inconsequential situations, to transfer meaning accurately to another person in every precise dimension in which it was experienced.

We are all unique individuals. Countless factors and influences in each person's upbringing, background, education, and life experience make an individual a unique person. Because of our differences, we relate to the world in our own particular ways. Whenever we communicate with others, we are attempting to describe what has happened within us as a result of experiences coming from outside of us. As long as each of us can sense with only a single mind—our own—the process will remain imperfect. We have no control over the mind of another; rather than directly transferring a thought or feeling, the best we can do is put it into words and hope those words create a similar thought or feeling in someone else.

Interpersonal communication frequently fails because of the imperfections in the process. Too often communication fails simply because we assume the person we are talking with knows and understands what we happen to be talking about—after all, we know what we are talking about. Also, the process is fully as susceptible to failure when viewed from the other side; we assume we know what the other person means without taking steps to make certain this is so. The greatest number of communication failures probably occur in simple interchanges between people: You say something to another person and the two of you part, each with a meaning in mind. You believe you have been understood, and the other person believes he or she understands; yet you have parted with completely different meanings in mind.

## THE TWO-WAY STREET

Communication within the supervisor-employee relationship must be a two-way street that is heavily traveled in both directions. You are the supervisor; the authority of your position and the number of people with whom you must be concerned will limit the amount of communication flowing from employees to you. Therefore, it is generally up to you consistently to go more than halfway in the communication process.

One-way communication—the simple delivery of orders and instructions in authoritarian fashion with no information flowing the other way—is not communication at all. There are occasions when one-way communication seems to work effectively. Giving orders in a military situation or snapping out instructions in a prison emergency are good examples of this type of communication. However, these one-way transactions work only because they have been preceded by a significant amount of two-way communication in the form of instruction, training, and practice.

The undeniable pressure of time encourages managers to communicate in a one-way fashion, that is, simply to deliver orders or instructions in a few words before moving on to other problems. It always seems faster to deliver an instruction than it is to engage in discussion or encourage a few simple words of feedback. One-way communication that is clean and neat does not waste time or words—at least it seems that way, until the misunderstanding begins to surface.

One-way communication is often the refuge of the insecure manager. It discourages feedback and suppresses discussion. The manager is considerably less likely to be challenged and therefore cannot be found "wrong." One-way communication is also the province of an authoritarian manager, the individual who behaves as though all meaning must flow from the "boss" downward and that nothing valid can be expected to flow in the opposite direction. This mode of communication will be familiar to those already in corrections; it is all too common. True two-way communication, on the other hand, takes time, often considerably more time than a corresponding one-way contact would have taken. It is a simple trade-off: more time is invested for the sake of achieving greater accuracy in the transfer of meaning.

Consider the originator of a message in a two-way communication situation. The "sender" of the message experiences a certain vulnerability by virtue of being open to feedback and thus open to question, discussion, and perhaps disagreement. This position of vulnerability is not acceptable to all people in their communicating relationships, but feedback is the all-important element in two-way communication. It is feedback that helps clarify what has been said and indicates whether the message has been correctly received.

## BARRIERS TO EFFECTIVE COMMUNICATION

### Semantics

Words, our most actively used tools of communication, are in truth quite inadequate for the role we make them play. We expect far too much of these small bits of language. A word is simply a symbol we use to stand for something; it is not the thing itself. The only true meanings words have are the meanings we give them through active use.

Words are inconsistent in their meanings; many of them possess a variety of "definitions." In fact, the 500 most frequently used words in the English language have a total of nearly 15,000 dictionary definitions. This suggests that the "average" word, if we can say there is such a thing, can have 30 definitions, some quite similar to each other but some extremely different from all others.

Words are also likely to mean different things to different people. For instance, how long or short a span of time does *prompt* mean to you? Some words can even mean different things to the same person at different times or under different circumstances. For example, *fix* may mean one thing if you happen to be repairing an automobile and something else entirely if your immediate interest is locating a reference point for navigation purposes.

We have words in our language that can be described only as fuzzy in terms of meaning and usage. Take a good look at a few of the words that fill our organizational communication to the point of overflowing. Again, we have *prompt*. We also have *sufficient, appropriate, adequate,* and other similarly vague terms. What meaning are you going to get if the last sentence of the memorandum you just received says: "You are requested to take prompt action, employing adequate measures to ensure appropriate response sufficient to the situation"?

You can sample many of the problems of semantics by pondering your reaction to a simple question long used in discussions on this subject: How tall is a tall man? Over six feet? Six feet six inches or taller? Five feet nine inches or taller? Your answer probably depends in part on how tall you are, and ultimately the answer to the question depends entirely on who is doing the judging.

## Emotion

Words often carry emotional overtones that vary from person to person and create additional barriers to interpersonal communication. Words that register neutrally or perhaps favorably on some people are likely to hit "sore spots" in other people. Aside from the obvious—profanity, obscenity, ethnic slurs, and downright insults—many words used without malicious intent will trigger negative emotional responses in listeners. Perhaps the word *stubborn* does not bother you, but the person you are talking with may resent being referred to as stubborn. Perhaps your boss places a favorable connotation on the term *eager beaver* and applies this to you; however, you may resent the term as suggesting you are trying too hard or bordering on being annoying. (You would prefer to be called a "loyal and energetic employee.")

Positive emotions can be good to some extent in interpersonal communication. However, even positive emotions (for instance, joy or enthusiasm) can cloud individual judgment and impair communication when they are experienced to a degree that the feelings themselves become more important than the message being communicated.

Negative emotions—hurt and anger and all their variations—definitely tend to impair effective communication. The prison setting presents ample opportunities for these emotions to charge an otherwise neutral conversation. No matter how inoffensive you try to keep your language, you are likely (perhaps frequently) to touch one of someone's sore spots and trigger an emotional reaction.

A line employee may have just been involved in a stressful situation involving name-calling by an inmate; you may unknowingly reap the emotional residue of that conversation when you talk to that person a few minutes later. Consider the times you may have turned away from a conversation with the impression that you have somehow hurt, offended, or angered the other person, and you honestly had not had the slightest idea of what you might have said to cause that reaction. You do this unintentionally, and it is not likely that you will ever be able to eliminate this from your communication entirely. However, what you can do is to be aware that this occurs with all people in interpersonal situations and that by exercising empathy you may better understand the other person's position. Also, since you may hurt, offend, or anger someone unintentionally, always extend to the other person the benefit of the doubt. Remember that when someone touches one of your little sore spots and you are hurt, offended, or angered, chances are that it was completely accidental and no injury was intended.

Generally, the higher the negative emotional level of one or both parties to an interpersonal exchange, the less are the chances of meaningful communication. When emotion threatens to turn a discussion into an argument, it is time to back away from the situation as diplomatically as possible and try again when tempers have abated.

Emotion in interpersonal exchange also tends to polarize views and drive participants toward opposite positions. Anger or its variations are also likely to be evident in the behavior of someone who has been put on the defensive and who is using emotion unconsciously to cover a weakness or shield a position from attack.

It would be easy, but quite useless, for us to say we should not allow ourselves to be hurt or angry. You cannot help experiencing a feeling, and feelings themselves are neither right nor wrong—they are just there. However, be aware of the destructive potential of negative feelings.

In all dealings with your employees and others, be reasonably careful of the words you use, remain normally polite and friendly, and do not hesitate to be conciliatory if it appears necessary or helpful. Although you happen to be the manager and occupy a so-called position of authority, never consider yourself too self-important to apologize when you err in your interpersonal communication.

In all dealings with others, and especially in dealing with employees on critical issues and points of difference, avoid sweeping generalizations that are by their nature untrue. Two of the worst words you can use are *always* and *never,* as in "You're always late," or "You never submit it correctly." Rarely are *always* and *never* strictly true, but both are usually inflammatory.

## LISTENING

The following words of wisdom have appeared on many office walls: "How come it takes 2 years to learn to talk and 60 or 70 to learn to be quiet?" How much of the talking do you do in any interchange with an employee? This is a valid question because you cannot truly listen while you are talking.

Of our four verbal means of communication—writing, reading, speaking, and listening—listening, when effectively practiced, requires most of our communication time. Yet listening is the single verbal communication skill for which the least amount of solid, practical help is available. Although listening skills are not easy to describe or define, these skills can nevertheless be learned. Conscientious attention to the following suggestions and precautions can make you a better listener.

### Be Attentive

Force yourself to concentrate on what the other person is saying. Do not turn off your attention because the speaker is uninteresting or reject close attention to the subject because you "know it already." Some people speak in ways that fail to grab and hold your attention automatically, and if you are really to listen to what is being said, you will find it necessary to apply some conscious effort. Knowing that your forced attention may be required is often more than half the battle; the remainder becomes a matter of actually applying your undivided attention. Also, keep in mind that even though a topic may not seem interesting or important to you, it usually is important to the person doing the speaking.

### Wait Before Responding

All but trained listeners are likely to rush their responses by reacting to only a portion of what is being said. The temptation is great; you hear a few words that trigger a response in you and your mind begins to race ahead to form the comment you will deliver as soon as the other person pauses. Resist this temptation. While your mind is busy forming your response, your listening capacity is reduced, sometimes to the point where you will interrupt the other person. Instead, deal with one complete thought or idea at a time, hearing the person out completely before offering a response.

### Get the Whole Message

Many people have a habit of listening only for "facts"—specific bits of information. Facts are useful, of course, but their usefulness is diminished if they are not considered within the context of the entire message. Listen to the whole message before making decisions or rendering judgments.

### Keep Interruptions to a Minimum

If you can possibly avoid doing so, try not to interrupt the other person to offer a correction of something you think has been improperly stated. Certainly avoid interrupting to offer advice or to scold or otherwise criticize. This is especially important in face-to-face communication within the supervisor-employee relationship. Generally, interruptions are in order only if you make them to ask for expansion or clarification of something that has been said or to ask related questions intended to encourage more relevant comments.

### Be Aware of Your Emotional Sore Spots

While you are listening, be aware of the possibility of emotional reactions within you. Know that the other person can unintentionally trigger an emotional reaction in you. Give the other person the benefit of the doubt and force yourself to concentrate on the message as being distinctly separate from its emotional overtones. You cannot help what you feel, but you can control what you do with those feelings. If you allow negative feelings to come to the foreground and dominate your reaction, your listening capacity will be sharply reduced.

## SOME GUIDELINES FOR EFFECTIVE INTERPERSONAL COMMUNICATION

### When You Are Doing the Talking

- Before speaking up, put some effort into structuring the communication you are about to deliver. First think out the what and why of the communication. When you know what you are going to say and what you are trying to accomplish, you can consider how best to communicate it.
- Consider your listener's needs, interests, and attitudes. Try to exercise empathy at all times, constantly judging what you are saying from your listener's point of view.
- Deliver your comments in language properly suited to the level of knowledge, education, and experience of your listener. Never talk down to or over the head of the other person.
- Except in the direst of emergencies (and even then if your listener is not prepared to respond appropriately), follow up your communication immediately with a request for feedback. Ask to have the message played back to you in the listener's own words. This could be as simple as: "How would you describe what I've just asked you to do?" Ideally, your approach should not be one that suggests you are trying to find out if the other person understood you—although that is a major purpose—but rather that you are trying to assure yourself that you communicated your thoughts clearly and fully.

### When You Are Doing the Listening

- Pay attention. Really listen—your undivided attention conquers many potential problems.
- Listen always for meaning, striving constantly to determine what is being said and why it is being said.
- Consider the whole person, searching out attitudes and feelings as well as meanings. Keep in mind that words and other signs—the nonverbal signals given out by the other person—cannot be separated from attitudes and feelings.

- Be as patient as necessary to encourage the individual to try to communicate fully.
- Be prepared to compromise as necessary to achieve agreement or understanding, and consider yielding completely on minor points or unimportant details. Compromise is not the dirty word some regarded it to be; rather, reasonable compromise is often the most important step in establishing mutual understanding.
- Return the message to the speaker in your own words, using discussion to iron out differences until you both agree that the message sent and the message received are the same.

## THE OPEN-DOOR ATTITUDE

Every manager has probably said at one time or another, "My door is always open." This is an easy statement to make, but it takes effort to assure that these words reflect an honest attitude, not a timeworn platitude.

Your job is to help your employees get their work done. In addition to guiding and directing their overall efforts, you must answer questions, deal with problems, silence rumors, and put fears and suspicions to rest. Remember that your employees do not work for you as much as they work with you and that a large part of your function is to "run interference" for your employees so that they can accomplish their work as efficiently as possible. To do all of this, you must be visible and readily available to your employees and have an always growing one-to-one relationship with each employee. It is your responsibility to consider the employee as a whole person, not simply as just a producer. To do so often requires you to be a person first and a manager second. Successful supervision requires human sensitivity. Without sensitivity, a supervisor has only rules, policies, and procedures, which are useful, but which by themselves are grossly inadequate for the complete fulfillment of the supervisory role.

Effective one-to-one communication with each employee is the basis for mutual understanding between supervisor and employee. A healthy attitude for the supervisor assumes a Golden Rule approach to communication: Deal with others as you would wish to be dealt with yourself.

Your one-to-one relationship with each employee is critical to the institution as a whole. The way each employee sees you—available, friendly, caring, and helpful, or perhaps the opposite—so may he or she come to see the entire organization. As a member of management, you represent the organization to the employee. The impression you create as a person will contribute, for good or ill, to the individual employee's impression of the organization.

---

## CASE 9–1: WHAT'S IN A PHRASE?

Mort Harriman accepted the position of industrial procurement supervisor at a major state prison that had a large metal factory. He was to be responsible for not only purchasing but warehousing raw and finished goods and staging material flow to the factory floor.

In his middle 30s, Mort had considerable experience in material management and procurement. Years before, following his graduation with a degree in general business, he was floor supervisor in the largest paint warehouse in a major metropolitan area. After five years there he moved on to become manager of purchasing for a sheet metal fabrication firm. Now, after eight years, the economy had soured, and he had really felt lucky to have been hired at the nearby 1,000-bed state prison, although at a lower wage. He had never before worked for a government agency.

Mort reported to Art Reynolds, the factory manager, and was impressed with him because he seemed to have his finger on everything on the factory floor, as well as being on top of the other details of running a factory inside a maximum-security prison. Mort was impressed by the tempo, tone, and general enthusiasm of the prison factory. His new job was a significant change from the relaxed environment from which he had come, but Mort was sure he would do well.

Mort had come to work at the prison during an extremely busy period. Not only did he have the expected task of getting to know the workers in the warehouse and business office, but there was also the problem of relocating the factory's largest storeroom to a newly completed area. Also, it was the time of annual budget preparation and during Mort's first week each department's initial budget drafts were due.

On Monday, Mort's first day, Reynolds gave him considerable orientation along with several instructions. The last item concerned the budget. As Reynolds put it to Mort, "I realize you are new, but you've walked right into the annual budget cycle. All of the other department heads are expected to have their first-cut budgets to me on Wednesday. You're going to be involved enough as it is, so let's say I'll expect to have your first rough cut as soon as you can do it, but no later than noon Friday."

Later that day Mort began assembling preliminary numbers for the budget draft. He took it home with him and did a small amount of work on it.

On Tuesday some severe problems developed with the transfer of goods to the enlarged storage area and Mort found himself deeply involved. At the same time he was pursuing a series of face-to-face meetings with employees, in order to get to know them. By mid week Mort was thinking that never in several years on his past job had the work come at such an unexpected pace.

Shortly after noon on Friday Mort was seated at his desk handling a few items of correspondence when his phone rang. It was Reynolds, who asked, "Mort, where is that draft budget?"

Mort suddenly realized that he had not touched the budget since Monday evening. Recalling Reynolds' words, he said defensively, "You told me to get it to you as soon as I could. I've been buried; I just haven't been able to get at it."

"I did say as soon as possible," Reynolds replied. "I could have used it Wednesday. I also said 'no later than Friday noon.' It's now Friday, past noon, and I don't have your draft."

Mort said, "I'm sorry I let it slip. I'll get it to you as soon as—" he stopped and caught himself for he had almost said, "as soon as I can." Instead he said, "I'll get it to you as quickly as I can put it together."

After a few seconds of silence, Reynolds said, "I'll be here until about 6:00 tonight. I expect your budget draft on my desk before I go home."

Mort cleared his desk and prepared to work on the budget, thinking somewhat glumly: "First week on the job and I'm already on the list." He could also not help thinking that his boss on his previous job would never have expected a new employee to get up and running so rapidly.

### Instructions

Isolate the particular words or phrases that got Mort into trouble. Explore the likely reason why trouble resulted from a few seemingly innocent words.

What does this tell you about:

- The context within which a message is delivered?
- The apparent meanings of simple words?

### CASE 9–2: THE EMPLOYEE WHO IS NEVER WRONG

"I know what I heard, and that's that," correctional officer Craig Masterson said in the no-nonsense tone that shift supervisor Harry Anderson had come to know so well.

"Captain Steele says otherwise, Craig," said Anderson. "He told me in no uncertain terms that the instructions he gave you were just the opposite of what you did."

"He's wrong," snapped Craig.

"He says that you were wrong, and he seemed quite sure about it." Harry paused thoughtfully before adding, "He took the trouble to explain the whole situation to me, and I have to say that I understood his instructions. At least I was able to give them back in my own words so he was satisfied that I understood."

Craig scowled, then shrugged and said, "Then he changed his story."

"You're suggesting that he lied to me?"

"I didn't say that. I'm just saying that he told me one thing and then apparently told you something else. Maybe he didn't understand what he was telling me. You know how he just kind of rattles off something quickly and runs away."

Harry sighed and said, "Craig, did you consider the possibility that you didn't understand? It isn't hard to misinterpret when everything happens so fast and. . . ."

"I know what I heard," interrupted Craig. "When I know I'm wrong, I'll say so. If I even think I may be wrong, I'll say so. But in this case I know I'm right. It's not even remotely possible that I could have misinterpreted him."

Feeling that Craig had given him cause to say something that had been nagging at him for quite some time, Harry said, "It seems to me that you're never wrong, Craig."

Craig glared at his supervisor. "What do you mean by that?" he asked.

Harry took a deep breath and plunged in: "I've been watching you work various posts for three years, and in that time I've never known you to admit to being wrong about anything. This business with Captain Steele is just one more example. You always turn everything around so you come up clean. Is it so necessary that you be right about everything? Do you ever make a mistake?"

Craig's tone, already cool, became colder. "Like I said, I'll admit I'm wrong—but only when I am wrong. And I want to know the other times you're talking about, the times when I supposedly turned everything around."

Harry began, "Well, there was—" he stopped, shook his head, and said, "No, that was something else. In any case, you ought to know what I'm talking about. Think about it, and you'll know what I'm saying. You've got an answer for everything, an answer that always places you in the right."

"You can't think of any specific incidents because there haven't been any," said Craig. He rose from his chair and continued, "You may be my supervisor, but I don't have to listen to this. Is there anything else you wanted to say about the Captain's problem?" he glared down at Harry.

Harry rose to his feet. "Well, it's just that this incident isn't really closed. Captain Steele told me to write it up for your performance record as a verbal warning."

"Well, you can bet I'll fight that," said Craig. "I won't sign a warning I don't deserve, and I won't say I'm wrong when I know I'm right."

When Craig left the office, Harry began to regret having spoken to Craig as he did. He was convinced, however, that he had to try to get through to Craig about his apparent need to be "right" about everything.

## Questions

1. When Harry "took the plunge" and went beyond the specific incident to talk about Craig's overall conduct, he made a mistake that is embodied in the statement "You always turn everything around so you come up clean." What was Harry's mistake?

2. How would you recommend attempting to determine the cause for the misunderstanding between Craig and Captain Steele?

3. Taking Craig's departure from Harry's office at the end of the case description as your starting point, how could you propose to deal in the future with the employee who is "never wrong"?

## CHAPTER 10

# Leadership: Style and Substance

*Real leaders are ordinary people with extraordinary determinations.*

*—John Seaman Garns*

*Be willing to make decisions. That's the most important quality in a good leader. Don't fall victim to what I call the ready-aim-aim-aim-aim syndrome. You must be willing to fire.*

*—T. Boone Pickens*

### Chapter Objectives

☛ Describe patterns of leadership, or leadership "styles," ranging from rigid (autocratic) to open (participative).

☛ Review opposing sets of assumptions about people that give rise to different leadership styles.

☛ Establish the necessity for sufficient flexibility in leadership to vary style according to circumstances.

☛ Determine the primary characteristic of effective leadership.

☛ Relate the employees' view of the supervisor to critical elements of leadership performance.

## INTRODUCING LEADERSHIP

Most people have some potential for leadership, although in some people this potential may be limited. The essential difference between the leader and the nonleader is determined by the degree to which a person succeeds in learning about leadership and applying what has been learned.

Leadership is like many other human endeavors—talent helps, but it is not necessary to be extraordinarily talented to be successful. You may not be a "natural leader"; you may not be able to run a large organization or get hundreds of people to follow you in some undertaking. However, you stand at least an average chance of being able to furnish true leadership to the employees in a department or other work group.

Since there are vast differences in perceptions of what characterizes a leader and how a leader should behave, our discussion of leadership will begin with the consideration of style—the patterns of behavior projected by leaders as they work. And although it is tempting to talk about leadership on a grand scale (since most of the great leaders we learn about led armies, nations, churches, or corporations) we will better serve our needs by limiting the discussion to the context of the correctional manager's environment.

## PATTERNS OF LEADERSHIP

Leadership styles range along a continuous scale from purely authoritarian at one extreme to fully participative at the other. In the scale in Figure 10–1 from left to right the following styles are delineated.

- Exploitative autocracy describes the harshest style of leadership. The exploitative autocrat not only wields absolute power over the people in the group, but also uses the group primarily to serve personal interests. This type of leader literally exploits the followers.

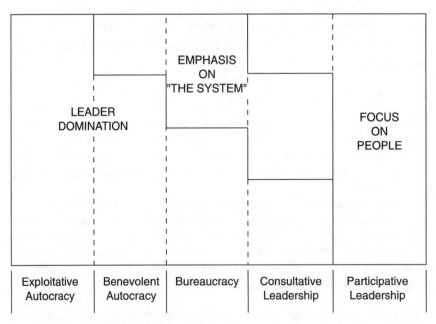

**Figure 10–1** Patterns of Leadership

- Benevolent autocracy exists when the leader wields absolute power, often with an iron hand, but is generally sincere in believing that the behavior of those in the group must be closely ordered and regulated for the good of the organization. References to autocratic leadership throughout the remainder of this chapter will refer generally to this particular leadership pattern.

- Bureaucracy is a term that immediately raises visions of large federal and state government agencies (especially where correctional organizations dealing with confinement are concerned, since most are organized in a quasi-military manner). As a leadership pattern, it refers to the primary emphasis on rules and regulations. The bureaucratic leader "goes by the book," creating new rules and regulations as new situations arise to such an extent that the "book" itself often becomes more important than the purpose it is intended to serve.

- Consultative leadership is exhibited when the leader remains open to input from members of the group, but, through either pronouncement, attitude, or practice, retains full decision-making authority. In many instances consultative leadership is appropriate (as even autocratic leadership of the benevolent kind is sometimes appropriate), but often the practice of consultative leadership is qualified under a participative label. Some supervisors claim they are open to participation, but in practice they are "open" only as long as the employees come up with the same decisions they would have made themselves.

- Full participative leadership exists when plans or decisions are made by all of the department's employees as a group or team. The supervisor is a key member of the group, providing advice, information, and assistance in any way possible and who has made a prior decision to accept the outcome of the group process.

With the exception of exploitative autocracy (which serves the leader's goals rather than those of the organization), no particular leadership pattern can be labeled "wrong." What is right for one department may be wrong for another; what is right in one particular situation may be wrong under a different set of circumstances. What was right in the past may be wrong today.

Changing social conditions have lessened the need for autocratic leadership over the years; yet autocratic leadership patterns prevail in many organizations. Gone are the days when the average worker was uneducated and completely dependent on orders from above. Autocratic leadership was the rule when the average worker was illiterate, or at best, semiliterate, but even today many outmoded organizational assumptions prevail. Autocratic and bureaucratic leadership hold forth when they should have given way to more consultative and participative styles. This shift in leadership patterns is an issue of note in corrections, as line security staff in many agencies are increasingly college-educated, and others have worked in noncorrectional organizations that use less regimented forms of management.

We will briefly examine some of the assumptions on which so-called modern organizations are based. More complete consideration of the reasons why people work is provided in the discussion of motivation in Chapter 11.

## SOME ASSUMPTIONS ABOUT PEOPLE

Douglas McGregor, in his work "The Human Side of Enterprise,"[1] wrote of two opposing approaches to management: Theory X and Theory Y. Theory X in its pure state is what we have been calling autocratic leadership. Pure Theory Y is participative leadership. Each of these management theories is based on a number of assumptions. The first assumption, and the only one common to both theories, is that management remains responsible for organizing the elements of all productive activity, that is, bringing together the money, people, equipment, and supplies needed to accomplish the organization's goals. Beyond this assumption, however, the two theories proceed in opposite directions. Theory X assumes the following.

- People must be actively managed. They must be directed and motivated, and their actions must be controlled and their behavior modified to fit the needs of the organization. Without this active intervention by management, people would be passive and even resistant to organizational needs. Therefore, people must be persuaded, controlled, rewarded, or punished as necessary to accomplish the aims of the organization.
- The average person is by nature indolent, working as little as possible. The average person lacks ambition, shuns responsibility, and in general prefers to be led.
- The average person is inherently self-centered, resistant to change, and indifferent to the needs of the organization.

Theory Y, on the other hand, includes the following assumptions:

- People are not naturally passive or resistant to organizational needs. If they appear to have become so, this condition is the result of experience in organizations.

- Motivation, development potential, willingness to assume responsibility, and readiness to work toward organizational goals are present in most people. It is management's responsibility to make it possible for people to recognize and develop these characteristics for themselves.

- The essential task of management is to arrange organizational conditions and methods of operation so people can best achieve their own goals by directing their efforts toward the goals of the organization.

## STYLE AND CIRCUMSTANCES

If you are an autocratic leader, you are operating under Theory X assumptions. You choose to make all the decisions and hand them down as orders and instructions. If you are a participative leader, you are generally ascribing to Theory Y assumptions and encouraging your employees to participate in joint decisions.

Some situations—institutional emergencies for instance—call for a highly directive Theory X approach. However, in most cases, you have a choice of leadership styles available to you, ranging from extremely closed to extremely open. The trick is to know which style to apply and when to apply it. You may have some "Theory X people" in your department; they will likely be a minority—those few who actually prefer to be led and have their thinking done for them. However, you may also have a number of "Theory Y people" who are self-motivated and capable of significant self-direction. This is especially likely in departments employing large numbers of professionals, such as the medical or case management departments. Although the same "rules" (meaning personnel policies) apply uniformly to all employees, you will deal differently with individuals. Some you will consult and invite their participation; others you will simply direct.

Avoid making assumptions about people. Know your employees and try to understand each one as both a producer and a person. By working with people over a period of time, and especially by working at the business of getting to know them, you can learn a great deal about individual likes and dislikes and capabilities. Learn about your people as individuals and when necessary, lead accordingly. If you are convinced that a certain employee genuinely prefers orders and instructions and this attitude is not inconsistent with job requirements, then use orders and instructions. Although many employees of correctional organizations seem to prefer participative leadership, not everyone will. Maintain sufficient flexibility to accommodate the employee who wants or requires authoritarian supervision. It is just as unfair to expect people to become what they do not want to be as it is to allow a rigid structure to stifle those other employees who feel they have something more to contribute.

Whereas there is no single style of leadership that is appropriate to all people and situations at all times, consultative and participative leadership is most appropriate to modern organizations and today's educated workers.

## OUTMODED VIEWS

In addition to harboring erroneous assumptions about people, many managers cling to outmoded notions of how a manager should behave. The prison environment is particularly susceptible to fostering these stereotypical views. In all likelihood, this mind-set started with the historical role of the warden as a "mini-god" with virtually unbounded power within the institution. Even today, prison staff see the warden in particular, and other top managers in general, as being "boss"—the giver of orders: "I'm the boss. I'm paid to make decisions and I'm responsible for the results of those decisions, so I will make those decisions." Because the prison culture places a high value on strength and assertiveness, some managers equate strong leadership with an autocratic style and see participative leadership as "passing the buck" or "spreading the blame." In general they view participative leadership as a shirking of responsibilities.

However, participative leadership is anything but abrogation of responsibility. Recall from the material on delegation that although you can parcel out your management authority and spread it among a number of employees, you remain responsible for the decisions and actions of your employees. The true participative leader, who willingly remains responsible for the decisions of the group, is displaying considerably more courage than the autocrat who simply decides and gives orders. To trust your employees with a share of your authority while you retain full responsibility is a sign of strength, not a sign of weakness.

Another outmoded view of leadership is reflected in the belief that the leader should always know best, that employees look to the leader to "tell them how to do it." The true function of the leader is to help the employees find the best way to do it themselves. The leader does not take up a position at the rear of the pack and shove. Neither does the leader move in front of the crew and urge them to follow. Rather, the leader is somewhere in the pack—a facilitator, a remover of obstacles, and in general a catalytic agent that causes the entire group to move forward in the proper direction. The true leader is not the master of a department, but rather its busiest, most responsible servant.

## LEADERSHIP'S PRIMARY CHARACTERISTIC

Many attempts have been made at creating detailed listings of qualities that characterize leaders. It is done all the time; great lists are generated that include standard noble but intangible characteristics such as honesty, integrity, and initiative, and slightly more measurable criteria such as academic qualifications. People who write hiring requirements for managerial positions create job specifications as full of noble characteristics as the Boy Scout Law. However, there is hardly a characteristic we can name—education, experience, integrity, communication ability, energy, conscientiousness—that we cannot find completely lacking in some successful leaders. In short, you cannot make even a brief list, and truly say that a leader must have these characteristics.

Is there anything, then, that truly defines a leader? A leader is certainly not defined by organizational appointment or the simple conferring of a management title. A title may describe a position but not a person; a great many so-called leadership positions are occupied by people who are anything but leaders in the true sense of the word.

The single factor that defines or characterizes a true leader is the acceptance by the followers. This means acceptance of the individual as a leader, not simply acceptance of obedience to the position the individual occupies. You have undoubtedly known managers who were not especially respected, were perhaps even ridiculed or joked about when not present, but were nevertheless obeyed. Obedience, although it may be grudging, will often be extended to the position because of the authority of the position itself. However, willing obedience will be extended consistently only by those employees who have accepted the supervisor's leadership.

This positive, persuasive style of leadership is effective. As Alan Greenspan, chairman of the Federal Reserve Board, said, "You can lead an organization through persuasion or formal edict. I have never found the arbitrary use of authority to control an organization either effective or, for that matter, personally interesting. If you cannot persuade your colleagues of the correctness of your decision, it is probably worthwhile to rethink your own."

Acceptance by one's followers cannot be mandated; it must be earned. Without this acceptance, a supervisor is a manager in title only and a leader not at all.

## WORD PLAY: LEADERSHIP VERSUS "MANAGEMENT"

Leadership has been attracting a great deal of attention and acquiring newer shades of meaning in the total quality management (TQM) movement. As empowerment is "in" and delegation attracts little concern—although empowerment is no more than proper delegation with a slick new finish on it (see Chapter 5)—so is leadership "in" at present and likely to remain that way for several years. Many concerned with the quality movement speak of the need for "not management, but leadership."

With this highly positive connotation placed on the word *leadership,* we are left with an eroded connotation of management, conveying the impression that somehow mere management does not measure up to leadership. However, *management* and *leadership* remain two words that are generally synonymous and freely interchangeable in many uses.

As suggested above, someone can be a manager—or supervisor, director, coordinator, administrator, chief executive officer, or whatever—in title without being a true leader. However, this in no way renders management as a whole anything less than, nor anything significantly different from, leadership. There is poor management and there is good management; there is poor leadership and there is good leadership. One can be a manager in title without being a leader, but in terms of function one cannot manage without leading and cannot lead without managing. Good leadership and good management go together, as do poor leadership and poor management.

We frequently hear management described as both art and science. We might say the same about leadership, but we are usually ready to consider leadership more as art. Leadership is more likely to inspire thoughts of the human element, whereas management conjures up images of "techniques" and "tools." Whether we are speaking of management or leadership, however, we are dealing with the process of accomplishing goals through the efforts of people. Only so much of this process can be quantified and reduced to rules and techniques; the remainder will come from the heart and the gut. It can be developed from within, but it can never be instilled from without. Whether leadership or management, it is this unquantifiable, frequently elusive "soft" side that puts the word "good" or another adjective in front of management or leadership. And leadership and management cannot be justly compared without the use of qualifying adjectives.

## AN EMPLOYEE'S VIEW

Not all the employees in a department will view the supervisor in the same light or develop the same impression of the supervisor as a leader. Each of your employees will experience your leadership "style" in bits and pieces that add up to a total impression. As long as you are convinced you are doing the best job you know how to do, there is little to be gained from worrying about the opinions your employees hold of you. However, it pays to remember that your view of yourself as a leader is rarely the same as the view of you that your employees hold. What you see as your strengths may not be seen as strong points by your employees. Conversely, what your employees see as your strong points may not even have occurred to you as significant characteristics of your style.

There are several aspects of supervisory performance that are likely to influence your employees' assessment of you. Your employees may not use the same terms we use to describe these aspects of performance, nor use labels such as "autocratic," "authoritarian," or "participative." However, the view your employees form of you is usually related to the way you come across in regard to some or all of the following.

- Do you communicate openly, sharing all necessary or helpful information with the employee group? Openness to communication is associated more with consultative or participative leadership, and a closed communication posture is associated more with autocratic leadership. Granted, there are occasions in prison when sensitive information must be closely held, but those occasions usually are rare.
- Do you display awareness of people's problems and needs? The participative leader tends more toward awareness of individual

problems while the autocratic leader often appears unaware or even uncaring.

- Do you display trust and confidence in employees? The autocratic leader displays little trust or confidence, relying mostly on close supervision. The true participative leader is able to extend trust and confidence.
- What means do you use to motivate employees? The autocratic leader frequently relies on fear and punishment to move people forward. The participative leader motivates through involvement and reward whenever possible.
- Do you provide support to employees? The employees of the autocratic leader often find they stand alone when things go wrong and they need the supervisor's backing. Support for employees and their decisions and actions is a hallmark of the participative leader.
- Do you request input on job problems? The autocratic leader tends to go it alone, but the consultative or participative leader is generally open to input from the work group.

## THE VISIBLE SUPERVISOR

Supervisors experience many pressures that encourage them to "face upward" in the organization toward higher management. After all, the supervisor's praise, reward, and recognition come from this upward direction. It is natural for supervisors who seek career growth to recognize that advancement is often facilitated by the extent to which they are organizationally visible outside of their own areas of responsibility. Opportunities to serve as acting associate warden or to participate in cross-training in other prison departments can be legitimate developmental tools used in this light.

In facing upward, however, the supervisor runs the risk of losing sight of the rank-and-file members of his or her own department. In the long run the employees and their day-to-day performance have the greatest effect on the performance of the supervisor, but it is all too easy for supervisors to be so busy facing upward—meeting with the boss, serving on committees, attending outside functions, and such—that they lose touch with the people who, by how they perform, can truly make or break supervisors.

To provide true leadership to the work group, the supervisor must be an integral part of the work unit and be perceived as such by employees. To get things done effectively through employees, as supervisor you should: (1) be visible and available, spending most of your time where you are really needed; (2) show concern for the employees' problems; (3) maintain a true open-door attitude so that your employees can always reach you when they need you; and (4) rely on immediate feedback to let all of your employees know exactly where they stand. Much of true leadership is provided by visible example, and the more visible you are to your employees, the greater the chance of your gaining their acceptance.

Indeed, personal visibility is thought by some to be a key to successful management—correctional or otherwise. That is the heart of the MBWA (Management by Walking Around) school of thought—one that is highly regarded in prison work.

One of the most respected correctional administrators in the United States, James D. Henderson, spoke to this issue, saying, ". . . personal visibility builds staff confidence in their leaders. Instead of visualizing some front office paper-pushers, line staff can relate to managers they see regularly, have an opportunity to talk to, and who listen to their concerns and problems. I'm talking about personal contacts with staff in every area of the institution. I have toured institutions where neither staff nor inmates knew the warden who was walking along with me, providing a clear indication of the problems existing in that facility. In another location, the unit log in segregation indicated that the warden visited there for a total of three minutes. That's simply not enough time in such a critical area of the institution. In yet another case involving a serious escape, supervisory personnel had avoided visiting death row for weeks at a time."[2]

## TRUE LEADERSHIP

The only factor that truly defines a leader is the acceptance of leadership by the followers. A style that leans toward participative leadership is more likely to be found acceptable by the majority of today's workers than a style that leans toward autocratic behavior. However, no single pattern of leadership behavior is appropriate to all situations at all times. You may lean toward participative leadership most of the time. However, there still may be times when the situation calls for autocratic behavior—you need to be able to make a decision, issue an order, and expect results; crisis intervention is a reality in prison. A good manager must be able to rapidly shift gears to this mode, even if it is not his or her normal pattern. Also, there may be times when bureaucratic behavior (strict interpretation and application of the rules and regulations) may be required. True leadership is flexible; it responds to both individual and organizational needs and is shaped to fit the needs of the moment.

---

## CASE 10–1: THE BUCK STOPS HERE

As a chief correctional supervisor in a small minimum-security prison, you report to the warden.

The plaque on the warden's desk saying "The Buck Stops Here" describes her approach to the job. She never avoids a decision or a problem, even of the most controversial or unpleasant sort, and for this you respect her.

However, the warden makes her decisions in a vacuum with no input from other department heads involved in the issue at hand. She is apparently conscientious in her attempts to come up with the best solution each time. But when she transmits the instructions for carrying out her decisions, she does so without giving you or anyone else the opportunity to provide the perspective of the person who has to translate the order into action.

### Question

When you receive an order from the warden which you know is inappropriate—and assume you know so because you are much closer to the problem—how can you make yourself heard without deliberately rejecting her style of leadership?

---

## EXERCISE 10–1: A VIEW OF YOU AS A LEADER

This exercise may be difficult for you—not difficult to accomplish, but difficult to accept what you learn from it. However, it can be helpful in suggesting areas in which your employees' view of your leadership style differs from your view.

The six questions appearing below are taken from the six points discussed in Chapter 10 under "An Employee's View." Each is provided with its own scale, extending from 0 (fully autocratic) to 10 (completely participative).

1. Do I communicate fully and openly?
   0  1  2  3  4  5  6  7  8  9  10
   (Not at all)           (Completely)

2. Am I aware of people's problems and needs?
   0  1  2  3  4  5  6  7  8  9  10
   (Unaware)              (Fully aware)

3. Do I display trust and confidence?
   0  1  2  3  4  5  6  7  8  9  10
   (Not at all)                 (Fully)

4. Do I motivate using
   | fear and | appreciation and |
   | punishment? | reward? |
   0   1   2   3   4   5   6   7   8   9   10

5. Do I furnish backing and support in a pinch?
   0   1   2   3   4   5   6   7   8   9   10
   (Never)                      (Always)

6. Am I open to employees' input on problems?
   0   1   2   3   4   5   6   7   8   9   10
   (Rarely if ever)             (Usually)

Prepare a simple handout sheet including the questions and the scales as they appear above and a few lines of instructions. You need only instruct employees on how to use the scales, explaining that you are seeking—related to a management development exercise, if you wish—an employee view of the department's leader. Stress that completing the form is optional and that they should not use their names. Provide a drop-off point so you will be unable to determine who did or did not complete a form.

Before you receive any completed forms, rate yourself on the same six questions using the same form.

After you receive the completed forms, compare the employee ratings with your own, both individually and by taking an average rating offered by all employees on each question.

You and your employees may not see your strong or weak points in the same light. If you are unhappy with a particular response, remember that a poor rating does not mean you are that way, but it can mean that you are viewed that way because it is "how you are coming across" to people. The results may suggest aspects of your "style" that could use your attention.

---

**NOTES**

1. D.M. McGregor, The Human Side of Enterprise, *Management Review 46,* no. 11 (1957): 22–28, 88–92.
2. J.D. Henderson and R.L. Phillips, Developing a Safe, Humane Institution through the Basics of Corrections, *Federal Prison Journal,* 1, no. 1:15–19.

## CHAPTER 11

# Motivation: Intangible Forces and Slippery Rules

*The only way to motivate an employee is to give him challenging work in which he can assume responsibility.*
—*Frederick R. Herzberg*

## Chapter Objectives

☛ Establish a perspective on what employees want from the organizations they work for.

☛ Review the basic forces at work in human motivation and their influences on employees in today's organizations.

☛ Examine the value of material rewards as motivators.

☛ Describe the supervisor's role in creating the environment in which employees become self-motivated.

## SATISFACTION IN WORK

We can describe motivation as the initiative or drive causing a person to direct behavior toward satisfaction of some personal need. Each of us has needs, and many of these needs are the reasons why we work. Depending on how well our needs are met through our employment, we may be more or less satisfied with our role in the organization.

We will begin with the premise that, in the long run, the satisfied employee will more likely be a better producer than the employee who is generally dissatisfied. A satisfied employee is usually more enthusiastic, more willing to work, and more of a self-starter.

Unfortunately, traditional organizations have done much to assure that a fair amount of dissatisfaction will exist at many organizational levels. We find that so much work has been structured, subdivided, and systematized that human factors beyond mere job performance are ignored and the inherent challenge of work as a normal human activity is diluted or dissipated. Prison work tends to display these characteristics, even though individual action and interaction with inmates is a key element in many prison jobs. Even in prison, people respond to work in terms of personal needs and desires. It becomes necessary for

171

management to seek ways and means of allowing employees to satisfy those basic needs through their work.

## THE REAL REASONS PEOPLE QUIT

A report issued by the Administrative Management Society presented the results of an extensive survey intended to determine the reasons most frequently given by people quitting jobs.[1] Seven reasons were identified.

1. **Lack of recognition.** The number one reason for people leaving jobs involved lack of recognition, the feeling that what they did was not fully appreciated and that their contributions were not acknowledged.

2. **Lack of advancement.** The second most cited reason for making a job change was the desire to go to an organization with more opportunities for advancement, promotion, or professional growth.

3. **Money.** Monetary reasons were generally twofold, with a split between people seeking more income and people seeking change because they believed they were paid unfairly relative to others.

4. **Too many bosses.** Although likely to include a number of people who legitimately worked for more than one boss, this reason largely involved hazy lines of authority under which workers were unclear as to who they were actually answerable to much of the time.

5. **Personality conflicts.** This general reason for quitting included personality conflicts with co-workers as well as conflicts with immediate supervisors and other members of management.

6. **Underqualification.** People who quit jobs for this reason were those not fully qualified for their positions to begin with. Placed in such jobs through poor selection practices and perhaps weak personal decisions, such persons resigned generally to escape the feeling of "being in over their heads."

7. **Overqualification.** People who were more qualified or capable than what the job required generally cited lack of challenge and lack of interest in the work.

These reasons give us a picture of what people feel they need from their work. It is not a clear picture; many people who leave jobs for any of the above reasons would probably not be able to say clearly if they did so because they were seeking something or trying to escape something. However, we can see in the seven reasons the reflections of a number of basic human needs. People have material needs and thus the need for money. People also have needs related to recognition as individuals and needs that relate to their regard for themselves.

## DEMANDS ON THE ORGANIZATION

People want the organizations they work for to supply them with a number of things. We cannot list these in any particular order; what is important to one person may matter very little to another. The following list encompasses most of what employees expect of their employers:

- Capable leadership that can be respected and admired
- Decent working conditions—surroundings that promote safety and physical well-being; this is particularly important in the prison setting
- Acceptance as a member of a group
- Recognition as an individual or partner, not simply as a servant of the "system"
- Fair and equitable treatment
- A reasonable degree of job security; this would be considered a plus for government employment, although this is less of a factor in private sector prison operations
- Knowledge of the results of individual efforts
- Knowledge of the organization's policies, rules, and regulations
- Recognition for special effort or good performance
- Respect for individual religious, moral, and political beliefs
- Assurance that all others are doing their share of the work
- Fair monetary compensation

## MOTIVATING FORCES: THE BASIC NEEDS

We should say something about a small word—*needs*. It is necessary, in considering human motivation, to take as broad a view of this term as possible. If someone is pursuing a promotion or other reward, you might be tempted to say that the person does not really need this but rather may simply want it (considering a need as something essential). However, we are not speaking of needs in such a way that we are forced into defining absolute essentials and separating them from other things we could call wants, desires, wishes, or aims. Rather, we are referring to those things you pursue simply because they represent fulfillment to you. In this sense they are indeed "needs" because we see them as essential to our fulfillment as individuals.

In his well-known "need hierarchy," A.H. Maslow described the basic human needs as follows.[2]

- **Physiological needs.** These are the most fundamental needs—those things we require to sustain life, such as food and shelter.
- **Safety needs.** These include our needs to feel reasonably free from harm from others and reasonably free from economic deprivation (call this "job security").
- **Love needs.** These include our need to be liked by others and to be accepted as part of a group—be it a work group, family, or social group. Needs at this level involve a sense of belonging.
- **Esteem needs.** At this level in the hierarchy we experience needs for recognition, for approval, for assurance that what we are doing is appreciated.
- **Self-actualization.** According to Maslow, the need for self-actualization represents "a pressure toward unity of personality, toward spontaneous expressiveness—toward being creative, toward being good, and a lot else."

Maslow states that we proceed through the need hierarchy from the most fundamental needs toward the highest order needs. Once a need is satisfied, another arises to take its place, and thus we experience needs of increasingly higher order. If we are in need of food, clothing, and shelter, then the basic physiological and safety needs are motivating our behavior. When we experience unmet physiological and safety needs, factors like job satisfaction and interesting work experiences will not mean a great deal to us. At that level we are most interested in generating an income with which to buy the basics of life. However, once these lower-order needs have been satisfied to a reasonable extent, we begin to experience the love needs, to look for acceptance, and to take our places in various groups. Thus, we progress through the hierarchy until we find that ultimately we are motivated by the need for self-actualization.

Whereas the need hierarchy has been firmly established, there are vast differences among people as to individual needs and thus corresponding differences in what is required to satisfy those needs. For instance, one person's need for assurance of reasonable job security may be filled by the knowledge that the job will last at least another three months, while another person may feel uneasy unless assured the job will last until retirement. Love needs and esteem needs may be quite powerful in an individual who requires constant reassurance of worth and capability, while another person with a higher degree of confidence and more sense of self-worth may experience much lesser need at this level. Regardless of the needs actually experienced by any given individual, the matter of progression through the need hierarchy holds true: as a need is reasonably satisfied, another, higher order need arises to take its place.

People have vastly different reasons for working. When people concentrate most of their energies on simply remaining fed, clothed, and sheltered at a minimal level, they rarely go beyond the satisfaction of basic physiological and safety needs. In our modern industrial society, however, these lower order needs are satisfied for most people most of the time. We then experience higher order needs and proceed to seek satisfaction. Even the person who feels continually driven by the same goal—for instance, money—will be doing so for changing reasons. Once reasonable economic security is no longer a concern, money may be seen as the means of securing leisure time, social acceptability, status, prestige, perhaps even power and influence, all expressions of higher order needs.

## WHAT MAKES THEM PERFORM?

In a survey conducted by the United States Chamber of Commerce, the first-line supervisors in 24 organizations were asked to rate ten morale factors in the order in which they believed these factors would be important to their employees.[3] In short, they were asked to rank these factors as motivating forces. A second phase of the survey required all the employees of the same supervisors to rank the same ten factors in order of importance to them as individual workers.

**The supervisors guessed that the ten factors would appeal to their employees in this order of importance:**

1. Good wages
2. Job security
3. Opportunity for promotion and growth
4. Good working conditions

5. Interesting work
6. Organizational loyalty to employees
7. Tactful disciplining
8. Full appreciation of work done
9. Understanding of personal problems
10. Being included in on things.

**The employees placed the same morale factors in the following order of importance:**

1. Full appreciation of work done
2. Being included in on things
3. Understanding of personal problems
4. Job security
5. Good wages
6. Interesting work
7. Opportunity for promotion and growth
8. Organizational loyalty to workers
9. Good working conditions
10. Tactful disciplining.

Note that the order of importance expressed by the employees places primary emphasis on satisfaction of higher order needs rather than those usually associated with materialistic factors. Certain economic motives such as wages and job security were considered important enough to appear in the upper middle portion of the employees' list. However, for these people who were employed and had normal expectations of remaining employed, the economically related factors had no appeal as primary expectations of their work.

Note also that the three factors rated highest by the employees were rated lowest by the supervisors. This raises some obvious questions about the importance of higher order needs and job satisfaction and about the relative value of money as a motivator.

Note the apparent inconsistencies between the results of this survey and "The Real Reasons People Quit" listed earlier in this chapter. One of the more glaring inconsistencies involves the employee's view of the opportunity for advancement or for "promotion and growth." The opportunity for promotion and growth earned only seventh place in the employees' order of importance. However, lack of advancement opportunity was the second most cited reason for people leaving their jobs. This suggests that some particular forces might be dissatisfiers if they are weak or absent but might not be particularly strong motivators if they are present. In other words, advancement opportunity, if it is there, may not cause people to work harder to fulfill certain needs; however, the absence of such opportunity may cause feelings of dissatisfaction that could lead a person to quit. Then, too, the strength of such a factor will vary according to individual needs. The person with strong desires for advancement may leave if opportunity is not present, but the person in whom this need is not as strong may stay and be happy regardless of the lack of advancement opportunities.

A survey of a much smaller scale than that described, yet using the same ten morale factors, was conducted with supervisors and employees of a number of upstate New York hospitals.[4] There were some differences in results, ascribable in part to the characteristics of the population surveyed. In this survey all supervisors and workers were employed by hospitals, but nevertheless the economic factors were rated about the same in both surveys. Again, supervisors saw the economic factors as stronger than the employees saw them, and again some of the factors that rated high with employees rated low with supervisors.

## MONEY AS A MOTIVATOR

Whereas we can probably all agree that money is an important reason for working, it has frequently been shown that money does not necessarily motivate people to work more effectively. Yet many managers continue to regard money as the principal key to motivation.

The factors leading to job satisfaction are not necessarily the same factors that can lead to dissatisfaction. We can separate the factors that have a bearing on job satisfaction or dissatisfaction into two types: (1) those inherent in the job itself and (2) those external to the job (occurring in the job environment). The true motivators, it appears, are those factors inherent in the job and realized through the workers' own efforts at accomplishment. True motivators include such things as achievement, the opportunity for achievement, the opportunity to assume responsibility, the actual performance of meaningful work, and the opportunity to learn, develop, and grow. All these are parts of the job itself. Their presence in a given job does not guarantee that the worker will necessarily take advantage of the opportunity to pursue them; however, if they are not there, the worker who might otherwise be motivated cannot put them there and the chances for job satisfaction are greatly reduced.

Among the external factors (those occurring in the job environment) are organization policy, salary, fringe benefits, character of supervision, and working conditions. When these factors are not met to an individual's level of expectation, they can lead to dissatisfaction. However, even when environmental factors are well satisfied, they generally provide no sustained motivation. The true motivators grow on and from themselves, but the environmental factors need to be continually increased or reinforced to provide any lasting benefit.

Money is important, and many of us would not be against receiving more money for doing what we now do. However, money's main functions are primarily to help us avoid pain or discomfort. Our salaries help us to avoid the feeling of economic deprivation we experience when we "don't have enough to live on" as we see that need. Our salaries help assure us—given that we are being paid equitably (relative to others doing the same kind of work)—that we are not being treated unfairly. It should be noted that since all public prison systems operate within a civil service structure that classifies jobs in a rational way, this pay/job equity may not be a major factor in those facilities. Whether or not that is the case in private corrections is not evident at this early stage of the development of that field.

Money and those other external factors that relate to money have one desirable characteristic that the true motivating factors do not possess: They can be measured on an objective scale. How do you begin to measure such intangibles as achievement and the feeling of worth resulting from the doing of meaningful work? How do we apportion such "rewards" among the work force? The fact is we cannot. Money, however, can be measured, so it constantly is measured and used as a "motivator."

## MOTIVATION AND THE FIRST-LINE SUPERVISOR

The age-old carrot-and-stick approach, alternating reward and punishment for certain behavior, simply fails to work once people have reached an adequate subsistence level and are motivated primarily by higher-order needs. The supervisor could do well to remember that economic rewards are but a portion of the total reward the employee works for.

Leadership and employee motivation are directly related to each other. The quality of supervision will generally have a significant bearing on the willingness with which employees perform. Leadership that employees can respect and admire is far more likely to produce positive performance than leadership that employees see as harsh or arbitrary.

One of the keys to motivating employees is the supervisor's motivation of self. You set the example for your employees. If you are genuinely interested, stimulated, energetic, and caring, this will show and some of your employees will respond in kind.

All of your employees are unique individuals and their "motives" are actually stable personality characteristics that each brings to work. Some may be ambitious and desire money and leadership positions; some may be fulfilled largely by helping others; some may satisfy their needs through overcoming obstacles to accomplish difficult tasks. These drives remain much the same within each person, so what you are actually attempting to influence in your employees is "aroused motivation." You wish to awaken in them the drive to seek fulfillment of certain needs.

Generally, we provide aroused motivation by:

- Valuing employees as individuals and treating each as such
- Providing challenge in the work situation whenever possible
- Increasing or varying job responsibilities when possible
- Helping employees to grow in ways that benefit both them and the organization

Although it is not always possible to provide a great deal of challenge in certain jobs or provide certain workers with increased responsibility, it is always possible to bring one or two of the prominent motivating forces into play in any situation. A simple "You did a good job" can be a powerful motivator, and a "Thank you" can be valued compensation for someone's efforts. You cannot "motivate" an individual as such. Rather, you can only create the climate within which the person will become self-motivated.

---

### CASE 11–1: "WHAT'S THIS PLACE COMING TO?"

Like most other states, this one was experiencing a major increase in the number of convicted felons sentenced and awaiting transfer to its prisons. The strategy used for several years of allowing shorter-term cases to "back up" in county jails was no longer viable. Sheriffs were exerting a great deal of pressure on the legislature to do something to give them more space for their misdemeanant cases by removing the felons.

With state prisons seriously crowded, there didn't seem to be any way out of the crisis but to contract beds with a private corrections firm. The newspapers in the major communities throughout the state carried occasional stories about the efforts of the Department of Corrections to acquire more beds from the private sector. More than one of these articles had suggested that youth offenders and lower-security adult inmates would be sent to those private prisons while the institutions housing them would be renovated for confining more dangerous, higher-security cases.

A number of employees at the state's medium-security youth reformatory—especially those who had worked there a long time—were concerned about the future. One of these was Mark Patterson, who had been supervisor of education for the last 14 years. He ran a very large school and vocational training complex to meet the needs of the young people confined at his facility.

Patterson had expressed his concern more than once about these reported plans to various members of administration, including the warden. He received no answers from his immediate supervisor, the associate warden, who seemed to know little more about the future than Patterson. From the other members of the administration he received only references to published documents describing how the legislature was considering this plan, and what some of the implications might be. These references only raised more questions in his mind because they suggested the reformatory would be a prime candidate for upgrading to a medium-security adult facility.

One morning before work Patterson encountered a neighbor at the local gas station. They talked a few minutes before the neighbor said, "Oh, that thing about the reformatory in the paper today—what is it going to do to your job?"

Mark was puzzled, but rather than display his lack of specific knowledge he said, "Oh, I don't really know yet. We'll have to wait and see." After the neighbor paid for his gas, Mark picked up a copy of the local paper.

According to the lead story, the Department of Corrections had made some far-reaching recommendations for redistribution of bedspace in various locations. All of the youth offenders at the reformatory would be sent to a contract facility and the institution would indeed be converted to an adult institution. The article said that there would be some staff adjustments, since adult offenders needed different kinds of programs than the youth cases.

When Patterson went to work he noticed solemn faces wherever he went, and particularly in his department. Before the morning was over, he discovered that several of his best teachers were already talking about applying for jobs at the juvenile training school, which was not mentioned in the article as being involved in the plan. Several others wondered out loud if they could move to the private facility and continue doing what they were doing. Without exception, they voiced misgivings and outright concerns over working with a higher-security adult offender.

Patterson met briefly with the associate warden, who indicated he had no prior knowledge of the change. He further suggested that Mark was under consideration for an upcoming opening as executive assistant to the warden, but even this news had little effect on Mark's disposition.

## Questions

1. What are some of the possible short-range effects on the morale, performance, and individual effectiveness of the education personnel and staff throughout the reformatory?

2. What morale factors (refer to the section, "What Makes Them Perform?") are most affected by the impending changes at the reformatory?

3. Keeping in mind that the employees' need to be "included in on things" must be balanced against the institution's inability to know precisely what is happening outside of the prison, how might this matter have been approached so as to minimize negative reactions among the employees?

---

## CASE 11–2: THE PROMOTION

With considerable advance notice, your prison's records supervisor retired. Although the job was advertised under normal civil service procedures, within the institution it was assumed that you (the assistant supervisor) would be appointed to the supervisor's job. However, a month after your boss' departure the department was still running without a full-fledged supervisor. Day-to-day operations had been left in your hands as acting supervisor, but the prison's associate warden had begun to make some of the administrative decisions affecting records operations.

After another month passed you learned through the grapevine that the prison had interviewed several candidates from other institutions for the supervisor's position. Nobody had been hired, however.

During the next several weeks you tried several times to discuss your uncertain status with the associate warden. Each time you tried you were put off; once you were told simply to "keep doing what you're doing."

Four months after the supervisor's departure, you were promoted to records supervisor. The first instruction you received from the associate warden was to abolish the position of assistant supervisor.

## Questions

1. What can you say about the likely state of your ability to motivate yourself in your "new" position? What can you say about your level of confidence in the relative stability of your position, and how might this affect your performance?

2. At the time you assume the supervisor's position officially, what is likely to be the motivational state of your staff? Why?

---

**NOTES**

1. F. Fournies, The Real Reason People Quit, *Administrative Management* (October 1969): 45–46.

2. A.H. Maslow, A Theory of Human Motivation, *Psychological Review* 50(1943):370–396.

3. Chamber of Commerce of the United States, *Washington Review,* 1966.

4. C.R. McConnell, "What Makes Them Perform?" Unpublished survey, Hospital Association of New York State, 1975.

## CHAPTER 12

# Performance Appraisal:
# The Supervisor's Darkest Hour

*The privilege of encouragement is one that may be exercised by
every executive and supervisor and it should be cultivated, not
so much as a working tool to be employed objectively, but as an
act of deserved kindness and intelligent leadership.*

*—Anonymous*

## Chapter Objectives

☞ Establish the objectives of performance appraisal as a management
technique.

☞ Identify and review common approaches to employee performance
appraisal.

☞ Assess common appraisal problems and suggest why many appraisal
programs fail.

☞ Outline the requirements of an effective performance appraisal system.

☞ Highlight the requirements or characteristics necessary to make the
organization's performance appraisal system as legally defensible as
possible.

☞ Introduce standard-based appraisal as a desirable long-range consideration in improving the organization's evaluation process.

☞ Introduce the concept of "constructive performance appraisal."

☞ Suggest how the supervisor can make any existing appraisal system
better serve the true objectives of performance appraisal.

## DARKEST HOUR?*

Why refer to performance appraisal as "the supervisor's darkest
hour"? The evaluation of employee performance through the application of some formal appraisal system is part of almost every supervisor's job. Yet as common as the requirement for performance appraisal may be, supervisors often dread that process and all that goes

---

*Adapted from "Employee Evaluation" by C.R. McConnell in *Human Resources Man-
agement in Pharmacy Practice* by M.W. Noel and J.L. Bootman (Eds.), pp. 104–106, Aspen Publishers, Inc. (1986).

with it. In all modern organizations—corrections included—employee appraisal remains a basic responsibility of all persons who direct the work of others. In prisons where the origin and structure of the performance evaluation process is closely tied to the collective bargaining process, it is an even more critical activity for supervisors to carry out properly and effectively.

Performance appraisal operates both inside and outside of whatever formal system the correctional agency may have. The supervisor who formally reprimands an employee for a breach of policy is, in effect, appraising performance. The supervisor who compliments an employee for a task well done or who criticizes an employee for committing an error and provides the employee with directions for correcting the error or avoiding its recurrence is also appraising performance. Any instance of criticism or praise, whether offered within or outside the context of a formal performance appraisal system, constitutes employee evaluation.

Pursued within the context of a formal, mandated system, as it is in most prisons, performance appraisal requires a great deal of the supervisor's time and attention. Most supervisors discover that there is not enough time to do everything they must do, so appraisal is left to compete with many other activities. Since appraisal requires information that the supervisor must accumulate over time, difficult elements of the appraisal process are always competing for space on the supervisor's list of priorities. Since performance appraisal appears to have no direct impact on the accomplishment of the day-to-day work in the department, it often gravitates to the lower part of the supervisor's priority list until attention is required.

Some appraisal systems call for the evaluation of all employees at the same time, ordinarily once each year; interim reviews may occur quarterly or every six months. Under the all-at-once approach, the supervisor often views the performance appraisal task as overwhelming; other essential tasks may suffer because appraisals must be done. Under the pressure created by the knowledge that important work is being left undone, the supervisor may fail to do justice to the appraisals. If the supervisor has a large number of appraisals to do, perhaps the ones undertaken first receive the most care while the later appraisals receive less time and attention. Because a number of appraisals within a specified number of days or weeks is required of them at what is usually an inappropriate time (and rarely is there an appropriate time for a task that intrudes so deeply into the daily routine), many supervisors come to regard appraisal as a necessary evil or an unnecessary and resented intrusion.

Fortunately, not all appraisal systems call for the evaluation of all employees at the same time. Many call for the appraisal of employees on their employment anniversary dates. Although this approach is to be preferred over the all-at-once approach, it too can have its problems. The supervisor who must evaluate every employee at once may be extremely busy for a few weeks, but he or she knows that once the appraisals are finished, the process will go away for the greatest part of the year. However, when appraisals are done on employees' anniversary dates, the manager still has the same number of appraisals to do, but they are staggered throughout the year. Under this approach, appraisals are never "caught up" and the process hangs over the supervisor as a nagging task.

Less subtle performance appraisal pressures from higher management, usually by way of the personnel or human resources department, aim at getting appraisals accomplished according to some schedule. Because the human resources people must invariably remind evaluators of due dates and otherwise ride herd on the process, many supervisors come to view appraisal in a decidedly unfavorable light as "the personnel department's system" or "just more of personnel's paperwork."

Discomfort with performance appraisal also arises from the understandable reaction of many supervisors to the uncertainties inherent in the appraisal process. Supervisors know they are expected to advance opinions and render judgments and are made uncomfortable by this necessity. Furthermore, to pursue the process to any truly conscientious extent, they may have to discuss unfavorable judgments with employees. Thus in addition to reacting negatively to what they see as a requirement imposed upon them from above, supervisors may also react negatively to what they see as a highly subjective process in which their opinions and judgments may ultimately be challenged and thus must be defended.

In short, in many organizations the supervisors tend to view performance appraisal primarily as a requirement of "the system" rather than as a key element of the essential supervisor-employee relationship.

## THE OBJECTIVES OF APPRAISAL

The primary objectives of performance appraisal should be:

- To encourage improved performance in the job each employee presently holds

- To provide growth opportunity for those employees who wish to pursue possibilities for promotion, and, conversely, provide the organization with people qualified for promotion to more responsible positions

In general, the true objectives of appraisal are not well served. An appalling number of appraisal systems function as criticism and fault-finding. Certainly these systems were not intended to be used in this fashion, but their weaknesses, primarily their focus on the past, have brought about their general misuse. Rather than simply looking at the past and stopping there, an effective performance appraisal system should seek to utilize the past only as a starting point from which to move into the future. When the appraisal interview becomes history and the form finds a home in the personnel file, the employee should be able to reasonably answer these two questions:

1. How am I doing in the eyes of my supervisor (and thus in the eyes of the organization)?
2. What are my future possibilities?

In this brief review of performance appraisal we will describe the common approaches to employee evaluation, consider some reasons why appraisal programs frequently fail, comment on the need for performance appraisal, and consider ways of more fully utilizing performance appraisal as an effective management technique.

## TRADITIONAL APPRAISAL METHODS

Over the years a number of appraisal systems have evolved, some depending on a greater amount of structure than others. Your agency probably has a specific appraisal method that you are required to use. In this chapter, we hope to show generally how a variety of systems work and the continuing efforts to make appraisal systems more objective, more reliable, and less dependent on the unsupported judgment of the people doing the evaluating. The major approaches to performance appraisal are discussed below.

### Rating Scales

Rating scales, the oldest and most widely used appraisal procedures, are of two general types. In continuous scales, in reference to a particular evaluation characteristic, the evaluator places a mark somewhere along a continuous scale (Figure 12–1). There is usually a numerical scale involved, so the evaluator is actually assigning a certain number of "points" to the individual for that particular characteristic. Generally, the evaluator is aware of some position on the scale that constitutes "average" or "satisfactory" performance. In discrete scales, each characteristic is associated with a number of descriptions covering the possible range of employee performance. The evaluator simply checks the box, or perhaps the column, accompanying the most appropriate description (Figure 12–2).

Rating scale methods are easy to understand and easy to use, at least in a superficial manner. They permit numerical tabulation of scores in terms of measures of average tendency, skewness (the tendency of a group of employees to cluster on either side of a so-called average), and dispersion.

Rating scales are relatively easy to construct, and they permit ready comparison of scores among employees. However, rating scales have severe disadvantages. Do total scores of 78 for Barbara and 83 for Carlos really mean anything significant? These systems are also subject to assumptions that the ability of a high score on one characteristic compensates for a low score on another. For instance, if an employee scores low relative to quantity of work produced, can this really be counterbalanced by high scores for attendance, attitude, and job knowledge?

Ratings frequently tend to cluster on the high side when rating scales are used. Supervisors may tend to rate their employees high because they want them to receive promotional consideration and their fair share of pay raises. They want employees to feel good about themselves. Also it is easier to praise than it is to leave oneself open to the

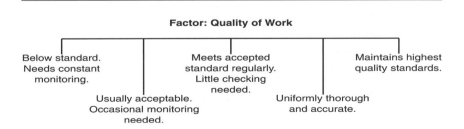

**Factor: Quality of Work**

Below standard. Needs constant monitoring.

Usually acceptable. Occasional monitoring needed.

Meets accepted standard regularly. Little checking needed.

Uniformly thorough and accurate.

Maintains highest quality standards.

**Figure 12–1** One Characteristic from a Continuous-Type Rating Scale

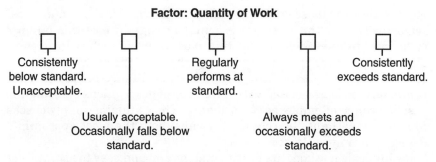

**Figure 12–2** One Characteristic from a Discrete-Type Rating Scale

appearance of being critical. Different supervisors tend to rate differently. Some consider average as precisely that—average acceptable work, nothing to be ashamed of. Other supervisors seem to think of average as something of a dirty word and tend to rate most employees on the high side of the scale.

## Employee Comparison

Employee comparison methods were developed to overcome certain disadvantages of the rating scale approaches. Employee comparison may involve the ranking method or the forced distribution method.

### Ranking

The ranking method forces the supervisor to rate all employees on an overall basis according to their job performance and value to the institution. One approach is simply to look at your subordinates and decide initially who is the best and who is the poorest performer and then to pick the second and next-to-last persons in your rank order and so on, applying the same judgment to the remaining employees. This is simple enough to accomplish, but the process is highly judgmental and strongly influenced by personality factors. Also, some employee must end up as "low person on the totem pole," and this may not be a fair assessment overall. It also is somewhat difficult to apply to a large department. The chief of security in a major penitentiary with several hundred correctional officers is going to find it difficult to use this method, even if the strategy is to apply it at the shift level rather than across the entire department.

*Forced Distribution*

The forced distribution method prevents the supervisor from clustering all employees in any particular part of the scale. It requires the evaluator to distribute the ratings in a pattern conforming with a normal frequency distribution. The supervisor must place, for instance, 10 percent of the employees in the top category, 20 percent in the next higher category, 40 percent in the middle bracket, and so on (Figure 12–3). The objective of this technique is to spread out the evaluations. However, while it is true that the general population may be distributed according to a normal curve, in an organization we are dealing with a select group of persons. If employees have been properly trained and probationary periods correctly used to eliminate the genuine misfits, then the true distribution of abilities and performance in the work group should be decidedly skewed. That is, your group's "average" should be better than the general average assumed by the so-called normal distribution (Figure 12–4).

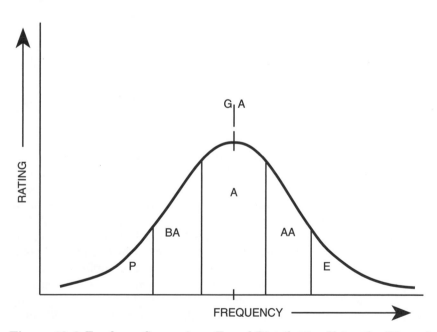

**Figure 12–3** Employee Comparison: Forced Distribution Using the "Normal Curve"

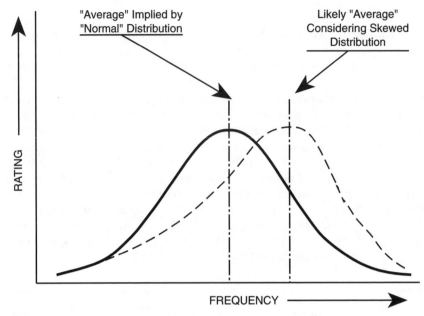

**Figure 12–4** Effects of a "Skewed" Normal Distribution

## Checklists

### Weighted Checklist

The weighted checklist consists of a number of statements that describe various modes and levels of behavior for a particular job or category of jobs. Every statement has a weight or scale value associated with it, and when rating an employee, the supervisor checks those statements that most closely describe the behavior exhibited by the individual. The completed rating sheet is then scored by averaging the weights of all the descriptive statements checked by the rater. This is much like the rating scale approach except for the application of the weights. Some evaluation characteristics are worth more than others. Often in checklist evaluation systems the weights are intentionally kept secret from the supervisor. This is done supposedly to avoid deliberate bias on the part of the supervisor; it is not possible to "slant" a rating to make the final score come out in some predetermined manner.

*Forced Choice*

Like the pure checklist approach, the forced choice method requires the development of a significant number of statements describing various types of behavior for a particular job or general category of jobs. These statements are arranged in groups of four or five each, and within each group the evaluator must check the one statement that is most descriptive of the performance of the employee and the one statement that is least descriptive of the employee's performance. The groups are so designed that each will contain two statements that appear favorable and two that appear unfavorable. A set of five statements from among which the supervisor must make the choice just described is shown in Exhibit 12–1. While statements A and B both appear favorable, only statement B actually differentiates between high and low performance employees. Statement C is actually descriptive of low performance employees. Although E also appears to be unfavorable, it is inconsequential in this set because of the presence of C. Statement D is neutral. Once again, the actual value or weight of the statements is kept secret from the supervisor.

## Critical Incident

The critical incident method requires a supervisor to adopt the practice of recording all those significant incidents in each employee's behavior that indicate either effective or successful action or ineffective action or poor behavior. The use of a notebook or card system provides reminders of performance characteristics under which various incidents can be recorded. For instance, if an employee saved the day by

---

**Exhibit 12–1** Illustrative Group of Statements from a Forced-Choice Appraisal

Circle the letter for the statement that is most descriptive of the employee's performance and the letter for the statement that is least descriptive of the employee's performance:

| Most | Least | |
|------|-------|---|
| A | A | Makes mistakes only infrequently |
| B | B | Is respected by fellow employees |
| C | C | Fails to follow instructions completely |
| D | D | Feels own job is more important than other jobs |
| E | E | Does not exhibit self-reliance when expressing own views |

spotting an inmate scaling a fence and taking appropriate action to stop the escape attempt, you might want to record the incident under "initiative."

There is a potential hazard in the use of the critical incident method. Supervisors are busy people, and often everything that should be recorded does not reach the notebook, particularly the positive or constructive episodes. However, negative incidents, because of their "seriousness," are more likely to reach the pages of the book than are many occasions of positive performance. This approach can lead to overly close supervision, with the employees feeling that the supervisor is watching over their shoulders and that everything they do will be written down in the "little black book" or on their "5 × 8 card."

## Field Review

Under the field review appraisal method the supervisor has no forms to fill out. The supervisor is interviewed by a representative of the personnel department who asks questions about the performance of each employee. The interviewer writes up the results of the interview in narrative form and reviews them with the supervisor for suggestions, modifications, and approval. No rating forms or factors or degrees or weights are involved; rather, simple overall ratings are obtained.

The field review approach relieves the supervisor of paperwork. It also assures a greater likelihood that supervisors will give adequate and timely attention to appraisals because the personnel department largely controls the process. However, the process takes the valuable time of two management representatives (the supervisor and the personnel interviewer), and it requires the presence of far more personnel department manpower than most institutions feel they can afford.

## Free-Form Essay

This method simply requires the supervisor to write down impressions about the employee in essay fashion. If desired by the organization, comments can be grouped under headings such as: job performance, job knowledge, and goals for future consideration, for example. To do a creditable job under this method, the supervisor must devote considerable time and thought to the evaluation. On the plus side, this process encourages the supervisor to become more observant and analytical. On the other hand, the free-form essay approach generally demands more time than the average supervisor is willing or able to spend. Also, appraisals generated by this method are often more reflective of the skill and effort of the writer than of the true performance of the employees.

## Group Appraisal

Under this approach an employee is evaluated at the same time by the immediate supervisor plus three or four other supervisors who have knowledge of that employee's work performance. This method may be particularly adaptable to prison shift work, where staff are likely to be assigned to multiple posts and work for multiple supervisors over the course of a rating period.

The virtue of this method is its thoroughness. It is also possible for multiple evaluators to modify or cancel out bias displayed by the immediate supervisor. The drawbacks of this approach are such that it is rarely used: it is extremely time consuming, tying up perhaps four or five members of management to evaluate a single employee. It is often inapplicable because there may be few managers beyond the immediate supervisor who are sufficiently familiar with the employee's performance.

## Common Appraisal Problems

A common problem encountered in performance evaluation is the "halo effect." This refers to the tendency of an evaluator to allow the rating assigned to one or more characteristics, or recent events, to influence excessively the rating on other performance characteristics. The rating scale methods are particularly susceptible to the halo effect. For instance, if you have declared an employee to be excellent in terms of "initiative" and "dependability," so might you be inclined to rate high relative to "judgment" and "adaptability." Since it is extremely difficult to completely separate consideration of one performance factor from the others (many performance characteristics actually include shades of others), there is no guaranteed way of eliminating the halo effect.

A common problem in most rating systems is the tendency of many supervisors to be liberal in their evaluations, that is, to give their employees consistently high ratings. Most approaches to rating are partially based on the assumption that the majority of the work force will be "average" performers. However, many people (supervisors included) do not like to be considered "only average."

Central tendency or clustering is another problem, one that some of the rating methods just described have attempted to overcome. Some supervisors are reluctant to evaluate people in terms of the outer ends of the scale. To many supervisors it is "safest" to evaluate all employees consistently. This often leads to a situation in which "everyone is average," contrary to the likelihood that in a work group of any considerable size there are, in fact, performers who are better or worse than the so-called average. Some performance evaluation systems rely on an informal method of structuring the number of evaluations in each category in order to avoid both this situation and the prior problem of overly liberal evaluation systems.

Interpersonal relationships pose a considerable problem in performance evaluation. The supervisor cannot help but be influenced, if only unconsciously, by personal likes and dislikes. Often a significant part of an evaluation will be based on how well the supervisor likes the employee rather than how well the employee actually performs. This longer-term influence based on personal relationship is somewhat different than the halo effect, which refers to a short-term impact of performance on evaluation.

## WHY APPRAISAL PROGRAMS OFTEN FAIL

Many performance appraisal programs fail outright or partially fail to do the jobs they were intended to do. A number of the reasons for appraisal program failure stem from weaknesses in the systems as already described, and some result from deeper-seated reasons.

Although most appraisal programs are supposed to be based on observable behavior and performance, many often fail because they actually require the supervisor to render personality judgments. Consider the difficulty of truly evaluating a number of employees relative to each other as they relate to their work in terms of "characteristics" that are often actually personality characteristics. There are many appraisal systems in which the performance characteristics defy objective assessment (Exhibit 12–2). How can a supervisor truly rate someone on a

---

**Exhibit 12–2** Listing of Rating Characteristics from an Actual Appraisal Form

| | | |
|---|---|---|
| 1. Quality of work | 6. Initiative | 7. Dependability |
| 2. Volume of work | 4. Job knowledge | 8. Attitude |
| 3. Effectiveness | 5. Adaptability | 9. Attendance |

characteristic such as "adaptability"? The problems are compounded by problems of semantics—what in fact are "initiative," "judgment," and so on?

Another reason for failure is that supervisors are unqualified to judge personality characteristics. Very few people are qualified to render personality judgments, yet supervisors are put into a position of having to do so time and time again.

Many systems fail to allow for distinguishing between the cause and results of behavior. For instance, an employee who comes across as irritable and who constantly argues with others is likely to get marked down on "attitude." However, the results of the behavior (the clashes with other people) are the only real evidence the supervisor has to go on. To say that these interpersonal clashes result from a poor attitude is to try to assign a cause to the behavior. This assignment of cause to result is an unqualified leap for the supervisor; it is inappropriate to call an employee who appears unwilling to adapt to your ideas "stubborn," but our appraisal systems constantly require us to second-guess cause in this fashion.

Programs also fail because of the uncomfortable position of the person doing the evaluating. It is an extremely serious matter to probe the personality of an employee in a fashion that results in a permanent record in the employee's personnel file. The supervisor is put into a position of power over the employee's potential for promotion, pay increases, and favorable references in the future. Many supervisors dislike being put into this position and compensate by keeping all their evaluations high or at least harmless.

Some systems fail mechanically, owing to poor system administration. Perhaps appraisal forms and notices do not come out on time, are not followed up, do not get discussed with employees, or perhaps do not get completed at all. The mechanics of any appraisal system must be such that a system is "kept moving"; because of natural resistance to the uncomfortable task of appraisal, a system can die of its own weight unless it is continually nudged along.

Poor follow-up on appraisals can weaken a program, if not cause the program to fail entirely. This suggests that an appraisal should not be an evaluation of the past to be filed away and forgotten. Since it should ideally be a guide to future action, a performance appraisal should be reflected in an active document that is used in the employee-supervisor relationship during the months to come. That is a strong attribute of the critical incident system, if it is properly structured. Calling in the employee on a scheduled basis to review all performance entries in the notebook or on the index card is a perfect opportunity for the supervisor to scan prior entries and follow up on both positive and negative episodes, picking up on both functional and dysfunctional trends. In many systems, unfortunately, the only time the last performance appraisal is pulled out of the file is when the next appraisal is due.

## WHY APPRAISE AT ALL?

As discussed in Chapter 11, most employees are not very well motivated by only the visible rewards that exist as part of the organizational setting. Those "environmental factors" (such as salary, fringe benefits, and working conditions) are not the only things that employees work for.

Recall the position of "full appreciation of work done" as a potentially powerful motivator of employee performance. People who are doing good work need to know they are doing good work, and they need to know that what they do is appreciated. This knowledge and appreciation are essential parts of the "psychic income" that every employee needs to receive in some measure in addition to the real income associated with the position.

In addition to knowing they are doing well and that their work is appreciated, employees need to know when they are not doing particularly well and what they can do to correct their behavior. Criticism itself, even so-called constructive criticism, does not bring about longlasting behavioral change. It is one thing to criticize; however, it is something else entirely to criticize and be able to supply alternatives for behavioral change and improvement.

Performance appraisal is needed because all employees deserve to know where they stand in the eyes of the supervisor and the organization. Beyond this, however, the employees need to know where they stand so as to be able to do something positive about future performance.

## REQUIREMENTS OF AN EFFECTIVE APPRAISAL SYSTEM

Although every correctional agency's appraisal system is different, any performance appraisal system must meet a number of conditions to have a realistic chance of being effective. If it does not, it will do less than it should be expected to do. However, even if the system does meet all the conditions, success is not necessarily guaranteed. To be fully effective, a system requires thorough, conscientious application by managers who believe in the value of performance appraisal. Careless or indifferent application can kill even the best systems or turn them into mere paper exercises. The requirements of an effective performance appraisal system are:

## System Objectives

The primary objectives of performance appraisal should be:

- to encourage improved performance in the job each employee presently holds
- to provide growth opportunity for those employees who wish to pursue possibilities for promotion, and, conversely, provide the organization with people qualified for promotion to more responsible positions

Overall, the system must serve the true objectives of performance appraisal as previously described.

## Appropriateness of Criteria

System criteria—those characteristics upon which the employees are evaluated—must be as closely related as possible to the kinds of work being evaluated. Never does a single approach fit all of the jobs to be evaluated within a single organization, especially a prison with its many and varied occupations.

## Standards of Performance

The majority of the evaluations made of any individual employee should reflect specific performance standards that are established based on the employee's job description. These standards should be set in terms of objective measurements; that is, the supervisor should be able, for a significant number of evaluation criteria, to come up with a numerical measure of results that may be compared with an established standard.

## Employee Knowledge of Criteria

Well in advance of being evaluated, employees must know the criteria on which they will be evaluated. Employees must be fully aware of the job description tasks as they are presently known to the manager, and they should be fully aware of all applicable job standards. The usual method for establishing this base is by providing each employee with a copy of the standards at the beginning of the rating period.

## Management Education

Managers throughout the organization should be thoroughly oriented in the use of the system and thoroughly trained in the consistent application of the process.

## A Working Tool

Once it is completed, an evaluation should serve as a live, working record to be used as a starting point for monitoring progress. This is especially important for unfavorable evaluations, which should be sufficiently complete as to spell out specific steps and time frames to be involved in correction and improvement.

## Appraisal Interview

The appraisal interview should be meaningful; it should not be avoided because the manager is uncomfortable nor should it be treated once-over-lightly and disposed of quickly simply because the manager feels the pressures of time. The appraisal interview should be a true two-way exchange and receive the manager's full attention for whatever time is required.

## Self-contained Record

Once it is placed in the employee's personnel file, a completed performance appraisal should stand on its own. Cross-reference to an appraisal manual, evaluation key, or list of explanations should not be necessary in determining what any particular rating means.

## System Administration

The system must be administered appropriately and effectively. All scheduled review dates must be observed. Managers must receive appraisal forms and reminders a reasonable amount of time before appraisals are due, and they must receive interim reminders as necessary to assure that appraisals are not allowed to run late. In short, someone needs to pay constant attention to the process of keeping the system moving.

The fact that this kind of auxiliary support system seem to be necessary in almost every correctional organization (and others as well) is in itself a testimony to the problem most supervisors have with this portion of their jobs. For any other aspect of a supervisor's job, this level of hand-holding, or external monitoring, would be considered evidence of a performance problem on the part of the supervisor. And yet, it is an almost universal phenomenon.

## LEGAL ASPECTS OF PERFORMANCE APPRAISAL

Performance appraisal now carries with it many potential legal traps. An increasing number of wrongful termination lawsuits or individual labor-management disputes are an outgrowth of inadequate performance appraisal procedures. If an employee is let go for any performance-related reason, but the evaluations on file show "good" or "standard" or "satisfactory" performance, the stage is set for a wrongful discharge complaint.

Performance appraisal information is also playing an increasingly active role in complaints filed under the Age Discrimination in Employment Act (ADEA). Such actions most commonly involve complaints concerning promotions, retirements or layoffs, and discharges.[1] In all of these kinds of actions there are questions of employee performance. Regardless of what the defendant organizations say about the performance of the individuals who complain they were discriminated against, the courts generally rely on the documentation of performance found in the personnel file—that is, the written performance appraisals.

In these situations, the biggest trap in performance appraisal, referred to earlier in this chapter under "Common Appraisal Problems," comes back to haunt many appraisers. That trap is the lenient appraisal—stating on the record that the individual's work is acceptable when in truth it is unsatisfactory in some respect.

Drawing on how performance appraisal has fared in the legal system through a significant number of cases, we can make some reasonable conclusions as to the characteristics of a legally defensible system. No matter what prison system you work for, an effective, legally defensible appraisal system would include the following elements.

1. The system is based on the job, with the appraisal criteria arising from an analysis of the legitimate requirements of the position.

This is the embodiment of the oft-repeated admonition to focus on the job itself and not the person who does the job.

2. Performance is assessed using objective criteria as much as possible given the unique requirements of the job. The reasons behind the assessments must amount to more than simply the unsupported subjective assessment of the appraiser. These criteria must be known to the employee in advance of the rating period.

3. The appraisers have been trained in the use of the system and possess written instructions on how the appraisal is to be completed. This establishes that any appraiser is as reasonably capable of evaluating performance as any other appraiser using the same system, and that the system can be expected to be applied as intended.

4. The results of each appraisal are reviewed and discussed with the employee. This is a major concern. Documentation of performance problems and of efforts to correct them are necessary if an employee fails to improve and must be let go, but it is also necessary to prove that the employee knew about the difficulties. The legally defensible appraisal system can be used to demonstrate that the employee knew of the problems and was given the opportunity to correct them.[2]

## STANDARD-BASED APPRAISAL: A LONG-RANGE TARGET

The difficulty often encountered in the setting of performance standards and the sheer volume of work sometimes involved in this process should not be taken lightly. Going to the standard-based appraisal on an organization-wide basis requires that performance standards be developed for the majority of the tasks in every active job category in the organization. More often than not, this first requires that the organization's job descriptions be updated and revised so that most of the individual task descriptions lend themselves to the development of standards. It also means that the organization must adopt—which usually means install from scratch—some form of work measurement system. However, with sufficient effort, it is usually possible to come up with several measures that are applicable to various aspects of each employee's work.

Effective job standards ordinarily reflect a concern for four major dimensions of an employee's work: (1) quantity, (2) quality, (3) use of time, and (4) use of financial resources (cost). These four areas are, of course, interrelated—time is money, quantity is related to time, and so on—but it is nevertheless possible to focus performance standards in each of these four key areas. An employee performance standard may take any of the following general forms:

1. **Quantity**
    (a) Number of reports, inmates, or other items processed
    (b) Number or percentage of occurrences of specific types of acts
2. **Quality**
    (a) Number of errors, repeats, or rejections (as in reviewing clerical output)
    (b) Employee turnover rate (as could apply in evaluating a supervisor)
3. **Time**
    (a) Deadlines missed, turnaround time (actual as compared with desired)
    (b) Acceptable work accomplished within a time unit
4. **Cost**
    (a) Amount of cost savings or cost per inmate (as in food service operations)
    (b) Cost per item (as in production in prison industries)
    (c) Budget variance, both bottom line and line item (again applying to the appraisal of supervisors, to include things like overtime management)

Consider an example of a performance standard that relates to quality of work. Suppose an acceptable error rate for a particular activity has been determined to be four mistakes per month (each necessitating, of course, rework or repeat). Suppose further that the normal anticipated range of error has been determined to be three to five mistakes per month. The performance standard for the particular activity is set at three to five errors per month, so the individual who generated three, four, or five errors in a month for this activity may be said to have met the standard.

It will not always be possible to attach a measurable standard of performance to every last task on an employee's job description. There is no way of establishing that the average performance for a correctional officer will involve finding an average of 5 prison-make knives for every 100 cells searched, for instance. For most employees, however, it will in fact be possible to come up with performance standards that measure most of the major tasks an employee performs.

It should be noted that the preceding simple example used only three outcomes in comparing performance with a standard. The employee either failed to meet the standard, met the standard, or exceeded the standard. Little else is needed, least of all the judgmental variations suggested by the rating-scale approach and several of the appraisal ratings appearing in Exhibit 12–2. Rarely are more than three simple outcomes required, and often it is possible to rely on only two outcomes; many employees have job responsibilities, the fulfillment of which can be assessed simply by noting whether these tasks did or did not get accomplished. In some cases there are only two outcomes—yes or no. Did the officer search at least five cells on each shift and were those searches logged in the unit log? *Yes* or *no* tells the story.

The essential intent in using standards of performance in appraisal is to quantify the outcomes of performance as much as possible and thus reduce the necessity for managerial judgment to the lowest possible level. This can be accomplished only when appraisal is not based on general personality or performance characteristics, but is based rather on specific job responsibilities and the standards of performance to fulfill those responsibilities.

## CONSTRUCTIVE APPRAISAL

There is another performance appraisal method available in addition to those already discussed—the constructive appraisal approach. This is not a specific system, but rather a broad approach that may be used in place of a more formal system under certain circumstances or perhaps used as part of or in support of an existing system. Before an approach such as this is used in any formal way as a supplement to an official evaluation system, the supervisor must be sure that there are not labor-management, statutory, or regulatory constraints to doing so.

The constructive approach to performance appraisal involves those employees who are capable of setting goals for themselves to help determine the basis on which they will be evaluated. This approach is workable in most institutions and is particularly applicable to managerial, professional, and technical personnel. It is also applicable to most other employees who have a reasonable degree of self-determination or control over their immediate work environment and the order and manner of performance of their tasks. For instance, many record staff, business office and finance employees, and even many secretaries and clerks, can be appropriately evaluated using the approach.

There are four elements of constructive appraisal.

1. **Job description analysis.** To set the stage for future activity, the employee is asked to analyze the job description and to indicate where it should be expanded, contracted, or altered in any way. While the employee is doing this, the supervisor should also be reviewing the job description. When a supervisor and employee have thoroughly reviewed the job as it exists on paper, they meet to discuss all elements of the job and work on correcting or modifying the job description until they agree on job content and on the relative emphasis each part of the job should receive. This step allows supervisor and employee to come to agreement on what the employee should be doing. As a by-product of this process, the department is assured of having job descriptions that are as current as they can reasonably be made.

2. **Employee performance objectives.** Working independently, the employee develops a few simple targets or objectives covering some key aspects of the job. Within reason, these objectives should be: manageable—attainable through the employee's own effort and not dependent in any way on forces beyond the employee's control; realistic—attainable within a reasonable period of time; and challenging—representing at least a modest improvement over past performance.

   These objectives should be expressed in a few simple statements that cover several aspects of the employee's job, but do not necessarily try to cover everything. They should simply constitute a modest plan of improvement that the employee will pursue while still concentrating primarily on day-to-day activities.

   The objectives suggested by the employee should be as specific as possible. Ideally an objective will embody statements of what, how much, and when. For instance, an objective formulated by a secretary may look like: "To reduce typographical errors (what) by at least 50 percent (how much) before the end of the year (when)." Another example could be a caseworker developing an objective that states, "To submit all classification studies on new inmates to the chief of classification within 30 days of the inmates' commitment to the institution."

3. **Negotiated objectives.** Once the employee has developed the objectives, these should be discussed with the supervisor. The supervisor should make no effort to impose any personal objectives on the employee. Rather, it is the supervisor's job to help the

employee keep the objectives realistic, manageable, and challenging, while also assuring they remain consistent with the overall objectives of the department and the organization.

Once the supervisor and employee have agreed on a program of objectives, this program should be committed to writing, perhaps in a separate memorandum or in a space available on the employee appraisal form.

4. **Discussion of results.** Periodically the supervisor and employee should meet to discuss where the employee is in terms of progress toward the objectives. This will not necessarily occur at the time of the next scheduled performance appraisal; some objectives may be realizable within two or three months, and some may take two or three years to attain. This approach usually requires the supervisor and employee to get together on the subject of employee performance more often than a rigid performance appraisal program would require.

Certainly the employee will not always achieve the objectives set. Some objectives will be exceeded; some will barely be approached. Most important in this appraisal method is how it involves the employee, who sets objectives, works to attain them, and works with the supervisor to analyze the differences between planned performance and actual results. You can see that the structure of this method lends itself more to smaller departments rather than large ones.

Under the constructive appraisal approach, the employee knows well in advance the basis for evaluation. Having participated in establishing the objectives, the employee is better able to understand the goal to be attained and is usually more willing to work for improvement.

This appraisal approach also encourages the employee and supervisor to come to complete agreement on the content of the employee's job—no small accomplishment in many departments. Without such agreement, it often appears that a job exists in three distinctly different forms: (1) as the supervisor envisions the job, (2) as the employee sees it, and (3) as it exists "on paper."

Most importantly, because constructive appraisal takes place entirely within the context of the supervisor-employee relationship, it strengthens that relationship, provides opportunities for growth and job satisfaction, and supports open communication between supervisor and employee.

The more often constructive appraisal contacts occur between employee and supervisor, the stronger the supervisor-employee relationship becomes. When the ideal employee-supervisor relationship exists, performance appraisal becomes a mere formality, because under these conditions both supervisor and employee know fully where the employee stands at any given time.

## THE APPRAISAL INTERVIEW

Much of what was said about the mechanics of interviewing in Chapter 8 is pertinent to the formal performance appraisal interview. The appraisal interview should occur when it was scheduled to occur or when the employee was told it would occur. The setting should be one that allows for privacy, freedom from interruptions, and free and open discussion. The appraisal interview should focus on joint problem solving.

## LIVING WITH AN EXISTING SYSTEM

More often than not the particular approach to performance appraisal used in your organization is decided elsewhere. You may be using an appraisal method that was in place before you arrived in the agency, or you may be required to use an appraisal system that was designed and implemented by others (usually a personnel administration section or sometimes at the state level rather than within the department of corrections).

Many performance appraisal systems make use of some variation of the rating scale method. If that is the case in your agency, accept what we have said about the pitfalls of checklists (especially those that require you to render personality judgments) and be aware that you are required to operate in risky territory. Try to make the best use possible of the system you are required to use, and whenever possible to have solid behavioral or performance-based data to back your judgments. Use the system because you must, but make every effort to use it wisely and fairly. Awareness of the pitfalls of standard appraisal approaches, such as the halo effect, central tendency, and the making of unqualified judgments will protect you from falling into these traps. Regardless of the system used, make every effort to emphasize performance or production (that is, results) rather than personality traits.

Even within the confines of an existing system it is possible for you to get away from scales and boxes at least partly by going beyond checklist requirements. With supervisory and professional employees it may be possible to use constructive appraisal along with the checklist method, since these employees may not be covered by a specific managerial appraisal system nor be subject to a collective bargaining agreement that specifies a particular appraisal system. Even with lower-grade-level employees, those doing repetitive, manual, or clerical jobs, it may be possible to open the appraisal process to some degree of input. Consider asking some of your employees one or both of the following questions.

1. What do you do now that you believe you could do better?
2. How would you change your job if you could?

You may get nothing in response to your questions, but at least you will have made the effort to let someone know you are interested. On the other hand, you may get far more than you could ever hope for in terms of positive suggestions. Some of the best suggestions for improving performance in these more repetitive tasks come from the people who do the jobs day in and day out. After all, regardless of how you, the supervisor, may view the job from the outside, when it comes to the inside details, there is no one who knows more about the job than the person who does it.

If you are permitted to do so, consider also the use of self-appraisal along with your existing performance appraisal system. Give the employee a blank copy of the appraisal form, and ask for a self-rating to be brought to the appraisal interview (so you do not see it prior to generating your own evaluation of the employee).

There are, of course, some weaknesses in self-appraisal. Some employees use the opportunity to "ego trip," giving themselves high marks in many areas. However, you will find that in practice most employees tend to be more critical of themselves than you are. In any case, the process will help you gain some insight into an employee's self-concept.

Self-appraisal also gives you insight into employee strengths and weaknesses, both as observed by you and perceived by the employee. The process can also suggest where you and the employee might best concentrate your efforts at joint problem solving. For instance, if your rating system calls for assessment of the employee on 12 characteristics and if you and the employee are reasonably close together in your independent assessment of 9 or 10 of these characteristics, you know that the 2 or 3 characteristics on which you are far apart constitute the most productive starting ground for joint problem solving.

The agency's performance appraisal system and how you use it may relate directly to the general philosophy of leadership in the organization. If permitted the latitude by statute or policy, autocratic leadership will usually perpetuate the use of a highly structured, rigid appraisal system, leaving little room for constructive appraisal or employee input in any form. Conversely, a more participative leadership style may encourage appraisal methods that are correspondingly more open to employee input and involvement. Regardless of the organization's formal appraisal system, however, within your own department you generally have the freedom to back up the system with some constructive steps of your own and turn appraisal into a more constructive process.

## A SIMPLE OBJECTIVE

It indeed is true that appraisal is intended to improve performance in the job the employee now holds and to develop the employee for possible promotion. However, consider an employee who performs, and perhaps has been performing for years, a simple job in quite acceptable fashion, a job that leaves little room for improvement and no opportunity for growth or advancement. Even in this limited set of circumstances, performance appraisal has a simple but still extremely important objective—to encourage the employee to continue delivering the same acceptable performance.

Performance appraisal is essential to employees at all levels. Proper appraisal stimulates improvement, encourages growth and advancement, and conveys your appreciation of individual effort.

---

### CASE 12–1: IT'S REVIEW TIME AGAIN

"Well, Jack, I'm sure you know why you're here—it's performance appraisal time again. I want you to know that I've seen a lot of good work coming from you these past 12 months—well, 14 months really, since we're a little off schedule as usual. I appreciate it, and I'm sure the warden appreciates it, too. There's always room for improvement, of course, but let me hit the good stuff first.

"Your output has been great, and I'm especially satisfied with the way you tackled the special classification project when we got that big transfer of inmates from the reformatory. You showed plenty of good judgment in the decisions you made and in your recommendations.

"There are a couple of things that bother me, however. But I know I can speak straight from the shoulder. Your aggressiveness is still something of a problem. I can think of two, maybe three times, when

I've had to work real hard with the captain and lieutenants to get them calmed down after you were interviewing inmates and didn't get the inmates back to the unit in time for count. It wasn't so much that you forgot to call in the outcounts as it was the way you got so defensive when the shift supervisor called you about it. I'm sure you'll agree that tact and diplomacy aren't your strong suits. I point this out because your lack of sensitivity to working smoothly with other people isn't going to do you any good if you're thinking about moving up someday.

"And another thing. . . ."

## Instructions

Analyze and critique the foregoing "opener" of Jack's annual appraisal interview. Be especially sensitive to:

- Apparent "system" weaknesses
- The rendering of personality judgments
- The treatment of the causes and results of behavior

---

### ROLE-PLAY 12–1: MS. PARKER'S APPRAISAL

Mr. Haskins, an ambitious, young physician's assistant recently promoted to administrator of a mid-sized prison hospital, recognized the importance of running an efficient medical operation. Haskins inherited a subordinate, Ms. Parker, head nurse of the secure medical/surgical ward. Having worked at the prison for seven years and proven herself to be quite capable, Ms. Parker required minimal direct supervision; she was considered a competent manager. Staff assigned to her section were loyal, stable, and highly motivated; they worked well together and seemed to emphasize quality care.

Ms. Parker and her staff were acutely aware of Mr. Haskins' promotion. Within a few days there were frequent references to Haskins as "the new kid on the block" and "the snoopervisor." Ms. Parker quickly came to resent the flurry of questions, criticisms, and suggestions that surfaced in every discussion she had with Mr. Haskins.

In formally appraising Ms. Parker, Haskins made some critical comments. While not complaining specifically about her work, Haskins rendered some harsh judgments concerning "negative attitude." Ms.

Parker was referred to as "resistant," "sarcastic," and "irritating." Their concepts of supervision clearly differed. A basic clash of personalities was evident in the performance appraisal itself.

The potential for turning the appraisal interview from the learning situation it should be into a conflict is clear in this example. Your task is to consider the possibility of avoiding the personality clash and imagining the meeting in a way that would facilitate a positive approach to appraisal.

To the person designated as Mr. Haskins: You honestly believe that Ms. Parker is automatically resistant to change regardless of the nature of a particular change. She truly strikes you as irritable and generally sarcastic. You realize, however, that some of her behavior may result from a combination of factors, including your "new ideas" and your relative youth.

To the person designated as Ms. Parker: You have been distressed by the steady stream of communications from Mr. Haskins, including many items you consider unnecessary, nitpicking, and change merely for the sake of change. You have worked in this prison hospital setting for years. You feel you know much about quality inmate-patient care and you know that you have much to contribute. You would welcome a setting that gives you the opportunity to present what you know in such a way that it would be considered fairly.

Mr. Haskins and Ms. Parker are to assume they have already had one tentative appraisal contact during which many of their hard feelings came out. They are ready to try again.

The role-play participants are to conduct an appraisal meeting intended to establish a desirable new beginning for the relationship between Mr. Haskins and Ms. Parker. It is suggested that the participants consider the positive approach to appraisal and attempt to reach agreement on two or more sample performance targets. (Participants may use tasks from their own areas of responsibility in the appraisal discussion—and may even move the setting from nursing to some other functional area to accommodate participants' backgrounds—as long as the two primary role players agree in advance on the ground rules.)

The remaining members of the group should take either side of the appraisal in a discussion. (It works best if group members "choose sides" before starting and do not change during the exercise.) Afterward, all participants should critique the results of the role play in general discussion.

**NOTES**

1. M.H. Schuster and C.S. Miller. Performance Appraisal and the Age Discrimination in Employment Act. *Personnel Administrator* 29, no. 3 (1984):48.
2. C.R. McConnell. *The Health Care Manager's Guide to Performance Appraisal* (Gaithersburg, Md.: Aspen Publishers, Inc., 1993), 207.

## CHAPTER 13

# Criticism and Discipline: Guts, Tact, and Justice

*Indifference is probably the severest criticism that can be applied to anything.*

—*Ann Schade*

*I never gave them hell. I just tell the truth and they think it's hell.*

—*Harry S. Truman*

## Chapter Objectives

☛ Establish the need for rules and regulations in the operation of any organization.

☛ Suggest some self-improvement guidelines for taking—as well as delivering—criticism.

☛ Introduce the concept of progressive discipline.

☛ Distinguish between problems of conduct and problems of performance and describe how each should be addressed.

☛ Provide guidance for the use of fair and effective disciplinary action.

## THE NEED FOR RULES

Rules do not exist solely to benefit the correctional organization in some abstract way, nor are they traps set by management to snare the unwary employee. However, neither are rules, as the old saying might suggest, "made to be broken." They exist for good reasons. And in some respects, there is no workplace more driven by rules and structure than the prison.

Rules outline a general pattern of behavior that we are expected to observe and practice. Ordinarily created with the rights and needs of the majority in mind, rules exist to protect us in a number of ways. In terms of the prison organization, rules exist to safeguard the institution and its inmates and staff. They are guidelines for individual and group behavior and action, and as such they represent the organization's expectations of its employees.

Rules should be reasonable both as to their stringency and as to the number of them that exist. Because prisons organize and supervise the lives of individuals who, by definition, are not particularly good at following rules and laws, the regulation of their conduct by institutional rules is a particularly important issue. Today's legal environment certainly requires that the structure of prison life be spelled out clearly—for staff and inmates. But this need to clearly and minutely spell out the rules and regulations for inmates can carry over into staff issues as well. And when organizations give way to the temptation to write a rule or regulation to cover every last contingency, the result is an unworkable bureaucratic structure. Many prisons seem to operate in a virtual policy maze in which it is sometimes impossible for staff to do anything without running afoul of some regulation.

As well as being reasonable in quantity and strictness, rules should attempt to serve the common good without infringing on individual rights and freedoms. Since nothing remains constant for long, rules should be regularly examined for their applicability to present circumstances and conscientiously updated as real needs change. For instance, it would be helpful for the "rules of the organization" (perhaps called the employee handbook or the personnel policy and procedure manual) to be thoroughly reviewed for possible changes at least once each year. This review can easily fit into the annual policy review that most correctional organizations conduct for all inmate and administrative management policies.

Just as most prisons provide inmates with a copy of the rules and regulations that apply to them, the employee rules and regulations should be made known to every staff member. The organization should assure that every employee has had the opportunity to become thoroughly familiar with the rules. It has been proven that many employees are not familiar with their own organization's rules. Even in systems that require each new employee to sign a statement indicating receipt and review of the employee handbook, many people will sign without reading the rules.

Rules and their enforcement are but a part of our concern with criticism and discipline. Many forms of behavior, often involving marginal, questionable, or otherwise hazy aspects of job performance, are deserving of criticism, such as personal mannerisms that disrupt the workplace or actions that could create a safety problem. There are few rules for the supervisor to use in criticizing an employee except rules of the broadest possible kind, or rules of reason or judgment. Even specific rules defining employee conduct—rules that can result in disciplinary action if they are not followed—are not always as clear cut as we would like to think they are.

## CRITICISM

Anyone who has been a supervisor for any length of time will have found it necessary to criticize someone because of conduct or work performance. Also, persons with experience in supervisory positions will have found they are sometimes targets, rather than sources, of criticism. The first-line supervisor is in the position of having to take criticism from above for "everything that's wrong" with worker conduct and performance, and to take criticism from below for "everything that's wrong" with the organization and its policies and practices.

Think about the last time you were criticized. Try to remember how you felt, how fair or unfair the criticism seemed to be, and how the critic's attitude and words actually struck you. Then keeping in mind how you believe the criticism should actually have been handled, try to put yourself in the position of the critic. You are likely to find that criticism is no more pleasant to give than it is to receive.

Also, think about the tone of the criticism. Was it conveyed in a rational way, or in the heat of the moment after a mistake or a poorly-handled situation came to light? The tone and manner in which criticism is conveyed is critical to how it is received and how effective it is in bringing about the desired correction in performance.

When you are criticized, learn from it. Learn what you should do and what you should avoid in criticizing others by carefully reviewing how you have been criticized under certain circumstances and how you reacted to that criticism. Learning to take criticism is the first step toward learning how to criticize others appropriately.

When you are criticized, whether by an employee, your supervisor, or another member of management, or someone from outside the institution, remember the following:

- **Keep Your Temper**

   Make up your mind that no matter what is said you are going to remain calm. Do not jump to conclusions based on the possibly harsh, uncomplimentary, or unfair remarks you may be hearing. If you allow your critic to "get to you," you will experience emotional reactions that will serve only to diminish your true listening capacity and hamper your ability to deal effectively with what you are hearing. Whatever you do, stay calm.

- **Listen Completely**

   When criticized, a person's natural temptation is to start developing a defensive stance while the critic is still speaking. To strive for an open mind and the ability to listen completely, try imagining yourself in the position of a neutral third party—act as though you were hearing about someone else, not about yourself.

- **Consider the Source**

    "Consider the source," as a suggestion to shrug off anything coming your way may be a cliche. However, this expression retains a degree of validity. Ask yourself the following questions:
    — What are the person's credentials? Is this person qualified to criticize in this instance?
    — What are this person's motives? Are there any vested interests involved?
    — Are the comments valid, or do I just happen to be a convenient target?

    Whenever you are criticized, especially by your supervisor or another member of management, try to determine whether the person is genuinely trying to help you improve.

- **Evaluate the Criticism**

    Try to judge whether your critic had all the facts available and whether or not, quite simply, the criticism made sense. Search for positive suggestions in the criticism, and try to determine whether you will benefit by following your critic's advice.

- **Keep It in Perspective**

    Some people—and it does not pay for a supervisor to be among them—do not take criticism well. They can be absolutely crushed by a few harsh or critical words. Realize, however, that criticism, no matter how harsh or ill directed, is not the end of the world. More often than not it is "business as usual" and interpersonal relationships drift back toward their original state. Criticism, unless carried to destructive extremes, is simply words strung together. As Mark Twain said, "If criticism had any real power to destroy, the skunk would have been extinct long ago."

- **Follow Up**

    Having evaluated criticism directed at you, you can do with it what you wish, depending on how deserved you believe it was. If you can honestly accept what you have heard, then take steps to change your behavior accordingly. Even if you feel you honestly cannot accept the criticism, that it is perhaps misdirected, undeserved, or unduly harsh, you have at least learned a bit more about the person who did the criticizing.

### Giving Criticism

Supervisors are often reluctant to criticize employees. This reluctance may be rationalized as unwillingness to hurt others' feelings. However, it is just as readily attributable to the supervisor's natural resistance to performing an unpleasant task.

Certain kinds of behavior may deserve criticism or even disciplinary action—criticism plus warning or punishment. The reasons for criticism are generally incidents of misconduct or poor performance or the manifestation of a poor attitude.

Misconduct, hinging largely on the existence and application of rules, is often clear-cut. Poor performance, on the other hand, often relates to assessments of quality and other judgments that are partly subjective, so the line separating what is deserved from what is undeserved is likely to be indistinct. Problems of employee attitude, especially if not immediately reflected in misconduct or poor performance, are the most difficult to deal with and call for the greatest care on the supervisor's part.

Few of us would deny the value of receiving constructive criticism when it is due. However, criticism is still criticism, and regardless of the sugar coating afforded by the word *constructive,* it is still likely to have a bit of a sting to it.

Criticism is necessary, but only if it is truly constructive. First and foremost, criticism should always include guides for correction. Simply telling people what they have done wrong without suggesting how they might do it correctly amounts to no more than placing blame. Criticism should always focus on the problem—on the results of a person's behavior and not on the person who created the problem. Criticism should also allow the supervisor and employee to work together to develop a new approach. Criticism, properly applied, can be the first step to shared problem-solving in the supervisor-employee relationship.

**Criticism should also be:**

- **Timely.** It should be delivered as soon as possible after the behavior occurs or the results are discovered. Saving up criticism for some special upcoming contact (for instance, a performance appraisal interview) is ineffective and possibly destructive.
- **Private.** Never criticize an employee in the presence of other people. The words that pass between the two of you are no one else's business. Even when you walk in on a situation in which a number of people are present, after you take whatever steps are

necessary to stop what is going on, you should meet with the problem employee in private before delivering criticism.

- **Rational.** Never criticize in anger. Take the risk of blunting the impact of your criticism by allowing yourself time to cool down and assess the situation calmly before criticizing. Often when your anger has dissipated, you will be able to see dimensions of the problem that were previously hidden by your emotional state.

Consider some of the more common causes of incidents, errors, and omissions leading to criticism of employees: lack of adequate job knowledge, poor understanding of management's expectations, inability to perform as expected, and attitude problems. Recognize that each of these embodies some reflection of the supervisor's responsibility for the knowledge, understanding, capability, and attitude of the employee. Before confronting the employee, the supervisor should ask: Have I fulfilled all of my responsibilities to this employee?

## DISCIPLINE

The word *discipline* comes from the same root as the word *disciple* and means "to teach so as to mold." Originally, teaching was the key to discipline—to shaping or molding the disciple. However, we have come to think of discipline, and disciplinary action, as punishment.

The true objective of discipline should not be punishment. It should be correction. One of the primary requirements of disciplinary action is to give the employee the opportunity to correct the behavior that prompted the action.

### Conduct versus Performance: Separate Progressive Paths

Except in the few legitimate instances where immediate termination is appropriate, corrective action must be progressive. That is, it must follow through a number of steps in which subsequent similar infractions are addressed with increasing severity. Most government agencies have incorporated progressive discipline procedures in their personnel management regulations, and some even have established tables of sanctions that include recommended action to be taken for first, second, and third infractions.

At each step in the progressive process two pieces of information must be made clear to the employee: what the person must do to correct the problem, and what may follow if the problem is not corrected.

Throughout the process it is essential to view the sequence of occurrences exactly as it would be viewed—and often is viewed—by outside entities such as a labor-management review panel or even a judge, by asking: Was the employee given every opportunity to correct the offending behavior?

In applying corrective action it is also necessary to make a distinction between problems of conduct and problems of performance. Although traditional progressive disciplinary processes may work well for problems of conduct, such processes are not appropriate for performance problems. The employee who has broken no work rules and violated no policies is not appropriately handled with a progressive disciplinary process, for work performance that falls short of standard or expectation.

The supervisor always needs to ask: Is the employee not capable of performing as expected under present circumstances? If the employee cannot, for one reason or another, perform as expected, it is not a discipline problem, and to treat it as one is to burden the process with a layer of negativity that only impedes correction.

### Conduct Problems: Traditional Progressive Discipline Plus

*Counseling*

The first step taken to address a specific kind of errant behavior should be counseling. One to one, supervisor to employee, the employee should be told what was done that was wrong, why it was wrong, what the organization's rules are concerning this behavior (with specific use of handbooks, policy manuals, and other written references), what the possible consequences of this kind of behavior are, and the period of time within which correction is expected. All of this needs to be accomplished without reference to any kind of "warning"; it is simply an important, job-related discussion between supervisor and employee.

Any such counseling session should be thoroughly documented by the supervisor in notes retained in departmental files.

*Oral Warning*

Repeated errant behavior following counseling should be addressed using the early stages of the more formal progressive disciplinary process, specifically the oral warning. It should be stressed that the oral warning stage (also regarded as another type of counseling session) should be used only after the employee has failed to respond to counseling.

The oral warning should be documented by the supervisor on a form created for that purpose by the agency. If it is documented, is this not actually a written warning? It certainly may seem so, but the difference between a written and oral warning lies in what goes into the employee's personnel file. The record of an oral warning should be retained in department files; it should go into the official personnel files only as part of a subsequent warning following counseling for the same kind of behavior.

If it is truly to be an "oral" warning, why document it at all? Because the oral warning is a step in the progressive disciplinary process, and when an employment relationship breaks down and legal problems result, it can become necessary to provide evidence that each step in the process was followed.

### Written Warning

The written warning follows in turn as necessary. This documentation is placed in the employee's personnel file.

An employee whose improper behavior has not been corrected following counseling, oral warning, and written warning is in a position in which failure to change will lead to loss of income via suspension or loss of employment. By this stage the supervisor and employee have been together on the subject of the employee's behavior problem three or more times. The supervisor must now bring other organizational resources into the process.

### Before Suspension

At this stage, each agency will have different procedures to follow. If no specific steps are required prior to suspending an employee, the supervisor may at this point consider referring the employee to one of three available sources of further assistance: the employee assistance program (if the agency or institution has one), a medical resource for a physical examination, or the personnel department.

If, in any of their numerous contacts, the employee has given the supervisor reason to believe he or she may be experiencing mental health problems of any kind, a referral to the employee assistance program may be in order. If a physical problem related to the employment situation may be involved, then a referral for a physical examination may disclose reasons for the poor performance. If the problem appears to be unrelated to these two factors, the referral should be to personnel, an employee relations specialist, or employee ombudsman, if the agency has such a position.

This referral puts the employee in contact with someone who can point the way toward resolution of some underlying problem. Also, a knowledgeable person other than the supervisor is brought into the process, and this new participant may be able to get through to the employee where the supervisor could not. Finally, this step gives the employee one more distinct opportunity to correct the problem behavior.

### Suspension and Discharge

If the referral step is unsuccessful, suspension without pay and eventual discharge may follow, as necessary. However, a well-functioning referral program for employee behavior problems will significantly reduce the use of the clearly punitive steps of suspension and discharge.

Should you feel you have cause to discharge an employee, you should take your case to the personnel department for thorough review before taking action. In today's legal environment, virtually all government agencies require human resource or administrative review and concurrence in such cases. A review of this type would be prudent in the private sector as well. This review should be aimed at determining whether or not all bases have been covered from a legal perspective and whether or not the record clearly demonstrates that the employee was given the opportunity to correct the inappropriate behavior. Because of the time required, this review serves another extremely important function: It assures that no employee is ever fired on the spot or otherwise terminated in the anger of the moment.

Some severe infractions must of course be dealt with as they occur. An employee caught bringing drugs into the institution should not be allowed back in. However, an immediate firing is never the answer. The offending employee should instead be removed from his or her post, sent home, and placed on home duty or indefinite suspension pending investigation and resolution.

Not all infractions will require the application of all the foregoing steps. If a mild problem, such as tardiness (within a few minutes of starting time), becomes chronic, it may require all of the steps described above. A more serious infraction, such as a tower officer caught sleeping on post, may call for a written warning or suspension on the first violation and discharge on the second violation. The organization's personnel department ordinarily provides guidance for determining the severity of disciplinary action for specific infractions.

**Performance Problems: "Warnings" Not Applicable**

It is inappropriate to apply a progressive disciplinary process to an employee who is exhibiting substandard work. The substandard performer has not "broken the rules"; to group this person with the supposed rule breakers is to lend a negative aspect to a process that must be as positively oriented as possible.

Substandard performance can be simply described as the production of unsatisfactory results that prevent an employee from attaining or maintaining job standard. The job standard may be defined as the acceptable level of output achieved by employees in the same or similar job classification, or defined as the standard level of results, determined in advance by the supervisor and clearly identifying the quantity and quality of output expected.

*The Newly Identified Substandard Performer*

The supervisor's primary objective should not be to get rid of the substandard performer, as is frequently the case, but rather to show the substandard performer how to perform acceptably. The supervisor should:

- review the job standard with the employee, ensuring that the standard is known and understood and, ideally, that the employee accepts this as a reasonable expectation;
- counsel the employee, developing an action plan specifying what must be done to attain an acceptable level of performance and a timetable for doing so. Document this thoroughly (as any counseling session should be documented) with a copy of the complete plan supplied to the employee;
- conscientiously monitor the employee's progress against the improvement plan, providing assistance as necessary;
- remove apparent obstacles to the employee's success when possible and make reasonable accommodations to enhance employee performance.

If this process does not correct the problem within the agreed upon time period, it should be repeated in identical fashion. A mutually acceptable plan of correction should be created, with necessary modifications from the earlier plan (based on what was encountered in the process) and an agreed upon target date.

## *The Important "Plus"*

The second time the employee is taken through the corrective counseling and instruction, the process should include the same referral process as for a progressive discipline case. The advantages of doing this are that a new person who can possibly help is brought into the process, and the employee is given the chance to address any underlying problem that is causing the unsatisfactory performance.

## *How Many Times?*

Depending on how much improvement is noted from one time to the next, the foregoing process might be applied three or four times. When finally every reasonable opportunity to improve has been extended multiple times without lasting improvement, a last-ditch deadline should be set. When this deadline arrives, employment should end, unless all conditions of the plan of improvement have been met. Of course, a wise supervisor who has reached this stage has already told the personnel department that a problem is developing, and that adverse action may result.

## *Dismissal, Not Discharge*

When it is necessary to release an employee for reasons of substandard performance, the action should be identified as a dismissal for failure to meet job standards, and not as a discharge. The distinction is important: A discharge for cause is a "firing," and a person so terminated has lost employment through inappropriate conduct. In most parts of the country the person would not be eligible for unemployment compensation. The individual who is dismissed for inability to meet the standards of the job is not considered wholly responsible for the termination, so the action is regarded more as a layoff than a discharge. The dismissed employee is usually eligible for unemployment compensation.

## Guidelines for Fair and Effective Discipline

- **Be Reasonable**

   At all times strive to keep the severity of disciplinary action consistent with the infraction. Many agencies have established explicit guidelines for applying discipline in specific categories of offenses. If yours is an agency that maintains data on the sanctions applied for given charges brought against an employee, try to access that information. If you are on your own, however, remember the particular action you associated with a certain infraction in the past and try to avoid any unjustified variation in the scope of the punishment involved.

- **Avoid Making Examples**

  Every employee deserves fair, consistent treatment relative to all other employees. Resist the occasional temptation to make an example of an individual for the sake of discouraging the same kind of behavior by others. Making examples serves only to create fear and resentment, and it destroys the effectiveness of discipline. Should an employee challenge the rationale of the action in an administrative hearing or in court, making an example will probably be indefensible.

- **Follow the Rules**

  The rules in the employee handbook will not cover every situation, but they will apply to many occasions when disciplinary action is warranted. Use the rules, and use them consistently. What applies to one employee should apply to all others for the same offense. Use written warnings when the system calls for them. Do not simply slide over an incident deserving a warning without actually issuing the warning; this omission may return to haunt you later.

- **Respect Privacy**

  Do not meddle in the life of an employee outside of the institution. What an employee does on off hours is ordinarily none of your business. The only time you can be concerned with an employee's private life is when you know that the person is engaged in something that can harm job performance or negatively affect the reputation of the agency.

  Even then you must be cautious to avoid violating someone's privacy and to be sure there is a "nexus," or logical connection, between the questionable off-duty conduct and the employee's role and performance in the workplace. This is often easy to establish for law enforcement positions—such as the case of a prison employee or police officer using illegal drugs off duty. But you cannot assume automatically that every objectionable or unconventional personal act is connected with the workplace in a way that would justify some form of personnel action.

- **Avoid Favoritism**

  Under no circumstances should you allow yourself to favor any employees over others. Undoubtedly there will be some employees you personally like better than others; people are different and your reactions are natural. However, you must make every effort to assure that disciplinary actions you dispense are consistent among your employees regardless of your personal feelings toward various people.

- **Act Only on Clear Evidence**

  Take disciplinary action only when absolutely certain you are dealing with a truly guilty party. Hearsay or secondhand evidence is totally inadequate and undeserving of more than your passing attention. It is far better to run the risk of allowing someone who warrants disciplinary action to slip through rather than to discipline an innocent person unjustly. Many agencies require some form of investigation and multilayered review to ensure that disciplinary actions are fully supported in fact.

## *Avoid Dwelling on History*

When an incident is over and disciplinary action has been taken, forget it. Do not bring the incident up again; do not continually remind the employee that you remember what happened. Unless the nature of the misconduct itself requires supervisory follow-up, the only extent to which you can justifiably deal with history in most cases of disciplinary action is through the necessary accumulation of written warnings. This practice, of course, must be spelled out in agency rules and regulations.

## The Inevitable Documentation

At several points in the processes described in the preceding paragraphs the need to provide documentation was mentioned, even to the extent of calling for documentation of so-called "oral" warnings. It is often too easy to delay the documentation and perhaps forget about it entirely, because documentation is not usually an immediate concern. Most of the time documentation is never used again, whether immediately or later. But when it is needed to defend a personnel action, it is worth its weight in gold.

After most employment actions take place, the involved parties go forward to other concerns and never look back. Occasionally, however, an employment action is challenged, either internally through a griev-ance or appeal process, or externally through a labor-management pro-ceeding or a lawsuit. And when an action is challenged, all of the docu-mentation related to it in any way is brought to the foreground.

Documents related to performance or conduct problems are used to reasonably establish: whether something did or actually did not occur; whether an employee was or was not spoken with about a certain prob-lem; whether the employee agreed or disagreed with a certain course of action, and so on. These documents are used to establish whether or not the employee was given the opportunity to improve or correct. Human memories fade or become selective regarding certain kinds of informa-tion, and documentation is essential to either support or refute certain contentions. The importance of the documentation of employment ac-tions cannot be stressed too strongly. In the words of one investigator for an employee advocacy agency, "If it's not properly documented, all signed and dated, we assume it never happened."

## GUTS, TACT, AND JUSTICE

Criticizing employees and parceling out disciplinary action takes courage. In most instances it is normal for the supervisor to feel un-easy. We can go so far as to suggest that a manager should never want to reach the point of becoming completely comfortable with criticism and discipline; this might suggest a callousness that runs contrary to the character of an effective supervisor.

An employee who has done something deserving of criticism or disci-plinary action nevertheless deserves your full consideration as an indi-vidual. You must continually be aware of feelings—your own as well as others. However, regardless of individual feelings, what you say and what you do must be said and done out of consideration for the needs of the institution, its inmates, and its employees.

---

## CASE 13–1: DID HE HAVE IT COMING?

"That was a stupid thing to do," said Ron Walker, food service admin-istrator at a large medium-security prison.

"What do you mean?" asked the recently promoted assistant food ser-vice administrator, Susan Aldred, flushing noticeably at the words.

"You fiddled around making those bulk vegetable purchases so long that you stalled us right into a price hike. This late in the budget year there's no way we'll recover that much in other purchases; thanks to you, we'll go about $4,500 over budget for the year."

"So I made a mistake," Aldred retorted.

"Mistake? More like a colossal blunder. Forty-five hundred bucks! I don't know what ever convinced you that you know the vegetable market. The way prices have been going, you should know you've got to get in and cut a contract fast." Walker shook his head and repeated, "Forty-five hundred!"

Aldred stood and glared down at Walker. "So I slipped, and I know it. In the two months I've been in this job, I've saved twice that in other areas—how come I don't hear about that?"

"Because that's your job," Walker replied curtly.

"Well, maybe I need a new one," Aldred said, and stormed out of the office.

## Questions

1. Do you believe Aldred "had it coming" or that some criticism was deserved?
2. What essential element is missing from Walker's criticism of Aldred?
3. How might this situation have been approached to minimize the chances of an emotional interchange?

---

### CASE 13–2: A GOOD EMPLOYEE, BUT . . .

Lieutenant Rich Patterson was uncomfortable about a personnel action he was considering. He decided to discuss it with Marcia Saenz, another lieutenant. He began with, "I have no idea how I should deal with Pat Nelson. I just don't recall ever facing one like this before."

Marcia asked, "What's the problem?"

"Excessive absenteeism," Rich answered. "Pat has used up all of her sick time virtually overnight, and most of her sick days have been before or after scheduled days off. You know what that looks like!"

"What's unusual about that? Unfortunately, we've got several people who use their sick time as fast as they earn it. And most of them get 'sick' on very convenient days."

"What's unusual is the fact that it's Pat Nelson. She's been a pretty good officer for more than seven years, but all of a sudden she starts what looks a lot like sick leave abuse. She's used up all of her sick leave in seven months. And recently, she was out for three days without even calling in."

Marcia said, "You can terminate her for that."

"I know," said Rich.

"Especially when you take her other absences into account. You've warned her about them?"

After a moment's silence Rich said, "No, not in writing. Just once, face-to-face."

"Any record of it? Fill out a disciplinary dialogue form for her to sign?"

"No," said Rich. "I really hated to. I know I should have taken some kind of action by now, but I can't seem to make myself do it."

Marcia asked, "Why not?"

"Because she's always been such a good employee. She's always shown up on time and done what she's told to do, she handles inmates well, and until this came up she was one of our best officers. She's still that way, except for her attendance problems the past seven months."

Rich shrugged and continued, "I guess what I'm really hung up on is: How do I discipline someone who is usually a good employee, and do it in such a way that it doesn't destroy any of what is good about her?"

Marcia shook her head and said, "Good officer or not, I'd say you ought to be going by policy. That's all I can suggest."

### Questions

1. How would you advise Lieutenant Patterson to proceed in the matter of Pat Nelson?
2. Do you feel that Patterson's failure to take action thus far affects his ability to take action now? Why, or why not?

## CHAPTER 14

# The Problem Employee and Employee Problems

*In so complex a thing as human nature, we must consider it
hard to find rules without exception.*

*—George Eliot*

## Chapter Objectives

☛ Qualify the term *problem employee* and review the hazards involved in applying labels to people.

☛ Provide suggestions as to why the problem employee may present problems for the supervisor.

☛ Present general guidelines for handling troublesome employees.

☛ Recognize the "plateaued employee" as a special case and suggest approaches for dealing with this person.

☛ Offer guidelines for the control of absenteeism.

☛ Provide guidance for relating to employees whose performance is affected by personal problems.

## IS THERE SUCH A PERSON?

We might legitimately ask whether or not there really is such a person we can call the "problem employee." Considering your answer in practical terms—from the viewpoint of a correctional manager—you might be tempted to say there is such a person and offer several real-life examples from among the employees in your department. Indeed, sometimes there may seem to be many problem employees.

In actuality, however, who knows how many, or how few, problem employees there really are in a given institution? A person may be a true problem employee, but you may see only the apparent problem. Also, you, by your leadership style and through your expectations of the individual, may well be part of the problem that an individual employee displays.

Usually the problem employee will be neither a very good nor a very poor performer. Rarely can outstanding workers—that is, those exceeding management's expectations in terms of quality of work, amount of

227

work, and interpersonal relations—be considered problems. In addition, the worker whose performance has been chronically substandard and generally unacceptable should no longer be there to present a problem, assuming that persons who turn out to be simply unable to do their jobs are properly "weeded out" after being given every reasonable opportunity to learn. Rather, the problem employee is usually a worker whose performance, both functionally and interpersonally, falls in the mid range and perhaps a bit short of the average. The problem employee is tough to instruct and correct, tough to motivate, and generally troublesome to handle. There are days when employees in this category make you wish for nothing but inmate problems to deal with!

Problem employees are sometimes typed or labeled by terms such as "know-it-all," "wise guy," "blabbermouth," and "complainer." These terms tend to magnify one or two narrow behavioral characteristics so they overshadow the whole person. Also, when we categorize a person, we tend to assume that the person is, in fact, that way. Our thinking then channels our relationship with the individual along certain narrow lines.

For instance, if you need something from the chief of security but you know that "that stubborn so-and-so" is difficult to deal with, you may readily adopt a hard-line approach to making your request without realizing you are doing so. You may know that one of your employees is undergoing personal stress because of a serious illness in the family; your approach to that individual may be more gentle and you may be inclined to give the person more latitude in their job performance.

People, and thus employees, are all different. The majority of your staff behave in somewhat the same fashion, owing largely to the rules, methods, and procedures they are required to follow as prison employees. But this common behavior in no way means that they are alike. Each has a particular personality, and each is a collection of attitudes and feelings that add up to a unique individual.

Some supervisors are unaware of, or perhaps ignore, the differences between staff that mark some as so-called problem employees. They may decide that it is easier to stand on the authority of the supervisory position and use orders and ultimatums for handling the problem employee.

The problem employee, however, can be a particularly interesting challenge for the supervisor. Yes, a particular employee may be difficult to get along with, but learning to get along with one so-called problem employee can improve skills at relating with people all the way around.

Supervisors should make every effort to avoid pigeonholing, or categorizing, employees. Even our use of the term *problem employee* is unfair; although it is a broad category, it still is a category, and we are grouping people together under that single label. Categorizing employees, which we cannot help doing to some extent, often leads to a gradual narrowing of the categories and eventually to stereotyping. In addition to being hazardously unreliable, stereotyping is unfair: It almost always constitutes unwarranted generalization. As G. K. Chesterton said, "All generalizations are dangerous, including this one."

Watch out for labels you would apply to employees, especially labels with negative connotations, such as stubborn, grouchy, lazy, undependable, and dull. When we use such labels we are erecting obstacles that may prevent us from seeing more favorable, but perhaps less obvious, characteristics that are also present. When we apply labels, we are rendering personality judgments that most of us are unqualified to make.

Often we are unwittingly led into accepting a label generated by someone else. For instance, a new supervisor coming in from the outside may get a rundown on all employees from the departing supervisor: "This one is cooperative, that one is a grouch, this one is headstrong and insists on doing things the wrong way, that one is a crybaby," and so on. It is bad enough that we are inclined to form our own shaky judgments, let alone that we compound the problem by accepting those of another supervisor. By automatically accepting a label, we are setting ourselves up to think of the person as actually being that way and to expect the person to behave according to that label. Our impressions of individuals should be formed through personal observation and interaction.

## DEALING WITH THE PROBLEM EMPLOYEE

### Ups and Downs

Recognize that everyone in your department, including you, has good days and bad days. The mood of the day, how things have been going, how one feels physically, and many other factors have a bearing on how one comes across to others. If you have worked in an institution for any length of time, you know that one nose-to-nose confrontation with an inmate can affect your entire day, and not for the good. So it is with your employees.

Try to be empathic. Try putting yourself in the employee's position, and try to appreciate fully why that person feels and acts in such a way. When you see the visible signs of problems in your employees, give serious thought to your own behavior under similar circumstances. What would cause your coolness, distance, irritability, or other less-than-desirable behavior?

Direct, forceful attempts to alter behavior of the problem employee will probably fail. For instance, meeting deep-seated stubbornness head-on with hard-nosed determination is more likely to be destructive than constructive. Recognize that very often we cannot change so-called difficult people, but that often we can accept and perhaps even use their peculiarities.

### Time To Be Troublesome

One of the keys to dealing with the problem employee is to keep the person constructively occupied. The act of doing meaningful work, with energies directed into obviously useful channels, is by far the best cure for many problem employees. Activity can remove some problems, such as irritability, boredom, or frustration owing to inactivity, and it can "keep the lid on" other problems. When we have time on our hands, we tend to dwell on ourselves and our troubles, and the things that bother employees are more likely to come to the surface and be magnified when they are idle.

Whenever possible, use your employees in the capacities for which they are best suited. Not everyone does everything with the same degree of success, or is equally suited to all assignments. While the needs of the institution often require that people be placed in less-than-ideal assignments, it is management's responsibility to see that employees' talents and preferences are applied to best advantage. Then, problems are less likely to develop.

Many employees are troublesome because they are not challenged by their work. Some simply do not care for what they are doing—there are many tasks in a prison that few people would enjoy doing day in and day out. Keeping employees constructively occupied could include offering increased responsibility to those who are able to assume it and rotating job duties to spread around the least desirable tasks so they have minimum negative impact. Many security departments base their entire staff assignment system on this premise, with highly structured rosters that ensure that all staff work each shift and each post over a period of time.

## The Whole Person

You will find that, to some degree, people bring their outside problems to the job and carry their job-related problems off the job. For some employees, this crossover is minimal. With others a small crisis in either facet of their existence can affect attitudes and behavior in the other. The employee who becomes sullen and withdrawn may have done so because of some job-related experience or because of something that happened off the job. If someone has become "moody" or "stubborn" or invited the application of some similar label, that alone should give you cause to wonder what is behind the behavior.

The behavior of an employee can be an emotional defense against perceived treatment received on the job. The same supervisory approach will not be interpreted in the same way by all employees. As a supervisor, do you make it a practice to remain on friendly terms with everyone—friendly, but impersonal and businesslike—conscientiously trying to play no favorites while you avoid getting "too close" to your employees? To some of your employees this will be appropriate behavior; you will be seen as a good supervisor. However, some employees will see this same behavior as artificial and perhaps label you as "cold" or "phony." (It is not just the supervisors who do the labeling.)

Do you make an effort to get to know all your employees, openly expressing interest in them as individuals and inquiring into their personal interests? In the eyes of some employees, this behavior will make you a good supervisor. To others you will seem nosy, inquiring into things that are "none of your business." Is it your practice to circulate about the group during the workday or tour your part of the institution, in order to simply show people you are there, available, and interested? If so, this behavior will be accepted by some employees as appropriate supervisory behavior, while others may see you as distrustful because you are constantly "checking up" on them.

Whatever you do in your efforts to be a good supervisor, a few employees will react negatively. These negative reactors are likely to be your "problem employees."

## SEVEN GUIDELINES

**In dealing with problem employees, adhere to these guidelines.**

1. **Listen.** Make it clear that you are always available to hear what is bothering your employees. Display an open attitude. Conscien-

tiously avoid the tendency to shut out possible unpleasantries because you "don't want to hear them." Many employees' doubts, fears, and complaints are created or magnified by a closed attitude of the supervisor. Your obvious willingness to listen will go a long way toward putting some troubles to rest.

2. **Always be patient, fair, and consistent.** But retain sufficient latitude in your behavior to allow for individual differences among people. Use agency rules as they were intended, stressing corrective aspects rather than punishment. Apply disciplinary action when truly deserved, but do not use the threat of such action to attempt to force employees to change.

3. **Recognize and respect individual feelings.** Recognize that a feeling is neither right nor wrong—it is simply there. What a person does with a feeling may be right or wrong, but the feeling itself cannot be helped. Do not ever say, "You shouldn't feel that way." Respect people's feelings, and restrict your supervisory interest to what each employee does with those feelings.

4. **Avoid arguments.** Problem employees are frequently ready and willing to argue in defense of their feelings or beliefs. However, by arguing with an employee, you simply solidify that person in a defensive position and reduce the chances of effective communication.

5. **Let your supposedly stubborn or resistant employees try something their own way, when possible.** As a supervisor you are interested first in results and only secondarily in how those results are achieved (as long as they are achieved by reasonable, permissible methods). There is no better way to clear the air with the employee who "knows better" than to provide the flexibility for that person to try it that way and either succeed or fail. In other words, the employee who appears stubborn or resistant may not be so by nature, but may be reacting to authoritarian leadership. More participative leadership might be the answer.

6. **Pay special attention to the chronic complainers.** These employees grouch and grumble all through the day and spread their gloom and doom to anyone who will listen. Chronic complaining is not only a sign of several potential problems but breeds new problems as well. The chronic complainer can affect departmental morale and drag down the entire work group. You should make every effort to find out what is behind the complain-

ing. Altering assignments to limit the opportunity to spread complaints may be called for.

7. **Give each employee some special attention.** The supervisor-employee relationship remains at the heart of the supervisor's job, and each employee deserves to be recognized as an individual as well as a producer of output. Honest recognition is all that some of our so-called problem employees really need to enable them to stop being problems.

## A SPECIAL CASE: THE PLATEAUED EMPLOYEE

The plateaued employee is discussed in this chapter because this person is caught up in a set of circumstances that can lead to problems. This employee can go no further in the organization. A move to a supervisory position may not be possible because he or she lacks the basic qualifications. Further promotion and significant pay raises may not be possible because the employee is already at the top of the grade. The supervisor may be limited organizationally from making any significant changes that would enhance job satisfaction for the employee. The plateaued employee is blocked from growth and advancement in all channels. Because there are no more material rewards left to prevent creeping dissatisfaction, and other rewards, the true motivators that should be inherent in the job, are limited, this employee presents a special motivation problem.

It is unfortunate that many plateaued employees become problems, because these employees very often have much to offer the organization. Their experience often surpasses that of others in the department. Yet because their professional advancement is stymied, the organization is not getting the full benefit of their abilities. The supervisor must appeal to the individual through true motivating forces that stress job factors rather than environmental factors.

**In dealing with the plateaued employee, try the following suggestions:**

- Consult the employee on various problems and aspects of the department's work. Ask for advice. An employee with years of experience in the same capacity may have a great deal to offer and react favorably to the opportunity to do so.
- Give the employee a bit of additional responsibility when possible, and let the person earn the opportunity to be more responsible. Some freedom and flexibility may be seen as recognition for the employee's past experience and contributions.

- Delegate special one-time assignments. Years of experience may have prepared the employee to handle special jobs above and beyond ordinary assignments.
- Use the plateaued employee as a teacher. The experienced employee may be quite valuable in one-on-one situations, helping to orient new employees or teaching present employees new and different tasks.
- Point the plateaued employee toward prestige assignments, such as committee assignments, special projects, attendance at an occasional seminar or educational program, or the coordination of a social activity, such as a retirement party or other gathering.

These ways of putting interest, challenge, variety, and responsibility into the work itself may not involve formal job description duties, but collateral or informal tasks. In dealing with the plateaued employee, special attention must be given to true motivating forces because the potential dissatisfiers, that is, the environmental factors such as wages, fringe benefits, and working conditions, are present in force. If the employee has come to regard an occasional pay increase as deserved reward for putting up with the same old nonsense, what happens when the top of the scale has been reached and pay raises stop? Dissatisfaction will begin. These suggestions can help the person find sufficient motivation in the work itself while offsetting the dissatisfying factors that are often beyond the supervisor's control.

There are other potential solutions to the problem of the plateaued employee, conditions permitting. Maybe it is possible to transfer the person to a completely different assignment or to set up a rotational scheme in which several employees trade assignments on a regular basis. The plateaued employee may be cross-trained on several other jobs within the department, getting the chance to do a variety of work while becoming more valuable to the department.

Perhaps it is unfair to discuss the plateaued employee in a chapter on problem employees, since many such employees present no problem at all. However, it is to the supervisor's advantage to recognize the plateaued employee as a special case that a bit of conscientious supervisory attention can keep from becoming a real problem.

## ABSENTEEISM

To the supervisor, absenteeism is an immediate problem of sometimes significant dimensions. Even a modest percentage of absenteeism in the department is likely to upset schedules. The supervisor must then divert supervisory time and effort to juggle personnel and assignments to cover necessary tasks. As well as being a significant problem in its own right—particularly in prison departments that operate on rigidly-scheduled rosters—absenteeism is usually a symptom of other problems. The employee who develops a pattern of chronic absenteeism becomes a problem employee. Chronic absenteeism, in turn, should suggest that this employee may have problems, personal or otherwise.

To some extent absenteeism plagues supervisors and managers in every industry and organizational setting, not just corrections. Absenteeism may be legitimate; people get sick and have other difficulties that sometimes keep them away from work. A considerable amount of absenteeism, however, is not legitimate—in terms of organizationally recognized reasons for employee absence. In addition, there is no sure way of determining how much absenteeism is legitimate and how much is not.

It has been estimated that absenteeism costs the country over 10 billion dollars per year in lost output and other costs. When someone fails to show up for work, one of two things usually happens: (1) the employee's work goes undone that day or (2) someone else must be assigned to do the absent employee's work. In both cases significant cost can be involved. Perhaps sick leave benefits are paid to the absentee, wages are paid to a replacement employee (often at an overtime rate), or revenue is lost because the employee was not there to perform. Numerous rippling inefficiencies also have a dollar impact on the organization. In departments like security, absenteeism within a fixed-post, fixed-shift structure can be a major disruption.

Employee attitude and supervisory behavior can combine to increase absenteeism. An employee experiencing a negative turn in attitude is likely to discover that unwarranted absence, once indulged in, is just that much easier the next time around. Such absenteeism is aided by silent or tolerant supervision.

Since there are legitimate reasons for employees to be absent, absenteeism is a problem that can never be completely cured. However, absenteeism can be reduced and controlled through conscientious supervisory attention.

## Guidelines for Reduced Absenteeism

For control of absenteeism in your department, consider the following eight guidelines.

1. **Stress to employees that employment is a two-way street.** Sick leave is an employee benefit with an associated cost, one that is provided for use only when needed. It is a privilege, not a right, that should not be taken for granted. Tell them how absences affect your department in terms of added cost and lost output.

2. **Let your employees know how their attendance is important to the operation of the department.** Openly publicize your concern for absenteeism and its effects on department performance.

3. **Start new employees the right way.** Include your expectation of regular attendance in their orientation. Make sure they clearly understand all the rules governing absenteeism and the use of sick leave benefits.

4. **Keep accurate attendance records, and let each employee know you do so.** Do not put yourself in the position of having another department (for instance, personnel or payroll) research an employee's attendance record when a question arises.

5. **Have absentees report to you when returning to work.** This generally will not bother legitimate absentees, but it puts a certain amount of pressure on the healthy "stay aways." In any case, you should be sufficiently interested in your employees' well-being to briefly check with someone returning from a day or two of absence. You may want to insist that the employee speak to you personally when they are calling in sick, in order to put additional pressure on the individual.

6. **Do not allow your system to reward for absenteeism.** In some departments where rotating shift and weekend coverage is built into the work roster, there may be people who claim illness only when scheduled to work on Saturday or Sunday. If possible, arrange your scheduling so that a person who calls in sick on a scheduled Saturday or Sunday will be rescheduled to work that day on the following weekend. The employee's fair share of weekend duty cannot be avoided through the use of sick leave.

7. **Discuss unusual patterns of absence with the employees involved.** If someone's supposed illness or personal problem always creates a long weekend or stretches a holiday into two days, make it known that you are aware of the pattern and feel it would be more than coincidence if the pattern continues. If your personnel regulations allow, insist that the employee bring in a written explanation from a doctor for persistent absences.

8. **Use incentives available to you as a supervisor to discourage absenteeism.** For instance, it would make sense to delegate a special assignment or a particularly interesting or appealing task to someone you can count on to show up regularly for work; make it known that this measure of dependability is one of your reasons for selecting this person. Also, make appropriate use of employee's attendance records at performance appraisal time. Whereas attendance is not likely to weigh heaviest in a performance appraisal, it can certainly add its weight to other appraisal factors in extending or withholding praise and reward.

### Morale and Motivation

Employee morale and individual motivation to perform are key factors in a department's rate of absenteeism. Generally, low morale and lack of individual motivation will encourage increased absenteeism. Some people stay away from work because they are ill. However, many absences happen when employees are feeling "on the fence"—neither especially sick nor particularly well. If this "blah" feeling happens to coincide with a "blah" attitude toward the job, the employee will stay home as long as sick-time benefits remain available.

All the factors having a bearing on the employee's attitude toward the organization, the job, and the work—the motivators and dissatisfiers discussed in Chapter 11—can influence attendance. Some of the most frequent causes of unwarranted absences are boredom, repetition, lack of interest, lack of challenge, and the inability to see positive results from one's efforts. Anything the supervisor can do to improve the chances of employee self-motivation will also be positive steps toward reducing and controlling absenteeism.

### THE TROUBLED EMPLOYEE

Employees with personal problems that they cannot help but bring to work with them are rarely able to do their best work. As a supervisor your position is difficult. Getting the work of the department done well is your responsibility. How your employees perform their duties in completing the department's tasks is also your business. As an appropriately caring supervisor, you should be interested in the employee as a whole person, but the employee's private life and personal problems are none of your business; they represent an area you cannot enter without specific invitation.

In dealing with the apparently troubled employee, do not prod and do not push. Make yourself available to the employee, and make known your willingness to listen. You may have to go as far as to provide the time, the place, and the opportunity for the employee to talk with you, without specifically asking the employee to "open up." Quite often, if your openness is evident, the troubled employee will turn to you.

### In relating to the troubled employee:

- **Listen.** But do not give advice. Some of the most useless statements you can make begin with, "If I were you. . . ." Although many troubled employees could use advice, it is usually advice that you are not qualified to deliver. The best you can do under most circumstances is gently suggest that the employee seek help from qualified professionals.

- **Be patient.** Show your concern for the employee as an individual. Although you should naturally be concerned with an individual's impairment as a productive employee, do not parade this before the troubled person. Rather, be patient and understanding. When possible, you might even ease off on tight deadlines and extra work requirements until the person is able to work through a problem.

- **Do not argue.** Do not criticize an employee for holding certain feelings or reflecting certain attitudes. Avoid passing judgment on the employee based on what you are seeing and hearing.

- **Be discreet.** Let nothing a troubled employee tells you go beyond you. Be extra cautious if an employee opens up to the extent of revealing much that is extremely personal and private. While it often does good for someone to be able to simply talk to someone else about a problem, a person runs the risk of saying too much and might afterward feel extremely uncomfortable about having done so. If you can, try to demonstrate that you sympathize and understand, without allowing the employee to go too far. Always provide assurance that what you have heard in such an exchange is safe with you.

- **Reassure.** When you are honestly able to do so, provide the employee with assurance of the security of the employee's job, the absence of undue pressure while problems get worked out, and the presence of a friendly and sympathetic ear when needed. You need not know the nature of the employee's outside problem in order to supply very real assistance by reducing the job-related pressures on the individual.

In general, the good supervisor will listen honestly and sympathetically to the troubled employee. A supervisor can reduce pressure on the employee, but will leave the giving of specific advice to persons qualified to deal with such problems.

## Employee Assistance Programs

A typical agency employee assistance program (EAP) will:

> . . . motivate employees in need of assistance to accept early counseling to help them regain their productive capability; minimize absenteeism, sick leave, and grievances; reduce the need for disciplinary action; and improve morale. The EAP is a confidential program available to all (agency) employees and when feasible, to immediate families of employees who have alcohol, drug, or emotional problems, and to employees with immediate family members with alcohol, drug, or emotional problems.[1]

Originating during the 1970s, EAPs continue to proliferate steadily throughout government as well as in private industry. Should your organization have an EAP in place, your troubled employees may find that they have sources of appropriate help at hand.

A well-functioning EAP can help increase work quality, reduce productivity losses, and control tardiness, absenteeism, and other undesirable conditions that affect job performance when employees' personal problems carry over into the work environment. A great many kinds of personal problems—drug abuse, alcoholism, and compulsive gambling, as well as marital, legal, financial, and emotional difficulties—can harm an employee's performance. The EAP is intended to provide employees who are troubled by such problems with personal, confidential assistance.

Ordinarily, the EAP consists of a network of service providers, or a referral system to such providers, available to employees in need of specific kinds of assistance. For confidentiality, few of the actual treatment services are provided by a component of the institution or agency where the employees work. All employees will know about the EAP, but the institution's only direct involvement will be through the services provided by the organization's EAP coordinator.

As a supervisor in an organization that operates an EAP, you should be trained to recognize job-performance problems that result from personal difficulties. As an alternative to normal disciplinary processes, you can suggest that the employee consider visiting the EAP coordinator.

An employee might enter the program independently, without referral. Most EAPs encourage self-referrals from employees. Beyond management referral and self-referral, third-party referral is also possible—perhaps from a family member, clergyman, personal physician, or other concerned party.

Although employees' lives outside of the workplace are truly none of your legitimate concern, employees' work performance indeed is. Knowing the common signs that indicate serious personal problems that affect job performance, you are able to tell employees how to gain access to the EAP should they desire help. The supervisor neither commands nor directs; the supervisor simply recognizes the signs and reminds employees of the availability of the EAP. However, in some organizations an employee's refusal to comply with a supervisory referral to an EAP can be used to support the disciplinary or termination process. Refusal to seek help may imply that the employee is not trying to correct performance problems.

Over time, as employee acceptance grows, more troubled employees seek help on their own. With more self-referrals, the focus moves from crisis intervention to preventive care. A mature, well-functioning EAP can be the most comprehensive resource available for dealing with the troubled employee.

## THE REAL "PROBLEM"

The true people problem of the supervisor is not the problem employee, but the basic challenge presented by the vast differences among people. Everybody is different, so there is no single right way of dealing with all employees. Should you have 12 employees reporting to you, there may be 12 different "right ways" of dealing with these employees.

A good general rule for supervision is to give as much time to a new employee as you would devote to a new major assignment. Get to know your people even better than you know your work. Your employees are your greatest resource. Your humane and understanding use of the human resource will determine your success as a manager.

---

## CASE 14–1: THE GREAT STONE FACE

Six months ago you were hired from another, smaller state prison as a supervisor for a business office with 20 employees in the state's largest penitentiary. Most of your staff have been at that institution for several years. One of your employees, Paul Steiner, is assigned to maintain a complex accounting system for your prison industry operation. His job requires considerable training. Your predecessor never trained anyone else in the job.

Paul strikes you as good at what he does. However, he has days—at least one a week—on which he refuses to speak with his coworkers. His silences are well known; the other employees refer to him as "the great stone face." Since his regular duties require contact with other employees, when one of his silent moods strikes, the department's work flow is impaired and people begin to complain.

On several occasions you have given Paul the opportunity to talk with you, but so far he has given you no clue as to any difficulty that might be behind his moods. All of your indirect offers of help have been ignored, and when directly asked if anything is bothering him, he ducks the question.

### Instructions

Develop a tentative approach to the overall problem presented by Paul's behavior, including the effects of his mood changes on the department. (An "if—then" approach is suggested. For instance, "If I try this particular direction and such a response is forthcoming, then I'll go on to try. . . .")

Share your thoughts on the problem in a discussion group.

---

### CASE 14–2: THE FIRST-CLASS GROUCH

"As your assistant, I'm certainly not trying to tell you what to do," said Carol Ames. "You're the boss, and I'm only pointing out—again—a problem that's leading us into lots of grief."

"I know," Sam Henson, administrative services manager, said with more than a trace of annoyance. "I'm trying to take it the way you mean it. I've heard it from several people and I know we've got a problem with Nancy. I just don't know how to deal with it, that's all."

"It has to be dealt with," Carol said. "The institution's receptionist/switchboard operator is in a position to leave a first and lasting impression on a lot of people, and she's generating an endless trail of complaints. I've heard from visitors, staff, and the headquarters office, and a lot of other people—just about anyone you care to name—about her curt, rude treatment of them. It's been going on for months, and it's getting worse. And now she's starting to mix up phone numbers—routing calls to the wrong offices."

Sam said, "I know. I had hoped that whatever was bugging her would pass. But it hasn't. She's gone from bad to worse. And it's too bad—she's been here a long time, and this problem is relatively recent."

"One of us needs to talk with her. Or at least make some attempt to find out what's wrong."

Sam spread his hands, palms up, and said, "I've tried to talk with her. Just a week ago I gave her a chance to talk in private. I even asked if I could help out in any way, but. . . ." He shrugged helplessly.

"But what?"

"She told me nothing was wrong, or something like that. I got the impression that she was telling me—kind of roundabout—to mind my own business."

"Well, something is wrong," Carol said, "and we need to do something about it. She's coming across as a first-class grouch and the whole prison is suffering."

## Instructions

Develop a tentative approach for dealing with the apparent attitude problem presented by the receptionist/switchboard operator. Address:

- Possible ways of assisting the employee with "the problem"
- Opportunities to correct behavior
- The necessarily progressive nature of any disciplinary action considered
- The needs of the department.

---

**NOTE**

1. Federal Bureau of Prisons, U.S. Department of Justice, "Employee Assistance Program," Program Statement 3792.06.

## CHAPTER 15

# The Supervisor and the Human Resource Department

*I use not only all the brains I have, but all I can borrow.*

*—Anonymous*

### Chapter Objectives

☞ Introduce the human resource department as a vital staff function that supports operating management and the employees of an institution.

☞ Outline the functions of human resources and show how these functions relate to the role of the supervisor.

☞ Describe a number of action steps the supervisor can take to ensure that he or she will obtain appropriate service from human resources when needed.

☞ Suggest what the supervisor can do to establish a working relationship with human resources that will lead to improved human resource service to the organization.

## A VITAL STAFF FUNCTION

Human resources facilitates the work of the prison organization by concerning itself with the organization's most important resource—people. The names *human resources* and *personnel* are often used interchangeably. Other familiar designations are *employee relations* and *labor-management relations,* two labels that today describe subfunctions of modern human resources—employee problems and problem employees, and union matters, respectively. Regardless of label, the mission of this particular support department remains the same—to assist line departments in acquiring, maintaining, and retaining employees so that the objectives of the organization may be fulfilled.

The supervisor's greatest source of assistance is the human resource (HR) department. The supervisor who knows exactly what should be expected from human resources and how to get it when needed, has a distinct managerial advantage.

## A SERVICE OF INCREASING VALUE

The human resource department has become increasingly valuable to organizations and to supervisors as its tasks increase in response to

243

a number of internal and external forces. In corrections, two of these are the proliferation of laws affecting employment and privatization. Personnel management laws that formerly applied only to private business apply to private prisons, whereas a totally different statutory and regulatory structure may apply to public correctional facilities.

## Increase in Employee-Related Tasks

There was a time when HR did not exist. HR arose to fill a need in the modern organizations of government and the private sector, where the earliest human resource departments were commonly known as employment offices. As businesses grew large, they recognized the advantages of centralizing the process of acquiring employees. Employment and record keeping made up all the work of the employment office. When wage and hour laws came into being, the employment office absorbed much of the concern for establishing standard rates of pay and monitoring their application relative to hours worked. This began the compensation function.

In response to new laws and other pressures (both internal and external), organizations began to provide compensation in forms other than wages, and the employment office took over the administration of what became known as fringe benefits. As organizations responded to labor legislation and labor unions, labor relations functions were added to the growing list of activities that shared a common theme: All had something to do with acquiring, maintaining, or retaining employees.

Other people activities were added as needed, and what had once been the employment office became personnel, literally, "the body of people employed by the agency." During the last two decades the term *personnel* began to be replaced by the term *human resources*, but the essential meaning remains the same. All the while, the HR function grew in value as it took on an increasing number of employee-related functions.

## Proliferation of Laws Pertaining to Employment

A number of laws were the primary cause of the increase in employee-related tasks described above. For example, the establishment of Social Security, worker's compensation, and unemployment all created benefits tasks for HR. A great deal of labor relations activity was brought about by these laws. In addition, various antidiscrimination laws, including the Civil Rights Act of 1964, the Age Discrimination in Employment Act, and the Equal Pay Act, brought with them an increased volume of work for HR.

Antidiscrimination laws have forever changed the way most organizations work. This category of legislation has created a strongly law-oriented environment in which lawsuits and other formal discrimination complaints have become routine HR business. They have also turned employee recruitment, performance evaluation, and disciplinary action into legal minefields for the unwary. These laws have created more work for HR, and more reasons for the individual supervisor to turn to HR.

### Tendency toward Decentralization

There is a tendency toward decentralization in prison administration, in the form of what most systems call "unit management." Unit management calls for increased first-line manager responsibility and for moving decision-making as close as possible to the bottom of the hierarchy. Unit management means that certain decisions that might once have been made by an associate warden—for instance, inmate classification decisions or deciding how far to proceed in a particular disciplinary action against an employee—have been moved down to the level of the supervisor. As more employee-related decisions migrate to the first line of management in this fashion, the more the first-line manager—the individual supervisor—has to depend on the guidance and support of the human resource department. This tendency toward decentralization in the form of unit management has increased the value of HR to the supervisor.

### LEARNING ABOUT YOUR HUMAN RESOURCE DEPARTMENT

To be able to get the most out of the prison's human resource department, it is first necessary to understand its function, to know how it relates to the organization, and to be familiar with the functions performed by your particular HR department.

### The Nature of the Function: Staff versus Line

Human resources has already been described in these pages as a staff function. As opposed to a line activity, a function in which people actually perform the work of the organization (for example, correctional officers or food service staff), a staff function enhances and supports the performance of the organization's work. The presence of a staff function should make a difference to the extent that the organization's work is more effectively accomplished with the staff function than without it.

The distinction between line and staff is critical to appreciate because a staff function cannot legitimately make decisions that are the province of line management. Operating decisions belong to operating managers; they must be made within the chains of command of the line departments. The business manager of a prison is not the person who actually makes the decision to expend money for new floor buffers in a housing unit; the unit manager or perhaps the safety and sanitation officer makes that decision. The primary purpose of human resources is to enhance and support work performance by recommending courses of action that are (1) consistent with legislation, regulation, and principles of fairness, and (2) in the best interests of the organization as a whole.

When managers' preferred decisions are altered by human resources' recommendations, complaints such as "Personnel made me do it," or "This is the HR department's decision," are not uncommon. However, human resources generally does not—and should never—have the authority to overrule line management in any matter, personnel or otherwise. If, as occasionally is the case, a personnel-related decision made by line management must be reversed for the good of the organization, that reversal is by higher line management. Human resources may reach out and bring higher management into the process when a supervisor insists on pursuing a decision that HR has recommended against (for cause). But line management at some level actually must make the decision, not HR staff. Whether or not line management readily listens to its advisors in human resources depends largely on their professionalism and track record in making solid recommendations.

## The Human Resource Reporting Relationship

In virtually all agencies, the HR department reports to top management. Generally, human resources should report to the level that has authority over all of the organization's line or operating functions. At the institutional level, depending on the particular organizational scheme employed, the human resource manager might report to either the warden or the associate warden.

Human resources must be in a position to serve all of the organization's departments equally. Independence and impartiality are essential for human resources services to be provided to the whole organization. If the HR function is organized directly under the warden or a single associate warden, there is a relatively low risk that the organizational structure itself will bias the provision of services toward one department or portion of the organization. If the HR manager reports to one of several associate wardens, as is the case in many prisons, then extra care should be exercised to ensure that the other departments supervised by that associate warden do not receive any form of preferential treatment by HR staff. In such situations, the warden must be alert that this dynamic does not develop.

Also be wary of the occasional practice of duplicating HR functions within the same facility. For example, there is an argument to be made for the health services department to be delegated some HR functions (medical staff recruitment, for instance) while the institution's regular HR office serves all other departments. Although there may be advantages to be gained from this approach, splitting or subdividing other HR activities tends to create duplication of effort while increasing the organization's exposure to legal risks.

## The Human Resource Functions

There are almost as many possible combinations of human resource functions as there are HR departments. A great many activities that may be generally described as "administrative" can find their way into the human resource department. However, we will here be concerned with the significant activities or groups of functions that are often identified as the tasks of human resources.

**There are four basic human resource functions:**

- **Employment, often referred to as recruiting.** This is the overall process of acquiring employees—advertising and otherwise soliciting applicants, screening applicants, referring candidates to managers, checking references, extending offers of employment, and bringing employees into the organization.

- **Compensation, or wage and salary administration.** This is the process of creating and/or maintaining a wage structure and ensuring that it is administered fairly and consistently. Related to compensation, as well as to other HR task groupings, are job evaluation, the creation of job descriptions, and maintenance of a system of employee performance evaluation. When the correctional agency develops these standards and procedures, it is the local HR department's responsibility to administer them.

- **Benefits administration.** This activity is a natural offshoot of wage and salary administration, since benefits are actually a part of an employee's total compensation. Benefits administration consists of maintaining the organization's benefit structure and assisting employees in understanding and accessing their benefits.
- **Employee relations.** This activity may be generally described as dealing with problem employees and employees who have problems. It may range from handling employee complaints or appeals through processing disciplinary actions to arranging employee recognition and recreation activities.

One can see these four general activities at work in every human resource function regardless of size and overall scope. In a very large institution or correctional agency these may be separate sections within HR, each with its own head and its own staff and perhaps including subdivisions of those functions. In a very small institution, these are likely to be the tasks of a single person with multiple duties.

One additional basic function that may be encountered is labor-management relations. Although this may be a functional title that identifies a whole department in a very large prison, or simply a function of the human resource department, it is also a relatively generic label that applies to the maintenance of a continuing relationship with a bargaining unit, that is, a labor union. Again, depending on size, labor-management relations ordinarily is a subdivision of human resources or simply one of several responsibilities assigned to one person.

**Other activities may be found within human resources:**

- **Employee Assistance Program.** Often this is part of human resources, although it also can be managed by the institution's chief of mental health.
- **Training, for both managers and rank-and-file employees.** With the exception of continuing education for some specialties such as medical staff, formal training functions most often are part of human resources.
- **Payroll.** In the past this often has been part of personnel, but payroll functions also may be organized under the business office. However, a working relationship between HR and business office personnel has always been essential. In recent years, integrated

personnel/payroll systems have started a shift of the payroll function back toward HR.

### Rounding Out Your Knowledge

Using the foregoing paragraphs as a guide, determine exactly which functions are performed by your prison's human resource department. Further, take steps to attach a person's name to each function. You should seek to be in a position in which you understand how the HR department is organized, so you know generally who does what, who reports to whom, and who bears overall responsibility. Moreover, you should also make certain that you are aware of human resource functions (for example, employee assistance functions) that may belong elsewhere in your particular organization, so you can ensure that you always take certain matters to the correct department.

Next, take the time to make a list of the supervisory functions or activities you encounter that can lead you to seek information or assistance from human resources. The lists of most supervisors may have a great deal in common. They might include:

- **employment:** finding sufficient qualified candidates from whom to fill an open position
- **benefits:** providing information in response to employees' questions about benefits
- **compensation:** providing information responding to employees' pay questions
- **employee problems:** determining where to send a particular employee who is having difficulty with a specific problem
- **job descriptions/job evaluations:** determining how to proceed in assessing the grade or pay step of any particular position
- **policy interpretations:** determining the appropriate interpretation of personnel policy for any particular situation
- **disciplinary actions:** determining how to proceed in dealing with what appear to be violations of work rules
- **performance problems:** determining how to proceed in dealing with employees whose work performances are consistently below the agency's standards
- **performance appraisals:** securing guidance in completing appropriate performance appraisals and finding out how much one can depend on human resources to coordinate the overall appraisal process

This list can doubtless be expanded. One helpful method of expanding your list includes leafing through your agency's personnel policy manual and employee handbook; this process will bring to mind additional areas of concern that you encounter in your work.

## PUTTING THE HUMAN RESOURCE DEPARTMENT TO WORK

### A Universal Approach

The first, simplest, and most valuable advice to be offered for getting the most out of your human resource department involves the age-old two-step process of initiation and follow-up. It is but a slight variation on a practice followed by most successful supervisors.

The successful supervisor knows that any task worth assigning is worth having a specific deadline. The "do-it-when-you-have-a-chance" or "when-you-think-about-it" approach breeds procrastination, delay, and inaction. An assignment—necessarily a well-thought-out, specific assignment—must be accompanied by a target for completion, a deadline which, though it may be generous or even loose, leaves no doubt as to expected completion. And when that deadline arrives and no results have been forthcoming, the supervisor then exercises the most important part of the total process—faithful follow-up. Faithful follow-up is the key; the behavior of supervisor who always waits a week beyond the deadline is telling the employees that they always have at least an extra week.

Anything needed from the human resource department should be addressed in a similar manner. The process might be summarized as follows.

- Make certain the issue is part of human resources' responsibilities, and determine, if possible, who in the department would be the best person to approach on the topic.
- Be specific in your question or need to facilitate a specific response.
- If you make contact and convey your need to the appropriate person and the answer is not immediately available, ask when an answer will be supplied.
- If the promised reply date occurs later than your legitimate need date, negotiate a deadline agreeable to both you and human resources.
- If your agreed-upon deadline arrives and you have not received your answer, follow up with the department. Follow up politely,

follow up diplomatically, but follow up faithfully. Never let an un-answered deadline pass without following up.

This process should be applied not only to problems, issues, and concerns that you as a supervisor would consider taking to human resources. It should especially be applied to questions and concerns that your employees bring to you. If an employee's question in any way involves human resource concerns, and if you are unable to respond appropriately, then you need to take the question to HR as though it were your own.

## Some Specific Action Steps

Any number of supervisory needs presents opportunities to put the human resource department to work. The more frequently encountered of these include the following.

### Finding New Employees

There are any number of points in the employment process at which the supervisor and HR must work together. Fulfill your end of the working relationship, and expect HR staff to fulfill theirs. Tracking vacancies in each department ordinarily is an HR function, but you as a supervisor also need to monitor vacancies and give the HR department prompt notice when you become aware that a vacancy is about to occur.

Screening prospective job candidates is another area in which supervisors and HR staff must work together. For example, if none of the five candidates HR has supplied for a particular position is truly appropriate, ask for more; do not settle for only what you are given, if what you are given is not enough. (For your part of the arrangement, do not continue to call for more applicants in your search for the "perfect" candidate if you have already seen two or three who meet the posted requirements of the job.) Also, stay in touch with HR concerning extending offers, checking references, and scheduling pre-employment physical examinations and starting dates. Do not be unreasonable: recognize that these activities take time. By making your interest and attention known, however, you will encourage completion of the process.

### Bringing Job Descriptions Up to Date

The supervisor ordinarily has a significant responsibility in maintaining current job descriptions for the department. The HR department usually also has the responsibility for associating a pay level with each job and for maintaining official files of up-to-date job descriptions. Your part is best done within your department; to the extent possible, job descriptions should be written by those who do the work and those who supervise the work. However, if you deliberately involve HR, it will contribute consistency to job descriptions and ensure each job is placed on the proper pay scale. Once again, your visible interest in the process will encourage timely completion of HR's activities.

### Disciplining Employees

Regardless of the extent of human resource involvement in processing a disciplinary action, that department does not actually take the action. The HR department disciplines nobody (except employees of the HR department, as necessary). Any employee deserving of disciplinary action must be disciplined through his or her immediate chain of command. In most organizations the supervisor is required to submit proposed disciplinary actions through the human resources department before implementation. Whether or not this is so for your organization, you need to take your best assessment to HR and ask for advice. And you should expect to receive sound advice—whether a single recommendation (complete with rationale for doing so) or multiple alternatives, each with its own explanation of possible consequences. The decision is theoretically all yours, and if it is a poor decision, you probably will bear the brunt of the consequences. Do not let HR avoid responsibility by failing to provide specific direction; insist on complete HR input in deciding upon disciplinary action.

### Evaluating Employees

One of the most important tasks of the supervisor is the appraisal of employee performance. No formal system of performance appraisal can function consistently throughout the agency without the central guidance usually provided by human resources staff. Although you can certainly evaluate your employees' performance alone, you can do a much more consistently acceptable job of evaluation with HR involvement.

The HR department should automatically provide forms, instructions, schedules, and reminders throughout the process. However, if the HR department is not always on top of the supervisor's employee appraisal needs, then the supervisor should take certain steps.

- Keep track of scheduled review dates and ask HR for forms and timetables.
- Ask for periodic instruction in how to apply rating criteria, especially if criteria have changed and refresher instruction is not supplied.
- Advise human resources of changing job requirements that may affect rating criteria.
- Periodically ask HR for rating profile information (if the agency or institution maintains it) that can reveal patterns in the supervisor's rating practices, show whether or not those patterns are changing with time, and show how this specific supervisor's rating patterns compare with those of other supervisors.

### Dealing with Training Needs

If the human resource department has responsibility for any kinds of employee training—and in most prisons this is so—do not wait for needed training to come to you. If there are training needs in your work group, take them to HR. If, for example, you feel several of your employees require training in basic inmate management techniques, take a well-developed request for meeting that need to human resources, negotiate a timetable for providing the training, and offer to become personally involved in the training. (With appropriate HR involvement, every supervisor is a potentially valuable instructor in some topic.)

The foregoing suggestions are offered primarily to convey a general idea to the supervisor: the human resource department exists as a service function for all employees. It remains for the supervisor to take each legitimate personnel-related need to HR and to ask for—and expect—an honest response.

### WANTED: WELL-CONSIDERED INPUT

The most effective human resource departments are not one-way dispensers of information and assistance; they interact with managers and respond to the needs of the prison's work force. However, the HR department can go only so far in anticipating needs and meeting them within the limits of available resources. To be fully effective, the HR department must learn of employee needs from employees and supervisors and must in turn go to top management with solid proposals for meeting the most pressing needs.

Some employees, although usually a minority, take their own questions, concerns, and suggestions to the human resource department. However, many employees will never do so for themselves; their needs, whether conveyed through words, actions, or attitudes, must find their way to human resources and eventually to top management through their supervisors.

**Among the kinds of information that the supervisor should pass to human resources are:**

- reactions to various personnel policies, especially when policies seem to have become less appropriate under changing conditions
- employee attitudes concerning pay and benefits, especially perceptions of inequities and alleged instances of unfair treatment
- complaints—and compliments as well—about employee services such as locker room conditions, quality of uniforms provided by the agency, or other related issues
- comments on the appropriateness of various employee benefits, and on benefits needed or desired
- potential changes in methods of acquiring, maintaining, or retaining employees that might afford the agency a competitive edge in those areas

## UNDERSTANDING WHY AS WELL AS WHAT

It is relatively easy to determine what human resources as a department does within the organization. However, it is necessary to go beyond what and develop an appreciation of why this department does what it does and why human resources sometimes must take a position opposing a line department's position.

Consider the case of the supervisor who decides termination is the solution to resolve a seemingly unending series of difficulties with an employee. The supervisor appeals to the human resources department to agree to termination. The supervisor says, "I simply can't do any more with this person. He's chronically late in spite of all my warnings. His absenteeism disrupts staffing; he uses up his sick time as fast as he earns it. His attitude is absolutely terrible; he's been overly aggressive with inmates and rude to inmate families during visits; and the way he talks to me borders on insubordination most of the time. His people skills are marginal and he's a disruptive influence when he's working housing units. I've been patient longer than anyone has the right to expect of me, but nothing has changed. I want to terminate him."

As often occurs in such circumstances, the human resource practitioner hearing the supervisor's request briefly reviews the employee's background and immediately recommends against termination. This may disappoint and upset the supervisor and leave him displeased with the HR department. He may complain, with some justification, that he ought to be supported in his efforts to get rid of an unsatisfactory employee. He may well view HR as obstructive, adopt an adversarial position, and perhaps even attempt to solicit the assistance of his own higher management to oppose the human resource position.

Why would human resources be automatically protective of an employee like that described above? The differences lie in, first, the supervisor's perspective versus the human resource perspective, and second, the frequently cited employee personnel file—"the record."

The supervisor is legitimately focused on the good of the prison's operation at the unit or department level, and the employee in question threatens it. Human resources' view conflicts with the supervisor's in two ways. In micro terms, HR must be concerned with the rights of the individual employee; in macro terms, HR must be concerned with the good of the total organization. The organization is of course no more than the sum total of a number of individuals. But in focusing on the total organization, the HR perspective is different than that of the supervisor—who is concerned with more than one employee but much less than the total workforce.

Then there is "the record" to consider. In this case it turns out that all of the supervisor's warnings concerning tardiness were unrecorded oral warnings. Likewise, there are no warnings on absenteeism, except for a single written warning that is too old to be effective in a current disciplinary action. No other warnings appear in the personnel file, and although in the mind of the supervisor this employee has always been less than satisfactory, the personnel file includes several performance evaluations which—although not glowing with praise—suggest at least minimally acceptable performance. In short, there is no basis for termination except in the supervisor's mind.

In regard to problems such as that just described, the HR department is:

- defending the rights of the individual, not only because doing so arises from a sense of fairness but also because there are many laws requiring the agency to do so
- protecting the agency from numerous legal risks

Whenever there is a risk that an employee problem or complaint will be taken outside of the agency, it is best to think of any criticism of employee conduct or performance in a single light: If it is not in "the record," it never happened. Except in instances of termination for major infractions calling for immediate discharge (and these days even many of these actions are successfully challenged), a discharge must be backed up with a written trail describing all that occurred. It is legally necessary to be able to demonstrate that the employee was given every reasonable opportunity to correct the offending behavior or improve the unsatisfactory performance.

## EMPHASIS ON SERVICE

As a staff function, human resources is organized as a service activity. Service departments provide no inmate supervision or productivity in the prison factory; they do not directly advance the work of the organization. However, because they support the performance of the organization's work, they become necessary in a practical sense. For example, if a pure service such as the facility maintenance shop did not exist, the prison's physical plant would gradually self-destruct. Similarly, without human resources to see to the maintenance of the work force, the overall suitability and capability of that work force would steadily erode.

Recognize human resources for what it is: an essential service function required to help the organization run as efficiently as possible. Learn what the HR department does, and especially learn why the department does what it does. Provide input to the human resource department. Forge a continuing working relationship with the HR department, making it clear that you expect service from this essential department. Challenge the HR department to do more, to do better, and to continually improve service. Put the human resource department to work for you and your employees.

---

### EXERCISE 15–1: WHERE CAN HUMAN RESOURCES HELP?

Review the human resource functions as outlined in this chapter. Within each major function, identify the subfunctions that involve you as a supervisor. For example, under the employment or recruiting function, you will probably not locate or screen applicants, but you will interview job candidates. As another example, you will have no responsibility for administering benefits, but you will often be expected to come up with answers to your employees' questions about benefits.

When you have generated a complete list of human resource subfunctions that require your involvement, determine who in your human resource department is most involved with each and associate one or two names with each subfunction. Most supervisors' lists will be likely to include selection, interviewing, answering benefit questions, doing performance evaluations, and taking disciplinary action. This can become the basis of a reference list to help familiarize you with the individual specialties and strengths of the organization's human resource practitioners.

As an additional activity, review your list of pertinent human resource subfunctions against Chapter 24, "The Supervisor and the Law." For each human resource subfunction with which you are involved, indicate the major areas of legislation (for example, "antidiscrimination laws") and the specific laws (for example, "Immigration Reform and Control Act") that concern your performance of the subfunction.

---

## CASE 15–1: A FAVOR—OR A TRAP?

You are the receiving and discharge department supervisor in a medium-security prison. One morning well before the start of your department's normal working hours, you were enjoying a cup of coffee in the employees' lounge/locker room, sorting out some notes on your plans for the day, when you were approached by Cerese Carter, one of your two most senior employees in terms of service. She seated herself across from you and said, "There's something going on in the department that you need to know about, and I've waited way too long to tell you." Cerese proceeded to tell you ("In strictest confidence, please, I know you'll understand why.") that another long-term employee, Marge Jenson, had been making a great many derogatory comments about you throughout the department and generally questioning your competence.

For nearly ten minutes Cerese showered you with criticism of you, your management style, and your approach to individual employees, all attributed to Marge Jenson. On exhausting her litany, Cerese proclaimed that she did not ordinarily "carry tales" but that she felt you "had a right to know, for the good of the department—but please don't tell her I said anything."

Although Cerese's comments were filled with "she saids" and "she dids," (she being Marge) and generally twice-told tales without connection to specific incidents, something extremely disturbing clicked in your mind while you were listening. Recently your posted departmental schedule had been altered, without your knowledge, in a way indicating that someone had tried to copy your handwriting and forge your initials. Two separate, seemingly unconnected comments by Cerese together revealed that one of only two people could have altered your schedule. Those two people were Marge Jenson—and Cerese Carter herself.

As Cerese finally fell silent, you were left with an intense feeling of disappointment. You wondered if you could ever again fully trust two of your key employees.

## Questions

1. What should be your immediate response to Cerese Carter? Why?
2. Do you believe you have the basis on which to proceed with disciplinary action?
3. How can the human resource department help you in these circumstances?

# PART IV

# The Supervisor and the Task

## CHAPTER 16

# Decisions, Decisions

*As a rule. . . the person who has the most information will have the greatest success in life.*

*—Benjamin Disraeli*

*All decisions should be made as low as possible in the organization. The Charge of the Light Brigade was ordered by an officer who wasn't there looking at the territory.*

*—Robert Townsend*

## Chapter Objectives

☞ Establish a direct relationship between the amount of effort going into a decision and the potential consequences of that decision.

☞ Identify the elements of the basic decision-making process and describe the steps followed in rational decision-making.

☞ Define constraints and identify the various forms in which they appear.

☞ Establish perspectives on risk and uncertainty in decision-making.

☞ Discuss the implications of the "no-decision option."

☞ Review decision-making authority and responsibility.

## A FACT OF LIFE

Decision-making is a fact of life for correctional managers and nonsupervisors in both working and nonworking situations. We all make decisions every day, sometimes a great many of them. Many of these decisions are small and inconsequential and are made automatically or very nearly so. Some are larger, potentially significant, and require considerably more time and effort.

The potential consequences generally govern the amount of effort we put into making any particular decision. This stands to reason; decisions involving appreciable risk should not be made lightly, nor can they usually be made with speed and ease. A decision to authorize an evening educational class for inmates who work during the day is far different than a decision to determine the best way to resolve a hostage situation. Lee Iacocca said, "If I had to run up in one word what makes a good manager, I'd say decisiveness. You can use the fanciest computers to gather the numbers, but in the end you have to set a timetable and act."

Most of us are self-programmed to make some decisions, especially small decisions of little consequence and those we make on a regular basis. You probably do not consciously think of yourself as making a decision when you decide what to have for lunch or which shoes you will wear to work, but you nevertheless are following the basic decision-making process: You are receiving information, forming and comparing alternatives and selecting one of these, and translating your choice into action.

The more often we make certain kinds of decisions, the better we get at it. For instance, if you are the manager of the security department of a new institution that is about to open, your job could include ordering chemical agents and munitions for the armory and towers. If you had no other guidance (in the form of headquarters procurement specifications, for instance), then you may have gathered information about several brands and carefully evaluated it for cost and other features. This could have taken you a significant amount of time, and you might have switched to a second or perhaps even a third brand later on as you accumulated information based on experience during training exercises or even in actual usage. However, chances are that each time you repeated the ordering process the task became quicker and easier. Eventually you may have reached a point where your decision to order these chemicals and munitions became no more than the simple act of reordering a product that you had already accepted as meeting your needs. Similarly, you become self-programmed to make many decisions that come your way periodically. Regardless of preprogramming, however, and regardless of the existence of comprehensive policies and procedures, as a supervisor you are going to face numerous situations that require original decision-making.

Policies and procedures never cover everything. What, then, do you do when you discover that a necessary decision cannot be made "by the book," as often is the case in prison. What do you do when no one is immediately available to tell you what you should do? When a situation requiring action is left up to you—and there are plenty of these in supervision—you have to take some kind of action. Your supervisory position requires you to exercise judgment as to whether the situation is in fact your problem and to exercise judgment in arriving at a solution.

## THE BASIC DECISION-MAKING PROCESS

The six elements of the basic decision-making process are (1) identifying the problem, (2) gathering information, (3) analyzing information and arranging it into alternatives, (4) choosing an alternative, (5) implementing the chosen alternative, and (6) following up on implementation.

Regardless of the scope or potential impact of any particular decision, most of the foregoing elements are present to some extent in every decision-making situation. In minor situations the problem or need may be self-evident and require no attention beyond simple recognition. You still gather information, analyze it and form alternatives, and make a choice. Of course in simple, repetitive situations—deciding what shoes to wear to work, for instance—your preprogramming may compress these steps considerably. Implementation is always present, since your decision is nothing without it—you must eventually make a choice and put the shoes on. Follow-up is also always present, fleeting though it may be—do the shoes really match the outfit, and does that little scuff mark show?

As decision-making situations grow in scope and complexity, however, the importance of each element of the process looms greater.

### Identifying the Problem

Before tackling any problem requiring a decision, it is necessary to consider whether you are dealing with a real problem, something that is based on fact and not the result of opinion, misinterpretation, or bias. Do not simply "jump into" every apparent problem that comes along; investigate to determine whether it is indeed a problem deserving your attention.

Look also at the nature of the apparent problem. Is it a unique situation, not previously encountered and not covered by existing policies and procedures? Is it a common, recurring problem, one for which specific procedures exist? Is it perhaps self-solving, one of those rare but nevertheless genuine situations that correct themselves when left alone?

Also be mindful of whether the issue you are confronting really is the problem or is simply a symptom of the real problem, which is hidden. Finding a cut bar is a problem all right, but it also is an indicator of a larger problem—an attempt to escape, to break into the commissary, or to engage in some other unauthorized activity. Being led astray by symptoms, which are the obvious, surface indications of trouble, is a hazard inherent in supervisory decision-making. Effective treatment of a symptom may lead to immediate improvement. However, the symptom may soon reappear, suggesting that what you thought was the problem may not be the problem at all. If, for instance, a backlog occurs in the sentence computation process, you may feel the need to do something about it. Perhaps you authorize overtime or give the employee involved some temporary help. In a few days the backlog is gone and the computation specialist is current with incoming work. A few days later, however, you notice that a backlog is again growing; there is a three-day, then a five-day accumulation of uncomputed sentences. In reducing the backlog you treated a symptom; the return of the backlog suggests the problem is elsewhere, perhaps in staffing itself, distribution of work, inmate commitment patterns, or somewhere else.

You cannot always tell if a symptom is a symptom until you deal with it once and it returns. However, by scratching beneath the surface indications of trouble, you can often determine where the real difficulty lies before you on corrective action.

### Gathering Information

Volumes have been written on this and the next stage of the decision-making process. Elaborate quantitative approaches to decision-making concentrate on the collection of information and the arrangement of this information into alternative choices.

Colin Powell, General, U.S. Army (Retired) once said, "Information is the lifeblood of an organization. If you're not on top of that information system, you're not dealing with the lifeblood of the organization." Essentially, your task is to gather enough information to give you some degree of assurance that you are making a decision consistent with reasonable risks. Your broad objective in gathering information is to gather everything that has a bearing on your decision-to-be, that is, everything you can collect considering the time and effort you can or should devote to the decision. You will be researching and observing with a specific purpose in mind: to get as much information as you feel you need to help you make an intelligent decision.

Recognize that often you will never have "enough" information and nobody can tell you how much information is enough. We can only suggest that your information-gathering effort should be consistent with the potential impact of the decision you have to make. If you happen to be selecting a new booking camera for the receiving and discharge area, you may spend a great deal of time talking with salespeople and study-ing the prices, operating costs, and features of many different ma-chines. You might talk to staff in other institutions who use various cameras. Your activity could consume a number of hours spread out over days or weeks, and this effort may be justified because of the amount of money at risk. However, if you happen to be trying to decide what brand of pencils to buy for the office, you had best not spend three days gathering data about brands and prices.

In gathering information for decisions, work with facts and not with opinions. Much so-called information comes to you directly or indirectly from other people. As you gather your decision-making building blocks, take care to separate the factual from the subjective. While researching the booking camera issue, ask staff at other institutions for specific figures on their patterns of film usage, frequency of equipment break-down, and other factors that are important to your operation. Facts and opinions both may be useful, but the latter will more readily lead you astray.

### Analyzing Information and Arranging It into Alternatives

This, along with gathering information, constitutes a cyclic process. You will find you are arranging and evaluating bits and pieces of infor-mation while you are still collecting more information. You tend to "fill in the gaps" as you go along, going back for more information whenever questions arise or you discover weaknesses in your data. This cyclic process can go on for quite some time in decisions of considerable im-pact; you want as much information as you can acquire when the poten-tial consequences are significant.

However, this is the stage where the process begins to break down in the hands of some so-called decision makers. Projecting the impression of being conscientious, cautious, and thorough, some people continue gathering more and more information and keep refining the alterna-tives further and further, taking forever to make the decision. As al-ready suggested, however, in a decision of importance you will never truly have "enough" information. You may never reach the stage where you are 100 percent comfortable taking a risk based on the information you have in hand. However, you cannot "if" a problem to a solution; somewhere along the way you must take a stand, accept some risk, and decide. Of course, the higher the degree of risk, the more information you will want, but even in a riot or hostage-taking situation, there will come a time when—often still lacking all of the information you really want—you will have to make a decision.

Any number of different kinds of information will greet you when you are researching a problem. Buying a booking camera you will learn about cost, size, operations, service and maintenance, warranties, color, and a dozen other factors; you may even learn about how computers and digitalizing processes can allow you to store inmate pictures on computer disks and then use them for nonbooking purposes. The cost and organizational implications of a decision like this are high. But even in low-cost activities, like buying pencils, you will encounter price, brand, color, hardness, and so on. It is the same in almost every decision-making situation: A number of factors are present, and all may or may not have a bearing on your choice.

The organization's needs, the department's needs, the inmates' needs, and your needs and preferences all have a bearing on the decisions you make. However, it is not often possible to achieve complete satisfaction of all needs and preferences. For instance, you might like a booking camera that gives you the lowest operating cost and the longest warranty, but it turns out that machine A has the lowest operating cost and machine C has the best warranty. You then find yourself in the position of having to make smaller decisions along the way. You are led to discover that trade-offs are necessary between and among decision factors and that you will settle for less in regard to the factors that mean the least to you for the sake of achieving satisfaction on certain other factors.

Ultimately your decision factors will be arranged into a number of alternatives, from which you will select one. The number of alternatives may be clearly limited and well-defined. Sometimes, however, the number of alternatives is up to you. If there are 5 brands of 12 gauge shotgun ammunition on the market and 8 makes of booking cameras available, you should not limit yourself to looking at only one or two possibilities. Neither, however, can you afford to perform an exhaustive analysis of every possible choice. Rather, you will scan the field of available choices using some broad criteria and concentrate on developing perhaps three or four of the more appealing choices as specific alternatives. You may look at several possibilities along the way but discard some because certain constraints rule them unsuitable (more about constraints later).

## Choosing an Alternative

Left with several reasonably well-defined alternatives, you make your decision by picking the one you feel best fills your needs and meets your preferences. It is a matter of comparing the possible choices and taking the one that "comes to the top"—both objectively and subjectively—for you, the decision maker. This becomes your solution (or at least your recommendation) and you should immediately question it from several directions:

- Does this answer deal with cause (the problem) rather than simply with effect (a symptom)?
- Does this answer have the effect of creating policy or establishing precedent, and as such should it be formally expressed as a guide for future decisions?
- Will this solution, if implemented, have adverse effects on any other aspects of the prison's operation?

### Implementing the Chosen Alternative

Implementation is action, putting the decision to work. Without implementation a decision is no decision at all; it is simply an academic exercise in "What if we did this?" A true decision is both choice and action.

From this point forward we could repeat, with added emphasis, most of what was said in Chapter 4 about the basic management functions. Planning, organizing, directing, coordinating, and controlling all come into active play in the implementation of a decision and in the follow-up.

### Following Up on Implementation

Follow-up is generally the weakest part of the decision-making process. Employees resist change for many reasons. Old habits persist, new habits are difficult to form, and, most important here, conditions surrounding the decision may change. The moment you obtain specific information and commit it to paper, it starts to become obsolete. Needs and preferences change, products change, people change, and the environment changes. Time goes on, and the more of it that passes—and with significant decision-making the lag between choice and complete implementation can be considerable—the more change is likely to accrue. You will need to clarify instructions, assess timing and make adjustments as necessary, and in general supervise the entire implementation effort.

During implementation be open to employee suggestions. Allow yourself to learn from the way implementation appears to be going. Do not be afraid to admit an error; be willing to reverse or withdraw the decision if experience shows it is turning out to have been a bad one. Sometimes, through no fault of your own, the alternative that appeared best on paper will go sour in practice, and it makes little sense to continue pushing a poor choice. On the other hand, however, if partial implementation only assures you that your decision was the best you could make under the circumstances, then stick to it and see it all the way through.

## CONSTRAINTS

Anything that is constrained is limited in some way. In decision-making, constraints are those limiting conditions that rule out certain alternatives as possible or desirable choices. Once identified, constraints let you know how far you may go in considering certain alternatives; they tell you what is practical and what is not.

The constraints commonly encountered in supervisory decision-making involve time, money, quality, personalities, and politics. Other factors such as limitations of physical space and shortages of various material resources may also appear as constraints; however, since it is possible to build space and buy material, these seeming constraints reduce themselves to limitations of money.

### Time

Everything done in the organization takes time. It takes time to process a request for an FBI fingerprint check, escort an inmate to an outside hospital, order and obtain ammunition from a supplier, design and build a new segregation unit, organize to react to a riot, perform a disciplinary hearing, and accomplish thousands of other activities. Time may be a critical factor in a decision, or it may matter not at all. If you are still wondering, for instance, about what brand of pencils to buy, it may not matter at all that you need to wait an extra week to get the best deal on the preferred brand. However, if you are deciding on alternative procedures for reacting to a hostage situation, you may be limited to considering only those alternatives that can be successfully activated within a tightly restricted amount of time. As it relates to health, safety, and the quality of inmate care—as it relates, in fact, to life and death—time is a key constraint in many supervisory decisions made in prison.

In situations when it may not be critical, time can be considered flexible: You may trade off timeliness with other factors. When time does not matter, you may choose to complete a given task more slowly for the sake of greater convenience or lower cost.

It is necessary to assess the decision situation for the importance of time in the outcome. Once realistic timing is determined, the alternatives shaping up as well outside the limit begin to rule themselves out.

## Money

Money—the full cost of implementing a decision—is a common constraint. Often the limits are clear, defined by the amount of money you know is available. For instance, when you go to lunch with just five dollars in your pocket you know that all meals costing more than five dollars are ruled out by financial constraints. The money constraint can also be put there by someone who is making decisions of another kind or from another perspective. For example, you would like to buy a new computer for your department, but your immediate supervisor says, "No, it's not in the budget, we have no money available, and you'll have to make the typewriter last another year." Although there might be money available in the organization, someone else has made a decision on the relative worth of your proposal versus other uses for the money, so you are fully as constrained as though the money did not exist at all.

In short, any time an otherwise workable alternative costs more than you have or can raise, you are subject to financial constraints and that alternative is effectively ruled out.

## Quality

Quality—as demonstrated in the form of effective safety, security, and inmate programs—is always a primary consideration in the operation of a prison, and it can be just as great a constraint as time or money. Generally, when we make decisions affecting inmate programs and services, we are faced with the necessity of considering only those alternatives that do not compromise the quality of the prison's safety and security systems. Often the "quick and dirty" solution to a problem is clearly the best in terms of time, money, or both; however, if quality of the prison's core functions (staff and inmate safety and security of the institution) is likely to suffer, then the solution is unacceptable.

## Personalities

Although personalities may not strike you as presenting legitimate constraints on decision alternatives, they nevertheless must be reckoned with. We must try to avoid getting tied too tightly to the belief that "people shouldn't be that way." The fact of the matter is that people are "that way," and the constraints presented by personalities can be fully as limiting as absolute financial constraints.

There are managers who will not buy a particular product that analysis shows to be the best available simply because they do not like the salesperson. Some employees will not work well with other employees because of personality clashes, so an alternative that might otherwise be the best solution may not work at all. Also, some people are more resistant to change than others; some are more solidly attached to old habits or have strong tendencies toward doing things their own way as opposed to anyone else's way.

Although personality constraints are usually not the most powerful forces shaping a decision, they are nevertheless important. People are themselves a key factor to consider in analyzing alternatives. Approval and implementation are accomplished only through people, and people's acceptance of the decision and their ability to work with it are fully as important as the elements of the decision itself. This "people" consideration flows into the labor-management arena, as well; if there are clear historical or current indications that the union will oppose a course of action, that fact will have implications for choosing, modifying, or abandoning an option.

## Politics

Politics may not strike you as a legitimate constraint on a decision. However, the political implications of a decision are fully as real as the personality factors, and they often have far greater impact.

While we will not discuss how partisan politics might affect high-level administrators in state agencies (in terms of programmatic decisions and job tenure), that factor certainly is a reality in many correctional systems.

In the ideal, prisons are organizations of people (employees) with a common purpose. The prison serves society, which itself is a body of people having certain wants, needs, and preferences. Within both prison and society are many subgroups organized along various social, economic, professional, vocational, and other lines, and each of these groups has its own desires. Hardly a supervisor has not said at one time or another, "Politics shouldn't matter in running the organization," but in reality political considerations do matter.

Politics (the word carries a negative connotation for many of us) is frequently described as "the art of the possible." Specifically in correctional organizations it is the art of the possible given the actions and characteristics of all the various groups involved. For instance, a particular decision that serves the financial interests of the agency may alienate the employees. A decision that may appear good for the state's budget, a personnel freeze for example, may be seen as bad for the prison and would thus alienate its staff. Within the organization, a decision that serves the needs of the security department may unavoidably make the job of the food service department more difficult and thus alienate those employees. A decision that serves the needs of the business office may legitimately upset relations with the maintenance staff.

This is not to say that political considerations should rule or that "pressure groups" should get their way simply because they are larger, stronger, or more vocal than other groups. However, it is necessary to consider political implications because a decision that is made in the face of the strongest opposition, whether that opposition is justified or not, generally requires far more in the way of resources and effort to implement. The foregoing examples show that playing "politics" often is a realistic acknowledgment of the fact that you have to find ways to accommodate to the legitimate needs and concerns of others in the organization, or even outside the organization. In short, it is the price we have to pay for functioning within a network of people and organizational entities.

## Absolute and Practical Constraints

Constraints may be absolute or practical in nature. An absolute constraint clearly defines a limit beyond which you cannot go. For instance, if you are choosing a booking camera and $2,000 is the absolute extent of what you can spend, then $2,000 is the limit for any camera you seriously consider. More often than not, however, constraints present themselves by limiting the practicality of a decision. A certain condition becomes a constraint because it renders an alternative impractical under the circumstances.

For example, if you decide it is important to have two particular functions located adjacent to each other in the booking area, you might be faced with considerable expense for altering physical layout. You may then look at other possibilities: There may be space available across the hall, in an adjacent room, or on the second floor of the receiving and discharge building. You can function under any of these alternatives, but you will obviously do better with some than with others. It may be that the closer together you bring the two functions (saving staff escort time in the process), the more financial resources you will consume implementing the decision. Given that finances are limited, but that you are still trying to achieve reasonable operating efficiency, you develop trade-offs and settle perhaps for the second or third most desirable choice. This kind of decision may be driven by the structure of your budget; you may have no construction/renovation funds but ample salary or overtime funds. Many constraints, then, are in effect not saying "You absolutely can't do this" but are rather saying "You're going to pass a point where you shouldn't do this because it's no longer practical"—like locating one function next door even though it costs a fortune, or locating it elsewhere because it costs nothing in terms of construction or renovation.

We need to assess the constraints inherent in the situation realistically, recognize our limitations, and focus our attention on realistic, practical alternatives. Alternatives that lie beyond the bounds of the constraints we have identified are really not alternatives at all.

## RISK, UNCERTAINTY, AND JUDGMENT

Some decision-making theorists speak of something called "perfect information." This is a state that exists only when you know all there is to know about all aspects of every available alternative. Some would argue that if there truly were such a thing as perfect information, there would be no decision at all: The "decision" would have made itself because the only true alternative would be self-evident.

Because there is no such thing as perfect information, there are always elements of risk and uncertainty in a decision-making situation. Risk is there because something may be lost—be it time, money, effectiveness, or perhaps life itself—if the wrong decision is made. Uncertainty also exists; since you do not know everything about all aspects of the situation and have no guarantees that things will come out right, you do not know that your choice is the right one.

One of our major objectives in the decision-making process is to minimize risk and uncertainty by learning as much as practical about each decision-making situation. Since risk and uncertainty are always present, there is always the need for judgment in decision-making. Decisions do not make themselves: people make decisions. All of our efforts at gathering and analyzing information, as well as all sophisticated quantitative decision-making techniques, are efforts to reduce the extent of pure randomness in decision-making. For instance, someone lines up three booking cameras for you and asks, "Which one do you want?" You might make a purely haphazard decision by pointing and saying, "I'll take the middle one." The probability that you have made the "right" decision is literally one-third, based on a random choice of three available alternatives, so you experience a two-thirds chance of being "wrong." However, if you analyze all the data you can obtain about the three cameras and allow your judgment to be influenced by quantitative information, although you might never be absolutely sure you are making the right decision, you could reduce the chance of being wrong to considerably less than two-thirds.

In the final analysis many decisions will be wrong—regardless of the amount of quantitative information involved. Your objective is to try to refine your judgment by learning as much as you can about the alternatives.

## THE NO-DECISION OPTION

In even the simplest of decision-making situations there are always at least two choices: to decide or not to decide. In the no-decision option you "decide not to decide." This does not have to be a consciously made decision, but it often occurs by default through procrastination. Taking no action on a problem amounts to the exercise of the no-decision option.

Appreciate that whether the no-decision option is exercised by choice or through procrastination, it is still a decision. Frequently it is the decision with the most potentially far-reaching consequences; making no decision in a riot situation would be disastrous. But in less dramatic circumstances, all too often we adopt an attitude, either consciously or unconsciously, that suggests: "If I'm really quiet maybe it'll go away." Sometimes it does indeed go away and things get better. However, things usually do not get better. Murphy's Law reminds us that, If anything can go wrong, it will.[1]

## THE RANGE OF DECISIONS

Decision-making situations may range from the highly (but rarely totally) objective, with plenty of factual information on which to decide, to the purely subjective decision. The decision-making process described in this chapter applies to all decisions; the differences lie in the kinds of information we use to develop alternatives.

We can usually be more comfortable with so-called objective decisions. We have facts, figures, and other data to work with. We compare prices, statistics, hours, positions, or some other specific indicators and make our choices. Orderly approaches to decision-making are possible, and improved facility at making such decisions comes with practice.

The highly subjective decision is another matter. Little or no data are available. We must make our choices based on rules and regulations, policies, procedures, and precedents, and very often on our basic sense of what is right or wrong, fair or unfair, or logical or illogical. Many personnel-related decisions fall in the area of the subjective. Here, too, improved decision-making ability comes largely through experience.

Many times decisions must be made under less than ideal conditions. The decision maker must often act within a very limited time period. It is one thing to face a situation in which you have more than adequate time to develop and assess all workable alternatives; working on your annual budget, deciding in a relatively calm environment how to prioritize your funding could be an example of this kind of decision. It is another matter entirely to realize that undesirable consequences will result if a decision is not made by a deadline—and that this deadline does not leave time enough for reasonable investigation; responding to a hostage-taker's ultimatum is in this category. Unfortunately many supervisory decisions are pressure decisions (albeit less critical than the last example), and we have to accept the fact that limited time will squeeze us into a less than desirable pattern of analysis and action. In this regard, time may constrain not only the alternatives but the entire decision-making process.

## RESPONSIBILITY AND LEADERSHIP

An anonymous saying goes, It's all right to pull decisions out of a hat as long as you're wearing it. While this statement is only partially true (it is not usually all right to pull decisions out of a hat), the point about responsibility is well made. If you are assuming the authority to make a decision, an equivalent level of responsibility should accompany that authority. In making decisions for your department, you are consistent with your charge as a supervisor; you are responsible for the output and actions of your employees. However, it is not your place to make a decision with which employees other than your own or the supervisors of other departments must comply. In accepting a given amount of responsibility you ordinarily acquire decision-making authority consistent with that responsibility. No supervisor's decisions should exceed the limits of designated authority.

When you are delegating certain decision-making powers to some of your employees, be sure to extend authority and responsibility in equivalent amounts. Authority and responsibility are each weakened, if not negated entirely, by the absence of the other. How much decision-making authority you delegate to your employees will be a direct reflection of your leadership style. Generally the autocratic, or authoritarian, leader will prefer to retain all such authority while the participative leader will involve the employees in shaping and choosing decision alternatives.

## NO MAGIC FORMULA

It is possible to create valid guidelines for making many decisions. We do it all the time: We generate rules, regulations, policies, and procedures to guide our decisions. Institution emergency plans for responding to riots, escapes, and other crises are examples of how some structured guidance can be provided for the most complex situations. However, in spite of what a few determined bureaucratic leaders may believe, it is not possible to anticipate all contingencies and predetermine all decisions. It is not possible to cover everything with rules that say, in effect, "When this situation arises, apply this remedy." A riot response plan does not tell what to do in every type of riot, it only provides broad response parameters within which the on-site crisis manager makes specific decisions. Good supervisory decisions always will remain a matter of arriving at a proper emphasis on all decision elements through judgment based on facts and figures, knowledge, experience, advice, intuition, and insight.

---

## CASE 16–1: THE NEW BOOKING CAMERA

You are the receiving and discharge supervisor, and you must select a new booking camera for the department. The need for the camera has already been established, but you do not yet know which particular machine to select.

You have investigated several cameras and discarded a number of them because they do not take the kind of pictures you need or their costs were far above what your equipment budget would allow. You are left with three cameras from which to choose. All three will give you the kinds of photos you want, and all three will fit in the available space and are compatible with available power sources.

Camera A is available for $1,500. It must be purchased outright; it is not available on a lease. It will last at least five years in normal operation.

Camera B costs $3,000. It is also available on an eight-year lease at $500 per year. The estimated useful life of camera B is eight years.

Camera C costs $2,500. This camera is also available on a lease at a cost of $450 per year for a term of six years. Camera C has an estimated useful life of six years.

## Questions

1. Based on the very limited information you are given above, which of the three cameras might you select? Why?

2. Would you alter your decision if you were constrained by the necessity to limit expenditures because of a severe fiscal problem in the agency?

3. What additional information would you like to have before making a decision? (In other words, what important information has been omitted?)

---

## CASE 16–2: DECIDING UNDER PRESSURE

You are facilities manager of a large prison complex that includes four separate facilities.

Several times over the past few months the power plant supervisor (whose plant supplies steam and electricity to all four prisons in the complex) has mentioned to you that the maintenance workload and asbestos abatement problems on steam lines throughout the complex have been increasing and that he needs more help. His requests have never been more specific than "more help," nor have they been very strongly stated, so you have not looked into the situation.

However, on Monday of this week the supervisor came to you and said: "The plumbing crew needs an additional pipefitter and I need more funds now to deal with the abatement problem. I'm tired of waiting and tired of being overworked and worrying about a lawsuit on this asbestos thing. If something isn't done this week, you can find yourself somebody else to run the power plant."

## Questions

1. List at least three courses of action that may be open to you. What are the apparent disadvantages of each course of action you listed?
2. What hazards are presented by the way the "pressure" was introduced, and as facilities manager, how are you "at risk" in this situation?

## CHAPTER 17

# Management of Change: Resistant—Who, Me?

*Have no fear of change as such and, on the other hand, no liking for it merely for its own sake.*

*—Robert Moses*

*Progress occurs when courageous, skillful leaders seize the opportunity to change things for the better.*

*—Harry S. Truman*

## Chapter Objectives

☞ Establish a perspective on "change" as an unavoidable feature of the prison environment.

☞ Consider the effects of change on the pursuit of careers in corrections.

☞ Identify likely sources of employee resistance to change.

☞ Suggest guidelines for the supervisor to consider in managing change and minimizing employee resistance.

## THE NATURE OF CHANGE

### The Only Constant

We have heard it said over and over again that the only constant in this world is change, and often we do feel, with good reason, that there are few permanent features in our everyday world. It is also no secret that, in many ways, change has become the dominant force in our lives. Stability is a thing of the past. No longer can we rely on the same reliable characteristics of living, the same technology, and the same social structures and values from generation to generation. Consider, for example, the technology of daily living. Compare the era of the Roman Empire with the period of Colonial America and consider how little true change occurred in some 2,000 years.

Methods of transportation remained about the same—if one wanted to go somewhere one did so in a conveyance with two or four wheels pulled by an animal. Means of communication differed little in effectiveness if not in availability. (It is true that the impact of the printing press was felt in Colonial America, but its effects were not widespread because the general literacy rate remained low.) Whether one lived in the days of the Caesars or in the days of America's founders, cooking, heating, lighting, and plumbing would have been accomplished in about the same way. In both societies slavery was an accepted practice. It is perhaps a sad commentary on human development to point out that one area in which noticeable advancements were made was warfare (since gunpowder was introduced and refined along the way). It seems we had learned how to end life more efficiently without learning how to improve it appreciably.

### How Times Have Changed

At the beginning of the twentieth century, technological knowledge began to take hold as new inventions forever changed the way humans live. For example, the advent of the railroads dramatically lessened the distance and time required for moving goods and information. Such changes launched a period of steady and irreversible technological expansion. From about 1830 to the mid-1940s—approximately 115 years—total knowledge increased about five times over. While it may be argued that in the centuries prior to this there had been a slow accumulation of fundamental knowledge that finally catalyzed in the early 1800s, there is no doubt that the rate of change in society greatly accelerated at that point and will continue to do so.

It might seem surprising to learn that knowledge could multiply some five times within 115 years after remaining practically static for thousands and thousands of years. That increase, however, pales by comparison with the rate of knowledge growth experienced since about 1945. With the splitting of the atom and giant strides in electronics, technology has literally exploded. Recent technological growth has been such that it cannot be satisfactorily measured; new knowledge is accruing so rapidly on so many fronts that nothing will "stand still" long enough to be measured. We need not be overly impressed with the fivefold growth occurring in the 115 years preceding 1945; in the relatively brief time that has elapsed since the mid-1940s, technology, that is, total knowledge, has grown by a factor of thousands!

This is true of corrections as well. The availability of many types of sophisticated electronic perimeter detection systems—while foreshadowed by what old-timers will remember as a "snitch wire" on the wall—could hardly have been envisioned 25 years ago. Electronic monitoring for nondangerous offenders; elaborate computerized records systems; motion detection circuitry in closed circuit television monitors for isolated areas; remote medical diagnostic procedures such that inmates do not have to leave the prison to be examined by a physician; and teleconferencing technology for use in remote court hearings—these and many other new applications of modern technology have given corrections new opportunities to manage facilities more effectively and cost-efficiently.

The point to be appreciated is that most of what we must work with, and most of what we have, use, and enjoy was developed within the lifetimes of the generations now alive. And just as technology is not stable, neither are careers. We find ourselves faced with constant change as a way of life; we must continually upgrade our knowledge and skills simply to stay even with the advances made in our own fields.

### Is There Any Security?

We tend to equate stability with security. Yet we are undeniably among the first generations on earth to experience such massive change within our own lifetimes. In the past there was security in being unchanging and inflexible—in adopting a set of values, a pattern of living, and an approach to our work that we could expect to pursue for life. However, this behavior is no longer truly appropriate. The times in which we live suggest that our security now lies in our ability to be flexible and adaptable.

### INFLEXIBILITY OR RESISTANCE?

Failure to keep up with legitimate change in our fields can severely diminish our effectiveness as producers. If you are in the early stages of your career, it is entirely likely that a great deal of what you or your employees do will change dramatically in the next 20 years. Today's methods, techniques, and requirements will give way to new and generally more sophisticated counterparts. It will become more and more likely that the work you are called on to perform in the latter stages of your career will bear little resemblance to the duties you performed when you first entered corrections. This suggests that flexibility could be essential to your continued usefulness to your agency.

Most of us are resistant to change to some extent. Sometimes our resistance is rightly founded; restraint is a stabilizer, a needed counterbalance to frivolous disruption and change for the sake of change. However, much resistance has its basis in human nature alone and forces the basic needs of the individual to take precedence over the common good.

Think for a moment of what your own reactions may have been 25 years ago to a few seemingly wild "crackpot" ideas. Actually telling whether an offender is in his house or not from 20 miles away? ("Impossible.") Activate a closed circuit television monitor in a control room when there is movement in the field of view of the camera? ("Never work.") Depend on some microwave gadget to tell me if an inmate is about to hit the fence? (Not on your life! We need live officers in towers to do that!) All of these and many more are realities today.

Most of us are not instant believers in drastically new techniques or in the workability of marvelous new gadgets. Often it is because we do not have sufficient grasp of the principles on which these advancements are based, and just as often it is because we are reluctant to accept principles or theories that have yet to be proved. Perhaps we fail to appreciate that much of today's technology that we take for granted was, in its day, subject to resistance of almost destructive proportions. When the Wright Brothers were still trying to get their plane off the ground, many supposedly knowledgeable people of the day, engineers and scientists among them, were publicly labeling powered flight as impossible. More than once the telephone was branded an out-and-out fraud, with one critic going so far as to say that even if it were possible to transmit the human voice over metallic wires, the thing would be of no practical value. Likewise, the automobile and the railroad locomotive had their detractors.

We view such past attacks on today's accepted technology as similar to someone saying to Columbus: "Don't try it, Chris—you'll sail off the edge." However, when our initial response to a seemingly far-fetched idea is "it can't be done," we are reacting in the same way.

Consider how many ideas suggested on the job are disposed of on the spot with supervisors' reactions like: "There's no budget for that"; "The warden won't like it"; "The security staff would kill me"; "They won't let us do it"; and "The old way's good enough for me." We have so many ready-made "nays" that it often requires extremely compelling "yeas" to get through to us.

## SIGNIFICANT TRENDS DRIVING CHANGE IN CORRECTIONS

In addition to constant technological change and continuing social and legislative change, two significant trends are bringing about accelerated change in corrections. They are the courts and privatization.

The scope of litigation affecting prison operations has greatly broadened over the last two decades. From a former "hands-off" attitude toward corrections, the courts—and particularly federal courts—have become much more involved in the oversight and actual operation of many prisons. A great many positive gains have been made in the conditions of confinement at many prisons as a result of this escalation of judicial activity. However, this trend clearly has had an impact on the day-to-day management of many prisons and has reached deep into many agencies to affect the way line managers do their jobs.

Privatization is the second significant trend having an impact on corrections. The debate on this issue is complex and significant. Setting aside the philosophical debate over the role of government in the correctional function in our society, private corrections is proving to be valuable in that it offers an important population relief function for today's criminal justice system. But it also provides a contrasting view of how a traditionally public function can be performed. This challenges traditional prison administrators to review how they do their jobs and manage their resources. If a private correctional organization can provide adequate services and programs to inmates at a reduced cost, one must ask if some of the economies that result in those cost savings can be implemented in the traditional prison. Questions stemming from private corrections can be threatening to those in public corrections. The resistance of labor organizations to privatization of prisons is a prime example.

## WHY RESISTANCE?

People resist change primarily because it disturbs their equilibrium and threatens their sense of security. For the most part we all seek a comfortable equilibrium of values, activities, and environment. To some people that equilibrium is a comfortable, dependable rut; to others, equilibrium is a pattern of change, but it is their change, ordered in their way. With equilibrium we seek a measure of security, and we shift and move against daily forces in small ways to reestablish and maintain equilibrium just as surely as water seeks its own level. However, change from outside the person intrudes; equilibrium is disturbed, security is threatened, and resistance results.

**In work organizations, most instances of resistance can be traced to one or more of the following general causes:**

- **Organizational changes.** Departments are altered or interdepartmental relationships or management reporting relationships are changed.

- **Management changes.** New management assumes control of an organization or department.
- **New methods and procedures.** People are expected to do new and different work or accomplish old tasks in new ways.
- **Job restructuring.** Tasks are added to or deleted from people's jobs.
- **New equipment.** New technology affects job skills and procedures.

If you can accept the claim that change disturbs equilibrium and threatens security, go a step further and accept one additional factor that seems borne out in practice: People most fear the unknown. It is the unknown that actually disturbs equilibrium and threatens security. When your employees seem to be resisting change it is usually because all of the implications of the change are not known, understood, or appreciated.

However, most available ways of improving supervisory effectiveness do involve changing the way things are accomplished in your department. To have improvement you usually need to have change—change in ways of doing things and especially change in attitude. In the last analysis the success of any particular change depends almost completely on employee attitude.

Our consideration of change, then, brings us once again to consideration of the supervisor's approach in dealing with employees.

## THE SUPERVISOR'S APPROACH

As a supervisor interested in implementing a particular change, you have three avenues along which to approach your employees. You can (1) tell them what to do, (2) convince them to do it, or (3) involve them in planning for the change.

### Tell Them

Specific orders—commands, if you will—have been described as one of the marks of the autocratic or authoritarian leader. The boss is the boss, a giver of orders who either makes a decision and orders its implementation or relays without expansion or clarification the orders that come down from above.

The authoritarian approach is sometimes necessary. Sometimes it is the only option available under the circumstances—you don't have time to convince or build a consensus when you are dealing with a riot. However, the "tell them" approach is the approach most likely to generate resistance and should be used in only those rare instances when it is the only means available.

## Convince Them

In most instances though, including those in which the change in question is a non-negotiable edict from the upper reaches of the agency, you have room for explanation and persuasion. At the very least you should endeavor to make each employee aware of the reasons for the change and the necessity for its implementation. It may be that you have to champion the cause of something clearly distasteful (to you as well as to some employees) because it may be good for the institution overall or good for the inmates or even perhaps because it is mandated by new regulations of some sort. Your employees may not like what they are called on to do, but they are more likely to respond as you need them to if they know and understand the why of the change.

Your employees deserve information, and information serves you well because it often removes the shadow of the unknown. Few if any changes cannot be approached by this "selling" means, while the authoritarian "tell them" approach should be reserved for those infrequent occasions when someone clearly cannot be "sold."

## Involve Them

Involve your employees in shaping the details of the change whenever possible, and especially as it affects the way they perform their assigned tasks. It has been proven that employees are far more likely to understand and comply when they have a role in determining the form and substance of the change. For instance, if you are considering new equipment and have sufficient lead time, get the input of the people who will have to work with the equipment once it is in place. If the prison is to be expanded or remodeled and your department will change its physical space and arrangement, get your employees' opinions on where things should be located and how work should flow. Through involvement, change can become a positive force. Your employees will be more likely to comply because the change is partly "theirs."

In *A Passion for Excellence,* Tom Peters comments, "People who are part of the team, who 'own' the company and 'own' their job, regularly perform a thousand percent better than the rest." This dynamic is not confined to the business world; it works just as effectively in the prison setting.

And there is another potential benefit to involvement as well: Your employees know the work in ways that you may perhaps never know it. You supervise a number of tasks, some of which you may once have done yourself. However, your employees do, in hands-on fashion, those tasks that you only supervise. Thus your employees know the details of the work far better than you and are in a much better position to provide the basis for positive change in task performance.

It is suggested here, as elsewhere, that participative or consultative approaches to management are the best ways of getting things done through your employees. The most effective ways of reducing or removing the fear of the unknown make full use of communication and involvement.

## GUIDELINES FOR EFFECTIVE MANAGEMENT OF CHANGE

- **Plan thoroughly.** Fully evaluate the potential change, examining all implications in regard to its potential impact on your department and the total organization.
- **Communicate fully.** Fully communicate the change, starting early, to assure that your employees are not taken by surprise. To the extent you can, make it two-way communication; pave the way for your employees' involvement by soliciting their comments or suggestions.
- **Convince employees.** Take steps as necessary to convince your employees of the value and benefits of the proposed change. Appeal to employee self-interest. Let them know how they stand to benefit from the change and how it may perhaps make their work easier.
- **Involve employees when possible.** Be especially aware of the value of your employees as a source of job knowledge, and tap this source not only for the acceptance of change but for the development of genuine improvements as well. Recognize that it is not possible to involve employees in all matters—for instance, you cannot do much about a mandate from above.
- **Monitor implementation.** Monitor the implementation of any change, especially one involving employee task performance, until the new way is established as part of the accepted work pattern. A new work method, dependent for its success on willing adoption by

individual employees, can be introduced in a burst of enthusiasm only to die of its own weight as the novelty wears off and old habits return. New habits are not easily formed, and your employees need the help you can furnish through conscientious follow-up.

## TRUE RESISTANCE

Resistance to change will never be completely eliminated. People possess differing degrees of flexibility and exhibit varying degrees of acceptance of ideas that are not purely their own. However, involvement helps, and you will eventually discover, if you have not already done so, that most employees are willing to cooperate and genuinely want to contribute. Beyond involvement, however, communication is the key. Sharing full knowledge and understanding of what is happening and why is the strongest force the supervisor can bring to bear on the problems of resistance to change. Ultimately you will discover that it is not that people resist change so much as they resist being changed.

---

## CASE 17–1: DELAYED CHANGE OF COMMAND

After giving a month's advance notice to the business manager and her supervising associate warden, and with the knowledge of her staff, the accounting supervisor left her position at a large prison complex for a better-paying job elsewhere. Within the department (which serviced the needs of five separate institutions) it was assumed that Mr. Parsons, the senior accountant, would become supervisor. However, a week passed and no appointment was made.

The one week became several weeks. The business manager, to whom the accounting supervisor normally reported, began to make the administrative decisions for the section. Mr. Parsons was left with the growing task of overseeing the day-to-day functions of the entire section in addition to performing his regular work.

The department became aware that the prison was advertising for a accounting supervisor and that the business manager was conducting interviews. However, no one was hired. Finally, after six months without a supervisor, Mr. Parsons was elevated to accounting supervisor and was immediately authorized to hire an accountant to replace himself.

## Questions

1. During the period without an accounting supervisor, how would you assess Mr. Parsons' position from the departmental staff's viewpoint? The business manager's viewpoint? Mr. Parsons' own viewpoint?

2. How would you assess Mr. Parsons' position after he was finally made accounting supervisor?

---

### CASE 17–2: SURPRISE!

On Monday morning when the business office employees arrived at the prison, they immediately noticed the absence of the business manager. This was not unusual; the manager was frequently absent on Monday. However, he rarely failed to call his department when he would not be there—but on this day he still had not called by noon.

Shortly after lunch the supervisors of the various sections of the business office were summoned to the associate warden's office. There they were told that the business manager was no longer employed by the prison. They—the supervisors—were told to look after things for the current week and that a new business manager, already hired, would be starting the following Monday. All the supervisors were told about the new business manager was that it was somebody from outside of the prison.

## Questions

1. What was right or wrong about the manner in which the change in business manager was made?

2. What would you suppose to be the attitudes of the business office staff upon hearing of the change?

3. With what attitudes do you suppose the staff will receive the new manager?

4. In what other ways might this change have been approached?

---

**NOTE**

1. A. Bloch. *Murphy's Law and Other Reasons Why Things Go Wrong* (Los Angeles, CA: Price/Stern/Sloan Publishers, 1979), 11.

## CHAPTER 18

# Communication: Not by Spoken Words Alone

*I have made this letter rather long because I have not had time to make it shorter.*

*—Blaise Pascal*

*I had heard you were a very great man, but I don't think so. I heard your speech and understood every word you said.*
*—Davy Crockett to Daniel Webster (attributed)*

## Chapter Objectives

☛ Review the essential elements of written communication in the supervisor's job.
☛ Provide guidelines for writing clearer, more concise letters and memoranda.
☛ Examine "old habits" in writing and suggest why some of these habits should be changed.

## THE WRITTEN WORD

Letters, memoranda, and other written communications are essential in the operation of any organization. Although it seems at times that we have to put up with far more paperwork than we care to handle—and this is certainly true in prisons where the paper tiger has become a beast of considerable proportions—much of this paper is nevertheless necessary. Many organizations function quite well in spite of hefty amounts of paperwork, but just try to run an organization without paper.

The written word possesses a serious drawback: A piece of writing is a one-way communication, providing no opportunity for immediate feedback. As you write you are unable to amend, correct, clarify, or defend what you are writing based on the reaction of your audience. The need for clarity in writing is critical. However, clarity is the attribute most often lacking in written communications in the organizational setting.

## SOURCES OF HELP

Far too many letters and memos resemble low-grade Thanksgiving turkeys: They are hefty and meaty looking, but when you cut into them, you discover they are mostly stuffing. This chapter will present some guidelines aimed at helping you take some of the stuffing out of your letters and memos. Although our guidelines will help improve the clarity of your writing, no single chapter in a work such as this will make you a "good" writer, especially if you experience basic difficulties with grammar, punctuation, and usage. To become an effective writer, you need two things: (1) the desire to improve your writing and (2) the help provided by writing teachers and good reference works on writing.

Numerous books on writing techniques are available. Several are described in the bibliography at the end of this book, but if you were to use only one of them, give first consideration to *The Elements of Style* by William Strunk, Jr., and E. B. White. This book has fewer than 100 pages yet contains more solid, usable advice per page than any other book available. It is a great place to start when you decide to get help in improving your writing. Another particularly good reference on how not to write in "bureaucratese" is *Gobbledy Gook Has Gotta Go,* a U.S. Department of the Interior publication.[1]

## GUIDELINES FOR BETTER LETTERS AND MEMOS

Written communications perform several important functions. They are used to advise (or inform), explain, request, convince, and provide permanent records. Many agencies have specific requirements for the format or style of written materials. Many managers have their own specific expectations (often unwritten) regarding style and content for material originating in their department or institution. As a writer, you must be aware of those formal and informal guidelines for your written work. Use the advice in this chapter with this in mind. If your supervisor will not accept written material with contractions in it, then by all means adjust to that condition. If first person usage is not acceptable, don't use it. But within the constraints of your particular situation, use of the following guidelines will help you improve your writing in a minimum amount of time.

### Write for a Specific Audience

Your letter or memo may be going to one person, or several people. You will need to decide who, specifically, you are writing to. The person who will receive your communication—that person for whom your message is primarily intended—is your primary audience. However, you may also have a sizeable secondary audience—others who will receive, read, and perhaps make use of your communication.

Many managers seem to believe they should write in such a way that anyone picking up a particular document will "get the message." However, this is a difficult task at best, and it becomes nearly impossible when there is a sizeable secondary audience including people of widely varying backgrounds and different degrees of familiarity with the subject.

Since you cannot write for everybody who might read the letter or memo, you should write specifically for your primary audience. If you have trouble identifying your primary audience, sift through the likely recipients of the message with this question in mind: Who of all these people needs this information for decision-making purposes? Often your primary audience will consist of a single person, but it could just as well be two, three, or more people. If you are a shift commander writing about the need for specific change in policy on recreation yard coverage, perhaps all of the other shift commanders and maybe even the heads of some other departments should be aware of the issue. However, it would be your immediate superior, the chief of security, who would be the primary audience because it is in that position where the decision-making authority concerning policy is located. On the other hand, if the chief of security is releasing a new policy with which all shift commanders are expected to comply, then the memo announcing the policy will have all shift commanders as its primary audience.

Use what you know about your primary audience in deciding how to structure your message. Can you do it on a friendly, first-name basis? Must it be a formal letter, or will a brief, casual note suffice? Does this person seem to prefer detail, or would a concise overview be enough? Let your knowledge of your primary audience suggest how you should communicate.

### Avoid Unneeded Words

We could fill volumes discussing the subject of unneeded words. However, understanding and exercising one simple concept—that of the "zero word"—will take you a long way toward removing excess words from your writing. Every word in a given piece of writing can be placed in one of three categories: Necessary, optional, or zero. A necessary word is one that is essential to getting your basic message across. An optional word, as the name suggests, can be used at your option to qualify or modify a necessary word or phrase. A zero word contributes nothing to the message and should be removed.

Consider the following sentence:

Harvey is certainly an exceptionally intelligent man.

This sentence contains only three necessary words: *Harvey is intelligent*. Note, however, that even with all zero words and optional words removed what remains is still a sentence.

The word *exceptionally* is the only optional word in the sentence. It may well make a difference in what you are trying to communicate to say that "Harvey is exceptionally intelligent" rather than simply, "Harvey is intelligent." While this is perfectly acceptable, watch out for the excess use of such modifiers and qualifiers; after a while they not only become tiresome, but they also begin to lose their impact.

The sentence includes three zero words: *certainly, an,* and *man*. At least they are zero under normal circumstances—assuming that Harvey is a man. Still, if Harvey were anything else, a dog, for instance, we would say so. The word *an* is there for structural reasons, and certainly is *certainly* unnecessary, since in terms of what we are trying to convey Harvey either is or is not intelligent and *certainly* does not make it any more binding. Zero words abound in most business communication. However, they are relatively easy to get rid of with conscientious editing.

This is not to say, however, that the zero word infests all writing to the same extent. In many uses of written language, writers are attempting to tell stories or create moods or impressions. However, in writing an interoffice memo you are not writing a poem, a novel, or even a textbook. Your primary objective is to get your message across with clarity. A memo can be correct in every sense of grammar and usage although stripped of every zero word.

Select a sample of your writing and go hunting for zero words. If in doubt about a word, sound out the sentence without it. If the sentence remains a sentence and continues to carry the message you wish it to carry, then the word is probably a zero word. Chances are you will find a surprising number of zero words.

Often we use unnecessary words in groups, applying several-word phrases to do the work that could be done by one or two words. This is especially common in business correspondence in which some phrases have reached cliché proportions. Consider these examples:

- The use of "due to the fact that" when the writer could simply say "because"

- Saying "be in a position to" when all that is needed is "can"
- Saying "in the state of California" when "in California" says the same
- Using the stuffy "with reference to" when the job can be done by "about."

Avoid roundabout phrases in your writing. They simply add bulk to your communication without adding clarity. In fact, such words not only fail to add clarity, but they also can actually harm your message by surrounding and obscuring your real meaning.

## Use Simple Words

Almost every technical and professional field has its own jargon, with jargon being defined in the dictionary as "the technical terminology or characteristic idiom of a special activity or group." This is the second definition of jargon carried in several dictionaries—the first is "confused unintelligible language."

It is one thing if you happen to be a prison doctor writing to an audience of one who happens also to be a prison doctor. In this case you can get away with the free use of the language of your field. However, as a group, prison employees usually include other highly educated, specialized professionals, as well as secretaries, tradespersons, and other workers at various levels in the organization. Many of these staff in different fields have their own "languages."

Medical, mental health, and other technical professionals are among the worst offenders when it comes to sprinkling their correspondence with jargon. This "in language" of a field should not be allowed to cross departmental lines to any considerable extent, for example, when a physician communicates to a business manager or a psychiatrist writes to a correctional officer. Consider your primary audience (in this case, the recipient's background and familiarity with your subject) in preparing to write.

If technical professionals are the worst offenders when it comes to jargon, then administrative personnel, consultants, and other managerial professionals are the worst offenders when it comes to made-up words. Management is cluttered with once sensible words to which have been appended the suffixes -ize and -wise. So now we stylize, prioritize, and regularize and speak of things as timewise or wordwise, for example. Consider, for instance, the increasing number of people who show an apparent fondness for the likes of "operationalization." Yet through use this clumsy word is now recognized in several dictionaries. However, this inclusion makes it no less awkward and overblown.

The use of words considered incorrect, or barbarism, can cloud communication. These language twists can get us into trouble when they create an unintended meaning. Take this classic example from the field of medicine. A young administrative staffer, assigned to study systems and staffing in a hospital pathology department, referred on paper to the staff of the department of pathology as the "pathological staff." The department's director, who was sensitive to the analysis in the first place, flew into a rage after reading the word *pathological*—literally referring to the department's employees as the sick staff—and it was days before the remainder of the report was read.

## Edit and Rewrite

When you edit your correspondence, take out the zero words, the roundabout phrases, and other verbal stuffing. There are few pieces of writing we cannot improve by careful editing or rewriting. Very few people—including professional writers—can put their thoughts into completely effective written messages in a single try. In fact, professional writers probably do far more editing and rewriting than do most writers of day-to-day business correspondence. Therein lies the problem: Much of what is wrong with our writing is wrong simply because we do not put enough time into it. As this chapter's opening quotation suggests, given a particular message to get across, we generally need more time to write a shorter letter than a longer, but less effective, one.

If you are thinking that better writing is too time-consuming, that you would have to double your correspondence time to provide that extra reading through every letter and memo you write, think of the cost of misunderstanding. Have you ever had to spend valuable time and effort smoothing out some problem that developed because a written message was misunderstood? You can edit many memos in the time it takes to solve a couple of knotty problems arising from missed communication.

## CHANGING OLD HABITS

In our day-to-day writing we are often unconsciously still trying to please dear Mrs. Smith who taught us English "way back when." Even in the 1940s, 1950s, and 1960s, we were taught how to write letters that sounded as though they were lifted from a Victorian secretarial handbook.

Most of what has been said so far in this chapter is "legal" in terms of what Mrs. Smith taught us. However, there are additional practices that would have been guaranteed to get us into trouble with the teacher even though they will definitely help us improve our business writing today.

### Be Friendly and Personal

Feel free to use personal pronouns in your letters and memos. We use *I, you,* and *we* when we talk to each other, so why not use them when we write? Many of us were taught to avoid personal pronouns in formal writing, and this warning sticks with us. We were once taught never to write *I*. For clarity and directness, however, *I* is far preferable to archaic affectations such as *the undersigned* or *the author*.

Most of your letters and memos should sound as you sound when you talk. Once you achieve that conversational tone, your correspondence will be direct, friendly, and personal.

### Use Direct, Active Language

Ask direct questions when the situation warrants it. You may have been taught to go out of your way to avoid questions and thus say things like, "Let me know whether or not you will attend." It is much more direct to ask, "Will you attend?"

The use of the passive voice is pervasive in government writing. Instead, keep your statements in the active voice, avoiding the likes of, "The contract was signed by your representative." How much cleaner it is to say, "Your representative signed the contract."

### Use Contractions

Use *don't, wouldn't, can't, shouldn't,* etc., even though the use of contractions may have been taboo in your education. Contractions contribute to the natural, conversational tone you should be working to achieve. Even so, many writers of official correspondence squeeze the contractions out of the writing without realizing what they are doing. The result is a formalistic style, stilted and stuffy, that serves only to create more distance between writer and reader.

### Write Short Sentences

You are not William Faulkner, who could get away with writing an opening sentence of some 180-plus words. Neither are you writing the Great American Novel.

It is difficult to lay down any firm guidelines for sentence length. But consider that any time you create a sentence much more than 20 words long you are edging into questionable territory. Some teachers of business writing have suggested 20 words as maximum sentence length. Others suggest that 14 or 15 words be considered maximum. It is safe to say that the longer the sentence, the more opportunities there are for misunderstanding.

## Forget Old Taboos about Prepositions and Conjunctions

It is likely that most of us were repeatedly and sternly warned against committing two terrible "no-nos": ending a sentence with a preposition and starting a sentence with a conjunction.

A story is told about Winston Churchill and the rule concerning prepositions. When reminded that it was improper to end a sentence with a preposition, Churchill replied, "This is something up with which I shall not put." An extreme example, for sure, but it cleanly illustrates how far out of the way you may be led in search of so-called structure. Go ahead and say, "This is something I won't put up with."

Remember when a sure-fire way to lose points on a composition was to begin sentences with conjunctions, especially *and* and *but*. Fortunately this archaic prohibition has been successfully shattered by professional writers. The freedom to open a sentence in this manner can save you from long sentences and needless repetition. Of course if every other sentence in your letter begins with *and,* you will have created a different kind of monster.

## Say What You Want To Say and Stop

Avoid starting your letter by repeating what was said in the letter you are answering. Also, avoid opening with standard stuffing such as "In response to yours of the. . . ."

Simply say what you are trying to say. If the point of your letter is to tell a potential supplier that the bid was not accepted, do not spend two paragraphs describing the evaluation process and building the rationale for the "no" you deliver in paragraph three. Deliver your answer in the opening paragraph, preferably in the first sentence. Then go on to explain your reasons why, if necessary.

Having delivered your message and explained it as necessary, do not spend another paragraph or two winding down by repeating what you have already said. Simply say it—and stop. Also, watch out for standard closing lines that mean little or nothing. It may be quite all right to say something like, "Call me if you need more information"—if you really mean it. It is thoughtful and it shows that you are interested, but avoid phrases such as, "We trust this arrangement meets with your complete satisfaction." For one thing, you are telling your reader you expect satisfaction to result—you are not just asking. If your reader is not completely satisfied, you are likely to hear about it.

Consider something else that appears in the last example: the use of the collective *we*. Few words are more likely to make a letter impersonal to a reader, who is made to feel that the communication is coming from a crowd. The *we* has its place, for instance, when you are writing to someone outside the prison and are speaking for the organization. However, rather than being agency-to-person or agency-to-agency, most of your writing will be person-to-person. As long as the thoughts are your own and yours is the only hand pushing the pen, say *I*.

## SAMPLE LETTER

To illustrate the application of some of the guidelines offered in this chapter, a sample letter is shown before and after editing. The letter in its original form (Exhibit 18–1) was received by the records section of a prison.

---

**Exhibit 18–1** Sample Letter: Before Editing

---

April 15, 1996

State Prison
Main Street
Someplace, New York

ATTN: Records Department
Re: John Doe

Gentlemen:

Please be advised that we are attorneys for the above named former inmate at your facility, John Doe. We are enclosing herewith authorization executed by Mr. Doe for which please forward to this office a copy of the prison record of the said John Doe.

Thanking you, I am,

Very truly yours,
Rayborn & Rayborn
Attorneys-at-Law

Several comments on Exhibit 18–1 include the following:

- The writer used *Gentlemen* as a salutation and many correctional personnel are not male. You can use "Dear Sir/Madam:" or "To the Manager of the Records Department"
- "Please be advised. . . ." is one of those bits of stuffing spoken of earlier. It went out of date before most of us even learned it.
- " We are enclosing herewith...." More pomposity. Much preferred is *enclosed is*, or simply *here is*.
- ". . . .the above named. . . ." *Above-named* is right; *within-named*, also. In fact, the unfortunate Mr. Doe is named three times in one brief letter.
- "thanking you, I am. . . ." What can be said about this? This is made all the sillier by the presence of two names in the signature block following *I am* (and the letter was received unsigned).

Now take a look at Exhibit 18–2, the same letter after reasonable editing. This letter is simple, straightforward, and to the point. This is but one of several acceptable ways the letter could be rewritten.

Why all the fuss? You say you got the message anyway, without the criticism and the editing? True, you may have gotten the message. The sample letter is extremely short, so the potential for serious misunder-

---

**Exhibit 18–2** Sample Letter: After Editing

---

April 15, 1996

Records Department
State Prison
Main Street
Someplace, New York

Dear ____,

We represent John Doe, who was an inmate at your institution between August 3, 1990, and May 17, 1995.

Please send a copy of Mr. Doe's prison records. Proper authorization is enclosed.

Thank you.

Sincerely,
Richard Rayborn
Rayborn & Rayborn
Attorneys-at-Law

standing may not be evident. However, the potential for misinterpretation builds rapidly with the number of words in a letter. The body of Exhibit 18–1 contains 52 words. The edited version in Exhibit 18–2 contains 31 words. The difference represents a 40 percent reduction in the number of words used to get the message across.

It has been estimated that most official correspondence contains from 25 to 100 percent more words than are needed to get the message across effectively. Each added word presents another unwanted opportunity for misunderstanding. If every document you received were properly written, the two-inch thick stack of paper awaiting your attention would be much thinner.

## OTHER WRITING

We have been discussing guidelines primarily for writing letters and memos, since these make up the bulk of most supervisors' writing chores. However, you may occasionally find it necessary or desirable to tackle larger writing tasks, such as informational or analytical reports, training presentations, speeches, or journal articles.

Many elements of the personal, direct style preferred for correspondence are applicable to other writing. For instance, some speeches or training presentations should be handled with the same personal touch. Additional rules may apply in writing more structured material such as formal reports, and still more rules apply when writing for publication in magazines or journals.

If you have to write a report, get a manual or handbook on the subject and do some studying. Take note if you need to use a commonly recommended format—one that calls for a tight summary of objectives, conclusions, and recommendations early in the report. Also, remember that the first step in preparing to write a report (or a letter, memo, or any other piece of writing) is to get a clear image of your audience.

If you are serious about improving your writing, start with the few suggestions presented in this chapter and go on to the information contained in published sources. Consider keeping a four-volume self-help library on your desk: Strunk and White's *The Elements of Style,* any other book about writing in general (preferably business writing), a reference book on report writing, and a current dictionary.

## A MATTER OF PRACTICE

Writing is much like any other skill in that the more you work at it, the better you get. If you enjoy writing, or feel that you could enjoy it, then you have a head start on the self-improvement process. But if you do not enjoy writing, if every letter, every memo, every report, every performance appraisal narrative looms before you as a painful, distasteful task, you had better examine your attitude toward writing. Is writing tough for you because you truly dislike it? Or is it the other way around—you dislike it primarily because it is difficult for you?

You may not have to write a great deal on your job, but chances are you write enough to make it worthwhile to try a modest self-improvement program. One thing is certain: You will never get better at writing unless you work at it.

---

### EXERCISE 18–1: THE MATTHEWSON MEMO

**To:** Ted Matthewson, Warden
**From:** William Abernathy, Director of Corrections
**Re:** Use of CS Chemical Agents

Please be advised that departmental audit staff have indicated to me that your institution has continued to stock, use in training, and maintain ready for tactical deployment a large quantity of CS gas. As you know, maintaining or using any form of CS gas has been prohibited by departmental regulations for a lengthy period of time because it has been irrefutably established that this type of chemical agent, when used in closed areas such as cellhouses and other buildings, can cause serious medical harm and in some cases where used indiscriminately could aggravate existing medical conditions even to the point of causing the death of an inmate. Enclosed is a copy of the controlling policy for your information.

Please consider this memo a formal directive for the discontinuation of all storage, training use, or tactical deployment of said CS chemical agents. You are required to make immediate arrangements to acquire sufficient supplies of CN-based chemical agents and to replace all CS gas supplies in your institution with the equivalent CN agents, also adjusting all emergency plans and other institutional inventories and regulations to reflect this change and the different usage requirements of CN versus CS.

If you have any questions regarding the application or interpretation of this directive, you certainly may feel free to contact me at your convenience.

**Instructions**

1. Shorten the Matthewson memo by reading through it once and eliminating excess words where possible.
2. Take the results of step one and rewrite the memo, re-arranging passages and condensing thoughts as necessary.
3. Determine the percentage reduction in number of words of your finished memo as compared with the original.
4. How many words are there in the longest sentence of the original? In your rewritten memo?

---

## EXERCISE 18–2: THE COPY MACHINE LETTER

Write a letter to Mr. Nathan Perkins, district manager of Repro, Inc., describing the trouble you are having with your copy machine. Include the following information. (Not all points are of equal significance, and they are not presented in any logical order.)

- You are records manager for the state penitentiary.
- The prison has one Repro CM-400 machine.
- You have had the machine for ten months.
- You have discovered that the local address for Repro service is a manufacturer's representative and that the nearest real service agency is 125 miles away.
- The machine has required outside service five times.
- For the last three breakdowns your machine was down for three days, two days, and four days, respectively, awaiting service.
- You bought the machine without a service contract.
- There is administrative pressure on you to replace the Repro machine with a better known machine.
- The machine gives off a strong odor when operating.
- The Repro CM-400 was the cheapest machine available.
- The sales representative promised prompt service.

## ADDITIONAL CONSIDERATIONS

1. Your letter should probably contain complaints (poor performance, poor service, and so on) and threats (to replace, and so on).

Before writing, decide which kind of message—complaint or threat—will be the dominant message.

2. You have admitted to yourself that your own organization caused much of the problem when it "bought cheap" (lowest price, no service contract). Carefully consider to what extent—if at all—you might admit this in your letter.

---

**NOTE**

1. United States Department of the Interior, *Gobbledy Gook Has Gotta Go* (Washington, DC: Government Printing Office, 1966).

## CHAPTER 19

# How To Conduct Effective Meetings

*Meetings: Where you go to learn how to do better the things you already know how to do anyway, but don't have time to do, because of too many meetings.*

*—Anonymous*

## Chapter Objectives

☛ Characterize various types of meetings by the purposes for which they may be held.

☛ Provide guidelines for determining the need for a meeting and for preparing to conduct an effective meeting.

☛ Offer suggestions on how to obtain maximum benefits from a meeting while consuming the least amount of time.

☛ Place meetings in general in perspective as an often misused but potentially effective management tool.

## MEETINGS ARE HERE TO STAY

Most of us in management have complained about meetings, especially in regard to their number, frequency, and value. Like them or not, we must meet in order to operate our organizations. We may often consider meetings costly, frustrating, and wasteful, but we should not label a gathering with any of these unkind descriptions simply because it is a meeting.

Although our complaints about meetings indicate our chronic discontent with such proceedings, we accept them as a regular part of work. We are conditioned to them as a characteristic of organizational life.

Generally, the higher we climb in the management structure, the more time we spend in meetings. At all managerial levels, however, the situations and pressures encouraging us either to hold or to attend meetings are many. We find it is not possible to do an effective supervisory job without occasionally (and for some supervisors, frequently) dealing with people in gatherings larger than the simple one-on-one encounter. Meetings often represent the best available technique for arriving at joint conclusions and determining joint actions. It is often possible to accomplish within minutes results that would require hours, days, or weeks by other means.

Meetings are also essential to consultative and participative leadership styles. Joint decisions and actions take longer to arrive at than do unilateral decisions and edicts, since true two-way communication, including discussion and feedback, requires more time than dictatorial one way communication. This extra time can represent a small price to pay for the benefits afforded by an honest, open, participative leadership style.

On the other hand, much of our grumbling about meetings is justified. Many meetings waste our time because they lack clear purpose or are poorly led. Some meetings waste time and resources—they should not be held at all.

The true cost of most questionable or unnecessary meetings is lost productivity. What would these people have been doing had they not been involved in a meeting?

Why meetings? This question can have any of several answers depending on the purpose of the particular gathering.

## TYPES OF MEETINGS

### Information Meetings

The information meeting is held simply for the transfer of information, and can range in size from a small, section-level session to a prison-wide "recall" of all employees who are not staffing housing units and towers. In such a meeting, you have something to pass along to your employees or others and you choose to do this by a meeting rather than by some other means. Since the basic purpose is to transfer information to the group, the leader may do most or all of the talking. Although there are usually questions and discussion for the sake of clarification, the transfer of information is essentially one-way communication.

### Discussion Meetings

The objective of a discussion meeting is to gain agreement on something through the exchange of information, ideas, and opinions among all participants.

#### Directed Discussion

A directed discussion meeting may be appropriate when a conclusion, solution, or decision has already been determined; yet it is not to be relayed to the group as straight information. The leader desires to gain the participants' acceptance of the solution. In effect, a directed discussion is a sales pitch.

*Problem-solving Discussion*

This type of meeting is held when a problem exists and a solution or decision must be determined by the group. The answer determined by joint action may evolve from the ideas of a single participant.

*Exploratory Discussion*

The purpose of an exploratory discussion meeting is to gain information on which you or others may eventually base a decision. The objective is not to develop a specific solution or recommendation but rather to generate and develop ideas and information for others (perhaps yourself, but possibly your boss or some other manager) who must make the decision.

### A Special Case: The Staff Meeting

The staff meeting may be an information meeting, a discussion meeting, or both. A staff meeting is usually held for the purpose of communication among the members of a group. Staff members may report on the status of their activities. This meeting form is also used to solve problems, sell ideas, and explore issues, and, depending on the business at hand, it may take on any or all of the three forms of the discussion meeting.

### MEETING PREPARATION

A few of the following suggestions are most pertinent to discussion meetings convened for dealing with specific situations. Most, however, apply generally to all types of meetings.

### Defining the Problem

To enable a group to begin dealing with a situation it is necessary to establish the nature of that situation. The first step to prepare for a meeting is to identify "what's wrong." Before your invited participants attend the meeting, they must understand what they are going to discuss when they get there. You must be able to supply a concise statement of the problem or other reason for the meeting in the written announcement.

### Determining the Need for a Meeting

Having defined the problem, do not automatically assume that a meeting is inevitable. Other means of organizational communication are available, and all are valid and may be preferred under certain circumstances. In determining the need for a meeting, consider the following.

- How many people are involved? If very few, perhaps you can use the telephone, letters, or memos.
- Will a meeting save time? Often a problem can be solved by a memorandum or report, but if an exchange of ideas is needed then a meeting may avoid a seemingly endless series of other contacts.
- Should everyone get the same story? Perhaps the issue is complex or technically involved, calling for different levels of participation by various categories of personnel. Perhaps there are policy issues to be considered at a policy-making level before they can be dealt with generally.

### Deciding What Should Be Accomplished

Before you convene the meeting, you should have a clear idea of what you want to achieve. Should the meeting give you the solution to a problem? Will the group accept an idea? What significant decision-making information do you expect to glean during the meeting?

### Selecting the Meeting Type

Based on your determination of what should be accomplished, you should then decide what type of meeting you are going to have. Your clear understanding as to whether the discussion should be directed, problem solving, or exploratory will assist you in controlling the meeting and keeping the discussion headed toward the result you wish to accomplish.

### Selecting the Participants

Again based on your best determination of what is to be accomplished, you next need to decide who should attend the meeting. This choice should be based on your best assessment of who has the knowledge to deal with the problem and the authority to make decisions and commit resources to solve the problem. Your objective in selecting people to attend the meeting should be to secure the broadest possible coverage of the problem without overloading the meeting.

### Distributing Advance Information

All those invited should receive, along with the meeting notification, all information that would be helpful in preparing for the meeting. If you can give them only a statement of the problem, then let them know this is all you have. If you have background information in the form of letters, memos, or reports, send it to them so they can consider all aspects of the problem in advance of the meeting. Give them also your expectations of the meeting. At the very least, those invited should know both the problem and the objective.

### Notifying and Reminding the Participants

For all but the most informal meetings, written notification should include time, place, preparations to make or materials to bring, the statement of the problem, and the meeting's objectives. Ideally, you should provide written notification a week or more in advance and plan on telephoning reminders a day or two before the meeting actually takes place. Generally, the more important the topic of the meeting and the busier the people you are inviting, the more advance notice you should provide.

It is also a good idea to clear the date and time in advance with the key people attending. Otherwise you are likely to find yourself having to notify everyone of a change in arrangements after some have already cleared their calendars to attend. Remember that you are not the only busy person in the institution; it may frequently be necessary for you to bend your schedule to accommodate the availability of other people.

### Arranging for Proper Facilities

This step should seem self-evident, but too often a dozen people find they are ready to meet but have no place to sit down. If you need a sizeable meeting room, make sure you reserve it for the preferred date and time before your notification goes out. It should also be said that you need sufficient space for all persons involved, reasonably comfortable surroundings, and reasonable freedom from interruptions. Also, advance arrangements should be made for needed equipment such as chalkboards, projectors, and other aids.

**Preparing an Agenda**

For all but the simplest of meetings you should use an agenda to guide you. If the meeting promises to be long and involved, the agenda should be worked out sufficiently in advance so it can be supplied to all attendees with the meeting notification. Whether or not it is supplied in advance, however, as meeting leader you need the agenda. It may consist of only a few broad points jotted in the corner of your note pad, but the process of writing it forces you to rethink your purpose in calling the meeting and consider how you will get from problem to objective.

Although you will not think of every necessary step or essential question ahead of time, with an agenda you can at least remind yourself of certain important points. When the meeting is underway, your agenda may well expand as issues are raised and information previously unknown to you is offered. This is all well and good, as long as all agenda additions or digressions contribute directly to moving the group from the problem toward the meeting's objective.

**LEADING A MEETING**

**Start on Time**

For a regularly scheduled meeting (for instance, your monthly staff meeting held at 3:00 P.M. on the third Thursday of each month), you should try to begin precisely on time. The more you defer to chronic latecomers, the more likely these people are to remain chronic latecomers. Also, chronic tardiness can often be an indication of other problems, such as hostility, disrespect, lack of interest, or perhaps inflated ego.

Making a habit of starting on time can go a long way toward curing chronic tardiness. If it is 3:00 P.M. and only half of your staff are present, start the meeting even though you know the remainder will be trickling in over the next several minutes. Out of respect for those who show up on time, do not repeat what has already been said for the sake of the latecomers. Rather, let the late arrivers know they have to wait until after the meeting to find out what they missed from those who were present. Make it plain, also, that the content of the early part of the meeting is not filler or warm-up material that people can afford to miss. Make it a habit to start your regularly scheduled meetings precisely on time, and most chronic latecomers will change their ways as they get the message and become accustomed to your pattern of behavior.

On the other hand, you may want to allow some flexibility in how closely you adhere to a rigid starting time if the meeting is a one-time affair involving a number of people who are organizationally scattered, perhaps including some who are your superiors in the management structure. You are likely to wait more than a few minutes for a tardy person to show, especially if that person happens to be your boss. Also, a one-shot meeting is not a regular part of someone's schedule or pattern of behavior. Therefore, give yourself some slack in scheduling; for instance, you schedule a session for 1:30 P.M. although you know full well it will not start until 1:45 P.M. Try not to overdo this practice; it suggests disrespect for those who do show up on time and deference to the latecomers.

### State the Purpose of the Meeting

First tell the group why they are there and what they need to accomplish. Also, give them your best estimate of the amount of time the meeting should require. Ending time can be fully as troublesome as starting time in some situations. A meeting can be a form of escape for some people who lead busy, hectic working lives. Some people may tend to prolong the session with irrelevancies if progress is not well controlled. (It has been suggested that an effective way to get a one-hour meeting concluded in one hour is to schedule it to start an hour before lunch or an hour before quitting time.)

### Encourage Discussion

Do not allow the meeting to move in such narrow lines that valuable input is lost. Ask for clarification of comments that are offered. Request opinions and ask direct questions, particularly of the few silent ones who frequently populate meetings. Remember, if you have structured your meeting wisely then everyone who is there is there for a good reason. It is part of your job as meeting leader to do everything you can to get those people talking who ordinarily tend to remain quiet.

### Exercise Control

*Of Yourself*

- Don't let your ego get in the way simply because you are the meeting leader. Don't assume automatic control of the proceedings.

- Don't lecture or otherwise dominate the proceedings. Remember, the setting is a meeting, not a speech or a class.
- Don't direct the others by telling them what to do or what they should say or conclude. This would amount to one-way communication, which is only marginally appropriate even when the purpose of the meeting is purely informational.
- Don't argue with participants. Discuss, yes. Argue, never.
- Don't attempt to be funny. What may be funny to one person may not be to another. The best laughs generated at a meeting are those that arise naturally from the discussion.

*Of the Group*

- Don't allow lengthy tangential digressions to pull you away from the subject of the meeting. Many legitimate problems are identified through tangential discussions, but if they do not relate to the problem at hand, they dilute the effectiveness of the meeting. Should a legitimate problem arise, make note of it, but sideline it for action at another time and proceed with the subject at hand.
- Don't allow monopolizers and ego-trippers to take over. Although certain talkative people may have significant contributions to make, their constant presence on center stage serves to narrow the discussion and discourage marginally vocal contributors from opening up at all. Overall, your effectiveness as a meeting leader will be determined by how effectively you control the discussion of the group.

**Summarize Periodically**

Agreement in a discussion meeting is usually not reached in a single, progressive series of exchanges. Rather, agreement accrues as discussion points are sifted, sorted, and merged, and a solution or recommendation begins to take form. Periodically summarize what has been said, giving the group a recounting of where you are and where you seem to be headed. If they can agree with your summary of progress, then the meeting is on the right track.

**End with a Specific Plan**

When the meeting is over, you should be able to deliver a final summary stating what has been decided and who is going to do what and by when. Far too many meetings are frustrating affairs that may feel productive while underway but afterward leave participants hanging with a sense of incompleteness. No one should leave your meeting without full understanding of the decisions made, the actions to be taken, the people responsible for implementation, and the timetable for implementation. If the subject is sufficiently complex, it may be to your advantage to call for understanding by going "around the table," asking everyone for their interpretations of what has been decided and how they see their roles, if any, in the implementation of the decision.

### Follow Up

As far as your authority over the problem extends, it is up to you to follow up to determine that what has been decided gets accomplished. It is also up to you to see that minutes of the meeting, should they be necessary, are prepared and distributed; to provide later assurance to all participants that what they decided has in fact been accomplished; and to schedule a follow-up meeting should one be necessary.

### USE OR ABUSE?

As with any other management tool or technique, meetings can be overused, underused, or used ineffectively. They can be expected to do far too much—meetings are certainly no substitute for effective individual decision-making in the presence of proper authority and responsibility. Meetings can also be missed opportunities to serve organizations appropriately.

Whether the meetings you call are used or abused is largely up to you, the supervisor. Meetings are often an unwieldy way of doing business, and as such it is easy for them to become wasteful and ineffective. However, the properly conducted meeting remains one of the most effective ways of accomplishing certain tasks. Whether meetings are effective or ineffective revolves around the issue of control: If we fail to control our meetings, our meetings proceed to control us.

---

### CASE 19-1: THE CONFERENCE

This case concerns a conference of five persons:

1. Sue Turner, executive assistant to the warden. She functions in a staff capacity and has no supervision responsibility except for her

secretary, Betty. One of her assignments is a long-term project to determine some of the reasons for correctional officer turnover. She called the meeting approximately ten days ago. Two of the other persons she notified by telephone, and two she invited in person.

2. Martin Calabro, personnel officer

3. Marv England, chief of security

4. Paul Stanfield, training officer

5. Mary Hanson, union president

The meeting was scheduled for 1:00 P.M. in Turner's office. Turner returned from lunch at 1:08 P.M. to find Calabro and Hanson already there. At 1:12 P.M. England entered and Turner said, "I'd like to get started, but where's Stanfield?"

"I don't know," somebody answered.

Turner dialed a number and received no answer. She then dialed the switchboard and asked for a page. A moment later a call came in and Turner spoke briefly with Stanfield.

Turning from the telephone Turner said, "He forgot. He'll be here in a minute."

"Sue, I wish you had a larger office or a better place to meet," said England. "I don't know how we're going to fit another person in here."

"I know it's small," Turner answered, "but both conference rooms are tied up and I couldn't find another place. Say, holler out to Betty and tell her to find another chair—we're going to need it."

Mary Hanson said, "Sue, can you open your window a little? It's already stuffy in here."

Sue responded by opening the window a few inches. Then the training officer entered, squeezing into the office with the chair that had just been located. It was 1:18 P.M.

Turner said, "I guess we can get started now." She shuffled through a stack of papers before her and said, "I've got a copy, if I can, ah—oh, here it is—of a recent turnover survey done by the personnel officers in each institution in the department of corrections." Looking at the personnel officer she asked, "I assume you have this?"

"Yes, I have it. There's a copy in my office, but I didn't know I needed to bring it with me."

Turner said, "Well, I think what we can get from this thing is ——"

The chief of security interrupted, "Sue, wouldn't it be better if we all could see it? Then you could go down it point-by-point."

Sue said, "I guess you're right. I just have this single copy." She turned toward the door and hollered, "Betty, can you come here a minute?"

Betty entered and Sue instructed her to run four copies of the survey at once.

Turning back to her pile of papers, Sue said to the group, "The last time we got together there were a number of things we decided to look for. I don't remember just what we assigned to whom, but I've got it here somewhere."

For a half-minute or so Sue leafed through the papers before her. Then she turned to the file drawer of her desk and began to go through folders.

While Sue was looking, Marv England turned to Calabro and said, "Say, what have you been doing about advertising for that vacant firearms instructor position? We notified you three weeks ago, and Eleanor is leaving in another week and we still haven't had any candidates to interview."

Martin Calabro responded. His tone sparked a defensive reaction and a lively discussion began.

Turner located the paper she was seeking and Betty returned with the requested photocopies. Turner distributed the copies and fixed her attention on the chief of security and personnel officer as he waited for an opening in the discussion, which was now something between a conversation and an argument. At approximately 1:32 P.M. they managed to return to the subject of officer turnover.

"Now, about this survey of the other institutions," Turner began.

Mary Hanson said, "What about the survey? I thought you wanted to start with the things we agreed to do the last time we were together."

"Who cares," said Calabro. "Let's just get started."

The chief of security looked at his watch and said, "We'd better hurry up and get started and finished. I have a staff meeting at two o'clock."

The meeting settled down to a discussion of the survey and the preliminary data each person had gathered since the previous meeting. At exactly two minutes before 2:00 P.M., the chief of security excused himself to attend his meeting. At 2:08 P.M. Stanfield was called over the paging system; he left Turner's office and did not return.

At 2:12 Turner said she felt they had tentatively decided on their next step but required some input from the two parties who had already left. She then started to excuse the other two participants with the suggestion that they get together again after two weeks.

At that point Turner's telephone rang. She answered it herself, her usual practice, and talked for some four to five minutes before returning her attention to the two persons left in the office. She said, "I guess that's about it for this time around. I'll get back to you and set a time for the next meeting."

When the last of the participants had left, Turner's secretary came into her office and asked if they were finished with the extra chair. Turner indicated they were, and as Betty removed the chair Turner thought gloomily of how difficult it was to get anything done in this institution, and wondered if the warden would be satisfied with her progress on this project.

### Instructions

- Perform a detailed critique of "The Conference." Make a list of points you consider errors and omissions in the way this meeting was arranged and conducted.

- After each item on your list indicate what positive steps could have been taken to avoid each of the errors and omissions.

---

### CASE 19–2: YOUR WORD AGAINST HIS

You are at a meeting chaired by your department head. Also present are another department head and four other supervisors. The subject of the meeting is the manner in which the prison's supervisors are to conduct themselves during the present union organizing campaign.

Your department head makes a statement concerning one way in which supervisors should behave. You are surprised to hear this because earlier that same day you read a legal opinion that described this particular action as probably illegal.

You interrupt with, "Pardon me, but I don't believe it can really be done that way. I'm certain it would leave us open to an unfair labor practice charge."

Obviously irritated with the interruption, your department head responds sharply, "This isn't open to discussion. You're wrong."

You open your mouth to speak again, but you are cut short by an angry glance.

You are certain that the boss is wrong; he had inadvertently turned around a pair of words and described a "cannot-do" as a "can-do." Unfortunately you are in a conference room full of people and the document that could prove your point is in your office.

## Questions

1. Recognizing that you are but an attendee at the meeting and that your immediate superior is running the meeting, what should you—or what can you—do to assure that the other participants do not act on critically incorrect information immediately after the meeting?

2. What fundamental requirements of effective meeting leadership appear to have been ignored in this meeting?

## CHAPTER 20

# Budgeting: The Annual Trauma

*A budget is a means of telling your money where to go—instead of wondering where it went.*

*—Anonymous*

## Chapter Objectives

☛ Introduce the basic concepts of budgeting and establish the importance of budget preparation to the individual manager.

☛ Describe the advantages of participative approaches to budgeting.

☛ Define operating budgets, capital budgets, and cash budgets.

☛ Describe the process of developing an institution's annual budget from the budgets of individual departments.

☛ Illustrate the fundamentals of the process of monitoring expenditures against budget allocations.

## INTRODUCING THE BUDGET

There are likely to be considerable differences in the ways supervisors approach this chapter. In some prisons, individual supervisors have been actively involved in the budgeting process for years. In others, however, the budget remains a mysterious collection of numbers assembled by the headquarters staff or the prison's business office with no supervisory involvement whatsoever. Even more variation is introduced into the budget process when private prisons are included in the discussion, because then it is tied more closely to a fluctuating revenue stream.

If you have often been directly involved in the preparation of departmental budgets, you will find little in this chapter that you have not encountered in practice. However, if your budget preparation experience is minimal or nonexistent, you are likely to benefit from this basic discussion of budgeting. By providing an overview of the budget and the budgeting process, this chapter offers some specifics for consideration by prison managers who do not have backgrounds in accounting and finance (certainly the vast majority of supervisors, both in and out of corrections).

A budget is a financial plan that serves as an estimate of future operations and, to some extent, as a means of control over those operations. It is a quantitative expression of the agency's or the prison's operating intentions. A budget translates intentions into numbers.

A budget can be several things to the institution and to the individual supervisor. Used as a control mechanism, it can be a cost-containment tool that helps keep costs in line with available resources. It can also be a basis for performance evaluation, since a budget provides a quantitative indication of how well a manager uses the resources under his or her control. Further, a budget can be a means for directing efforts toward productivity improvement—since comparing performance against budget reveals how well resources are used, and can give a manager the basis from which to work for better resource utilization.

### Participative Budgeting

In some states, the legislature is engaged in the budget process. A warden may have to appear before legislative committees to represent the needs of his or her institution in order to receive adequate funding and positions for the coming year's operations. Often, this is participative budgeting in name only, as the funding parameters are set in advance and the agency representative has only nominal impact on the final budget allocation.

In some agencies the budget is prepared "upstairs" in the headquarters office and handed down for wardens and their subordinates to carry out. This practice leaves a great deal to be desired, as it requires the supervisor to implement a plan without having participated in the plan's development. The supervisor may remain ignorant of many of the whys and wherefores of the budget and thus be in a position of weakness when it comes to translating the financial plan into action at the departmental level.

Other institutions bring their supervisors into the budgeting process, at least for the purpose of structured requests that will be presented as a consolidated package to the agency's headquarters. This more team-like approach to budgeting, requiring active participation of managers at all levels, calls for close coordination of many diverse inputs and activities. It takes considerably more time and effort to assemble a budget in this manner than it does simply to allow the administration and the business office to get their heads together and issue a budget. The results of the team approach are well worth the extra work though, because it provides several distinct advantages:

- The end item of the process, the budget, is usually a far more realistic and workable plan than any that could be developed by some other means.
- The involvement of individual supervisors in the process breeds their commitment; they are more likely to believe in the budget and strive to make it work because they took part in its development.
- The interdepartmental and intradepartmental activities and interpersonal contacts pursued during the process tend to strengthen supervisors in their jobs.
- A spirit and attitude of teamwork is created in getting managers at all levels to work together toward a common goal. Teamwork is, to a great extent, one of the keys to the successful operation of an organization.
- The encouragement of more realistic planning serves to sharpen the focus of management's efforts and produce more appropriate results a greater part of the time.

Involving you, the individual supervisor, in the creation of the budget helps to define clearly the authority you possess and the responsibility you are charged with in the operation of your department. Quite simply, you created your budget, so you are responsible for operating within it.

Although the responsibility for draft budget preparation may lie with the supervisor, there is no reason for involvement not to extend below that level. As you will discover in this chapter, there are certain budget-related activities (such as the accumulation of operating statistics) in which some of your employees could participate. Employees who understand the nature of the budget and the reasons behind its preparation are more likely to share actively in working toward the department's objectives.

## Accounting Concepts

Before we discuss how a budget is structured, explanations of a pair of simple but important concepts are in order: the *fiscal year* and *fixed versus flexible budgets*.

The fiscal year is simply your institution's or agency's 12-month accounting year. This may be any consecutive 12-month period established for accounting purposes; for instance, May 1 this year to April 30 of next year. This means that for accounting purposes your institution's "year" begins on May 1. However, your fiscal year is just as likely to be coincident with the calendar year beginning January 1. The governments of many states and the federal government use something other than the calendar year as their fiscal year. Private correctional firms are similarly free to adopt a fiscal year other than the calendar year.

Within the accounting year are a number of accounting periods. It is common practice to keep track of payroll and certain other expenses on a basis of one, two, or four weeks and to accumulate this information on the basis of the four-week "accounting period." Thus there are 13 such accounting periods in the year. However, other important facts and figures are accumulated by month either because it is necessary to do so or because this is clearly the best data collection period available. Accountants and others speak of the "monthly closing," the act of determining the financial results or status of operations for a given month.

One of the biggest headaches encountered in budgeting involves differences in the length of the periods for which some data are accumulated. Payroll data almost always are kept in two- or four-week periods; many other expenses and various operating statistics are accumulated by month. In developing a budget, and especially in examining the results of operations after the fact, it is frequently necessary to manipulate some of the figures by "adding in" or "backing out" certain numbers at either end of a given period so you have complete information for the period you are interested in.

The idea of fixed versus flexible budgeting refers to the structural character of the budget relative to activity throughout the year. A fixed budget, by far the simpler of the two, assumes a stable level of operations throughout the year and spreads all budgeted costs evenly across the 12 months. A flexible budget, however, recognizes that certain costs can vary as the level of operations varies and attempts to account for this variation in the budget. Utilities will fluctuate with the season. Inmate population levels and associated costs will rise and fall in response to factors outside the prison manager's control. A flexible budget may treat certain costs as fixed because they are in fact fixed or because this is simply the best way to handle them, but it will also attempt to identify and allow for costs that vary as departmental activity varies.

## THE TOTAL BUDGET

There are several parts to the institution's overall budget, some calling for the supervisor's involvement and some that the supervisor will rarely be concerned with. The parts and subparts of the total budget described in the following paragraphs are each properly identified as budgets in their own right. To say "a budget is a part of a budget" reflects how these financial plans have always been described.

## The Operating Budget

The operating budget usually consists of three parts.

### Statistical Budget

The statistical budget is made up of projections of activity for the coming budget year. Usually based on a combination of past activity, current trends, and some limited knowledge of future conditions and circumstances, this is the institution's or agency's best estimate of work activity for the coming 12-month period. These estimates are projections of statistics such as expected commitments or releases, inmate-days expected, number of meals to be served, pounds of laundry to be processed, and so on. These may be prepared as gross, fixed estimates of a year's activity, or they may be projected by month based on certain knowledge suggesting variations in activity.

If the appropriate data are not maintained in the individual department, the business office will compile and summarize the most recent historical data and projections available and supply this information to the various departments. It is often necessary for the departments to refine these figures into detailed estimates of activities for the coming budget year. You accomplish this refinement the same way the business office makes its projections—based on past activity in your department and your particular knowledge of future operations. The assistance of the agency's research department is particularly valuable for departments like food service, the laundry, and medical services where population projections drive many of the costs involved in budgets.

### Expense Budget

The expense budget attempts to account for actual cost of operations (personnel and all other costs) for each department individually and for the institution as a whole. The departmental expense budget is the major area of supervisory involvement in the budgeting process.

### Revenue Budget

While public correctional agencies know the amount appropriated for the various budget areas, the private sector must take into account a revenue component. Usually prepared by the organization's accounting department, the revenue budget projects income likely to be received by the institution during the budget year, based on contractual information or inmate-day revenue projections.

Keep in mind that the revenue budget must allow for the impact of a wide range of factors because it ultimately must cover all costs of operation (and estimated profit margins in the case of a private prison). A revenue budget for a private sector prison may have to reflect the impact of another state sending inmates to the prison; the effects of a program being eliminated or curtailed; changes in staffing levels that have a direct bearing on cost; the impact of decisions and recommendations of the contracting agency; and, the effects of changes in reimbursement regulations or a contract renegotiation.

## The Capital Budget

A capital budget is prepared to account for potential expenditures for major fixed and movable equipment. Fixed equipment (a building, a boiler, or a new roof) and major movable equipment (computers, copy machines, package X-ray machines) represent those costs that must be "capitalized." These costs apply to operations for considerably longer than just a single budget period, so they must be spread out over a number of periods.

Sometimes the boundary between capital purchases and items that can be allocated to operations in the budget period is hazy. The agency or state revenue department usually has its own rules (consistent with legal guidelines) for determining what should be called a capital purchase. That guide may be expressed as some specific amount of money, some useful-life criterion, or a combination of these. For instance, your institution may have decided that any purchased item having a useful life longer than one year and costing more than $200 must be capitalized. Thus a $250 rifle would be capitalized, but a $150 gas mask would not, although both will clearly last longer than one year.

As a supervisor you should make it a point to learn your agency's guidelines for identifying capital assets. You may either ask for a certain item in your capital budget request or attempt to secure it through your departmental expense budget depending on where it fits your agency's definition.

In capital budgeting, requests for purchases often outrun the money available. Requests may come from all directions: from the security staff, who would like new shotguns for the towers; from the legislature, which may pass a law requiring a certain vocational training program with attendant equipment costs; from supervisors and department heads, who would like to have newer and better equipment; and from the federal government, which may tell your institution there is something you need to buy to enable you to conform with some code, regulation, or requirement (such as most recently has been the case with the Americans with Disability Act).

Compiling a capital budget may also require the institution to develop short-range and long-range capital plans to determine best what new and replacement equipment will be required for future operations. This involves looking at all equipment and listing each piece along with its age, original cost, and estimated replacement date. When looking at capital equipment within your own department, you should at least list all items according to projected replacement date and then go on to add your ideas of what new equipment you may require in the foreseeable future. Automated information systems in many correctional agencies assist in this and other budget-related processes.

Capital budget requests usually receive close scrutiny. The competing interests of the safety manager (who says three new floor buffers are needed to properly maintain the new tile that was just installed in all the corridors), the food service managers (who wants a walk-in freezer that will help cut food costs), and the chief of security (who needs the new high-volume chemical agent dispersal machine that every other prison in the system already has), all must be balanced in the process. Therefore, a request for a substantial capital expenditure must usually be accompanied by:

- a realistic assessment of the urgency or priority of the purchase
- detailed projections of all costs involved in the acquisition
- a full description of the items involved and the rationale (justification)
- a statement as to whether the requested item represents an addition, replacement, or improvement
- the impact, in the case of a revenue-producing department such as prison industries, of the proposed acquisition on revenues.

Most capital budget requests are ordinarily subject to several levels of review and approval. As a supervisor you may have been assigned a certain dollar limit for capital purchases for your department, but this amount will usually be low when reckoned against the cost of desired capital purchases.

It is just as likely that you personally will have no capital budget approval authority in your department. Your immediate supervisor, or perhaps the warden, associate warden, or business manager, may retain the authority to approve capital purchases up to a given amount. Some very large capital expenditures, however, may be authorized only by the headquarters office. Large-scale computer purchases, for instance, may be controlled at the headquarters level in order to achieve economies of purchasing scale across the entire system and to ensure compatibility for all computer software or hardware used in the agency. In the private sector, the warden may be given authority for procurement up to certain levels. Procurements above that level must be approved at the company's headquarters in order to authorize the amortization of those costs over a period of time. Installation of a new fence system and razor wire would not be charged against a single year's revenues, for instance.

## The Cash Budget

The cash budget is prepared by the business office or accounting department and is usually done last in the budgeting process. It consists of estimates of the institution's cash needs as compared with allocated funding or (in the case of the private sector) projections of cash receipts over the term covered by the budget.

The pattern of cash-in versus cash-out examined in the cash budget is extremely important to the institution because of the need to remain financially solvent. Most governmental agencies have to comply with what is called an "anti-deficiency" law that requires that the agency spend no more than its allocated funding. This statutory requirement is a very compelling reason to carefully control all spending. For private prisons, of course, the impetus is to make sure there is a healthy bottom line for stockholders.

## THE BUDGETING PROCESS

We need not be reminded at this point that a departmental budget is far from precise. There are any number of management actions you can take when actual costs and activity begin to move one way or the other. For instance, you may wish to permit or even encourage the heaviest use of vacation time during periods when workload falls off, if there is such a period for your prison. Some prison systems structure their annual leave systems to take annual training and other similar factors into account. These proactive steps help reduce reliance on costly overtime to cover for staff vacancies.

Also, by highlighting all elements of cost in the department, the budget affords you an ongoing awareness of supply expenses and other variable costs. Should you see the cost of supplies suddenly exceeding the projected amount, you are alerted to the need for investigation and possible action. Without a budget, certain costs could run unexplainably high for perhaps months without your becoming aware of the situation.

A budget, remember, is a plan. As such it attempts to look into a time that is not yet here, and it is necessarily based on estimates and projections. In no way is it ever to be regarded as a preordained, concrete picture of future events. Your budget rarely will reflect your exact plans and priorities, and rarely will the results be exactly as predicted. In this respect the budget is much like any other management tool: It cannot do the management job for you, but chances are you will do a better management job with it than you would do without it.

### Responsibilities

The responsibility for preparing the budget rests in part with several individuals and groups. In the public sector, the head of the agency is ultimately responsible for everything in the budget and thus retains the authority for final approval of the budget, subject to the state's legislative authorization system. Although the director of corrections will not likely become involved in the details of budget preparation, he or she will probably rule on major proposed capital expenditures item by item, and review and approve the principal parts of the budget, subject to legislative review. In the private sector, overall budget authorization and profit targets often remain with the company's headquarters staff, but within those parameters the warden has considerable discretion in spending.

At the individual institution level, the warden must assure that the budget being submitted to the agency head is consistent with the goals of the prison. It also must be realistic and workable in the light of current knowledge of expected population levels, programs, and expenses.

The business manager has an active role in preparing the cash and revenue budgets and assembling all pieces of the operating budget into a total budget for the institution. Like the warden, the business manager must assure that budgeting guidelines are followed and that the resulting plan appears to be workable and realistic in terms of what is known about the coming budget year.

All managers and department heads, at least under a participative budgeting approach, are responsible for assembling the expense and capital budgets for their own departments. In accounting or budgeting terms, the smallest organizational unit for which a budget is prepared is usually identified as a "cost center." A cost center—an organizational unit for which costs are identified and collected—is usually provided with expense and capital budgets prepared by the supervisor. In the case of middle- or upper-level managers who may have charge of several cost centers, the task also includes assembling individual cost-center budgets into a budget for their total area of responsibility.

At both the institutional and headquarters levels, budget committees may be established each year to facilitate the preparation of the budget. The institutional committee will usually consist of the warden, the business manager, the associate warden(s), and key department heads. It is the role of the budget committee to establish and distribute the guidelines for budget preparation, to decide how particular problems should be solved and certain issues dealt with as they occur, and to keep all stages of budget preparation activity moving toward completion.

## The Budget Coordination Meeting

A budget coordination meeting may be used as a "kickoff" for the year's budget-building activity. If the target for forwarding the institution budget to headquarters is the end of October, the budget coordination meeting may take place in June or July. Convened and conducted by members of the budget committee, the coordination meeting should include all managers who have an active role in budget preparation. At this meeting current and expected cost-related operational factors are discussed (per diem food and other expenses, salary fund usage levels, etc.), policies affecting budgeting are reviewed, and any changes are noted. Planned organizational changes likely to affect budgeting factors are reviewed and clarified, and trends of likely future activity are discussed. In short, any known or suspected factor that may have a bearing on budget preparation is reviewed.

The use of a budget manual can assist in this process. The manual is a book of informational and instructional documents assembled by the budget committee for the current year's budget preparation activity. Given to each person who must prepare and present a budget for one or more cost centers, this manual contains all information, instructions, and forms necessary for budget preparation.

The budget manual describes the full scope and purpose of the budgeting program; outlines all procedures for preparation, review, and revision of budgets; and defines the duties and authority and responsibility of all persons involved in the process.

## The Budget Calendar

The preparation of the budget for a sizeable prison is an exercise in timing. Budgets for dozens of individual cost centers must be put together, and these must be assembled into budgets for larger organizational units and eventually into a budget for the whole institution. If two or three pieces are missing, the total budget is delayed. The budget calendar provides deadlines for all steps in the budget preparation process. The calendar will let a supervisor know when the department's draft budget must be submitted, when it is likely to be returned following initial review, when the revision must be submitted, and how much time must be allowed for the approval process.

Much of the trauma that can be encountered in the annual budgeting exercise is due to matters of timing. We often tend to get things done at the deadline or perhaps a little late, and our planning rarely anticipates all contingencies. As a result, it is often necessary to go through the whole process again, perhaps several times, on the way to a realistic, workable budget for the entire institution.

Supervisors can enter the budgeting process with the best of intentions. However, the results may be unsatisfactory the first time around because the key persons assembling the final budget simply do not know exactly where the totals are going to fall until all the pieces are put together for the first time. We then must shift resources in more appropriate directions to come up with a budget that is realistic under the circumstances.

## Review and Coordination

When all of the individual departments' draft budgets are submitted, the business office staff ordinarily prepare the total budget for review and approval. The budget may go through several drafts before the budget committee believes it has a document appropriate for submission to the warden, and ultimately to the agency head.

## Adoption

While procedures vary from one agency to another, ordinarily the budget is forwarded to the agency head for review and approval. The summary information provided generally includes:

- a narrative description of the budget, some of its key elements, and the reasons behind its preparation in this manner
- relevant appropriation information (or a condensed income statement in the case of private facilities) for the budget period
- a summary of capital expenditure requests
- a cash analysis covering the budget period
- the key factors used in forecasting
- estimates of the impact of this budget on the institution's services and fiscal status

The agency head will either approve or reject the budget in whole or in part. If adjustments are needed because of conflicting priorities between prisons or due to other agency needs, necessary elements of the process are repeated until the agency head approves a budget for the institution for the coming year.

## MONITORING EXPENDITURES

A budget should be a live, working plan. This requires timely and accurate reporting of operating results. Even though public prisons do not have to deal with the problem of variable cash flow related to per diem payments, they still must be mindful of the status of their appropriation account as the year progresses.

Tracking and reporting the results of operations is generally a responsibility of the accounting or business office staff. Timeliness is essential; it stands to reason that the more recent the feedback received on results, the more valuable the budget is for highlighting the need for management action. The information received each month—a comparison of operating results for the period with the budget projections for the period—allows you to make adjustments for those aspects of operations that are wholly or partly under direct supervisory control. For example, an extremely high increase in the cost of vegetables for a sustained period of time early in the budget year can throw the food service budget into a crisis late in the year if adjustments are not made as soon as possible.

## GENERAL TIPS FOR BUDGET REVIEW AND MANAGEMENT

Reporting is often done in a way that highlights exceptions. That is, the reporting system, built on recognition of the likely presence of natural variations between operating results and budget projections, will specifically flag items that appear to be out of line beyond normally expected variations.

In a financial sense, minus signs carry a negative connotation for many people, but their meaning in a budget report can be just the opposite. A minus sign after a variance (expressed as either a dollar amount or percentage) often indicates a favorable variance—being under budget by that amount. However, the use of minus signs in budget reports is not always consistent from organization to organization and one should be careful to learn what conventions are being used when reading any such document.

Often a budget report shows charges made against a "zero" budget—that is, an account for which the department has budgeted no expenditures. This happens because people in the department make errors filling out requisitions and other forms. Or, people filling out forms may not provide sufficient detail, leaving others to place the charges in specific accounts. To prevent these errors, the supervisor should assure that all the department's employees who trigger expenditures and charges supply full charging information, which usually includes both department number and specific account number.

Occasionally, charges to accounts for which there is no budget may be legitimate. If the account in question appears to be the most logical place for a particular charge, but there happens to be no budget, this should serve as a flag to consider that account as a legitimate line item for the coming budget year (if it appears as though such charges may occur again).

The supervisor is often provided with guidelines for analyzing the budget report and answering for variances. Such guidelines are usually expressed in terms of a variance threshold beyond which answers are expected.

- For personnel costs, explanation or justification must be provided for variances beyond plus or minus a certain percent or dollar amount for total departmental labor costs for the month.
- For nonpersonnel expense, explanation or justification must be provided for variances beyond plus or minus a certain percent or dollar amount for any specific account for the month.

Answering to variances under budget is almost as important as answering to variances over budget. Being under budget for a period does not necessarily mean that money is being saved or that a favorable condition is emerging. It can often indicate that expenditures are occurring in a pattern inconsistent with the budget allocation, and it can sometimes indicate that certain necessary or desirable expenditures have been overlooked. For instance, a low figure in a salary account (due to vacant positions) might be more than offset by higher expenses in an overtime category elsewhere in the budget.

Under a comprehensive financial control system, supervisors are usually expected to answer to their immediate supervisor for budget variances. In addition to being provided with a monthly report of expenditures versus budget, the supervisor usually receives detailed backup information about the individual charges made to each account. This backup makes it possible to assess the validity of most charges.

In working with budget reports you should make it a habit to question all details that you do not fully understand. Learning month by month where all the department's budget dollars are going will eventually enable you to alter patterns of expenditures (at least partially) in order to modify unfavorable trends as they develop.

## CONTROL: AWARENESS PLUS ACTION

Preparing a budget and working with it throughout the year heightens your awareness of how the department's resources—for which you are responsible—are used in fulfilling the department's responsibilities. Reports of actual results versus budget projections provide all-important information on which to base corrective action when needed. For instance, when productivity problems occur and the relationship between worked hours and the volume of work begins to change unfavorably, you can take positive steps that might include effective use of overtime, review of scheduling of vacations and other time off, and routine scheduling of personnel for day-to-day coverage.

What is the value of the budget process and feedback on actual operations from the perspective of a complete organizational unit—whether a small department, a prison, or even an entire agency? At any time you know where you are relative to where you thought you might be, and you also know where you must look for improvement.

## CHAPTER 21

# Quality, Excellence, and Productivity: Old Friends in Modern Times

*Quality never costs as much money as it saves.*

*—Anonymous*

*We are not at our best perched at the summit; we are climbers, at our best when the way is steep.*

*—John W. Gardner*

## Chapter Objectives

☛ Compare the total quality movement and traditional concerns for quality in corrections.

☛ Identify the conditions necessary for the success of a total quality management program.

☛ Review the progression of the concern for productivity in corrections and reinforce the need for attention to continuing productivity improvement.

☛ Interrelate the concerns for quality and productivity as dimensions of the same overall concern for organizational efficiency and identify these considerations as an ongoing part of the supervisory role.

## THE TOTAL QUALITY MOVEMENT: "EXCELLENCE" ALL OVER AGAIN?

It appears that "quality" has become the fashionable business term of the 1990s, in the way that "excellence" was management's fashionable word of the 1980s. Although the total quality movement (TQM) and the excellence movement of the recent past had somewhat different origins, both came from basically sound and well-intentioned philosophies that have been adopted, adapted, promoted, and implemented with extremely mixed results.

The excellence movement was sparked by a phenomenally successful nonfiction book, *In Search of Excellence.* This book was so successful that being concerned with excellence in the conduct of enterprise of all kinds suddenly became fashionable. The fundamental message of *In Search of Excellence* was copied, reworked, repackaged, and expanded

329

upon by countless authors, consultants, trainers, and others. Business organizations of all sizes began to claim excellence as a goal that they had attained or were on their way to attaining.

Peters and Waterman, in their now almost classic work about organization quality, *In Search of Excellence*,[1] outline eight key attributes of what they view as excellent companies:

1. A bias for action
2. Close to the customer
3. Autonomy and entrepreneurship
4. Productivity through people
5. Hands-on, value driven
6. Stick to the knitting (stick with something you know)
7. Simple form, lean staff
8. Simultaneous loose-tight properties

In many ways, these traits form the framework of the total quality management movement in the United States today.

Features of TQM include the following.

1. Emphasis on teams and teamwork means that employees work together and solve problems in collaborative groups or taskforces that may cut across traditionally isolated functions and levels.
2. Sources of defects, errors, or inefficiencies are continually sought with the objective of eliminating them before, rather than after, production.
3. Measurement through statistical quality control (measuring and analyzing inconsistencies in manufactured products) and statistical process control (analyzing deviations in manufacturing processes) may be emphasized. This characteristic applies to correctional facilities that manufacture a product.
4. Participative management delegates tasks and responsibility to employees. Supervisors manage through a supportive, coaching style of leadership that invites input from employees.
5. Benchmarking is a continuous rating of the institution's departments and processes against model operations.
6. An emphasis on satisfying customers ensures that every employee understands the overall mission of the institution and his or her part in reaching for objectives that ensure success in meeting specific and general objectives.

7. A long-term management commitment to total quality management is illustrated by active involvement, participative leadership, and open communication.
8. Continuous training and development of employees is offered at every level.

Organizations that attempt to adopt excellence as a guiding philosophy of operations sometimes run into a problem: how to instill a philosophy in people so that it will eventually drive them to behave in a desired manner. Between the philosophy, which may initially be accepted by a few members of management near the top of the organization, and the actual practice, which involves many employees living out the philosophy, there lies the matter of transferring the philosophy from the few to the many.

A great many people never truly adopt the philosophy. They simply go through the motions, appearing to do what they perceive top management wants them to do. Invariably, when a philosophy is proceduralized—that is, when a process is superimposed upon something as ethereal as a concept, idea, or belief—something is lost. And those who simply adopt the process as part of the job without adopting the philosophy as their own will not truly reflect the philosophy in their behavior.

When a philosophy of management is overproceduralized, overpromoted, overpublicized, and overpraised, it becomes a fad. It becomes fashionable for its own sake. We have reason to wonder, therefore, whether the total quality movement may be just the latest management fad, destined to go the way of management by objectives (MBO) and excellence. Many employees, including many experienced managers, seem to think so. Unless their understanding of quality management is more than superficial, any new program along these lines will be difficult.

## CAN THE IDEA OF QUALITY BE NEW?

For years, many of the manufacturing and service industries had what was referred to as quality control. Quality control ordinarily concentrated on finding defects, rejecting defective products, and providing information with which to alter processes so they would produce fewer defects.

Whereas some prisons and headquarters offices conducted periodic audits of each institution's departmental functioning, most correctional agencies had very little of what is called quality assurance. In this context, quality assurance consisted largely of scrutinizing records to detect and tally departures from some established standard. This provided a starting point for reducing the same kinds of errors in the future.

In addition to correcting the processes that produced the errors, both quality control and quality assurance were often responsible for instituting more frequent quality checkpoints during the work process itself, so that errors might be caught earlier. Both quality control and quality assurance focused primarily on finding errors after the fact. Both were, and still are, retrospective processes.

Recently—using philosophical grounding and methods exported from the United States to Japan decades earlier and later brought back as "new, revolutionary management techniques"—the emphasis on quality has begun to shift from "catch errors before they go out the door" to "avoid making the errors in the first place." Thus we have the "new" idea of quality embodied today in labels such as total quality management and continuous quality improvement (CQI).

## Old Friends in New Clothes?

Many of the tools and techniques utilized under the TQM umbrella should look familiar to some people who have been in the work force for a few years. Many of the so-called current tools and techniques have been around for decades. They are presently being resurrected and revitalized, and in some instances renamed.

For example, a number of TQM-implementation case histories mention the acronym TOPS, standing for team-oriented problem-solving. As the name suggests, workers who have active concerns with various aspects of particular problems approach problem solving as a team, with a common goal and purpose. These problem-solving teams espoused under total quality management look, sound, and function the same as the quality circles promoted during the brief popularity of "Japanese management." "Self-directed work teams" and "team-oriented process improvement" are essentially quality circles by another name.

Quality circles were themselves nothing new when they were so named. In years past many work organizations used what were called "work simplification project teams," in function and intent identical to quality circles and the problem-solving teams of total quality management. Written about in the 1950s and earlier, these teams began to find a place in some service organizations as early as 1956.[2]

Many of the specific tools used by today's TQM problem solvers go back 50, 60, 70 years or more. Serious managers who believe in the potential of total quality management are finding that these techniques are as valuable today as they have ever been.

## THE GREAT FACILITATOR

Regardless of how many previously popular techniques are returned to the spotlight or how many genuinely new wrinkles are added, there remains one ingredient that is fully as essential to TQM as it has been to any other approach by any other name. That crucial ingredient is top management commitment.

The primary condition necessary to establish total quality management is long-term management commitment illustrated by active involvement, participative leadership, and open communication. This should come as no surprise; top management commitment to new ideas and approaches is a prerequisite to success for any organized enterprise. Without it, most organized endeavors are destined to, at best, generate results that fall short of intentions or, at worst, fail altogether.

One cannot imagine any rational top manager openly avowing opposition to the principle of quality improvement. Ask any top manager whose organization has espoused TQM if he or she is truly committed to it. Or ask any top manager if quality is a personal commitment. Surely each will state unwavering support. We know that many enterprises fail because of insufficient top management commitment. But since most managers will voice commitment, there is but one conclusion to be drawn: Top management commitment is a matter of degree. And it is the degree of commitment that is critical.

None of today's total quality programs will work as intended unless top management is actively promoting the concept. Superficial, lip-service-only commitment at the top results in similar weak commitment at lower organizational levels. Beware the skyrocket commitment of the top manager who gets all fired up over TQM, distributes information to everyone, creates a TQM steering committee, advisory committee, and chairs the first few meetings—but then starts missing meetings because of "pressing business" and transfers the guiding role to subordinates.

Understanding and adopting total quality management requires basic changes in thought and behavior patterns of management and employees. No matter how sincerely one believes in the underlying philosophy or aspires to the proposed results, change is difficult. One of the greater challenges to many managers is the participative management style which delegates tasks and responsibilities to employees. (See Chapters 5 and 17.)

If managers, especially first-line supervisors, will not let go of some of their decision-making power and delegate to employees, a total quality management program has little hope of taking hold. Delegation means not simply giving employees the responsibility for doing different tasks or detraining more efficient methods; it means also giving them the authority to make the decisions necessary to implement their own decisions. Further, delegating means accepting what the employees decide and living with it.

Delegating is particularly difficult for managers who have habitually managed by authoritarianism, a style that expects unquestioning submission to authority on the part of employees. Authoritarianism remains a common management style even with the movement to an open participative management style in many areas.

Some managers simply have not been exposed to the benefits of participative management. Most learn about management from other managers, and these tend to be organizational superiors who, for good or ill, are role models to those newer in management.

Subtle proof of the existence of the authoritarian streak can be experienced by the manager who might ponder his or her reaction to being pushed abruptly into a fully participative management situation. The manager may feel that participative management equals weakness, and that delegating decision-making authority to subordinates is somehow surrendering one's responsibility.

Changes in management style and approach have to occur in order for a quality management program to be successful. In most instances the manager will need to shift from being the boss—from planning, telling, instructing, and controlling—to being the leader of a team— being counselor, teacher, coach, and facilitator. Management's commitment can be seen as a total commitment not only to participative management and employee empowerment but also to intra- and interdepartmental teamwork and improved communication throughout the organization.

### Convincing Staff TQM Applies to Prisons

Convincing staff that prison is not so different as to invalidate the core concepts of quality management is a key starting point for any

TQM program in corrections. It is easy to say that you can't measure output in relation to inmates in any meaningful way and thus the program is useless in prison.

That is far from true. The easiest examples to use are seen in jobs such as secretary or clerk. These positions involve performance of tasks that are easily observable, quantifiable to a certain degree, and thus easy to monitor. The quality of typing as measured by typographical errors, or the quality of filing as measured by the rate of misfiled documents, can be clear indicators of the performance level of the employees involved. And certainly there is no reason why staff in those categories cannot be included in a participatory scheme that solicits and incorporates their views on how their jobs can be done more effectively.

But even the performance of correctional officers can be brought into such a framework. There is nothing preventing supervisory staff from tracking the number of cell searches conducted each day, the manner in which pat searches are conducted as inmates go in and out of housing units, or the contents of safety and sanitation reports on those units, in order to assess correctional officer performance. And there is nothing to stop a TQM-oriented manager from structuring a participatory scheme that includes the input of those same officers. To a certain extent, the unit management system mentioned earlier is a solid starting point for just this kind of interaction and participation in the quality process.

But in any case, there is no validity to the claim that the principles of TQM cannot be put into place in prison. The old saying, "If you can't find time to do it right the first time, how are you going to find time to do it over?" is equally applicable when talking about a poorly-written memo about an inmate, a poorly-typed report on the prison's budget, a poorly-conducted cell search, or a poorly-repaired plumbing leak in the powerhouse.

## Will Total Quality Management Prevail?

Total quality management has every chance of working where previous and perhaps partial efforts undertaken under other names have failed. Activity undertaken in the name of quality improvement is presently so widespread that the impression that "everyone is doing it" places considerable pressure on the supposed few who have yet to undertake quality management. With so much happening in the name of TQM we will find that, in some organizations, top management commitment is real and lasting. Also, some organizations' genuine successes will inspire others to try following a similar path.

Within corrections specifically, it will be difficult to avoid considering the adoption of quality management because of growing pressure to control costs, which can be accomplished by improving quality. This can only be done when TQM is accepted, not as a "project" or one-time fix, but rather as a permanent philosophy of operations.

### More Than Just a Job

For total quality management to work, the majority of employees in the organization need to experience sufficient commitment to their employing institution to see it as more than just a place to work. This can be a tall order indeed in these times of staff shortages, increasing numbers of inmates, shrinking funding, and growing pressure from the courts.

Today, prisons are wrestling with increased population levels and limited fiscal resources, notwithstanding massive construction programs that have barely been able to keep pace with commitment activity in most states. It seems clear that the tools and techniques of total quality management offer a workable means of reconciling concerns about quality and cost, and to some extent helping corrections deal with explosive growth. Once again it comes down to a matter of commitment: If employees at all levels are sincerely committed to the organization, its mission, and its inmate population, there is no reasonable way that TQM can not work.

For reasons suggested throughout these pages, some attempts to implement total quality management will fail. For some people, quality will gather dust in the old-management-approach graveyard along with all the other techniques that were tried, half-heartedly applied, and discarded. Some attempts, however, will succeed. And those correctional organizations that successfully implement TQM in the years to come will find themselves among the stronger, more adaptable prisons, which translates operationally into a safer, more humane environment for staff and inmates, and a greater level of public safety overall.

## PRODUCTIVITY IN PRISONS

For public prison employees it is reasonable to ask why we should be concerned about this issue, especially in the face of government budget systems that only indirectly encourage concern for productivity. Of course, for private sector prisons the answer is obvious—the bottom line. However, for both private and public prisons, productivity deserves attention because:

- It is simply good management to want to apply available resources to best effect
- It is possible, in an organization as varied and complex as a modern prison, to redistribute resources from areas of savings to other essentials
- The inflationary spiral affects all business and financial activities, and when resource inputs grow at a rate faster than system outputs, costs increase
- There is increasing external pressure to hold costs down while continuing to provide quality programs to inmates

Further, concern about productivity needs to be ongoing. One of the common errors of productivity's heyday was to regard productivity improvement as a one-time effort that could sweep through an organization and make it more efficient for all time. Not so. Some of the larger, more obvious corrections are one-time changes, but the need for attention to productivity is ongoing. Left unto itself an activity will be subject to creeping inefficiencies that eventually grow to be a significant problem. Left unto themselves most human activities will suffer diminished productivity; regular attention is needed to keep them tuned and running efficiently.

Concern for productivity is not particular to the prison setting. The National Commission on Productivity and Work Quality came into being in 1970 because American productivity had declined in the late 1960s and had yet to show signs of recovering. Productivity statistics indicated gradual recovery through the 1970s; many people probably assumed the problem had gone away. However, more recent indications suggest that the problem has returned, if indeed it has ever been away.

A July 1991 news story from the Associated Press carried the headline, "U.S. Standard of Living Falls for First Time since '82."[3] The story reported that Americans' standard of living declined slightly in 1990 "as the country fell further behind in its ability to compete internationally," according to the Council on Competitiveness. Specifically, "The council said in its fourth annual competitiveness index that America lost ground in such key areas as living standards, productivity, and investment."

The council's index measures the relative performance of the world's seven richest industrial countries. According to the report the United

States was the only country to experience an outright drop in living standards the last year referenced, and for three consecutive years it had ranked last of the seven in terms of the share of its economy devoted to investment.

The Council on Competitiveness is of course dealing primarily with manufacturing concerns, but the references to living standard, productivity, and investment relate to the entire American economy. With corrections accounting for a growing portion of government budgets nationwide, there is no denying the impact of prison productivity on our society. States in particular are having to make difficult choices about whether to fund schools, bridges, or prisons.

Today's government fiscal crisis means that there inevitably will be calls for a close examination of prison operations for potential improvements in productivity in order to reduce costs. In the mid-1990s there were calls at the federal level to curtail prison programs perceived as amenities, although these initiatives were for punitive reasons as much as for alleged cost-cutting. Paradoxically, "three strikes" legislation was being enacted in many jurisdictions, which had the effect of driving prison populations—and costs—up even further. If a prison is expected to do more with the same or fewer resources, it follows that responsible management will seek all reasonable ways of improving productivity. That makes TQM something that every correctional manager should consider.

## SIDES OF THE SAME COIN

The total quality management movement has its concern for productivity at a time when a variety of other factors are also pointing toward the need for improved productivity. Indeed, the quality issue is inseparable from productivity; one has direct implications for the other, and there is a direct relationship between them.

In the future, however, concern for productivity may not be limited to just the methods-improvement, cost-cutting, staff-reduction activities frequently associated with management engineering. Although work measurement may play a large part in productivity improvement, the view of productivity, and the scope of future effort will likely be more global than past efforts.

In any activity productivity is represented by a relationship between input and output, that is:

$$\text{Output/Input} = \text{Productivity}$$

Any process or activity has associated with it a level of quality, broadly describing quality as the relative acceptability of the output. Any change in productivity involves changes between and among all of these factors. Thus productivity may be said to be improved if:

- output is increased while input is held constant or decreased and quality is held constant (doing more with the same or less)
- input is decreased while output is held constant or increased while quality is held constant (doing the same or more with less)
- quality is improved while input and output are held constant or reduced (doing better with the same or less)

It follows, then, that productivity is reduced if the opposite of any of the foregoing changes occurs; for example, if output decreases while input is held constant.

Productivity may have received more or less attention at various times, but the concept of productivity and the need for constant attention to it have always been with us. The overall objective of productivity improvement efforts will remain the enhancement of the accomplishment of work by doing things in less time or with less effort or at lower cost while maintaining or improving quality.

The principal factors influencing productivity, and thus quality, are:

1. capital investment
2. technological change
3. economies of scale
4. work methods, procedures, and systems
5. knowledge and skill of the work force
6. the willingness of the work force to excel at what they do, and in all instances to do the right things in the best possible way

Given the direction from which most of the forces urging organizational improvement are coming, for the decade of the 1990s and into the next century, we will hear much more about quality than about productivity. However, these concepts remain two sides of the same coin, and the supervisor's tools that have traditionally been associated with productivity improvement (see Chapter 22) are also the tools of total quality management.

---

## EXERCISE 21-1: IN SEARCH OF—?

Select one actual application of a new management approach for analysis and study. This could be an application of management by objectives (MBO), some formal program or process emanating from the excellence movement, a quality circles program, an organized methods improvement program, or any other change-oriented mechanism intended to improve organizational success. The ideal choice would be an application in which you were personally involved, but lacking such involvement you may use any application of which you have some knowledge.

For the application you chose to study, answer the following questions:

1. Expressed in no more than one or two sentences, what was the guiding philosophy of the program?
2. In your view, was the program's guiding philosophy successfully translated into practice? How was this done or not done?
3. Do you believe that overall the program succeeded or failed? In either case, identify what you believe to be the three most important reasons behind the outcome.
4. What do you consider to be the single most important lesson learned from the organization's experience with the program?

---

## EXERCISE 21-2: THE "ELEVATOR" SPEECH

You are a supervisor in a prison that has just announced the introduction of a total quality management process that will eventually involve all employees in all departments.

Write a short, informal speech, no longer than one or two paragraphs consisting of a half-dozen sentences in total, that you can use to explain concisely to someone who asks, "What's this quality stuff all about and how can you use it in a prison?" (Since the time in which people may communicate is often severely limited, it is helpful to have a clear, well thought-out response to such questions ready at all times. This kind of response is often referred to as an elevator speech because you can deliver it in full between elevator stops.)

## NOTES

1. T.J. Peters and R.H. Waterman, Jr., *In Search of Excellence* (New York: Harper & Row, 1982).

2. H.B. Maynard, Editor-in-Chief, *Industrial Engineering Handbook,* 2d ed. (New York: McGraw-Hill Publishing Company, 1963), Section 10, 183–191. H.E. Smalley and J.R. Freeman, *Hospital Industrial Engineering* (New York: Reinhold Publishing Corporation, 1966), 68–69.

3. "U.S. Standard of Living Falls for First Time Since '82," *Democrat and Chronicle,* Rochester, New York, 10 July 1991, 9(A).

## CHAPTER 22

# Methods Improvement: Making Work—and Life—Easier

*There's a way to do it better—find it.*

—*Thomas A. Edison*

## Chapter Objectives

☛ Convey the belief that there is usually "room for improvement" in the way most tasks are performed.

☛ Outline a simple, logical approach to the improvement of work methods.

☛ Introduce some of the more common tools and techniques of methods improvement and provide guidelines for their application.

☛ Outline an organized approach to methods improvement that is applicable prison-wide.

☛ Identify the role of the supervisor in encouraging a "methods-minded attitude" on the part of the department's employees.

## EDISON-PLUS

You will notice there is no hedging in Thomas Edison's statement quoted above, no qualifier that might keep the door to improvement closed. Edison did not say there is sometimes, often, or even usually a better way. Often there are several better ways.

Some of the pioneers of industrial engineering, the branch of engineering dealing with work methods, insisted on the need to seek something they called "the one best way." In recent years, however, the notion of a single best way to do something has come to be regarded as something of a theoretical ideal. Rather, we now recognize that there are usually several better ways of accomplishing a given task and that we must seek one of these better ways that meets our needs and fulfills our objectives.

We can describe *methods improvement* as the organized approach to determining how to accomplish a task with less effort, in less time, or at a lower cost, while maintaining or improving the quality of the outcome. You may find this process referred to in different organizations by other labels, among them *methods engineering, job improvement,* and *work simplification*. Regardless of label, however, the intent re-

342

mains the same: to alter the performance of a task in such a way that the results show a desired improvement.

Methods improvement is understandably a subject that is not near and dear to a great many supervisors. Rarely is the need for change in a specific work procedure so pressing that it takes priority over the day-to-day, hour-to-hour operating problems of a department. Yet if it is not made part of today's effort, we will never realize the benefits of methods management. Much like delegation, it is one of those activities we promise to get serious about "after the rush is over." Somehow, however, we never quite get around to it.

Even a modest methods improvement program can be a valuable part of any supervisor's pattern of management. There are economic benefits to be gained: when you manage to accomplish a job in less time, with less effort, or with fewer material resources, you are improving your department's efficiency by bettering the relationship between output and input. There are a few intangible benefits to consider as well. When methods improvement is approached with a spirit of participative management, making use of the contributions of the people who actually do the work, there are positive returns in employee attitude.

## ROOM FOR IMPROVEMENT

Methods improvement may exist as a formal program in the institution or the agency, coordinated by a specific department. Or it may exist at the department level, at the discretion of the supervisor, as an informal, ongoing effort to "tune up," or improve work procedures. At the very least, methods improvement should exist in the department as an attitude. Such a "methods-minded" attitude, a practiced belief in the possibility of continuing improvement, will itself encourage employees to use time and other resources more effectively.

Methods improvement applies largely to tasks, or to problems of things—such as procedures, processes, forms, equipment, and physical layout—as opposed to problems of people. Yet the people who do the work shape and influence work procedures. A certain procedure may lose efficiency over months or years because of the changing environment in which the job is performed, but efficiency may also be lost because the habits, attitudes, and preferences people bring to the job influence the way they work. Dig deeply enough into causes and you will often find that many apparent nonpeople problems have human origins.

Each person coming to work in your department is a unique individual and as such exerts a unique influence on the workplace. Thus a work procedure, especially one that was perhaps not particularly well defined in the first place, becomes in part a reflection of the worker. Run several consecutive individuals through a specific task and the result is a composite "procedure" that incorporates the subtle and perhaps not so subtle influences of these several people. Since we train many employees on the job using the example of the person actually doing the job, we pass along not only essential job knowledge but also the influences of other workers.

It is not unusual for the procedure for performing a given task to exist in the department in three distinctly different ways. It can exist in one form in the mind of the supervisor who, perhaps having done the job at one time, thinks of a specific (and quite likely outdated) collection of steps. The procedure can also exist in the mind of the worker in the form of all the steps this person actually performs to accomplish the task. It may also exist in written form in the department's procedure manual or as a set of post orders on a post somewhere in the prison, which will be different from either the supervisor's concept or the worker's practice.

In some organizations the concern for methods improvement techniques is left to a specific function, such as a management engineering specialist in the headquarters office. However, the power to improve procedures and make work easier need not be limited to some special staff. A simple philosophy of methods improvement might suggest the following:

- There are few, if any, existing tasks that cannot be improved.
- The people who actually do the work can contribute valuable improvements.
- The power of participative management can bring out the best in each employee.

From a healthy, participative management point of view, methods improvement may be simply described as applied common sense.

## AT THE CENTER OF TOTAL QUALITY MANAGEMENT

With variations in terminology and occasional differences in emphasis owing to the agency environment in which it is applied, the process described in the remainder of this chapter is largely the process that drives work improvement within a total quality management (TQM) program. You may find this process referred to as team oriented problem solving (TOPS) or as the mission of "self-directed work teams." It has also been called "team-oriented process improvement" and "work simplification," the latter label identifying an organized approach to work improvement dating back to 1932.[1] The overall process has also been known by the broad generic label of "methods improvement." Regardless of label, two critical characteristics run through all of these approaches.

- A multidisciplinary approach is taken to problem solving, involving all departments that have a relationship to the problem.
- Solutions are generated—and implemented—at the level of the people who actually do the work.

## THE METHODS IMPROVEMENT APPROACH

The steps to methods improvement below will be followed by a review of some of the simpler tools and techniques of methods analysis. Successful methods improvement ordinarily begins with concentration on a single, specific task. A supervisor has far too much to do to attempt to improve everything at once; a shotgun approach will lead to the start of many projects but the likely completion of few or none. Simply select one task or isolate one problem—one that is causing trouble or one that some members of the department feel could be done more efficiently—and go to work.

### Select a Task or Isolate a Problem

You must of course become aware of a problem before it can be solved. When you examine in detail the areas where the department's problems usually arise, significant signs often suggest a particular task deserves analysis and improvement.

- An activity is costing you more in staff time or dollars than you know or believe it should cost.
- Bottlenecks occur as work backs up at various stages of a process, or there are chronic backlogs of incomplete work.
- Confusion is evident as employees appear uncertain as to what a task involves, what happens next, how it happens, and why.
- Poor morale prevails in the work group.

- Labor-management problems begin to surface.
- Inappropriate staff conversations suggesting idleness and other nonproductive activities appear to occur in excess.

In locating and defining problems that may highlight the need for improvement, it is important to distinguish between symptoms of problems and true problems. For example, what appears to be a bottleneck of work caused by poor work methods might seem correctable through a small amount of overtime, a bit of extra effort, or a rearrangement of task assignments. However, if the true causal problem happens to lie in ineffective scheduling practices, the supposed fix is not likely to work for long, once conditions revert to "normal." When the area addressed is really only a symptom of the problem, the difficulty will probably return within a short time or resurface in an altered form. Thus it is necessary to look beyond the apparent immediate problem and identify the force or forces that lie behind it.

## Gather the Facts

The next step is to learn thoroughly how the task is done now. The total process involved in the task under consideration must be described through narratives, sketches, flowcharts, or whatever other techniques are available. Sketching out "the system" often increases understanding of the relationships among system components, since you can often observe a logical order or interrelationship among the pieces once they are all captured on paper. Recording the present method in full also allows others, who may be able to provide insight into the problem, to examine the problem and compare it with their understanding of the situation.

**Applying the information-gathering tools and techniques of methods improvement, one can gather information from:**

- written policies, procedures, and post orders, if they exist
- architectural and layout drawings, if the problem concerns layout or physical space in any way
- work schedules
- samples of pertinent forms and records
- accounting data, payroll data, purchasing information, and other financial records
- statistical reports and other records of operating results

Rest assured, however, that what you collect from any of the forego-ing sources will often be insufficient. You must usually expend addi-tional effort in the one major area of concern that you cannot learn from existing information: how the task is currently being performed.

### Reduce the Problem to Subproblems As Necessary

Often a single apparent methods-improvement problem may seem too large or complex to tackle as a whole. Such a problem can often be broken down into a number of smaller, discrete problems that can be solved independently. For example, suppose that you have a number of difficulties manifesting themselves in a significant, ongoing backlog of classification transcription work. Caseworkers often fail to provide clear, understandable dictation. They also fail consistently to complete it within the prison's required 15-day period. Suppose that certain facts have been identified: Many casemanagers are not doing their dictation within the required period, so they are not following the necessary pro-cedure; Many casemanagers have complained about dictating equip-ment that is unavailable or operates poorly, if at all. There have been numerous complaints about high noise levels in the unit offices where the dictation takes place. Thus the problem may be divided into several subproblems, each of which may be addressed separately: (1) the re-cording procedure, (2) the state of the dictating equipment, and (3) the physical environment of the dictation area. Once the problems have been separately addressed and tentative solutions developed, the subsolutions may be combined as a solution to the total problem.

### Challenge Everything

All of the information gathered to this point, and most especially the record of how the job is now being done, must be subjected to searching study. Take nothing for granted. At every step along the way, ask: What is actually being done? Where is it done? By whom is it done? How is it done? Always, for every step, ask: Why?

**Examine every step and challenge every detail in an effort to:**

- eliminate activities whenever possible. Just because something is being done is no reason it must be done. Ask of each step: If this were not done at all, what would be the result?
- combine steps whenever possible
- improve the manner of performing various steps

- change sequence of activities, location where work is performed, assignments of people involved, and any other factors that might have a bearing on efficient task performance

The process of challenging every last detail lies at the heart of methods improvement. At this point methods improvement, while appearing to be a logical "scientific approach," must become a wide-open, no-holds-barred creative process. It is here that participation and teamwork have far-reaching implications. A number of factors come together to challenge every detail of the problem thoroughly and carry the problem solvers toward the results of the next step: Creative idea-generating techniques such as brainstorming; optimism, and genuine belief in the necessity for improvement; willingness to experiment, innovate, and to fail occasionally as part of the learning process; application of the tools and techniques of information gathering and analysis; the complete involvement of all parties who have a stake in the problem, regardless of their level in the organization; and a healthy positive attitude toward the need for constructive change.

## Develop an Improved Method

Having learned thoroughly about the task, you can use the results of your analysis to develop and propose a new method. However, the process is not as simple as replacing the old method with the new method. Further preparation is necessary.

- Check out the proposed method thoroughly. Using flowcharts and other analytical techniques, subject it to the same kind of detailed examination that you applied to the present method until you can provide reasonable assurance that the difficulties leading to the consideration of this task have been corrected.
- Analyze how the proposed method will affect employees, since they will apply the new method to the work they do each day. The best methods-engineered procedure ever to hit the department is bound for eventual failure if it includes elements that the worker—the critical human factor—considers demeaning or dissatisfying. When combining the "perfect" solution—perfect in a technical sense—with the human element, you sometimes need to back off from technical perfection to accommodate the needs of employees. For example, productive efficiency in a large prison's highly automated personnel department might suggest that one personnel assistant should sit at a keyboard for eight hours a day

and feed the system. However, it is likely that such a rigid assignment will lead to the physical discomfort of backache and eyestrain and the intellectual numbness borne of repetition and boredom. This can lead to dissatisfaction, which in turn often leads to reduced efficiency and diminished productivity. It is far better to sacrifice some theoretical efficiency up front, perhaps by rearranging the work of two people so they alternately divide their time between the necessary keying activities and other nonkeyboard activities.

- If at all possible, make some trial runs of experimental applications to test proposed methods. In this way you can also test variations in methods to determine which might work better in practice or be more palatable to the employees who do the work.

- In general, assess the practicability of the proposed method in the light of any possible constraints. It is one thing to idealize a method; it is quite another matter to make that method work in the face of constraints of cost, time, and quality considerations. One can spend only so much, the task must be accomplished within a given length of time, and quality must ordinarily be maintained at present levels or perhaps even improved. The workable solution must fall within these limits. (See the discussion on constraints in Chapter 16.)

### Implement and Follow Up

*Action is a must.* The best work method ever devised is useless as long as it remains solely on paper. Be prepared to accept a certain amount of "tuning up" and "debugging." Modification may be required because needs and circumstances present at the time of implementation may be different from those existing when the analysis was started. Rarely is a plan of any consequence implemented as planned in every detail. Implementation should be monitored until all the hitches have been worked out of the method.

Be ever aware of potential human relations problems and of the value of employee participation in methods improvement. Often you will find that the extent of participation before implementation will determine the success or failure of a proposed new method. The human problems encountered in the implementation of new work procedures are often the classic problems of resistance to change. As for employee participation, there is usually an identifiable relationship between employee involvement and resistance to change: the more intimately involved employees are in determining the form and substance of a change, the more likely they are to accept rather than resist that change.

When it comes to implementing new methods or procedures or any other change, as supervisor you have three avenues of approach: You can tell the employees what to do, you can convince them of what must be done, or you can involve them in determining what must be done (see Chapter 17). Employee involvement in determining new and revised methods is advisable for a number of important reasons:

- The employee who is involved will thoroughly know the details of the new method as it is created.

- The involved employee will "own a piece" of the new method and will thus be more likely to accept it.

- The employee is one of the most valuable sources, if not the single most valuable source, of information on how the task is performed now and how it might be performed better. The supervisor, who might have the superior perspective of departmental operations, may be able to observe what pieces do not fit together well, seeing that a number of things need to be improved. However, when it comes to specific tasks, it is the employee performing these tasks day in and day out who knows how to do them most effectively and efficiently. Employees are a source of information that should not be allowed to go untapped in methods improvement.

Close follow-up on implementation is essential, and for many tasks it must be maintained for a considerable length of time. Time is necessary for new habits to form and to replace old habits completely, and for new methods to dominate employees' actions fully and erase any fond remembrances of "the way we used to do it." Also, any method installed today is immediately subject to unforeseen problems and "creeping changes" that can affect performance. Thus supervisors must follow up a new method until it has completely taken its place among the department's normal processes. Even then the new method—as every departmental procedure—should be subjected to a periodic audit of effectiveness and appropriateness.

## THE TOOLS AND TECHNIQUES OF METHODS IMPROVEMENT

A number of analytical methods are available to a person pursuing methods improvement. We will introduce only two such techniques in this chapter, the flow process chart and the flow diagram. These are easy to use and broadly applicable to many situations.

One of the most valuable tools for examining an activity is the flow process chart, used for tracking and recording the steps of an activity and assessing the nature of each step. Flow process charts appear in many forms, but most make use of the five basic activity symbols shown in Figure 22–1.

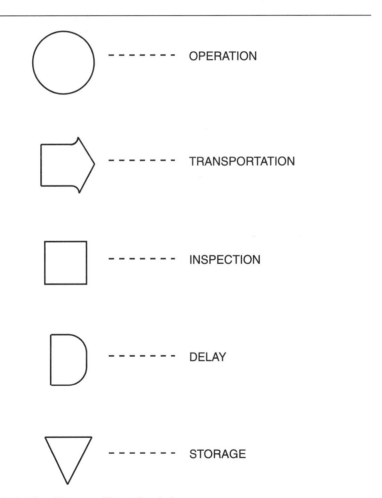

**Figure 22–1** Flow Process Chart Symbols

**For proper analysis all work activity should be divided into these five basic categories:**

1. An operation is any activity that advances the completion of the task. It is the actual doing of work, such as writing on a form, dialing a telephone, writing a report, searching an inmate, making a photocopy, or tightening a bolt.

2. Transportation represents any movement encountered in the activity. It may be moving an inmate from here to there, delivering a memo from you to your supervisor, carrying a record from here to the copy machine, or any other activity that has movement as its primary characteristic. Note that transportation involves only physical movement; except for the relocation of some person or thing from one place to another, nothing actually happens to advance the completion of the work—for instance, that chart that just arrived on person B's desk in the records office is just as incomplete as when it left person A's hands in the chief of security's office.

3. An inspection is an activity in which the primary emphasis is on verification of the results of prior operations. For instance, a housing unit supervisor may periodically check areas that have recently been cleaned; the supervisor in the receiving and discharge area may check a set of admission forms to assure they are appropriately completed; or, a business office supervisor may assign an employee to the task of verifying payments before they are mailed. Inspections, like transportations, do not advance the completion of the work. Rather, they are used to determine whether necessary work has been properly performed.

4. A delay is an unplanned interruption in the flow of necessary steps. A pencil breaks and must be replaced; a computer locks up and must be rebooted, losing some work; a beverage spills, necessitating cleanup and replacement; the person who must sign your hand-carried requisition is on the telephone—all of these are examples of delays that might be encountered in flow process analysis.

5. A storage is indicated whenever a step results in an anticipated interruption of the process, or it may represent the end of the process. More in-depth analysis than we are dealing with may distinguish between temporary and permanent storage. For instance, that completed invoice just dropped in the mailroom out-basket is in temporary storage; the process will be resumed after

some period of time. The completed inmate record just filed on the shelf is for all practical purposes in permanent storage (even though it may be retrieved some time in the future).

Although the activity symbols of Figure 22–1 can be used in charting activity in freehand fashion, they are ordinarily incorporated into prepared forms. A simplified version of a portion of a flow process chart form appears in Exhibit 22–1. If this form is used, it is necessary only to describe each activity, preferably in no more than two or three words; indicate the appropriate symbol for that activity; and, if you wish, connect the symbols to indicate sequential flow of activities.

A proper process chart should indicate whether the subject is the activities of a person or the flow of material. This decision must be made before beginning the analysis. For instance, if you are observing a clerk preparing and processing a three-part form, you may reach a point in the activity where the form is taken apart and goes in three directions while the clerk either remains working with one part of the form or perhaps goes off in a fourth direction. It is necessary for the user to make an early decision on the focus of the analysis (for example, either "purchasing requisition" or "purchasing clerk") and stick with it.

Note also the space on the chart form where you can summarize total work activities and total distances traveled in transportation steps. You can use this part of the form for comparing possible changes with present methods.

A second helpful tool is the flow diagram (see Figure 22–2). A flow diagram is simply a layout drawn to approximate scale on which lines are placed to indicate paths of personnel movement or material flow. Figure 22–2 illustrates the X-ray process in a prison infirmary.

A flow diagram can be especially helpful in determining how to rearrange equipment, furnishings, and work stations for improved effectiveness. It may be used to assess the approximate amount of movement necessitated by a particular layout, and to test a new layout to see if it represents improvement.

Numerous additional techniques are available for analyzing work activities of various kinds. Some of these are:

- **the operation process chart.** While a flow process chart captures an entire sequence of all operations, transportations, delays, inspections, and storages during a process or activity, an operation process chart typically focuses only on operations (the circular symbol) and inspections (the square symbol). It is most conveniently used to examine all the separate small activities or

**Exhibit 22–1** Flow Process Chart (Form)

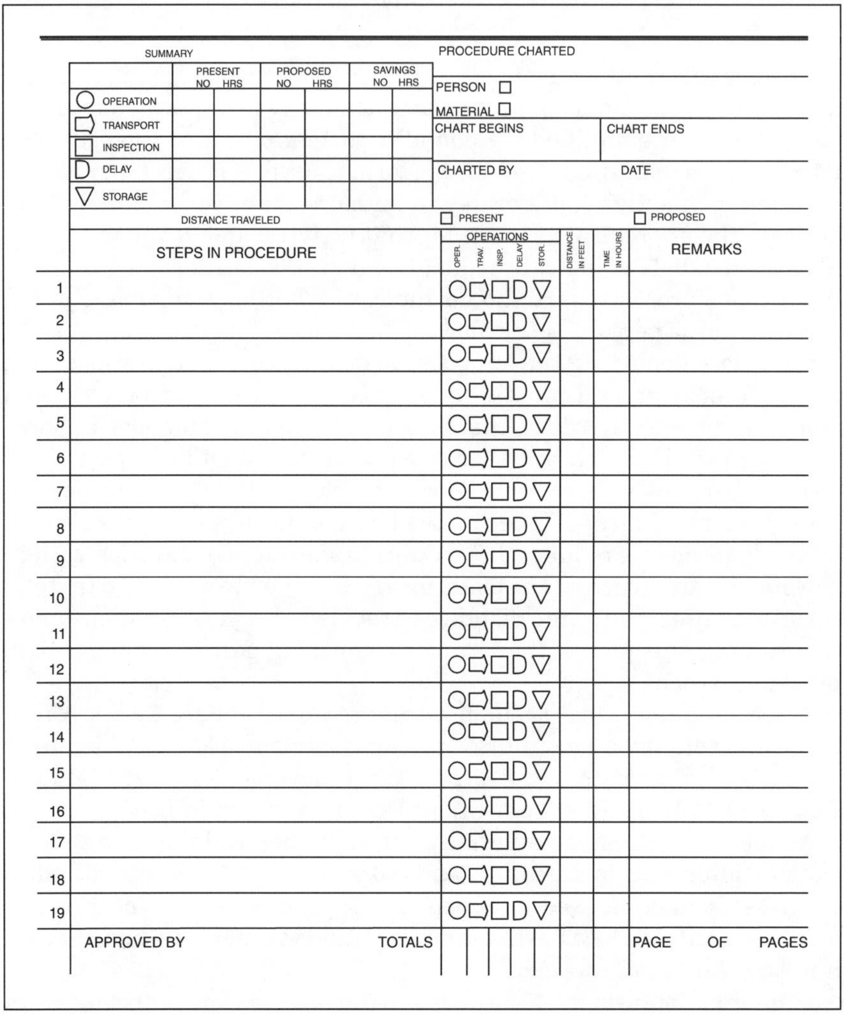
SUMMARY

| | PRESENT NO | PRESENT HRS | PROPOSED NO | PROPOSED HRS | SAVINGS NO | SAVINGS HRS |
|---|---|---|---|---|---|---|
| ○ OPERATION | | | | | | |
| TRANSPORT | | | | | | |
| □ INSPECTION | | | | | | |
| D DELAY | | | | | | |
| ▽ STORAGE | | | | | | |
| DISTANCE TRAVELED | | | | | | |

PROCEDURE CHARTED

PERSON □

MATERIAL □

CHART BEGINS | CHART ENDS

CHARTED BY | DATE

□ PRESENT □ PROPOSED

| | STEPS IN PROCEDURE | OPERATIONS (OPER. TRAV. INSP. DELAY STOR.) | DISTANCE IN FEET | TIME IN HOURS | REMARKS |
|---|---|---|---|---|---|
| 1 | | ○ ⇨ □ D ▽ | | | |
| 2 | | ○ ⇨ □ D ▽ | | | |
| 3 | | ○ ⇨ □ D ▽ | | | |
| 4 | | ○ ⇨ □ D ▽ | | | |
| 5 | | ○ ⇨ □ D ▽ | | | |
| 6 | | ○ ⇨ □ D ▽ | | | |
| 7 | | ○ ⇨ □ D ▽ | | | |
| 8 | | ○ ⇨ □ D ▽ | | | |
| 9 | | ○ ⇨ □ D ▽ | | | |
| 10 | | ○ ⇨ □ D ▽ | | | |
| 11 | | ○ ⇨ □ D ▽ | | | |
| 12 | | ○ ⇨ □ D ▽ | | | |
| 13 | | ○ ⇨ □ D ▽ | | | |
| 14 | | ○ ⇨ □ D ▽ | | | |
| 15 | | ○ ⇨ □ D ▽ | | | |
| 16 | | ○ ⇨ □ D ▽ | | | |
| 17 | | ○ ⇨ □ D ▽ | | | |
| 18 | | ○ ⇨ □ D ▽ | | | |
| 19 | | ○ ⇨ □ D ▽ | | | |
| | APPROVED BY | TOTALS | | | PAGE OF PAGES |

suboperations that may take place within a given larger task. For example, "take fingerprints" may appear as a single operation on a flow process chart covering the activities of a staff member in receiving and discharge. If you wish to examine "take fingerprints" in considerable detail, you might focus on this activity alone and create an operation process chart that breaks it into a number of

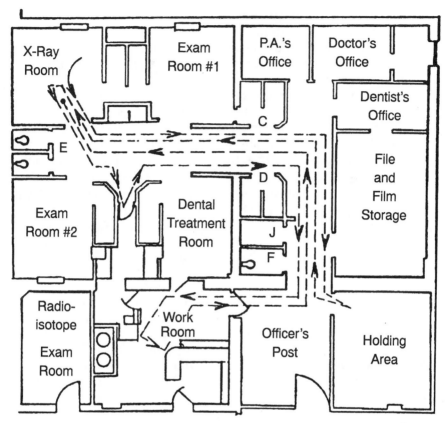

**Figure 22–2** Flow Diagram Charting Route of X-Ray Technician Travel

smaller work activities (operations) and verification steps (inspections).

- **the multiple activity flow process chart.** This tool is most useful if you wish to examine, for example, a multipart form that is processed over a period of days, such as an inmate's diagnostic form as he or she moves through the orientation process. Using the standard charting symbols, this chart would perhaps display the multiple parts of the subject form in a vertical column at the left and a time scale of perhaps several days of the week across the horizontal dimension. Using this technique you can illustrate, usually on a single sheet of paper, what happens to each part of the multipart form on each day of the processing cycle.

- **the multiple activity chart.** Formerly referred to as a man-and-machine chart, this form is used to chart the activities of an employee in conjunction with one or more pieces of equipment. The heart of this particular chart is a vertical time scale calibrated in either minutes or decimal parts of an hour. The activities of the worker and the utilization of the equipment are indicated parallel with this time scale. This technique makes it possible to identify times when worker or equipment is waiting or being productively applied and thus to consider rearrangements of activity that may reduce idle (nonproductive) time for workers, equipment, or both.

- **the gang process chart.** This flow process chart is applied to the analysis of the activities of a crew of two or more persons who must work together to accomplish a given task. The steps taken by each member of the crew are charted relative to each other on a time scale; that is, what worker A is doing at any particular time appears directly beside the activity that worker B is performing at the same time.

The foregoing overview of methods improvement barely scratches the surface of management engineering technology. For the supervisor who wishes to pursue methods analysis in considerably more detail, helpful published references are available. Two of the best such references are *Motion and Time Study* by Ralph M. Barnes and the *Industrial Engineering Handbook*, edited by H.B. Maynard. (*See the Annotated Bibliography.*)

## EXAMPLE: THE INFORMATION REQUEST

Exhibit 22–2 is a flow process chart of 17 steps illustrating the processing of a single information request in a prison records department. The activity begins when a request for information is pulled from the incoming mail; it ends when the fulfilled request is "filed," that is, placed in the inmate's file. The nature of the intervening steps should be evident from their brief descriptions.

With the complete task of answering an information request recorded on a flow process chart, we can begin to question the individual steps involved to determine whether there might be room for improvement. For instance, observation has revealed that considerable travel is involved in what would seem to be a small task—in all, about 100 feet of walking. This should raise questions as to whether any furniture or nonpermanent fixtures could be relocated to reduce personnel travel.

**Exhibit 22–2** Flow Process Chart: Information Request (Single)

| | | | | | |
|---|---|---|---|---|---|
| **SUMMARY** | | | | | **PROCEDURE CHARTED** *Information Request (Single)* |

| | | PRESENT | | PROPOSED | | SAVINGS | |
|---|---|---|---|---|---|---|---|
| | | NO | HRS | NO | HRS | NO | HRS |
| ○ | OPERATION | 10 | | | | | |
| ⬭ | TRANSPORT | 3 | | | | | |
| ☐ | INSPECTION | 1 | | | | | |
| D | DELAY | 1 | | | | | |
| ▽ | STORAGE | 2 | | | | | |

PERSON ☐
MATERIAL ☒
CHART BEGINS  *Get Request*    CHART ENDS  *File*
CHARTED BY  *CRM*    DATE  *3/9/91*
DISTANCE TRAVELED  *100 ft (for 1)*    ☒ PRESENT    ☐ PROPOSED

| # | STEPS IN PROCEDURE | OPER | TRAV | INSP | DELAY | STOR | DISTANCE IN FEET | TIME IN HOURS | REMARKS |
|---|---|---|---|---|---|---|---|---|---|
| 1 | Get, Open, & Read | ⊗ | � | ☐ | D | ▽ | | | |
| 2 | Verify Authorization | ○ | ⬭ | ☒ | D | ▽ | | | |
| 3 | Get File | ⊗ | ⬭ | ☐ | D | ▽ | 15 | | |
| 4 | File to Desk | ○ | ⊗ | ☐ | D | ▽ | 15 | | |
| 5 | Locate & Remove Pages | ⊗ | ⬭ | ☐ | D | ▽ | | | |
| 6 | To Copier | ○ | ⊗ | ☐ | D | ▽ | 20 | | |
| 7 | Start Copier | ⊗ | ⬭ | ☐ | D | ▽ | | | |
| 8 | Wait for Warm-Up | ○ | ⬭ | ☐ | ⊗ | ▽ | | | |
| 9 | Make Copies | ⊗ | ⬭ | ☐ | D | ▽ | | | |
| 10 | Return to Desk | ○ | ⊗ | ☐ | D | ▽ | 20 | | |
| 11 | Re-Assemble File | ⊗ | ⬭ | ☐ | D | ▽ | | | |
| 12 | Re-File File | ⊗ | ⬭ | ☐ | D | ▽ | 30 | | |
| 13 | Type Envelope | ⊗ | ⬭ | ☐ | D | ▽ | | | |
| 14 | Assemble to Mail | ⊗ | ⬭ | ☐ | D | ▽ | | | |
| 15 | Into Outgoing Mail | ○ | ⬭ | ☐ | D | ▼ | | | |
| 16 | Enter in Log | ⊗ | ⬭ | ☐ | D | ▽ | | | |
| 17 | File Request | ○ | ⬭ | ☐ | D | ▼ | | | |
| 18 | | ○ | ⬭ | ☐ | D | ▽ | | | |
| 19 | | ○ | ⬭ | ☐ | D | ▽ | | | |

APPROVED BY    TOTALS    PAGE    OF    PAGES

The delay recorded on line 8, waiting for the copy machine to warm up, should raise some questions. It may be perfectly legitimate—there are some copy machines that should be shut down between infrequent uses—but you will never discover this without probing to determine why.

In this example it is also reasonable to consider whether certain steps could be eliminated or combined. For instance, is it possible to obtain the inmate file (step 3), then go directly to the copy machine, perform the next several activities there, and thus eliminate a pair of transportations? Or if the copy machine warmup is required, would it be productive for the employee to turn the copy machine on before getting the file so the machine can be used without delay when needed?

Other pertinent questions should occur to you as you study the chart. However, we have not yet raised the most important question relative to this example: How many information requests are involved? If requests arrive at the clerk's in-basket in batches, then several additional questions become important:

- Can these requests be processed in batches, doing each step for several requests at a time?
- Can all necessary inmate files be obtained at once?
- Would it be practical to save all such activity for one time of day?
- Should all filing be done at the end of the day?
- Should you consider physical changes, such as moving a desk, to reduce transportation?

In the actual situation from which this example was taken, mail arrived in the records department once in the morning and once in the afternoon. The clerk was in the habit of handling information requests twice a day, usually within a few hours after the mail arrived, whether the "batch" consisted of a single request or several requests. A few simple changes in procedure were indicated:

- The copy machine was turned on at the beginning of the day and left on (a little investigation showed this to be the manufacturer's recommendation).
- It was decided to run the requests in batches, with little change in the steps indicated (trial runs involving a clerk doing several steps at the copy machine produced an awkward, counterproductive situation).
- An ideal batch size of 10 to 12 requests was established, thus providing that no request went unanswered longer than two days (the decision was simply to run 10 to 12 at once or a maximum of two days' requests, whichever accumulated first).
- A simple change in layout—turning the clerk's desk around and moving it about 8 feet—reduced total travel from 100 feet to about 70 feet. (A flow process chart of the resulting activity appears as Exhibit 22–3.)

**Exhibit 22–3** Flow Process Chart: Information Request (Batch)

| SUMMARY | | | | | | | PROCEDURE CHARTED *Information Request (Batch)* |
|---|---|---|---|---|---|---|---|

| | PRESENT NO / HRS | PROPOSED NO / HRS | SAVINGS NO / HRS |
|---|---|---|---|
| ○ OPERATION | 9 | | |
| ⇨ TRANSPORT | 3 | | |
| □ INSPECTION | 1 | | |
| D DELAY | 0 | | |
| ▽ STORAGE | 2 | | |

PERSON □
MATERIAL ☒
CHART BEGINS *Get Requests*   CHART ENDS *File*
CHARTED BY *CRM*   DATE *3/9/91*

DISTANCE TRAVELED *70 ft (for 10–12)*   □ PRESENT   ☒ PROPOSED

| | STEPS IN PROCEDURE | OPERATIONS (OPER / TRAN / INSP / DELAY / STOR) | DISTANCE IN FEET | TIME IN HOURS | REMARKS |
|---|---|---|---|---|---|
| 1 | Get, Open, Read & Sort by # | ⊗⇨□D▽ | | | Max. 10–12 / Batch |
| 2 | Verify Authorizations | O⇨☒D▽ | | | |
| 3 | Get Files | ⊗⇨□D▽ | 10 | | |
| 4 | Files to Desk | O⊗□D▽ | 10 | | |
| 5 | Locate & Remove Pages | ⊗⇨□D▽ | | | |
| 6 | To Copier | O⊗□D▽ | 15 | | |
| 7 | Make Copies | ⊗⇨□D▽ | | | |
| 8 | Return to Desk | O⊗□D▽ | 15 | | |
| 9 | Re-Assemble Files | ⊗⇨□D▽ | | | |
| 10 | Re-File Files | ⊗⇨□D▽ | 20 | | |
| 11 | Type Envelopes | ⊗⇨□D▽ | | | |
| 12 | Assemble to Mail | ⊗⇨□D▽ | | | |
| 13 | Into Outgoing Mail | O⇨□D▽ | | | |
| 14 | Enter in Log | ⊗⇨□D▽ | | | |
| 15 | File Requests | O⇨□D▽ | | | |
| 16 | | O⇨□D▽ | | | |
| 17 | | O⇨□D▽ | | | |
| 18 | | O⇨□D▽ | | | |
| 19 | | O⇨□D▽ | | | |

APPROVED BY   TOTALS   PAGE   OF   PAGES

The amount of effort put into such an analysis will depend on the total workload involved. In the situation just described, for instance, if information requests amounted to only one or two a day, as might be the case in a very small institution, there is little to be gained by shaving a minute or so from each repetition of the task. The time of the supervisor or other person analyzing the operation is fully as valuable as the time of the employee, and hours of effort can be wasted to produce minuscule returns. Under conditions of high volume, however, there may be significant gains to be made through a few hours' effort. If processing such requests required a full-time person or more, analysis could point to significant time savings. As early as possible in the methods improvement process, assess the potential savings in time and resources. Let your best efforts be directed toward improvements having the greatest potential for savings in time or other resources.

## AN ORGANIZED APPROACH TO METHODS IMPROVEMENT

A formal, institution-wide methods improvement program should ordinarily consist of three phases: philosophy, education, and application.

### Philosophy

For a methods improvement program to achieve long-run success, top management support should be active and visible. Regardless of where the idea begins, all employees must see top management as 100 percent supportive of an organized effort to maintain constant cost-containment pressure through regular, positive questioning of work methods. This commitment must be reflected in a shared belief that few if any activities cannot be improved.

The dissemination of the methods improvement philosophy throughout the organization may require much promotional effort. Promoting the benefits of the continuous oversight of work methods is a selling job that is never truly complete. However, once a program is underway and some positive results have been generated, these results will help to sell the philosophy.

Through meetings and printed matter, everyone in the organization should be encouraged to adopt the basic message that cost containment is here to stay. Every employee should realize that he or she can help the institution operate smoothly, safely, and cost-effectively. By paying continued attention to their use of time and resources, every employee can help produce higher-quality results.

### Education

Education in the tools and techniques of methods improvement should begin some weeks after the introduction of the philosophy. Management engineering professionals can begin to acquaint supervisors and middle managers with the ways and means of work analysis. Ideally, the educational process should include some pilot methods improvement projects taken from the jobs of the participants.

Once a number of supervisors and managers have been introduced to a working knowledge of methods improvement tools and techniques, selected nonsupervisory employees—especially those having skills applicable to potential projects—should be brought into the education process.

## Application

Ideally, an ongoing methods improvement program should be guided and monitored by either an administrative steering committee or a methods improvement coordinator who is a member of the administration, preferably with a background as a management engineer. Many agencies and individual institutions may not have the latter kind of specialist available, and may rely instead on a staff member who has received specialized training for this purpose.

In addition to assisting actively and coordinating necessary skills and resources, the primary task of the steering committee or coordinator is to keep the methods improvement projects moving. Methods improvement will not always be particularly high on the average supervisor's priority list; there is usually more than enough to do without it. By constantly monitoring the program, the committee or coordinator serves as an ever-present reminder that keeping methods improvement alive requires periodic activity. This monitoring also makes the process easier for supervisors who are involved in active projects.

Common sense suggests that it is best initially to pursue those projects that hold the greatest potential for returns or that are most readily completed. Although this may seem like "skimming" or going after just the "easy stuff," there is a distinct advantage in proceeding in this fashion: Some early, visible successes can often boost the momentum of the entire program.

Individual project teams may take two forms: the ad hoc group assembled for a single project, or the ongoing group formed to deal with a particular department or specific function.

**The ideal ad hoc project team consists of:**

- the supervisor responsible for the task being studied
- the assistant to the supervisor (if there is one)

- one or two of the persons who regularly perform the task
- one "expert" in the most prominent technical specialty related to the task (for example, an accountant to deal with aspects of a billing problem in the business office, a material management specialist to deal with a transportation problem in the prison factory, a personnel professional to deal with personnel policy issues)

**An ongoing project team formed to deal with a series of projects relating to a specific department or function might consist of:**

- The department head or assistant
- A representative of the administration
- A business office representative
- A management engineer or systems analyst
- One or more "experts," persons from particular technical specialties that might be involved in most projects
- One or two nonsupervisory employees of the department, including a representative of the bargaining unit

We realize that this discussion of methods improvement may seem idealistic, for many organizations have started programs only to see them gradually dwindle to nothing. Yet, whatever an organization's overall attitude toward methods improvement, the individual supervisors have the opportunity to pursue methods improvement strictly within the confines of their own departments.

Some projects can never be undertaken or successfully completed without interdepartmental cooperation. Still, in each department countless ways exist for a conscientious supervisor and a few positively motivated employees to improve work methods and contain costs. The average prison department can make many improvements. The supervisor has only to recognize the possibilities for improvement and provide an example of leadership to bring the employees into the improvement process.

### Total Quality Management in Action

We have of course, in the preceding few paragraphs, largely described the TQM process. Certainly the major phases of the process—philosophy, education, and application—are identical, as is the critical need for solid top management commitment. Much of the organization for TQM is the same, with a high-level "steering committee" providing guidance, and/or a methods improvement coordinator.

A true total quality management approach rightly calls upon the organization as a whole and each function or activity therein to identify its "mission"—the essential reasons for its existence—and further identify its "customers," both internal and external, and to pursue "quality," described in one of many of its current variations as meeting or exceeding customers' expectations.

Regardless of label or variation in application, however, the ultimate goals of TQM and methods improvement are identical: Ensure that the organization is doing the right things, and doing them right the first time.

## THE METHODS-MINDED ATTITUDE

The "methods-minded" attitude referred to earlier has its foundation in each employee's belief that improvement is always possible, and that, left to themselves for prolonged periods, work activities will experience "creeping changes," which usually are not changes for the better. Methods-mindedness is reflected in the person who develops efficient work habits and who always approaches a task in such a way as to achieve satisfactory results with minimum effort. Methods-mindedness might seem to be a talent. However, it is a habit or a collection of habits. And as a habit, methods-mindedness can be learned.

Your own attitude toward methods improvement will encourage your employees to become methods-minded. You need not plunge into methods improvement in a full-scale manner; rather, limit your attention to one or two troublesome tasks at a time—or simply to one activity or process that you feel has room for improvement. Even if you simply keep one such project open at a time, working on it as time allows or as you make time, you are bound to make noticeable progress and stimulate the interest of some of your employees.

Your employees are once again key to your success as a supervisor. You may be able to stand back at an objective distance and see problems your employees cannot see, but when you get into specific procedural details, the situation is reversed: Nobody knows most of the inner workings of a task better than the employees who do it day in and day out. Your employees can see much that is hidden from you.

Effective methods improvement in a department requires a merger of structural and human considerations. Referring to the organization types discussed in Chapter 1, methods improvement is able to produce an effective blend of the Job Organization System and the Cooperative Motivation System by tapping the individual enthusiasm and motivation of your employees to organize and refine the task they must perform.

---

### EXERCISE 22–1: "THE PENCIL"

**Using the basic flow charting symbols, chart the following simple activity.**

Get a wooden pencil from your desk, sharpen it at a sharpener located near the door of the room, and return to your place. Also, account for the following:

- Somebody else got to the sharpener a step ahead of you, so you had to wait

- The sharpener gave you a poor job; you found it packed with shavings that you had to clean out before you got an acceptable point.

Assuming "pencil sharpening" to be of sufficient importance to deserve a few minutes further study, sketch a flow diagram showing your relationship to the sharpener (use your actual surroundings). If you had to sharpen at least ten pencils each day, what could you do to reduce the time and effort spent on this task?

---

### EXERCISE 22–2: "THE FORM"

**Select one printed form that either originates or is largely processed in your department. Do the following:**

1. Utilizing the tools and techniques outlined in this chapter, record the flow of the form (and its copies, if it is a multipart form).
2. Further apply the tools and techniques to develop a new processing method. (This will be possible in most cases.)
3. Assess the form itself for possible changes in the arrangement of information that you might want to recommend.
4. Given that you might wish to alter the processing of the form or redesign the form itself in some way, outline the steps you would take in implementing your proposed changes.

## NOTE

1. H.B. Maynard, ed., *Industrial Engineering Handbook,* 2nd ed. (New York: McGraw-Hill Publishing Co., 1963), Section 1, 13.

## CHAPTER 23

# Training and Continuing Education: Your Employees and You

*The person who sees a career as one of perpetual investment in education stands a much better chance of surviving in today's world.*

*—Tom Peters*

## Chapter Objectives

☛ Establish the importance of training and continuing education as legitimate concerns of every supervisor.

☛ Stress the necessity for management commitment to training and continuing education.

☛ Describe various approaches to training and continuing education.

☛ Establish the role of the supervisor in providing and guiding the department's training and continuing education program.

☛ Identify avenues of training and continuing education available to the supervisor for self-development.

## WHY TRAINING AND CONTINUING EDUCATION?

It can be difficult and at times nearly impossible for people working in the field of corrections to keep up with all of the changes affecting their work. Some correctional workers, subject to continually changing techniques, procedures, and equipment, must feel as though the more they learn the more there remains to be learned.

Today's rate of technological change was discussed in Chapter 17. What we know and how we must apply knowledge today will not be the same tomorrow. Today's knowledge is not sufficient for the needs of tomorrow, so without a learning attitude we seem doomed to remain forever behind the times. The rate of technological change will not have equal impact on all skills and all professions. Yet no one can afford to stand still in one's field—however slowly developments may seem to accrue. In some areas of work activity, including administration, psychology, medical, finance, and automated technology, to name only a few, it is often necessary to absorb and react to change at a rapid pace simply to remain abreast of the times.

Continuing education (which for the purposes of this chapter includes both in-service training and formal coursework offered outside the institution) affords a significant means of bringing change under control, of making change work for you rather than against you. Continuing education provides the ability to increase knowledge, improve skills, and change attitudes as the needs of job performance change.

Continuing education also provides reinforcement through refresher education. Knowledge that lies unused or infrequently used can get rusty from lack of application, but relearning what one has learned before can revitalize knowledge and sharpen skills.

Continuing education can also increase individual capabilities and thus improve the effectiveness of all members of a work group. Later in this chapter we will highlight the benefits of cross-training, the practice of assuring that employees become proficient in the performance of jobs other than those to which they are regularly assigned.

In some segments of the prison setting, continuing education is required, or at least strongly encouraged, by accreditation and regulatory bodies. The American Correctional Association, in standard 3-4090 on Continuing Education, requires that "written policy, procedure, and practice encourage employees to continue their education," adding that "Employees who wish to continue their education should be given the opportunity to do so. Every effort should be made to coordinate educational activities with staff responsibilities. The institution's staff development and training program should promote and support employee participation in outside workshops, seminars, and other formal educational programs."[1]

Any prison that maintains a significant in-house medical capability must be concerned with continuing educational requirements for its staff. For example, in the 1988 Accreditation Manual for Hospitals, accreditation survey criteria for the continuing education of hospital staff appear in more than 50 places.[2] In the area of nursing, by way of an example, for a considerable number of years the education criteria of the Joint Commission on Accreditation of Healthcare Organizations (Joint Commission) has had the status of an accreditation standard, meaning that a number of continuing education criteria must be satisfied for the medical facility to receive accreditation.

Professional regulatory agencies of most states also require continuing education for teachers, psychologists, and other specialists. For instance, many state governments have long applied regulatory requirements to nursing in-service education, through their hospital codes. With the regulatory requirements of various governmental bodies increasing steadily, more legally mandated continuing education is certain during the coming years.

Thus people take part in continuing education—sometimes grudgingly—simply because it is required. However, much essential education—and specifically the education of supervisors and managers and the cross-training of employees—remains voluntary. It must therefore be accomplished through desire and commitment.

## COMMITMENT

Education receives a great deal of verbal tribute in our organizations; not many managers will deny the value of continuing education for working people. In practice, however, education in the work organization is often little more than a bit of superficial motion that produces little or no behavioral change.

It is true that education presents some problems in the functioning correctional organization. There are numerous activities of necessarily higher priority than education. It remains something that "we ought to do when we have time," but since it is eminently postponable it is usually put off until "after the current crunch is over." Also, continuing education costs money, a basic resource often in short supply. It is natural that various activities compete for available funds and just as natural that limited funds are channeled toward urgent needs and uses that generate readily measurable returns. Too often continuing education loses out to direct competition for management's time and the organization's resources. Top management often sees no immediate need for, nor an immediate return on investment from this kind of activity.

Much continuing education is undertaken without a great deal of out-of-pocket spending, so the principal commitments are time and effort. However, it is difficult for the individual supervisor to devote time and effort to education if not encouraged by higher management.

Regardless of the resources going into a program of education (the time you have available and the materials and assistance at your disposal), there is one critical element without which no educational undertaking can long succeed, an element that cannot be mandated. This is the personal and organizational commitment to training and continuing education. This commitment must be present and visible at a level and scope sufficient to support the training effort. That is, management training for department heads must have the support of administration; supervisory development for shift commanders must have the support of the chief of security; skilled training for case managers must have the support of the chief of case management; and so on. Some measure of commitment is behind every successful education endeavor, whether personal, departmental, or organizational.

## MANY OPTIONS

Continuing education may be a structured program of formal classes on specific topics. Less formal approaches include:

- a simple demonstration of manual skills or work methods for a small group of employees, or perhaps one-on-one for a single employee
- employee orientation and guided on-the-job training in which an employee learns while doing
- self-study, perhaps job-related reading, correspondence courses, or outside classes

Thoughts of continuing education tend to inspire visions of classes, teachers, and classrooms, and indeed much of continuing education is approached in "schoolroom" fashion. Such programs and classes, however, can vary considerably in type according to their purposes.

### Informational Programs

Informational programs are intended to implant specific information for later recall and application. Students receive information that they will be expected to absorb as received, recall when necessary, and apply as appropriate in the future. Informational programs are subject to evaluation by direct testing or examination. You are familiar with the pattern: students attend classes, participate in a number of assignments, and, finally, answer questions designed to test recall of the information received.

### Skill Programs

Skill programs are intended to impart specific skills: perhaps how to operate a computer, how to use a new type of gas gun, how to write a report, or how to cook using a new piece of equipment. To some extent, the results of skill programs can also be measured by test or examination, especially if these require the learner to demonstrate the skill.

## Concept Programs

In this type of program, the student studies concepts and concept-based patterns of behavior. The object is to develop skills based on these concepts as they are translated into action and refined through application in specific situations. Most management education falls under this heading. In a "supervisory skills development program," you may sit through a class or a series of classes to learn about the concept of delegation. You may also consider cases and exercises in delegation, reinforcing your knowledge of the concept, but the program does not allow you to benefit from real-world applications. When the applications are called for in real life, each situation itself becomes a learning process in which you must continually adjust the elements of the concept to suit reality. If you do this successfully often enough, you will have incorporated the delegation concept into your pattern of behavior. Thus you will have absorbed a concept in the classroom, carried it onto the job, and put it into practice in a number of situations, and developed the skill called delegation.

The problem with most concept programs, and thus with most management, supervisory, or leadership programs, is that they are treated by many learners and teachers alike as informational programs. As a result, concepts are absorbed as ideas but are not applied as true skills. Many supervisors can tell you about proper delegation, but not nearly as many practice delegation wisely and well.

For a concept program you can test for retained knowledge as you would with an informational program. However, the true success of a concept program depends largely on changes in behavior and attitude.

## YOUR EMPLOYEES

Regardless of how small the group you supervise may be, you will often find it difficult to meet all the educational needs of all your employees. Thus continuing education becomes an ongoing job—with the focus truly on continuing. Promotions, transfers, and replacements can create gaps in the capability of your work group. Even if all your employees do the same job or your group remains stable in terms of personnel transactions, there are always the gaps created by illness, vacations, and other time off.

A recommended objective for continuing education in any employee group is the achievement of the maximum possible amount of flexibility, through cross-training among employees working at comparable skill levels. For example, put yourself in the position of a records supervisor who has three records clerks assigned to three different areas. Although all three are classified as records clerks, one is assigned to compiling files on new inmates and filing and retrieval of file contents, a second to computing sentences, and the third to responding to correspondence and information requests. The absence of any one of these workers could mean that a disruptive backlog develops if no one else is able to step into that person's job for a day or two. However, if all three records clerks were trained in all three functions, the two on the job could be shifted around to serve the greatest needs. If all three clerks were present, similar positive action could be taken if one activity was backlogged, but the other two were current.

Versatility of coverage makes cross-training valuable to the supervisor. Employees also appreciate its benefits. They welcome the opportunity to learn different tasks, to undertake new activities, and to break away from long periods of performing the same tasks. The stimulation and the motivation they experience may encourage the supervisor to rotate employees through several different assignments at regular intervals. And of course, cross-training increases the potential for employee promotion. Take care, however, to assure that cross-training and job rotation are limited to employees and jobs in the same general job classification or pay range and that no labor agreements are breached by exchanging assignments in this way.

Your immediate goal in approaching continuing education with your employees is to impart knowledge or skill. Your long-range goal should be to create a learning attitude among your employees. Not all employees can be encouraged along these lines, so the creation of a learning attitude remains an ever-present goal that is never completely fulfilled. You will know that this goal is being served when some of your employees begin to seek out additional knowledge on their own, without supervisory urging.

### Getting Started

An excellent first step to pursuing continuing education in your department is to look about your institution for advice and assistance from other managers who are already involved in continuing education. If your institution is large enough or sufficiently committed to training and continuing education, you may have a training or staff development department. There also may be an in-service education function in the security department. If that is the case, the chief of security and the training officer can help with program structure and general approach. The training officer can provide plenty of advice, information, and assistance to another supervisor preparing to begin an in-house training or continuing education program.

Before launching any program of training or education, examine the needs of the work group and select some potentially fruitful starting points. It is best to begin with some form of learning-needs analysis.

## Determining Needs

A portion of a simple skills inventory matrix created for the employees in a food service department is shown in Exhibit 23–1. All of the employees in a particular job classification are listed in the column on the left side of the form. The remaining columns contain the supervisor's assessment of each employee's capabilities in the jobs identified at the tops of the columns. Note the simplicity of the breakdown: A number 1 indicates that the employee needs complete training in this activity; a number 2 indicates the need for some degree of refresher training; and a number 3 indicates that the employee now performs that particular job satisfactorily.

---

**Exhibit 23–1** Skills Inventory: Food Service

| Employees | Sanitation | Preparation | Dietary Knowledge | Inmate Supervision |
|-----------|:----------:|:-----------:|:-----------------:|:------------------:|
| P. Abel | 2 | 3 | 3 | 3 |
| C. Brown | 3 | 3 | 1 | 2 |
| N. Carter | 1 | 1 | 3 | 3 |
| J. Davis | 3 | 3 | 1 | 2 |
| D. Evans | 2 | 1 | 3 | 3 |

1. Needs complete training
2. Needs refresher
3. Satisfactory

Do not be misled by the simplicity of the matrix. To be sure, each number is a judgment call on your part. In creating the matrix (especially in determining the 2s and 3s, since a 1 is automatically indicated for an employee who has not done a particular job), it is necessary for you to speak with each employee and observe each at work. When you have completed such an exercise, you will have a good idea of where to focus your early training efforts.

Another form of the skills inventory, a variation applicable to the assessment of the learning needs of all employees' capabilities relative to all jobs in the department, is shown for secretarial staff in Exhibit 23–2. For each employee and each job you are really asking two questions: (1) Is training on this job applicable to this employee? (2) Can this employee, working under normal supervision and direction, perform this job satisfactorily?

A "not applicable" answer may be called for when a job is totally unrelated to an employee's general line of work or is of a different pay grade or classification. Be careful, however, of how freely you apply the "N/A" indicator: It may be to both your and the employee's advantage to consider training in completely different areas of activity as long as the jobs are consistent in classification and pay grade.

**Exhibit 23–2** Skills Inventory: Secretarial

| Employees | Transcription | Filing | Phone Contacts | Personal Contacts |
|-----------|---------------|--------|----------------|-------------------|
| R. Baker | Yes | No | Yes | Yes |
| P. Fredericks | N/A | Yes | Yes | No |
| M. George | Yes | Yes | Yes | Yes |
| N. Lori | N/A | No | No | Yes |
| D. Quincy | N/A | No | Yes | No |

Yes—Fully qualified
No—Training (or refresher) required
N/A—Not applicable to pay grade

Is your employee capable of performing the job with normal supervision and direction? Your answer, relying on your observation and judgment, is simply yes or no. If you do have doubts about an employee's ability to perform well, you may need to ask them some pertinent questions. All of your no answers indicate productive starting points for staff education.

## The Supervisor As a Teacher

You may teach in a continuing education program for your department. While you will be the most qualified, most readily available instructor for some of the topics and skills, chances are that a few topics will be better handled by others. For instance, if you are the records office manager and you are interested in cross-training several records office staff in sentence computation, it might be wise to use the employee who is regularly assigned to this task as an instructor. With encouragement and assistance, the person who best knows how to perform the details of a given task can become the best possible resource for teaching that task to others. You should not presume to do all of the teaching all of the time. However, your department's continuing education program will remain your responsibility and you will be fulfilling part of this responsibility by helping others develop as instructors.

Teaching a class can loom as a formidable task to a newcomer. If the idea of teaching a small class of employees frightens you, you can rest assured that you are not alone in that feeling: Just about everyone who teaches or speaks in public has experienced similar qualms. It helps to regard your early ventures into teaching as learning experiences in themselves, keeping in mind that you are not a professional teacher, that your employees are familiar to you and are not a group of unknown students, and that instruction in this environment is best accomplished in an informal, friendly atmosphere.

The keys to building your effectiveness as an instructor are preparation and practice. As long as you are reasonably comfortable with your knowledge of the subject and take care to organize your material for logical presentation, you can overcome your apprehensions about teaching. The more you teach a given subject, the better you will be able to teach it in the future. The more often you face a class of learners, the less bothersome your uneasiness about teaching will become.

*The Process*

In teaching nonsupervisory employees, you should be trying to do the following for your trainees:

- **Motivate them.** Attempt to reach them with reasons why they should want to learn. Let them know what is in it for them—new skills? something interesting for its own sake? opportunity for more interesting, challenging, or varied work? Let them know what they stand to gain and what the department stands to gain.

- **Tell and demonstrate.** Present your subject in logical order, and when teaching skill-related topics (for instance, how a particular task is performed) show them how it is done.

- **Check for their understanding.** Ask for questions, allow discussion, and generally encourage feedback. If you can hear what you have been saying coming back to you to your satisfaction in someone else's words, you are communicating effectively.

- **Let them try it.** After you have told and shown your students how a skill is applied and have received reasonable assurance that they understand, have them actually perform the task. Encourage feedback and work with them until they are able to perform the task to your satisfaction.

*Some Points To Remember*

While preparation is necessary to get your message across, your major task lies in dynamic instruction. Entertaining instruction can partially salvage thin material, but lackluster presentation can render the best-prepared material useless.

- *Combine your instructional methods whenever possible.* Teaching by telling, showing, or doing is most effective when two or all three methods are combined.

- *Use multiple modes of presentation.* Avoid reliance on a single medium of presentation. You might lecture for a while, support your comments with transparencies, show a brief film now and then, or use short segments of tape-recorded material. Use interactive techniques whenever possible—discussion, exercises, case studies, and in general anything that will draw your employees into the learning process.

- *Always be aware that your learners are workers, not students.* You are meeting with them in the middle of or perhaps after a regular workday, and chances are they have not come to your class fresh and relaxed. Never forget that they are full-time workers who probably have job problems on their minds.

- *Accept the high likelihood that you will rarely reach everyone in every way.* People are different; some are receptive to new information and new skills and some are not. But you must always try. Failure to reach everyone is not necessarily an indication of a teacher's shortcomings, but failure to try to do so is.

- Remember that for the instructor the process of teaching is itself a valuable form of learning. Most supervisors who have done some teaching have discovered that there is no better way to expand one's knowledge of a subject than to teach that subject.

## CONTINUING EDUCATION AND YOU

Formal continuing education programs for the supervisor often deal with matters of supervisory skill or management practice—usually the "concept programs" discussed earlier. Because these programs do not include practical applications, even the best prepared exercise or case problem is only a model of reality. Concept programs deal primarily with ideas and theories. As many people in management are constantly discovering, the gap between theory and practice can be broad and deep. Many managers may retain new information, but they never take the steps necessary to change their behavior based on this information.

Your opportunity to attend management programs usually comes about because administration, the personnel department, or staff development has made such training available. Although sometimes given the option of attending such a program you may sometimes find you are asked to attend in such a way that you clearly cannot refuse. Or you may simply be ordered to attend. Even if you feel your attendance is mandated or forced, do not allow this to influence you negatively toward the program.

Take advantage of the opportunity to attend supervisory and management programs whenever possible. You may feel inclined to bypass such opportunities because you are too busy, but if you approach management training with an open and receptive attitude, the experience practically guarantees that you will come away with something to help you do a better job.

Many of the better management programs are oriented more toward attitude change than toward imparting specific skills. To get the maximum benefit from such education, you must take the initiative to translate what you learn in the classroom into action on the job.

**Aside from management and supervisory programs provided by your organization, your continuing education can also include:**

- books, journals, professional bulletins and newsletters, and other publications
- courses offered outside of the institution, such as professional seminars, workshops, and management programs at local colleges
- audio- and videotape programs for self-instruction
- correspondence courses and conferences, seminars, and workshops offered by professional organizations

Whereas it is up to you to make continuing education available to your employees, it is not up to your superiors to make continuing education available to you. Your institution, if prompted by you and other supervisors, may make an occasional management program available. However, your access to most other forms of supervisor-oriented continuing education is largely controlled by you. In the last analysis, the most lasting and effective form of continuing education is self-education.

### YOUR KEY ROLE

Remember that it is your personal commitment to continuing education that will most influence how you and your employees develop educationally. If your commitment is verbal only—if, for instance, you simply launch a continuing education program for your employees and then back away—your employees are likely to follow your lead and participate only superficially. Your employees will take their cues from you. If they see you as truly "into education," they are much more likely to take your program seriously.

Stimulating and guiding your employees' continuing education while actively pursuing your own will give your department and institution competitive advantages in a world of rapid technological and social change. Continuing education is one of your crucial responsibilities as a manager.

## EXERCISE 23-1: THE SKILLS INVENTORY

Using the approach of either Exhibit 23–1 or Exhibit 23–2, prepare a preliminary skills inventory for your department or a portion of your department.

The technique of Exhibit 23–2 is adequate for a department of fewer than 10 employees and not more than 10 or 12 major tasks. If you supervise a larger department, concentrate on a single job classification or labor grade and apply the technique of Exhibit 23–1.

Do not simply render all judgments "off the top of your head"; when you have doubts concerning a person's ability to perform a certain task, spend a few minutes with the employee and ask some pertinent questions.

Use your skills inventory to develop a listing of learning needs for your employees based on: who must be trained in certain tasks and who would benefit the department by providing greater flexibility or improved task coverage by being trained in additional tasks, for example.

## EXERCISE 23-2: CROSS-TRAINING

If you supervise two or more persons in equivalent pay grades who perform somewhat different tasks, develop a plan for cross-training at least two (and preferably three) such persons in the others' tasks. If you do not yet supervise others, develop a hypothetical two- or three-person cross-training plan based on positions and tasks in the department in which you work. Your plan should include:

- a brief learning-needs analysis indicating who needs how much training in what functions
- who will do the training
- what training processes will most likely be used
- how long the training should require
- how you will assess the results of the training to decide when it is complete

**NOTES**

1. The American Correctional Association, *Standards for Adult Correctional Inst.,* 3rd ed. (Lanham, MD: 1990).
2. Joint Commission on Accreditation of Healthcare Organizations, *AMH/88: Accreditation Manual for Hospitals* (Chicago, Ill.: Joint Commission, 1987).

## CHAPTER 24

# The Supervisor and the Law

*Laws should be like clothes. They should be made to fit the people they are meant to serve.*
*—Clarence Darrow*

*Ignorance of the law, thoughtlessness, and, sometimes, plain stupidity cost U.S. organizations millions of dollars each year.*
*—Donald H. Weiss*

## Chapter Objective

☞ Provide a review of pertinent areas of legislation with which the supervisor should be generally familiar, with emphasis on the National Labor Relations Act, wage and hour laws, and laws dealing with affirmative action and equal employment opportunity.

## LEGAL GUIDES FOR SUPERVISORY BEHAVIOR

Correctional law relating to inmates, as a specialty area, is far too broad and complex to cover here. Major Supreme Court decisions and an ever-active judiciary at the state and federal levels make it critical that individual managers in the prison setting be aware of complex issues. These include: due process disciplinary hearings; First Amendment issues relating to visits, phone calls, and media access; the recently enacted Religious Freedom Restoration Act; tort law relating to the handling and disposition of inmate property; and numerous other issues that complicate a prison manager's job. The fact that the majority of states are under some form of court order or consent decree to limit population and/or improve conditions in either the entire state system or its major facilities is an eye-opening indication of the depth and breadth of judicial involvement in our profession.[1]

Each agency and institution has a carefully developed set of policies and procedures to cover areas such as these. Every manager should be aware of them, as well as the principles that underlie them, so that in new situations, informed decisions can be made. The alternative is costly, stressful litigation, and in some cases, monetary damage awards against individual staff. This is not an area to ignore.

Because this primarily is a book on how to manage employees, this chapter will provide general information relating to legal issues of personnel management. Individual states and the federal government have in place a variety of statutory structures that regulate labor relations and other management activities in prison.

In this chapter we will cover some of these prominent areas, and the way they influence supervisory behavior. We will discuss:

- the National Labor Relations Act. Comments will be limited to appropriate highlights of the act.
- wage and hour laws, for the benefit of the supervisor's familiarity with rates of pay, hours of work, and related matters.
- affirmative action and equal employment opportunity, and several laws that proscribe organizational behavior in regard to interviewing (see Chapter 8), hiring, and making certain work assignments.

First of all, you cannot read a small amount about the law and undertake to decide personnel-related legal issues for yourself. If you need just one reason to be convinced why this is true, go to a library that has a collection of the United States Code. Find Title 29—the labor law section. You will see that it consists of 11 volumes of 500–600 pages each (and each of those volumes has bulky supplements as well, which are updated periodically).

This massive body of law is just the tip of the legal iceberg when it comes to labor relations; the laws and court rulings that address specific issues are complex and constantly changing.[2] That is why your agency should have competent legal counsel to assist you on specific issues. Indeed, federal labor law, which is the overarching regulatory force for managers, could be the ultimate example of why we need attorneys and personnelists in our agencies. It simply is not possible for the average manager to know or understand the intricate details of this legislation.

The material in this chapter should, however, increase your general awareness of some of the things you should or should not do as a supervisor because of various legislation. When a true legal question arises, seek the answer through the personnel department, legal counsel, or some other administrative avenue.

## THE NATIONAL LABOR RELATIONS ACT

This legislation, amended by the Taft-Hartley Act and other related laws, is the central element of labor-management relations in the United States today.

These laws:

- Establish and protect basic employee rights to organize in the workplace, and to engage in collective bargaining with their employers.
- Outline employer rights and limitations with regard to organized labor activities.
- Set ground rules for mediation of labor disputes.
- Establish emergency Presidential powers to resolve disputes that impact vital national interests.
- Establish the National Labor Relations Board to monitor compliance with the Act.
- Govern other key activities in the labor-management arena.

This complex area of the law is covered in more detail in Chapter 26, but each agency or organization will have its own particular adaptation to this important body of legislation.

## WAGE AND HOUR LAWS

Of primary interest is the Fair Labor Standards Act, which is the federal wage and hour law and the model for the wage and hour laws of many states. Occasional points that might not be covered by federal law may be covered by pertinent state laws. Generally, if the same points are covered by both state and federal laws but differences exist between the two, the more stringent legislation will apply.

### Exempt Employees

Minimum wage and overtime requirements apply to prisons as in other industries. Three types of employees remain exempt and are identified as follows:

1. **Executives.** An executive employee must generally spend 50 percent or more of the time in direct management of an enterprise or an organizational subunit such as a department. In addi-

tion, an executive employee must direct the activities of two or more persons.

The executive definition may also require that a person possess the authority to hire and fire or so recommend; possess discretionary powers, rather than be assigned largely routine work; and from work week to work week spend no more than 40 percent of the time on nonmanagerial work.

2. **Administrative.** An administrative employee must spend 50 percent or more of the time on office or nonmanual work related in some way to policy, general business, or people in general and must be required to exercise discretion and independent judgment.

Other tests of the administrative classification may be assisting executive or administrative personnel; handling special assignments with only general supervision; working in a position requiring special training, experience, or knowledge; and spending not more than 40 percent of the time on nonadministrative work.

3. **Professional.** Professionals in institutions (for example, social workers, physicians, psychiatrists, psychologists, registered nurses, pharmacists) are so classified by virtue of spending 50 percent or more of the time in work that requires advanced specialized knowledge or is original or creative in nature. The definition may also require that the professional be consistently required to exercise discretion and independent judgment, be employed at intellectual and varied work, and be engaged in nonprofessional activities not more than 20 percent of the time.

The Fair Labor Standards Act specifies the minimum salary that virtually all executive, administrative, and professional personnel must be paid.

Arguments based on the applicability of a particular nonexempt definition are generally decided on the basis of the percentage of time spent on various activities. The time test applies on a work week to work week basis.

## Nonexempt Employees

All employees who do not fall under the executive, administrative, or professional category are considered nonexempt employees. They must be paid at least the prevailing legal minimum wage for each hour worked in a work week, and they must be paid at a rate of one and one-half times the regular rate for all overtime hours. In addition, they must be given equal pay for equal work unless there are legitimate factors that justify the establishment of different rates. (Gender is not a legitimate factor.) The organization is required to keep detailed records of hours worked and wages paid.

There are a few well-defined exceptions to the payment of the legal minimum wage. Special regulations allow the payment of lower rates to students, interns, and apprentices. Employment of such persons is also subject to additional requirements and restrictions.

## Overtime Compensation

### The Work Week

The Fair Labor Standards Act defines the work week as a fixed, re-curring period of 168 hours; that is, seven consecutive 24-hour periods. These 24-hour periods need not be calendar days, and the seven periods together need not be a calendar week. For instance, work weeks begin-ning and ending at midnight Friday or midnight Sunday are not un-common. The work week may be changed, and many organizations have done so to facilitate payroll accounting, but it cannot be changed in such a way as to avoid payment of overtime.

### Time and One-Half

The Fair Labor Standards Act requires payment of one and one-half times the regular rate for all overtime hours. Overtime hours are de-fined as those hours in excess of:

- 40 hours in a seven-day work week, where the usual seven-day work week is used
- 8 hours per day or 80 hours per 14-day period, when the use of the 14-day period has been approved and posted

The institution may use either or both methods for certain of its em-ployees but may use only one method at a time for a specific employee group. If the so-called 8 and 80 provision is used, overtime must be paid for all hours worked in excess of 8 in one day or in excess of 80 in the 14-day period, whichever results in the greater number of overtime hours.

In the following example, the employee worked a total of 80 hours. The employee is owed 3 hours of overtime that is derived from the fourth day, when 10 hours were worked, and the eighth day when 9 hours were worked (although on one day the employee worked only 5 hours).

| Day | Hours |
|---|---|
| 1 | 8 |
| 2 | 8 |
| 3 | 5 |
| 4 | 10 |
| 5 | 8 |
| 6 | 0 |
| 7 | 0 |
| 8 | 9 |
| 9 | 8 |
| 10 | 8 |
| 11 | 8 |
| 12 | 8 |
| 13 | 0 |
| 14 | 0 |
| 14 days | 80 hours |

**Overtime owed** = 3 hours (2 from day 4; 1 from day 8)

Next look at the next example:

| Day | Hours |
|---|---|
| 1 | 8 |
| 2 | 8 |
| 3 | 8 |
| 4 | 8 |
| 5 | 8 |
| 6 | 0 |
| 7 | 0 |
| 8 | 8 |
| 9 | 8 |
| 10 | 8 |
| 11 | 8 |
| 12 | 10 |
| 13 | 0 |
| 14 | 0 |
| 14 days | 82 hours |

**Overtime owed** = 2 hours (from day 12)

In this case the employee worked more than 8 hours on one or more days and more than 80 hours for the 14-day period. This example assumes that the employee worked 8 hours in each of nine days and 10 hours on the tenth day and thus is due 2 hours of overtime. Note that the employee has worked 2 hours in excess of both the 8 hours per day and 80 hours per work period provisions. However, this does not mean that the employee is owed overtime for 4 hours (based on 2 hours in excess of 8 and 2 hours in excess of 80). The employee is owed but 2 hours of overtime pay. Hours are not double counted; rather, when the totals of daily overtime and over-80 differ, it is the higher that must apply.

The Fair Labor Standards Act also specifies that only hours actually worked need to be counted toward determining overtime. That is, the institution is not required to count nonworked time such as vacation days, sick leave, holidays, and personal time as part of the 80 hours.

### The "Regular Rate"

The so-called regular rate referred to in the Fair Labor Standards Act includes the scheduled hourly rate plus on-call pay, call-in pay, and shift differential. The following presents an example of the effects of these additions on the rate:

Illustration of "Regular Rate"

**Overtime period:** 7 days, 40 hours

Employee worked 50 hours, including 4 hours of call-in time

| **Rates paid:** | Basic: $9.00/hour |
| | Shift differential: $0.60/hour |
| | Call-in: $50.00 (4 hours) |
| | On-call: $15.00 (flat) |

| **Calculation:** | $9.00 × 46 hours | = | $414.00 |
| | 0.60 × 46 hours | = | 27.60 |
| | 50.00 call-in | = | 50.00 |
| | 15.00 on-call | = | 15.00 |
| | | | $506.60 |

$\dfrac{\$506.60}{50} = \$10.132/\text{hour "regular rate"}$

$\$10.132 \times 1/2 = \$5.066/\text{hour overtime premium}$

| Basic Earnings (above) | $506.60 |
| Premium ($5.066 × 10 hours) | 50.66 |
| Total Earned | $557.26 |

Assume the employee in the example is paid overtime under the seven-day, 40-hour work week. The employee receives the following amounts: an hourly rate of $9.00, a flat rate of $15.00 for on-call time, $50.00 for 4 hours work on call-in, and 60 cents per hour shift differential. Assume the employee actually worked a total of 50 hours including the 4 hours of call-in time, and that shift differential was not used for the 4 hours of call-in time.

Since the employee worked a total of 50 hours, divide 50 into $506.60 to arrive at a "regular rate" of $10.132 per hour. Therefore, for the 10 hours of excess time the employee must be paid time and one-half this regular rate, or 10 hours at $15.198 per hour. Having already been paid the regular rate for each of the 50 hours, the employee is owed only the difference between that and $15.198 for the 10 excess hours, that is, $5.066 × 10 hours or $50.66. The total owed the employee in this example is $557.26.

Generally, hours spent at home "on call" are not counted as hours worked. This treatment depends on the employee's freedom of movement while on call. Pay received for such time, however, is counted in determining the regular rate. Note also, however, that when an employee who is "on call" is actually called to perform work, the hours actually worked are counted in the total hours worked. In determining whether on-call time must be counted as hours worked, the government will generally look to determine whether the employee must remain on the employer's premises or be sufficiently close that the time cannot be used as the individual chooses. If this is the case, the hours will be treated as working time for purposes of both minimum wage and overtime requirements.

## Equal Pay

A section of the Fair Labor Standards Act prohibits discrimination among employees on the basis of gender when the employees are doing equal work on jobs requiring equal skill, effort, and responsibility and performed under similar working conditions. In correcting unlawful differences in rates of pay, the act requires that the lower rate be increased; it is not permissible to decrease the higher rate. The act does make provision, however, for unequal pay if the inequality is directly attributable to a bona fide seniority system, merit system, incentive compensation system, or any other plan calling for a differential in pay based on any factor other than gender.

## AFFIRMATIVE ACTION AND EQUAL EMPLOYMENT OPPORTUNITY

### Title VII of the Civil Rights Act of 1964

As amended by the Equal Employment Opportunity Act of 1972, this legislation prohibits discrimination because of race, color, religion, sex, or national origin in any term, condition, or privilege of employment. The Equal Employment Opportunity Act of 1972 greatly strengthened the powers and expanded the jurisdiction of the Equal Employment Opportunity Commission (EEOC) in enforcement of this law.

As amended, Title VII now covers:

- all private employers of 15 or more persons
- all educational institutions, public as well as private
- state and local governments
- public and private employment agencies
- labor unions with 15 or more members
- joint labor-management committees for apprenticeship and training

The EEOC investigates job discrimination complaints, and when it finds reasonable cause that the charges are justified, attempts, through conciliation, to reach agreement by eliminating all aspects of discrimination revealed by the investigation. If conciliation fails, EEOC has the authority to go directly to court to enforce the law. Among other important provisions, the 1972 act also provides that discrimination charges may be filed by organizations on behalf of aggrieved individuals, as well as by employees and job applicants themselves. Applicants may also go to court directly to sue employers for alleged discrimination.

With these new powers, EEOC legal actions against employers violating the law have increased significantly. Regional litigation centers have been established with legal staff to provide more rapid and effective court action. Increased court-ordered affirmative action to remedy discrimination found under Title VII should emphasize to employers the need for effective affirmative action programs.

### Executive Order 11246 (Amended by Executive Order 11375)

Issued by the President in 1965, this order requires affirmative action programs by all federal contractors and subcontractors and requires that firms with contracts over $50,000 and 50 or more employees develop and implement written programs to be monitored by an assigned federal compliance agency. A recent U.S. Supreme Court decision on this issue (Adarand Constructors v. Pena)[3] means that some adjustments in the application of this Executive Order and other related regulations can be expected.

Specific requirements for result-oriented programs are spelled out in revised Order No. 4 issued by the Office of Federal Contract Compliance, U.S. Department of Labor. These requirements include identifying areas of minority and female underutilization, numerical hiring and promotion goals, and other actions to increase minority and female employment in job classifications where they are currently underutilized. Firms found not in compliance with Order No. 4 may face termination or cancellation of contracts or be barred from future contracts.

## The Equal Pay Act of 1963

The Equal Pay Act of 1963 requires all employers subject to the Fair Labor Standards Act (FLSA) to provide equal pay for men and women performing similar work. In 1972, coverage of this act was extended beyond employees covered by FLSA to an estimated 15 million additional executive, administrative, and professional employees (including academic, administrative personnel and teachers in elementary and secondary schools) and to outside salespeople.

## The Age Discrimination in Employment Act of 1967

The Age Discrimination in Employment Act (ADEA), covering age discrimination in essentially all aspects of employment, was first passed in 1967. Amended a number of times since its initial passage, ADEA applies to private employers and state and local governments having 20 or more employees and to labor unions having at least 25 members. The original act prohibited such employers from discriminating against persons in the 40- to 70-year-old age range in any area of employment because of age.

The Age Discrimination in Employment Amendments Act of 1986, effective for most employers on January 1, 1987, removed the age 70 limitation on ADEA protection. An employer can neither place an age limit on candidates for employment (except for those occupations for which it has been established that age is a bona fide occupational qualification, such as police officer, firefighter, and other select occupations) nor establish a mandatory retirement age for most employees.

The amended ADEA has also necessitated the amendment of numerous insurance plans and other employee benefits plans to permit their continued provision to all active employees regardless of their age. Essentially, ADEA in its present state requires employers to provide the same terms, conditions, and privileges of employment to all employees regardless of age.

### Title VI of the Civil Rights Act of 1964

Title VI of the Civil Rights Act of 1964 prohibits discrimination based on race, color, or national origin in all programs or activities receiving federal financial aid. Employment discrimination is prohibited because a primary purpose of federal assistance is the provision of employment, such as apprenticeship, training, work-study, or similar programs. Revised guidelines adopted in 1973 by 25 federal agencies prohibit discriminatory employment practices in all programs if such practices cause discrimination in services provided to program beneficiaries.

### The Americans with Disabilities Act

Passed in 1990 and largely effective in 1992, the Americans with Disabilities Act (ADA) affirmed the rights of persons with disabilities to equal access to employment, services and facilities available to the public (whether under public or private auspices), transportation, and telecommunications. Covered disabilities are defined in the law. This legislation provides a comprehensive mandate for barring discrimination against persons with disabilities and provides enforceable standards addressing such discrimination.

The ADA requires employers to provide reasonable accommodation for disabled individuals who are capable of performing the essential functions of the positions for which they apply. This may include altering physical facilities to make them usable by individuals with disabilities, restructuring jobs around functions they can perform, and altering or eliminating nonessential activities so that disabled persons can perform the work.

Regulations implementing ADA were issued by the Equal Employment Opportunity Commission (EEOC), the agency responsible for dealing with complaints of discrimination under all major federal anti-discrimination laws. Public and private organizations of all types are slowing learning the sometimes costly, but socially useful, impact of this legislation.

Of particular interest to employers today is the area of law concerning HIV-positive workers. This is a constantly changing portion of the managerial landscape, but the reader is referred to *Aids in the Workplace,* by William F. Banta (full reference in the annotated bibliography) for an excellent development of this increasingly important subject.

## Civil Rights Act of 1991

The Civil Rights Act of 1991 was essentially passed to reverse several Supreme Court decisions that had the effect of weakening (then) existing law. It provided for the most extensive modification of Title VII (of the Civil Rights Act of 1964) in more than twenty years. This newer law relies heavily upon jury trials, along with statutorily limited compensatory and punitive damages, as the basic litigation scenario under Title VII of the Civil Rights Act of 1964 and the Americans with Disabilities Act.

This act introduces jury trials into employment law to determine liability and compensatory and punitive damages for violations that are found to constitute intentional discrimination. The net effect of this legislation on employers is to increase the likelihood of legal action and increase legal costs associated with trials since potential plaintiffs and their attorneys are attracted by the prospect of damage awards and attorneys' fees (rather than simply compensation for losses, as under Title VII).

## State and Local Laws

Many state and local government laws prohibit employment discrimination. When EEOC receives discrimination charges, it defers them for a limited time to various state and local agencies having comparable jurisdiction and enforcement status. Determination of which agencies meet this deferral standard is a continuing process. These agencies' procedures and their requirements for affirmative action vary, but if satisfactory remedies are not achieved, the charges will revert to EEOC for resolution.

## The National Labor Relations Act and Related Laws

Discrimination on the basis of race, religion, or national origin may violate rights arising under these laws. It may be unlawful for employers to participate with unions in the commission of discriminatory practices unlawful under these acts, or to practice discrimination in a way that gives rise to racial or other divisions among employees to the detriment of organized union activity. It may also be unlawful for unions to exclude individuals from union membership, thereby causing them to lose job opportunities; to discriminate in the representation of members or nonmembers in collective bargaining or in the processing of grievances; or to cause or attempt to cause employers to enter into discriminatory agreements or otherwise discriminate against union members or nonmembers.

### Title IX, Education Amendments Act of 1972

In addition to extending coverage of the Equal Pay Act, this law prohibits discrimination on the basis of gender against employees or students of any educational institution receiving federal financial aid. Provisions covering students are similar to those of Title VI of the Civil Rights Act of 1964.

### The Rehabilitation Act of 1973

The Rehabilitation Act of 1973, as amended the following year, requires affected employers to maintain affirmative action programs to ensure the hiring and promotion of qualified handicapped persons.

### The Vietnam Era Veterans Readjustment Assistance Act of 1974

The Vietnam Era Veterans Readjustment Assistance Act of 1974 extends certain benefits, by way of affirmative action, to disabled veterans and veterans of the Vietnam period.

### Other Laws

Employment discrimination has also been ruled by the courts to be prohibited by the Civil Rights Acts of 1866 and 1870 and the Equal Protection Clause of the Fourteenth Amendment to the Constitution. Action under these laws on behalf of individuals or groups may be taken by individuals, private organizations, trade unions, and other groups.

## WHO NEEDS MORE RULES?

We have barely scratched the surface of the collection of personnel-related laws, rules, and regulations with which prisons must comply, by mentioning only the major areas that are likely to be of concern to correctional managers. The last decade has seen a dramatic increase in the amount of new and expanded federal legislation affecting employee benefits. Many of these changes will generally not be immediately visible to the individual supervisor, but they comprise the day-to-day concerns of the personnel department. You are likely to see many of the effects of this legislation in various aspects of your work, and, as a manager, you must be aware of and sensitive to them.

Remember that as supervisors we are also employees and that the protection afforded our employees under legislation, such as equal pay and affirmative action, also extends to us. As managers, we should be willing to recognize that certain laws represent well-defined and necessary boundaries within which we must work as we fulfil our daily responsibilities.

---

### EXERCISE 24–1: RATES, HOURS, AND OVERTIME

Your institution operates on the "8 and 80" basis for overtime.

One of your employees worked the following days and hours (mostly on the 11:00 P.M. to 7:00 A.M. shift):

| Day | Hours |
|-----|-------|
| 1 | 8 |
| 2 | 8 |
| 3 | 6 |
| 4 | 9 |
| 5 | 7 |
| 6 | 0 |
| 7 | 0 |
| 8 | 10 |
| 9 | 10 |
| 10 | 12 |
| 11 | 6 |
| 12 | 8 |
| 13 | 0 |
| 14 | 0 |

The employee's base rate is $18.60 per hour. Shift differential is $1.65 per hour. Day No. 10 included 4 hours of call-in, paid at a flat $80.00. (The employee was asked to come in at 7:00 P.M., 4 hours early.) Determine:

1. the hours of overtime due the employee
2. the "regular rate" for determining overtime premium
3. the employee's total earnings for the two-week period

---

## EXERCISE 24–2: ANOTHER ARRANGEMENT

Repeat Exercise 24–1, first making one important change: Instead of using the "8 and 80" basis, assume you are operating on the "standard" 7-day work week. Use days 1 through 7 for week 1 and days 8 through 14 for week 2.

Determine whether the resulting total overtime payment is the same as or different from the payment determined in Exercise 24–1.

---

**NOTES**

1. E. Koren, Status Report: State Prisons and the Courts—January 1, 1994, *National Prison Project Journal* 9, no. 1 (1994), 12.

2. Relevant legal requirements are changing all the time; the 1993 enactment of the Family and Medical Leave Act, for instance, has brought about significant changes in the leave policy of most organizations.

3. ___ U.S. ___, 115 S. Ct. 2097, 132 L.Ed. 2d 158 (1995).

## CHAPTER 25

# Organizational Communication: Looking Up, Down, and Laterally

*What we got here is failure to communicate....*
*—the Captain in the movie* Cool Hand Luke

## Chapter Objectives

☛ Compare and contrast the characteristics of upward communication and downward communication in the organizational setting, with special attention to the barriers to upward communication.

☛ Define and describe the supervisor's role in organizational communication.

☛ Provide suggestions for strengthening communications with other organizational elements including your immediate superior.

☛ Suggest ways of dealing with "the grapevine."

☛ Stress the importance of the supervisor's visibility to the department's employees.

## WHAT GOES DOWN MAY NOT COME UP

When he spoke out in those remarkably expressive tones, the Captain in the 1970s movie, *Cool Hand Luke* was speaking about his problems in getting a recalcitrant inmate to "get your mind right." But he spoke as well for the problems of supervising anyone—and keeping necessary information flowing—in the prison environment.

The chapter's leadoff quote actually is about a one-way communication problem. In any organization, communication must move both upward and downward through the structure. However, an informed management view of organizational communication will recognize that information does not flow both upward and downward with equal ease. Downward communication is facilitated largely by management's control of its own actions and by its control of most of the means of communication in the work setting. In contrast, much upward communication remains dependent on stimulation, encouragement, and the creation of a climate conducive to communication.

The essential difference between upward communication and downward communication can be highlighted by looking at a number of factors that inhibit upward communication.

## Organizational Concerns

Simple physical distance between supervisor and employee (as in the security department where staff are on posts throughout and even outside the prison) can inhibit upward communication. Simply put, the more time you spend physically separated from the location where most of your employees work, the tougher it is for them to communicate with you. Supervisors with employees who have considerable on-the-job mobility or are scattered over an extended physical area need to take steps to keep in touch. The more time you spend physically removed from your employees, the more likely you are to miss something that might have otherwise been communicated to you.

The number of levels in the organization structure can also inhibit upward communication. If a piece of information originating with a single food service employee truly deserves to reach the warden, the chances of it being properly and accurately communicated upward diminish with each managerial level it must go through. Each level that a message must pass through presents another set of opportunities for the message to be misinterpreted, sidetracked, or stopped entirely.

The relative complexity of a given problem or situation can also hamper upward communication. Some employees are often unable to define complex problems fully, especially if these problems appear to involve jobs or departments other than their own. Some employees may lack sufficient command of communication skills to enable them to translate their thoughts and observations into concise, understandable messages so they simply do not bother to try.

## Problems Involving Managers

The attitude exhibited by a supervisor or manager can have a great deal to do with how well information flows upward. If your manner and attitude should seem to say "no news is good news" or "don't tell me anything I don't want to hear," employees are likely to be discouraged from speaking up. Also, if the supervisor appears to react defensively—perhaps seeming to regard opinions, problems, or requests as personal jabs—employees will be inhibited in their need to communicate.

Some managers frequently exhibit resistance to becoming involved with the personal problems of employees. This resistance, which may stem from the supervisor's understandable uneasiness with hearing things that might be considered "confessional" in nature, serves as a wall that unfortunately keeps out desired feedback as well as unwanted information. Recall the notion of the employee as a "whole person," and learn to accept the high likelihood that many personal problems have their work-related sides.

The manager's available time can also be a factor inhibiting the upward flow of information. True, effective listening is a time-consuming process, and under the pressure of many high-priority tasks, it is easy to find yourself dealing with some items lightly, briefly, or not at all.

Probably one of the greatest inhibitors of upward communication lies in actions of the recent past: management's failure to respond to some earlier communication. A question, problem, or observation coming from an employee remains one-way communication and thus not true communication at all unless you make an effort to "close the loop" by providing the required feedback. This is not to say that employees should always expect to receive the responses they desire. Rather, they need simply to receive an indication that their messages have been considered and that management responses are offered. Your feedback, after proper investigation, consideration, or consultation as appropriate, may be simple: "Thanks very much for pointing it out; it's being taken care of"; "I'm sorry, but it can't be done (for such and such a reason)." Without feedback your employees are likely to think their concerns are "swallowed up by the system" and will be discouraged from communicating at all.

## Problems Involving Employees

Employees will see downward communication occurring more freely and frequently than upward communication. Tradition, authority, and prestige all favor the management hierarchy and downward communication over upward information flow. After all, you feel free to call on your employees at just about any time, just as your manager is likely to feel free to call on you at any time. However, rarely will nonsupervisory employees feel that same degree of freedom in their ability to call on the boss.

Most of the mechanisms and means of organizational communication are in the hands of management and favor the downward flow of communication. These include bulletin boards, public address systems, employee newsletters and other printed matter, and duplicating services. The individual employee with something to communicate must usually do so either by writing it out or relating it orally to another person. Some people simply will not relay a problem or concern to the supervisor because it has a personal dimension that they do not wish to reveal. Some may also hesitate to point out certain problems for fear of being blamed for causing them. For the same reason they will say nothing they might consider to be self-incriminating or self-deprecating in any way.

A final but sometimes insurmountable barrier to upward communication is found in emotion and prejudice on the part of a few employees. A limited number of nonsupervisory employees regard management—even the most enlightened, humane, and people-centered management—as exploitative and untrustworthy simply because it is management. Frequently this attitude extends so far as to regard the new supervisor moving up from the ranks as abandoning the "good guys" and joining the "bad guys." Rarely will an employee harboring such a view of management discuss any serious concerns with the supervisor—unless the supervisor has conscientiously worked to earn the employee's trust and confidence.

## YOUR ROLE IN ORGANIZATIONAL COMMUNICATION

Have you ever found yourself, perhaps in anger or frustration, saying, "The trouble with this place is there's no communication"? If the truth could be determined, we would probably discover that most supervisors have said this (or something very much like it) more than just a few times. However, the next time you feel inclined to cry "no communication," you might do well to consider that much of organizational communication depends on you and what you do and say. Before dwelling on the shortcomings that "they" exhibit—"they" being the often-blamed but never specifically identified villains of "they won't let me do it," "they didn't tell me," for example—it might prove more productive to work on your own communication practices. You cannot change someone else's habits and practices, but you can encourage them to change these for themselves and you can best do this by changing your own behavior.

Look at the simplified diagram of Figure 25–1. You, the supervisor, are in the middle. Your lines of communication run between you and other people in the organization. Your strictly formal lines of communication are those numbered 1, 2, 5, and 6; these depict the direct reporting relationships that exist between you and your employees and you and your immediate superior. Lines 3 and 4 suggest a large number of less rigid but still formal communicating relationships. These relationships are still formal because although you neither manage nor report to any of the people who work in or manage other functions and depart-

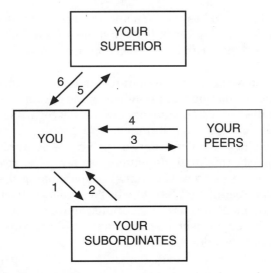

**Figure 25–1** Your Communication Channels

ments throughout the institution, you nevertheless require communication with many of them in the performance of your job.

First appreciate that communication along three of the six lines shown (those outgoing lines, numbered 1, 3, and 5) is completely in your hands. As the sender of a message, the originator of a communication, you have full control over all information leaving you. You control what is sent, when it is sent, why it is sent, how it is sent, to whom it is sent, and where it is sent. And you can always send something. Even when a communication you wish to send is dependent on your first receiving something from another party, you can at least say "I don't know yet," "I'm still waiting," or "I'll call you as soon as I hear."

The point of this discussion is twofold: (1) your outgoing channels of communication are completely under your control and (2) the best way to get information moving along your incoming lines of communication is to assure that the outgoing lines are open and operating.

Of your incoming lines of communication you have the greatest degree of control over number 2—information flowing from your employees. Some of this control is due to the authority of your position; these people report to you, so most of them expect to give you certain information at certain times.

An additional measure of control will stem from your degree of success in requesting and receiving feedback from your employees. This is where assignment completion targets and deadlines and periodic reports come into the picture, along with your effective use of follow-up. In short, you can manage in a way that assures you will receive a great deal of work-related communication simply because your style tells your employees you both need it and expect it. There remains, however, information you would like to know as a supervisor, such as individual complaints, claims of unfair treatment, and dissension between employees that cannot be mandated by structure or approach. You will receive this added information only by earning the trust and confidence of your employees and by showing through your actions that you are willing to communicate openly, honestly, and in confidence.

You have considerably less control over the information reaching you by way of line 4, the channel running from other organizational elements to you. You do not work for any of these people and they do not work for you. Because of your level or position you may possess some implied authority with some of these people, but you will have no authority at all with others. Therefore, your communicating relationship with these people has to be based on cooperation. You must display the willingness to communicate and the ability to decide, when you are ready to send something out, who truly needs it and who else should receive it as a matter of information or simple courtesy.

Again, the best way to get information moving in is first to see that it is freely moving out. Do so even if you have to shake off the old "50-50 ethic," the pressure suggesting that in our communication, as well as in other endeavors, it is only "fair" for each party to go halfway. Some people will respond to your conscientious efforts in kind; others, however, will respond inadequately or not at all. Nevertheless, you should be prepared consistently to go more than halfway more than half of the time. If this sounds unfair to you, then look at it from a selfish point of view: The person who is benefiting most from your extra communications effort is you.

The one channel of communication not yet discussed, number 6, leading from your superior to you, can present more problems than the others. It is on this channel that you stand the least chance of exerting some appreciable measure of control. Obviously, you do not have positional authority to help you in this relationship. Your communicating relationship with your boss, then, deserves special attention.

## Getting Your Boss To Communicate

If your immediate supervisor is a conscientious practitioner of the art of effective communication, you may be able to skim through these few paragraphs and not worry at all about what they contain. On the other hand, you may have sufficient problems with this particular relationship to make these few words worth considering.

Remember that how you are communicated with is, to some extent, a reflection of how you communicate. The following are a few ways in which you can tune up your communications to your supervisor in an attempt to stimulate more effective communication from your supervisor.

### Be Selective in What You Communicate

Do not expect your boss to do your job for you and take care of your problems. When something comes up, your initial impulse may be to turn to the boss for information, advice, or assistance. But before doing so make sure it is something you cannot take care of yourself. One of your legitimate functions as a supervisor is to be a "problem filter" for your boss, screening out those matters that should be resolved at a lower level.

### Do Your Homework

The existence of problems is one of the major reasons for the existence of managers. No manager really needs more problems than are already present. Many problems make themselves felt at all organizational levels, so what your boss needs are solutions. Even though many problems you encounter might be beyond the range of your decision-making authority, you can do more toward solving them than simply passing them one block up the organizational chart.

Remember that you are just one of several people reporting to the same superior, and what may look like a trickle of trouble to you may strike the boss as a flood of grief. When you must pass a problem up the line, first analyze it, assess its implications, prepare two or three alternative solutions, and recommend an answer, if you have one. In short, instead of saying, "Here's a problem. What do you what me to do?" you should be saying: "Here's a problem; here's why it's a problem; here are one or two possible solutions; here's the answer I think is best, and here's why."

### Structure Your Communications

When you need information, especially small bits of advice or minor decisions, put your questions in writing in such a way that they can be answered in one or two words. This will often make it easier for your supervisor to make a decision and to respond quickly.

For example, an education supervisor was having difficulty obtaining a few minutes discussion time with the associate warden about a program change she wanted to make. Unable to get time with her boss when she needed to, she re-examined the situation, expressing the problem in the form of three concise questions. After typing the questions on a single sheet of paper, she left them with the associate warden's secretary. The next morning the answers were on the education supervisor's desk (see Exhibit 25–1).

---

**Exhibit 25–1**  A Structured Communication

Mr. Parsons:

1. Can I go ahead with rescheduling the evening GED program as we discussed?

    *Yes*

2. Will I have at least a half an hour with the warden to discuss this after the next staff meeting?

    *Yes - schedule with his secretary*

3. Will you be available to talk with him at that time?

    *No - I'll be at another meeting then    B.P.*

    *5/17/96*

    Paul J. 5/16/96

## *Make Yourself Available*

Some bosses are thoughtful enough to say something like: "The best time to get me is first thing in the morning before the telephone starts to ring," or "I'm likely to be free between 4:00 and 4:30." Even without such assistance, however, you may often find you are in a position to know your manager's comings and goings and develop a sense for the better times to try for a brief audience. Remember, though, that in most cases you are not the only employee he or she supervises, and certainly not the only subordinate with problems. When you make yourself available to the boss, strive to consume as little time as possible. Remember, too, that although your boss's time is valuable, your time is also valuable. Most of your time belongs to your department, not to your boss.

## The Grapevine

Every organization has a formal structure, a network of reporting relationships described by the well-known organization chart. However, organizations also have a number of informal channels of communication—the "grapevine," based on informal relationships with friends, acquaintances, and others. These personal relationships characterize the informal organization, built upon the respect, acknowledgment, deference, or prestige people accord one another.

You have seen the informal organization at work when two or three nonsupervisory employees happen to stand out from the group, perhaps even speaking for others, although they have no official sanction to do so, or when a single supervisor is regarded as "senior" by the work group over a number of others at the same level because of some particular trait or combination of traits. In short, interpersonal relationships and people's regard for one another describe the informal organization, an invisible structure that is always shifting and realigning.

People will talk. The grapevine is not required by management, and it is certainly not controlled by management. It runs merrily back and forth across departmental lines and rapidly changes its course. The grapevine is dynamic but unreliable. It carries a great deal of information and misinformation. And it is here to stay.

Tune in; listen to what it is carrying and learn from it. As a supervisor you are likely to be isolated from some of the bits and pieces the grapevine carries, or at the very least you will learn of some things long after they have been known to your staff. How much you hear frequently depends on how well you relate to your employees and peers.

But beware the grapevine. When you are tuned in to it you are going to hear a few things that you know are simply not correct. When you hear something that is disturbing or strikes you as inappropriate, check it out if possible. As a supervisor you are responsible for setting the facts of the story right whenever you have the opportunity to do so. But be sure you have your story straight so you do not simply heap more speculation onto a growing rumor.

The grapevine sometimes possesses the distinct advantages of speed and depth of penetration. Some bits of news can travel through the institution at an astonishing rate, carried not only by staff, but inmates as well. It often reaches people who would never think to read a bulletin board or look at an employee newsletter. The grapevine can carry the good as well as the bad. The grapevine can carry useful, factual information. Using it can sometimes be to your advantage.

Sometimes it is not the truth or falsehood of a rumor that is so important as the fact that the story is out there on the grapevine at all. The grapevine network also telegraphs employee attitudes and beliefs. An astute manager will try to discern when this kind of dynamic is at work, and can use it to anticipate developments within the organization, such as the impending resignation of a key employee.

## WHICH WAY DO YOU FACE?

Your employees are likely to infer a great deal about your overall attitude as a supervisor according to how effectively you communicate. You will also be judged by your visibility and availability, that is, how much your employees see of you in and around the department and how readily they can get a few minutes of your time when they need it. Having the "management by walking around" ethic can help establish good communication between you and your employees.

However, in most organizations managers feel pressures to "face upward." They become more visible and available to superiors and other members of higher management than to their own employees and staff. After all, pay increases, promotions, and other rewards come from above. There are some traps in this reasoning, however. Not all higher managers are necessarily impressed by your ready availability to them. Effective top managers will begin to wonder who is running your department while you are busy looking upward.

Supervisors must develop and cultivate a variety of communicating relationships in the organization. The most important are those you establish with your employees. Regardless of the number and capability of the managers in any prison, it remains largely the nonmanagerial employees who do the hands-on work of running the institution. You are there to assure that the portion of the prison for which you are responsible is managed in the best possible way. Your primary attentions belong to the people who do the work. Among them you will find the real action, the real challenges, and the true opportunities. In the last analysis, it remains your employees who, through their job performance, can determine whether you succeed or fail as a manager.

---

## CASE 25–1: THE CRUNCH

You and four other department heads are at a meeting with your immediate boss, the associate warden to whom the five of you report. Two other department heads and the warden's executive assistant are also present. The subject of the meeting is sensitive.

Just minutes into the meeting the boss makes a statement that you know to be incorrect. You attempt to intervene, but the boss asks you to hold your comments. He seems to be focused almost entirely on the other department heads and the executive assistant.

Your boss proceeds to build an argument on his incorrect statement and you can sense that he is verbally "painting himself into a corner." Since you have already been silenced once you are hesitant to speak up again, and although you are sure of your information you have no way of "proving" anything without making a trip to your office and rummaging through some files. Within the confines of the conference room it would simply be your word against his, and he is the boss.

What should you do? In deciding on a possible course of action, consider the implications of:

1. keeping quiet and allowing the boss to proceed in apparent error
2. intruding, forcefully if necessary, until your information is heard by the group

---

## CASE 25–2: THE UNREQUESTED INFORMATION

One morning, about 15 minutes before your work day officially starts, you are enjoying a solitary cup of coffee when you are joined by Mr. Hatfield, one of your employees. Hatfield proceeds to advise you ("in strictest confidence; please don't say that I told you") that another employee, Mrs. Thomas has been passing derogatory remarks about your management style among members of the staff.

Mr. Hatfield proclaims that he doesn't ordinarily carry stories but felt that you "had a right to know, for the good of the department."

Should you:

1. thank Mr. Hatfield and ask him to report anything else he might hear?

2. acknowledge his concern "for the good of the department" but tell him to bring you no further such stories?

3. thank him, ask him to say nothing to anyone else, and decide for yourself to keep an eye on Mrs. Thomas?

Explain why you chose the particular answer you selected. You may modify, qualify, or further explain your answer as you believe may be necessary.

## CHAPTER 26

# Unions: Avoiding Them When Possible and Living with Them When Necessary

*If you don't have them, the best way to avoid them is to create a Theory Y environment where your people have a chance to realize their potential. If you already have unions, then deal with them openly and honestly.*

—*Robert Townsend*

### Chapter Objectives

☛ Explore the reasons for the organizing success of many unions, emphasizing that basic management errors often leading to unionization.

☛ Describe the typical union organizing approach.

☛ Define the supervisor's active role during a union organizing campaign.

☛ Stress the importance of the supervisor's role in effective two-way communication with employees—whether or not the employees belong to a union.

### THE SETTING

Labor management relations are an integral part of prison management; the question is whether you are dealing with the issue within a contractual bargaining structure or not. In the public sector, unions are a fact of life, while private prisons are largely nonunion.

Regardless of the situation you are in, you will have to deal with employees on matters that could involve a union, or could create a desire on the part of your staff to have one. Employees will object to your decisions. They will have grievances over a variety of issues. They will experience morale problems. They will be motivated toward increased pay and benefits.

How you as a manager deal with these issues can go a long way toward ensuring harmony and productivity in the workplace. Failing to adequately deal with them in a non-union prison can lead to a work environment that is ripe for union organization. Failing to deal fairly and legally with your union in a prison that already is organized can not only bring about serious operational problems, but be quite costly as well.

If you are working in a nonunionized setting, this section will be of particular interest. If your organization is already formally organized, then its principles will be important for you to be familiar with, in order to maintain good relations with your union (or unions) and its members.

## WHY UNIONS TAKE HOLD

In the early 1970s, a major study was made of 379 union elections, which extended over a period of three years and involved approximately 30 industries in nearly as many states. Of these 379 elections, 281, or 74 percent, were won by the unions. When researchers asked why the unions had such success, three conclusions were offered:

1. Most of the organizing campaigns focused on wages or other economic issues. Most of the initial demands were unreasonable, and most reflected ignorance about, or indifference to, the organization's financial position. Although in many cases the wage structure appeared to be a good organizing point, it was often not the real reason. The unions often won because of apparent management indifference to complaints, a lack of response (or even an effort to respond) to employee problems, and the organization's lack of credibility with employees about issues such as costs and operating circumstances.

2. In most of the cases in which the unions won, anti-management sentiment was initially brought about by employee perceptions of poor working conditions, exemplified by such things as substandard facilities, poor organizational communications, and arbitrary or uncaring management.

3. In many instances the anxiety produced by widespread lack of knowledge about what was truly taking place was helpful to the union cause.

Every lost election covered in the survey was related to serious morale problems among employees. In every such case, management was operating with little of no information about true employee feelings and opinions.

In testing the potential for unionization it is simply not enough for top management to have you talk to employees and report back on their feelings. True antimanagement sentiment—the kind that is potentially beneficial to a union organizer—is discovered only through effective listening. Many, if not most, employees would prefer to be loyal to the organization. But the organization's apparent indifference (from the employees's point of view) to upward communication can discourage such loyalty.

The price of management indifference can be extremely high. If a union loses a bargaining election, it may seek another election after one year has elapsed, and then may try again repeatedly until it succeeds. But management need lose only once. Odd are that if management does not listen to the employees, the union organizers eventually will win.

**There are three basic errors commonly committed by management in assessing the potential for success of union organizing efforts:**

1. The widely prevalent management notion that the causes of most worker dissatisfaction are wages, fringe benefits, and other economic concerns. However, initial organizing activity usually springs from noneconomic matters involving issues that are not as easily quantifiable as dollars. True, employee dissatisfaction will ultimately be expressed in the form of financial demands and a specific financial package can be obtained by contract. But there is no contractual way to achieve less tangible items such as sympathetic listening, open communications, and humane and respectful treatment.

2. Many top managers automatically assume that all supervisors are on the side of management. However, most supervisors came "up from the ranks" within the functions they supervise and as such are an integral part of the work group. Also, in many institutions first-line supervisors have been kept out of participation in real management decisionmaking. This may dispose them (informally) toward the union, even if they are members of the management team.

3. Frequently, no one at the top of the organization has any clear idea of what is really troubling the ranks of nonmanagerial employees. If you don't know what the real problem is, it is virtually impossible to craft a solution.

**Committing any of the following basic management errors in one form or another can pave the way for a successful union organizing drive:**

- Introducing major changes in organization structure, job content, equipment, or operating practices without providing advance notice or subsequent explanation to employees
- Giving employees little or no information about the status of important events at the institution, or about its plans, goals, or achievements
- Making key decisions without knowing the employees's true wants, needs, and feelings
- Using pressure (authoritarian or autocratic leadership) rather than true leadership (consultative or participative leadership) to obtain employee performance
- Disregarding or downplaying instances of employee dissatisfaction

## Corrections and Unions

Unionization of government employees is not a new phenomenon. If you are a public sector prison manager, you almost certainly are dealing with one or more unions already, while private prison managers probably are not. But it is an open question how long private prisons will remain unorganized. As the total number of jobs available in the manufacturing sector of the U.S. economy has been steadily declining for a number of years, unions have correspondingly lost the past source of most union membership. As this has taken place, unions have shifted much of their focus (which already had included government employees at all levels) to the service sector, which now employs 75 percent or more of the U.S. work force. This suggests that private prisons could be fertile grounds for union organizing in the future, particularly as more of these institutions are opened.

With the economy of the mid-1990s displaying a great deal of turmoil and uncertainty, employees are feeling more and more uneasy about the future. As many firms lay off staff, including mid-level managers, employees perceive a threat to their continued livelihood. One would think the continuing expansion of the correctional segment of the criminal justice system in the 1990s would reassure prison staff of their job security. But privatization has been cause for alarm among public sector employees, as they feel threatened by the possibility of losing jobs or job security to a nongovernment entity.

Corrections, at both the organizational and individual employee levels, is faced with some nearly overwhelming concerns—many of which seem to defy all attempts at resolution because of outside pressures and restrictions. When staff feel that their individual concerns are not being adequately addressed by management, these employees will turn to someone else who will seem to listen. Often this "someone else" is a union.

On the other hand, it may not be too strong a statement to say that the formation of a union is (at least in part) evidence of an inability on the part of managers to properly balance the equally legitimate needs of the workplace and the worker. Managerial insensitivity to proper concerns, use of inappropriate supervisory techniques, and the failure to regard employees as an important and valuable resource that requires tending—all of these factors can create a fertile environment for a union.

## THE SUPERVISOR'S POSITION

For the nonunionized institution to remain that way, the individual supervisor must play a key role. Several sections of this book have talked about the importance of the supervisor-employee relationship. As the supervisor you are the member of management whom your employees know best. Indeed, you may be the only member of this mysterious entity called management whom most of your employees know on a first-name basis or even know on speaking terms at all. Thus as your employees see you, so are they likely to see all of management and the organization itself. If they see you as unconcerned, uncaring, distant, or indifferent, they are likely to view the organization as a whole the same way.

It follows, then, that the supervisor is in a key position when it comes to dealing with the threat of unionization. You are the link that ties your employees to higher management and thus to the organization. Your long-term behavior will have a great deal to do with whether or not your department or institution is a fertile ground for union organizing activity. Your conduct and actions during an organizing campaign will exert a significant influence on your employees's reaction to the organizing drive.

### The Organizing Approach

If you are a public sector prison manager, most of this section will not apply to you. However, it could be applicable in situations where one union tried to usurp representation of bargaining unit members from another labor organization.

What do the first stages of a union organizing campaign look like? You might be inclined to answer this question by citing one of the first visible signs—leafleting, or the distribution of union literature to employees at walkways, driveways, and parking lot entrances. However, while serious leafleting is an undeniable indication of union activity it is ordinarily not the first step in an organizing campaign. Before the first literature appears, the union probably has been studying the institution for weeks or even months, to judge its organizing potential.

When organizing activity actually begins, management may know nothing about it. In fact, during the earliest stages the union may take great precautions to conceal their interest. Because the controlled access of a prison reduces the options to non-employee union organizers for activity of this type, any area where employees congregate informally can be used for this purpose. The union may send organizers to locations frequented by off-duty staff (restaurants or bars). There, they can contact employees and learn from casual conversations what some of the issues and concerns are at the institution.

The organizers will try to learn as much as possible about the institution before identifying themselves. They also may attempt to pinpoint employees who have the potential to serve as internal organizers. These would be employees who are popular, knowledgeable, reasonably articulate, and in some way unhappy with the organization.

Should their initial, unannounced assessment raise serious doubts about the feasibility of an organizational drive, the organizers might simply withdraw without ever announcing their presence. However, if they believe the union may succeed in organizing the prison, they will likely identify themselves to a few selected employees and begin preparations to carry their message to others. Leafleting is likely to begin at about this stage.

The major exception to the usual significance of leafleting occurs in a practice sometimes referred to as a "pass-through." This is when union organizers devote a day or two to distributing literature at several targeted installations in the same general area. These are generally "cold" visits, with little or no advance work. The union will simply "pass through" the area and drop off as much literature as possible with employees (usually at shift change time) and follow up only if they receive expressions of interest from employees. The pass-through literature usually includes a reply card to be returned "for more information."

Once the organizers are openly interested in the institution and their purpose is generally known, they will step up their activities in meeting with employees and contacting them in other ways. At some point, possibly through sympathetic employees, they will attempt to obtain a list of the names and addresses of all the institution's nonmanagerial staff. The union will most certainly be contacting many individual employees by telephone and will seek to visit the homes of others.

In talking with employees, the union will attempt to learn about issues that can be used as rallying points for employee sympathy and support. The organizers also may attempt to identify martyrs and victims of "the system" and will effectively play on emotions in spotlighting incidents of alleged unfair treatment and discrimination. The union organizers will go to great lengths to impress on employees their right to be treated as individuals. This may seem elementary, since most of us will express strong belief in the rights of the individual. However, if line employees see management as indifferent and the union organizer is the first person to discuss this, then this may provide the initial grounds for union credibility. Organizers will make every effort to develop a communicating relationship with your employees. This should sound familiar, since the development of such a relationship is part of your role as a supervisor.

You can be sure that most issues and incidents highlighted by the union are specially selected to make the prison's management look bad. Lacking sufficient factual material, organizers may stage incidents intended to make the union look good and make management look foolish. It is critical for the supervisor to be aware of this particular organizing tactic. It is all too easy to make an inappropriate statement or incorrect decision when confronted with a trumped-up grievance or problem. Often, this happens at an inconvenient time and under awkward circumstances—usually in the presence of employee witnesses.

Ideally, these situations should be dealt with by the administration, the personnel officer, or whoever else may be coordinating the institution's counter-organizing activities. However, the supervisor often must react on the spot. The key to a successful response in such a situation is to not make promises or commitments, and to not be seen as refusing to listen to an employee. Afterward, the incident can be promptly reported to the proper persons.

## Unequal Positions

Under the National Labor Relations Act, unions and employers are not on an equal footing in the organizing process; in many respects the union enjoys the upper hand. Under the Act, an employer can commit an unfair labor practice and such charges can be brought against the organization by the union. If the National Labor Relations Board (NLRB) rules on an unfair labor practice charge and upholds the union's claim, then the union may be automatically certified as a recognized bargaining agent without the necessity of a representation election.

The law, however, does not work the other way around. Generally, there is no such thing as an unfair labor practice committed by a union. Also, as noted earlier, if the union should lose a bargaining election it may petition for another election after one year has elapsed. The employer may well have to win year after year to remain nonunionized. However, the employer need lose only once and the union is in, permanently, for all practical purposes, since decertification of a union is difficult to achieve and occurs infrequently.

### Your Active Role

The guidelines relevant to supervisory behavior during a union organizing campaign make up a sizeable collection of do's and don'ts.

### What the Supervisor Can Do When a Union Beckons

1. Campaign against a union seeking to represent employees, and reply to union attacks on the institution's practices or policies.
2. Provide employees with your opinions about unions, union policies, and union leaders.
3. Advise employees of their legal rights during and after the organizing campaign, and advise them of the institution's legal position on matters that may arise.
4. Keep outside organizers off institution premises.
5. Tell employees of the disadvantages of belonging to a union, such as: strikes (for nongovernment employees) and picket-line duty; dues, fines, and assessments; rule by a single person or small group; and, possible domination of a local by its national governing union.
6. Remind employees of the benefits they enjoy without a union, and tell them how their wages and benefits compare with those at other prisons (both union and nonunion).
7. Let employees know that signing a union authorization card is not a commitment to vote for the union if there is an election.

8. Tell employees that you would rather deal directly with them than attempt to settle differences through a union or any other outsiders.

9. Give employees factual information concerning the union and its officials, even if such information is uncomplimentary.

10. Remind employees that no union can obtain more for them than the institution is able to give.

11. Correct any untrue or misleading claims or statements made by the union organizers.

12. Inform employees that the institution may legally hire a new employee to replace any employee who strikes for economic reasons.

13. Declare a fixed position against compulsory union membership contracts.

14. Insist that all organizing be conducted during non-working hours.

15. Question open, active union supporters in the workforce about their union sentiments, as long as you do so without direct or implied threats or promises (see "Shifting Ground Rules").

16. State that you do not like to deal with unions.

## What the Supervisor Cannot Do When a Union Beckons

1. Ask employees about their union sentiments in a manner that includes or implies threats, promises, or intimidation in any form. Employees may volunteer any such information and you may listen, but you may ask only with caution (see "Shifting Ground Rules").

2. Attend union meetings or participate in any undercover activities to find out who is or is not participating in union activities.

3. Attempt to prevent internal organizers from soliciting memberships during nonworking time.

4. Grant pay raises or make special concessions or promises to keep the union out.

5. Discriminate against pro-union employees in granting pay increases, apportioning overtime, making work assignments, promotions, layoffs, or demotions, or in the application of disciplinary action.

6. Intimidate, threaten, or punish employees who engage in union activity.

7. Suggest in any way that unionization will force the institution to close up, move, lay off employees, or reduce benefits.

8. Deviate from known institution policies for the primary purpose of eliminating a pro-union employee.

9. Provide financial support or other assistance to employees who oppose the union, or be a party to a petition or such action encouraging employees to organize to reject the union.

10. Visit employees at home to urge them to oppose the union.

11. Question prospective employees about past union affiliation.

12. Make statements to the effect that the institution "will not deal with a union."

13. Use a third party to threaten, coerce, or attempt to influence employees in exercising their right to vote concerning union representation.

14. Question employees on whether they have or have not signed a union authorization card.

15. Use the word "never" in any statements or predictions about dealings with the union.

It is to your advantage to be sensitive to the limitations these requirements place on your actions and comments in your dealings with employees. Ideally, the supervisors in an institution undergoing organizing pressure should receive formal training in these guidelines from a labor attorney or a labor relations expert.

It is also to your advantage—at all times, but especially during a union organizing campaign—to know your employees as individuals, and know them well. People cannot be stereotyped and there are few reliable generalizations concerning employees's receptiveness to a union. However, it is nevertheless possible for you to make some reasonable judgments as to how certain employees might react under organizing pressure.

**Often the staff member sympathetic to the union's cause may:**

• Feel unfairly treated by the organization and believe that reasonable work opportunities have been denied

• Feel that the organization has been unsympathetic regarding personal problems and pressures

- Express a lack of confidence in supervision or administration and be unwilling to talk openly with members of management
- Feel unequally treated in terms of pay and other economic benefits
- Take no apparent pride in affiliation with the institution
- Exhibit career-path problems, having either changed jobs frequently or reached the top in pay and classification while still having a significant number of working years remaining
- Be a source of complaints or grievances more often than other employees
- Exhibit a poor overall attitude

As a supervisor it is extremely important for you to know your employees's attitudes toward the institution and to develop a sense for how well you are communicating. Ultimately, a labor union has little to offer employees if they already feel the organization is responding to their needs.


## SHIFTING GROUND RULES

The above lists of what the supervisor can and cannot do in the presence of union organizing are based on interpretations of the National Labor Relations Act by the NLRB. Many of these interpretations are clear cut and have stood the test of time regardless of the composition of the NLRB. Some, however, are not clear cut and are likely to change as the board's composition changes. The matter of management's questioning of employees about union sentiments and activities is the best illustration of this possibility.

From 1980 it was relatively accurate to cite the so-called "TIPS Rule" in summarizing the most important elements of what a member of management could not do during union organizing: A manager could not Threaten, Interrogate, Promise, or Spy. (You may have encountered "TIPS" as "SPIT" or "PITS," depending on the arrangement of the four prohibitions.)

In the middle 1980s the NLRB loosened its interpretation of interrogation to suggest that it is lawful for an employer to question union supporters about their union sentiments as long as the questioning carries with it no threats or promises and in no way interferes with or restrains the employees in the exercise of their rights under the National Labor Relations Act.

The present posture on interrogation is hardly new; it had been an applied principle of labor relations for 30 years until 1980. In 1980, however, when the NLRB was dominated by one particular political party, the stricter interpretation of the interrogation prohibitions of the law was imposed. This stricter interpretation was reversed in 1984, when the NLRB composition changed again. However, even the principle as currently applied does not mean that most questioning of employees about union involvement is necessarily "safe." It essentially means that an unfair labor practice charge concerning interrogation will not automatically go against management but will likely be subjected to careful examination to determine whether any aspect of the questioning may have been coercive. The "TIPS Rule" remains valid in that interrogation still carries with it a fair amount of risk.

The lesson here is that the Do's and Don'ts found here are not cast in concrete; the ground rules for this type of activity change over time. Should you find yourself in the midst of a union organizing drive, pay strict attention to guidance provided by your agency's or organization's legal counsel and the administrator who is coordinating management's response.

## THE BARGAINING ELECTION

As it continues its activity, working through both outside and inside organizers, the union will try to secure enough employee interest to allow it to petition the NLRB for a bargaining election. The indications of such support generally will take the form of simple cards that employees sign to indicate interest in having an election. Employees should be aware that signing a card is not an automatic "yes" vote for union representation, but rather simply an expression of interest in having an election. When sufficient signatures are gathered (usually half or more of the number of employees in the unit that the union is seeking to represent), the union will petition the NLRB. After what is usually a cursory investigation, the Board will sanction an election and a date for voting will be set.

Election is by secret ballot, and all employees who work in the unit the union is seeking to represent are eligible to vote. If the union receives a simple majority of the vote, it will be certified by the Board as the legal bargaining agent for all persons who work in the unit. Although compulsory union membership is not required by law, this usually means that all persons working in the unit must eventually join the union. If the union fails to achieve a simple majority and any legal challenges leveled against the agency do not upset the results of the election, the union will withdraw. If the vote was close, a renewed drive may occur in relatively short order; a longer period may pass before another attempt if the results were clearly one-sided.

Keep in mind, however, that some elections are little more than formalities—they were lost long before the organizers ever arrived. If the relationship between employees and management is poor, then movement in the direction of a union could be difficult to reverse. This may, however, be accomplished through hard work and a great deal of open and honest communication. Even if a single unit of employees is lost to a union (for instance, a union representing correctional officers), new steps aimed at creating positive relationships can still pay off. A new atmosphere of improved communications can make contract bargaining easier, smooth out day-to-day labor relations matters, and help keep other bargaining units out of the institution.

## If the Union Wins

Shortly after the union is certified as a recognized bargaining unit, an initial contract will be negotiated. This gives supervisors a whole new set of rules and regulations to live with. Negotiations of this type are a very specialized activity, and ordinarily a line or mid-level manager would receive special training before becoming involved in them.

However, both private prison managers learning to work within a unionized environment or public prison managers dealing with a well-established union should know their union contracts inside out. Know what it says, know what it does not say, and know why it says what it says. More importantly, comply with it faithfully. Some contracts seem top-heavy with numerous details and exacting requirements. But that often makes some parts of your job easier, because the contract provides hard and fast rules for situations that were previously subject to interpretation and judgment.

No doubt management will have a formal labor-management committee or other structure to work through with the union on contractual and interim issues. In many institutions, monthly meetings between local union officials and designated management staff are used as a forum for working out problems and concerns as they develop. The union will probably have some input or comment opportunity for key recurring events, like formulation of quarterly rosters or other assignment-related matters. But those meetings do not mean that individual managers are relieved from their responsibility to communicate with their staff, or to work at individual department levels with union officials on matters of mutual concern. Above all, take the advice of Robert Townsend in the opening quotation: Be open and honest in your dealings with the union.

The presence of a union does not mean you can back off in your communications with employees and simply wave the contract at them. In fact, that probably is the worst thing a manager could do. Complete two-way communication remains essential in establishing and maintaining your relationships with all your employees, whether you do or do not have a union. After all, your employees work for the institution, not for the union. Generally the union will be the employees' voice only if the employees feel they are not recognized as individuals and are not being heard by management.

---

### CASE 26–1: THE ORGANIZER

You are the powerhouse supervisor in a prison presently under union organizing pressure. The power and steam plant, supporting shops, and supply areas you supervise are outside the secure perimeter of the prison.

The union's drive has reached the stage of signature cards. You are passing through the powerhouse's machine shop when you observe an individual who you believe is a union organizer backing one of the millwrights into a corner and waving what appears to be a union authorization card. The millwright looks worried and in considerable distress and also appears to be physically trapped in the corner by the other party. You cannot hear what the person with the card is saying, but you believe you recognize the kind of card this person is waving and you can tell this person is speaking quite forcefully.

**Describe what you would do under the following two sets of circumstances:**

1. You recognize the probable organizer as an employee of the prison but belonging to a department other than your own.
2. You are reasonably certain the probable organizer is not an employee of the prison.

---

## CASE 26–2: THE CONFRONTATION

You are unit manager of a fairly large private drug treatment facility for low-security offenders; the program has been operating under-staffed for a number of months. Times have been hectic, so you have been pitching in yourself much more than used to be necessary. On days when you have been short-staffed with floor officers you have taken to providing lunch reliefs personally. This practice has caused you to change your own lunchtime to the time when the staff lounge/dining area is most crowded.

Today you have just gotten your lunch and are about to take a seat when you are approached and very nearly circled by three of your staff members. One of them says to you, "We've been meaning to talk with you, but we're all so much on the run that we haven't gotten to you. Things have got to change around here. We can't keep going the way we're going. We're thinking of asking a union to come in, and we want to talk with you about it. Now."

There you stand in the middle of the lounge, tray in both hands, feel-ing surrounded. How do you believe you would handle this incident?

# Annotated Bibliography

**Addeo, E.G., and R.E. Burger.** *Egospeak.* Radnor, Pa.: Chilton Book Company, 1973.

The main point of *Egospeak: Why No One Listens to You* is: We don't listen effectively because we're too busy talking—either actively speaking or thinking of what to say next. Talking and listening, it is suggested, cannot happen at the same time. Of special interest to managers are the chapters concerning "JobSpeak" and "BusinessSpeak."

**American Correctional Association.** *Correctional Officer Resource Guide.* Laurel, Md., 1989.

This publication provides a broad range of information on practical issues faced by the correctional manager, not only in the security department of a prison, but in all departments. It begins with an overview of the criminal justice system and proceeds to cover all typical areas of institution operations, many of which are part of the day-to-day concerns of managers in other prison departments.

**American Correctional Association.** *Guidelines for the Development of Policies and Procedures.* Laurel, Md., 1991.

This book provides an inside view of the kinds of policies and procedures that a correctional manager must deal with on a daily basis. It keys model prison policies—covering virtually all institutional operations and departments—to professional standards promulgated by the American Correctional Association and thus provides the reader with a clear picture of the basic operational factors that a manager must incorporate into the administration of a prison department.

**Banta, W.F.** *AIDS in the Workplace.* Lexington, Mass.: Lexington Books, 1993.

AIDS is a topic of considerable concern in the correctional workplace, and not just in relation to inmates. Banta provides a very complete discussion of the supervisory implications of HIV. This book is an excellent starting point for anyone who wishes to learn more about the multifaceted impact that this disease is having in the U.S. workplace.

**Barnes, R.M.** *Motion and Time Study.* 7th ed. New York: John Wiley & Sons, Inc., 1980.

This book is probably the definitive work on the analysis of work motions and the establishment of time or performance standards. It is easily the most comprehensive volume available on the tools and techniques of methods analysis. Although the book is clearly intended as a text for industrial engineers or management engineers, a number of its sections, such as those on the general problem-solving process and human engineering, are useful to anyone interested in improving work methods. This volume clearly details all the known and proven tools applied in methods improvement.

**Berne, E.** *Games People Play.* New York: Grove Press, 1964.

Much of Berne's work presented in *Games People Play* formed the basis of the later work by Thomas Harris, *I'm O.K.—You're O.K.* essentially making Berne, a psychiatrist, one of the founders of transactional analysis. *Games People Play* is an interesting and important book in the study of the psychology of human relationships. It is not the easiest book to read, and the reading can be risky, since we are likely to recognize ourselves in the deadly serious little "games" we play with each other almost every day of our lives.

**Berne, E.** *The Structure and Dynamics of Organizations and Groups.* New York: Grove Press, 1963.

This book is about groups—from small informal groups to large formal organizations—and what can go wrong with them. It is not a handy leadership manual but rather a scientific work, and it is moderately difficult to read and absorb. There is much to be learned from this book concerning the psychology of the work group, but the approach and presentation are primarily academic.

**Block, P.** *The Empowered Manager: Positive Political Skills at Work.* San Francisco, Calif: Jossey-Bass, Inc., 1990.

While this book is something of an inspirational, rather than objective, work, Block provides some interesting views on the entrepreneurial and visionary aspects of management and leadership. For the manager caught in a bureaucracy or a bureaucratic mindset, Block's development of the issues of personal responsibility and initiative is important.

**Cribben, J.J.** *Leadership: Strategies for Organizational Effectiveness.* New York: AMACOM, A division of the American Management Association, 1981.

This is a clear and readable treatment of leadership that takes a fairly down-to-earth look at the essentials of leadership from the individual manager's point of view. Especially helpful are chapters concerned with organizational approaches to motivation and leadership values.

**Davis, B.L., et al.** *Successful Manager's Handbook.* Minneapolis, Minn.: Personnel Decisions, Inc., 1989.

A well-organized general work on a number of issues related to management development, this book contains a great deal of information on honing administrative skills, organizing, developing leadership skills, managing conflict, and other important management tasks.

**United States Department of the Interior.** *Gobbledy Gook Has Gotta Go.* Washington, DC: Government Printing Office, 1966.

A small (112 pages) but extremely interesting book that uses actual examples of some of the worst Government writing you will ever see to illustrate how official prose can be improved. This book is fun reading on its own—just to see the many ways our language can be butchered in the course of a government agency's operation—but it also contains many useful ideas on improving writing skills in general.

**DiIulio, J. Jr.** *Courts, Corrections, and the Constitution.* New York: Oxford University Press, Inc., 1990.

Dealing with legal issues is a reality for today's correctional manager. This excellent work summarizes the impact the courts have had on corrections in recent decades. It provides an insightful picture of how court interventions have actually worked out in several major correctional systems, both for good and bad.

_____. *Governing Prisons.* New York: The Free Press, 1987.

This book highlights some of the broader issues of managing prisons, through a comparative study of correctional management in three prison systems. DiIulio uses the categories of order, amenity, and service as bases for evaluating the quality of prison life (and therefore governance), and also delves into the issues of internal controls and bureaucracies that typify public prisons in the United States.

_____. *No Escape: The Future of American Corrections.* New York: Basic Books, Inc., 1991.

In this book, DiIulio combines scholarly information, on-site observation in numerous prisons, and a thoughtful practicality to produce an excellent picture of where our nation may be heading in the field of corrections. This work continues to emphasize the theme that DiIulio has developed in many of his writings—that the quality of management has a direct effect on the quality of imprisonment. This is must reading for correctional managers concerned with how their chosen careers are shaped and will continue to be affected by a variety of forces.

**DiIulio, J. Jr., et al.** *Improving Government Performance.* Washington, DC: Brookings Institution, 1993.

This book charts a course of thought parallel to that of the National Performance Review undertaken in the early 1990s by the federal government. It promotes the view that evolutionary, rather than revolutionary, change is a more effective way to streamline the bureaucracy and manage more efficiently. Geared more toward a macro view of management, and directed toward the federal level of government, it still makes for informative reading by the individual manager seeking to work effectively within the larger organization.

**Drucker, P.F.** *The Practice of Management.* New York: Harper & Row, 1954.

Along with Drucker's *Managing for Results* (Harper and Row, 1964), *The Practice of Management* is a highlight of Drucker's work. This is recommended reading for any supervisor who truly enjoys management and aspires to rise higher in the organization. One chapter of particular value is "Management by Objectives and Self-Control." (This portion of the book alone gave us a whole "new" approach to management—management by objectives.)

**Ewing, D.W.** *Writing for Results in Business, Government, the Sciences and the Professions.* 2nd ed. New York: John Wiley & Sons, Inc., 1979.

This is an excellent guidebook for persons who do the bulk of their writing in the institutional setting. The "situational approach" to writing—first examining the situation to determine what the writer wants to accomplish, with what readers, and under what circumstances—is promoted. It suggests strongly that effective writing means analyzing and planning as well as doing, and it is especially helpful in "targeting" written communications according to audience and purpose and in dealing with the often complex terminology of government, the sciences, and the professions.

**Fast, J.** *Body Language.* New York: M. Evans and Company, 1970.

This interesting and entertaining book deals with kinesics, the study of nonverbal human communication, or "body language," which can include any reflexive or nonreflexive movement of all or a part of the body used by a person to communicate an emotional message. The implications for interpersonal communication are significant; for instance, the book cites studies that reveal the extent to which body language can actually contradict verbal communications. *Body Language* will provide you with some interesting and potentially helpful insights into the actions that surround or accompany a person's words.

**Fournies, F.F.** *Coaching for Improved Work Performance.* Blue Ridge Summit, Pa.: Liberty House, 1978.

This book focuses on analytical and practical techniques for managers who want to improve their ability to motivate employees. It is filled with many example and case studies, as well as problem-solving techniques. While somewhat oriented toward a sales or marketing environment, many of its suggested approaches are quite applicable to the face-to-face interactions that characterize the correctional setting.

**Gold, M.E.** *An Introduction to the Law of Employment Discrimination.* Ithaca, NY: ILR Press, 1993.

A small, well organized book that covers key areas of employment discrimination law in a succinct, useful manner. A good "pocket guide" to the whys and wherefores of a complex field.

**Gordon, T.** *Leader Effectiveness Training (L.E.T.).* New York: Wyden Books, 1977.

If you seriously delve into only two or three books described in this bibliography, *Leader Effectiveness Training* should be one of your choices. Written in a clear, easily readable style, it takes a commonsense, humanistic approach to the task of getting things done through people. This book stresses cultivation and maintenance of open and honest interpersonal relationships. The chapter titles speak for themselves: "Doing it Yourself—Or with the Group's Help," "Making Everyday Use of Your Listening Skills," and "The No-Lose Method: Turning Conflict Into Cooperation."

**Harris, T.A.** *I'm O.K—You're O.K.* New York: Harper & Row, 1967.

This book is most appropriately read for improved understanding of human behavior—your own as well as others—and for deeper insight into the problems of interpersonal communication. Although much of the book consists of the definitive presentation of the field we call transactional analysis (TA), it can help you become more attuned to "where someone is coming from" in interpersonal dealings.

**Heckmann, I.L., Jr., and S.G. Huneryager, eds.** *Human Relations in Management.* Cincinnati, Ohio: South-Western Publishing Co., 1960.

Intended as a college text, this book is largely a collection of readings, questions, and bibliographies. Although moderately difficult to read in places, it is a gold mine of information for managers at all levels. Included, for instance, are A.H. Maslow's "A Theory of Human Motivation," Douglas McGregor's "The Human Side of Enterprise," and Gordon Allport's "The Psychology of Participation."

**Henderson, J., and W.H. Rauch.** *Guidelines for the Development of a Security Program.* Laurel, Md.: American Correctional Association, 1987.

A key resource work for the correctional manager, this book outlines the core functions around which every prison operates. Every section will not apply to every manager of a noncustodial department, but taken as a whole, the body of information contained in this publication would be essential to any manager who aspired to head an institution some day.

**Hersey, P.** *The Situational Leader.* New York: Warner Books, Inc., 1984.

This is a short, highly readable book based on a simple model that has been used to train managers at more than five hundred corporations. Using clear, interesting examples, this book reminds that it is not enough to simply describe your leadership style or communicate your intentions. Rather, a "situational leader" assesses the performance of others and takes responsibility for making things happen.

**Hersey, P., and K.H. Blanchard.** *Management of Organizational Behavior: Utilizing Human Resources.* Englewood Cliffs, NJ: Prentice-Hall, 1977.

This wide-ranging book focuses on linking management theory with practice and relies on a number of behavioral science frameworks. Drawing on examples from many areas of organizational life, it is well written, amply annotated, and provides a great deal of useful information for new and current managers.

**Jay, A.** *Management and Machiavelli.* New York: Holt, Rinehart & Winston, 1967.

Subtitled *An Inquiry into the Politics of Corporate Life,* this book is decidedly slanted toward the overall management of entire organizations. It has its basis in Jay's interpretation of the psychology and conduct of modern corporations paralleling the principles of management employed in the medieval political state. If you have an interest in the rights and wrongs of corporate management, you will get something from *Management and Machiavelli* that applies to all types of organizations, especially those of the bureaucratic and institutional form that we may work for (large hospitals, various associations, and with state and federal agencies).

**Kepner-Tregoe.** *Problem Analysis and Decision Making.* Princeton, NJ: Princeton Research Press, 1973.

This is a tersely written little book used in connection with management seminars conducted by Kepner-Tregoe, Inc. It is oriented toward a very rational, no-nonsense approach to the problem-solving and decision-making side of management.

**Likert, R.** *New Patterns of Management.* New York: McGraw-Hill Publishing Co, 1961.

This is a most valuable work in promoting understanding of the "systems of management" that exist in our work organizations. The basic organizational differences attributable to institutions are not the differences of "prison" versus "industry" but rather the differences between organizations doing repetitive work and those doing varied work. *New Patterns of Management* sheds considerable light on the matter of understanding the varying styles of supervision related to the different kinds of work the organization does.

**Maynard, H.B.,** Editor-in-chief. *Industrial Engineering Handbook.* 3rd ed. New York: McGraw-Hill Publishing Co., 1971.

This weighty volume, consisting of more than 1,500 pages containing the written contributions of more than 100 authors, is primarily a reference book for practicing industrial engineers. However, it is also especially useful to supervisors and managers whose work is affected by that of industrial or management engineers or who become actively involved in methods improvement projects. It makes an especially handy reference for a methods improvement project team involved in the analysis of manual tasks.

**McConnell, C.R.** *The Health Care Manager's Guide to Performance Appraisal.* Gaithersburg, Md.: Aspen Publishers, Inc., 1993.

This book is suggested as an adjunct to Chapter 12, "Performance Appraisal: The Supervisor's Darkest Hour," for those who wish to further pursue the topic of performance appraisal. Appraisal is briefly examined in philosophy and principle. Guidance is provided for handling the individual elements of appraisal and for designing and developing an appraisal system. Appraisal's relationship to job descriptions and other source documents is established, and basic variations in appraisal practices are examined.

**McGuigan, P.B., and J.S. Pascale, eds.** *Crime and Punishment in America.* Washington, DC: The Institute for Government and Politics, 1986.

This collection of contributed works covers the entire spectrum of criminal justice, from street enforcement to imprisonment. It provides the reader with a full-fledged primer that encompasses family and juvenile crime issues as well as judicial and correctional management concerns, such as alternatives to incarceration.

**Nierenberg, G., and H. Calero.** *Meta-Talk.* New York: Simon and Schuster, Inc., 1973.

If you are seriously interested in learning more about oral communication, this is a book to be re-read and studied. Subtitled *Guide to Hidden Meanings in Conversations,* the book deals with the kinds of things we say and why we probably say them—and not with the exact words we happen to be using but rather with the messages and meanings "between the words." One reading of Meta-Talk—or two or three readings, for that matter—will not make you an expert on hidden meanings. However, the book should provide insights that cannot help but enhance your ability to understand others better. The book's message is that no "meaning" is ever absolute, and that true meaning lies in the combination of speaker, listener, and circumstances.

**Odiorne, G.S.** *How Managers Make Things Happen.* Englewood Cliffs, NJ: Prentice Hall, 1982.

An excellent, easily readable rendering of the basics of management in modern work organizations, this work covers topics such as how to change poor work habits into good ones, how to develop a leadership approach that is solid, yet flexible when necessary, how to know when to criticize and when to praise, and how to combat carelessness and indifference. Odiorne's chapter on decision-making is especially well done.

**Osborn, A.F.** *Applied Imagination: Principles and Procedures of Creative Thinking.* New York: Charles Scribner's Sons, 1953.

This is one of the best books you could delve into for help in "getting your mind in gear." It may well stand yet as the definitive work on creativity; certainly it is among the most entertaining and readable works on the subject. Much of what the book contains may strike you as old, familiar stuff, but it is presented appealingly and most of it still holds true today.

**Parkinson, C.N.** *Parkinson's Law.* Boston, Mass.: Houghton Mifflin Co., 1957.

This book is essentially the forerunner of the many volumes that take a humor-in-the-bitter-truth approach to the problems of management and administration. Parkinson's elaborate and pompous style is exactly suited to the sometimes outlandish ideas he presents. Although you may be inclined to believe that the author rarely entertained a serious thought—for instance, he concedes that serious books on public or business administration have their place "provided only that these works are classified as fiction"—you may also find that a single reading provides a great deal of insight into organizational behavior. The best chapter is the first chapter, "Parkinson's Law or the Rising Pyramid." The "law" itself is stated in the book's opening sentence: Work expands so as to fill the time available for its completion.

**Peter, L.J., and R. Hull.** *The Peter Principle.* New York: William Morrow and Company, 1969.

This highly successful book presents some deadly serious messages in a wholly entertaining manner. The "Principle" states simply: In a hierarchy every employee tends to rise to his level of incompetence. The author is suggesting that we rise just so high, and no higher, in any organization, and that the level at which we stop is just a bit over our heads. It follows, Peter suggests, that eventually every position tends to be occupied by someone who is incompetent to carry out its duties, and that the real work is accomplished by people who are still on the way up to their levels of incompetence.

**Peter, L.J.** *The Peter Prescription.* New York: William Morrow and Company, 1972.

Whereas *The Peter Principle* is subtitled *Why Things Always Go Wrong,* this natural sequel is subtitled *How To Make Things Go Right.* As sequels often go, *The Peter Prescription* has neither the freshness of humor nor the fullness of insight that the first book has. Yet this is a valuable book since it is focused much more clearly on what the individual can do in the way of self-improvement. Especially recommended for reading and reflection is Part Two: Protect Your Competence.

**Peters, T., and Waterman, R.H., Jr.** *In Search of Excellence.* New York: Harper & Row, 1982.

In some ways, this book is viewed as a classic discussion of excellence in organizations. It is solid, useful reading for any manager, and contains excellent examples of the how and why of organizational excellence.

**Ring, C.R.** *Contracting for the Operation of Private Prisons: Pros and Cons.* College Park, Md.: The American Correctional Association, 1987.

Ring's small, easy-to-read analysis of the "pros and cons" of private corrections is must reading for corrections professionals as privatization continues to grow. Although private prisons are much more prevalent now than when this book was written and some material is dated, this still is a well-written exposition of the central issues involved.

**Schichor, David.** *Punishment for Profit: Private Prisons / Public Concerns.* Thousand Oaks, Calif: SAGE Publications, 1995.

Schichor makes no attempt to conceal his anti-privatization bias, but still presents a very complete picture of the issues surrounding privatization in corrections (and other social services as well). This book, read in connection with Charles Ring's work cited above, provides a great deal of thought-provoking information on this issue, which is of increasing importance in the field of corrections.

**Shave, G.A.** *Nuts, Bolts, and Gut-Level Management.* West Nyack, NY: Parker Publishing Company, 1974.

This book evolved from a series of interviews with a man described as "an extremely successful manager." Although the focus is primarily on the problems and responsibilities of middle and upper management in the manufacturing industry, there is plenty of commonsense advice applicable to managers at all levels in all lines of work. Supervisors who feel that there do not seem to be enough hours in the day would do well to read Chapter 4: "How To Vastly Increase Your Discretionary Time."

**Sherman, M., and G. Hawkins.** *Imprisonment in America.* Chicago, Ill.: The University of Chicago Press, 1981.

This book is policy oriented and within that context provides an overview of the evolution of correctional policies and practices in the United States. It concentrates on the issues of who should be locked up, for how long, and under what conditions, and concludes with a proposal for an integrated approach to imprisonment in the U.S.

**Stockard, J.G.** *Rethinking People Management.* New York: AMACOM, a Division of American Management Association, 1980.

This book generally lives up to its claim of being "constructively critical of personnel administration." In addition to providing the supervisor with insight into what an appropriately focused personnel function should be doing, it also suggests how the supervisor can act to enhance constructive responses from personnel.

**Strunk, W., and E.B. White.** *The Elements of Style.* 2nd ed. New York: Macmillan Publishing Co., Inc., 1972.

According to E.B. White, who in 1957 was commissioned to revise Strunk's original 1919 publication for the college market and the general trade, *The Elements of Style* was Strunk's attempt to "cut the vast tangle of English rhetoric down to size and write its rules and principles on the head of a pin." The attempt was successful; the book is a tight summation of the case for cleanliness, accuracy, and brevity in the use of written language. Should you limit yourself to only a single book about writing, *The Elements of Style* should be your choice.

**Terry, G.R.** *Supervisory Management.* Homewood, Ill.: Richard D. Irwin, 1974.

This book takes the view that behavioral objectives of the personnel involved are inseparable from getting the work out, so the goal of supervision is not a satisfactory work group but also a satisfied work group. The book's focus is primarily the first-line supervisor, making it one of the few works available to the lower levels of management. *Supervisory Management* touches upon all aspects of the supervisor's job, although some are necessarily treated once-over-lightly. Questions and cases accompany each of its 18 chapters, making it appropriate as a course text.

**Timm, P.R.** *Managerial Communication.* Englewood Cliffs, NJ: Prentice Hall, 1980.

This book is a refreshing exception to an old unwritten rule; it is a college textbook that reads as clearly and easily as a work of popular nonfiction. Although the topic of almost every chapter could well be a book or educational program in its own right, coverage of each aspect of organizational communication is more than adequate for the working supervisor. Chapters of special value to working managers at all levels include "Speaking Before Groups" and "Letters and Memos."

**Toffler, A.** *Future Shock.* New York: Random House, Inc., 1970.

An immensely popular book, *Future Shock* is most valuable in creating a full appreciation of the rate at which all aspects of life and living are changing around us. Also of note are the author's observations concerning the ways people cope—or fail to cope—with accelerating change. Anyone seeking insight into the impact of change and the origins of resistance to change would do well to examine the lengthy table of contents and read a few selected sections.

**Townsend, R.** *Up the Organization.* New York: Alfred A. Knopf, Inc., 1970.

*Up the Organization* is an entertaining book. It is arranged in alphabetical order by topic, and since no topic requires more than a few minutes reading time, it is a book that can be read in bits and pieces with no loss of impact. Townsend's approach is energetic and people centered; his is a management style that depends heavily on a basic belief in the willingness of most people to produce, given the proper environment. Although aimed largely at top management, there is much in the book's pages for first-line supervisors. Sections on "Delegation of Authority" and "People" are recommended. Read this book with some caution, however; much of its gutsy leadership style is personality based, and not everyone is a Robert Townsend. Although based largely in humanity and commonsense, in practical terms the Townsend style will reform an organization only when applied from the top down.

**Ward, D.A., and K.F. Schoen.** *Confinement in Maximum Custody.* Lexington, Mass.: Lexington Books, D.C. Heath and Company, 1981.

This book is a collection of presentations made at a conference held at the Spring Hill Center in Wayzata, Minnesota, in June 1978. While rather narrowly focused on the issues of maximum security confinement, it provides the reader with an excellent feel for the complexity of legal, psychological, and human issues that challenge managers in this very specific kind of correctional environment.

**Weiss, D.H.** *Fair, Square, and Legal.* New York: AMACOM, a division of American Management Association, 1991.

An excellent summary of applicable legal issues that managers must take into account to assure that they are engaged in lawful hiring, day-to-day supervision, and discharge practices. This work is particularly well organized and easy to read.

**Weiss, W.H.** *Supervisor's Standard Reference Handbook.* Englewood Cliffs, NJ: Prentice Hall, 1980.

This is an excellent book for first-line supervisors in any field. Its presentation is straightforward and very nearly person-to-person conversation. Despite its title it can be used effectively as a topic text as well as an occasional reference. Its emphasis is decidedly on dealing with day-to-day problems, and as such it does not delve deeply into longer-term processes such as planning.

**Zinsser, W.** *On Writing Well: An Informal Guide to Writing Nonfiction.* 2nd ed. New York: Harper & Row, 1980.

Lively and readable in its own right, this is also a helpful reference for people who are seriously interested in learning how to improve their writing in general. It is not a textbook, and certainly not an English grammar lesson. This book will give you valuable overall guidelines for writing for simplicity and clarity in today's world. The book's main theme is that there is no subject that cannot be made accessible if the writer writes with humanity and cares enough to write well.

# List of Quotations

**Chapter 1**    "The end product . . ."
*Source:* Rensis Likert, *New Patterns of Management* (New York: McGraw-Hill, 1961).

"So much of what we call management . . ."
*Source:* Insert from Speechwriter's Newsletter. (Lawrence Ragan Communications, Inc., Chicago, Ill., Undated).

**Chapter 2**    "Treat people as adults . . ."
*Source:* Insert from Speechwriter's Newsletter. (Lawrence Ragan Communications, Inc., Chicago, Ill., Undated).

**Chapter 3**    "As we are born . . ."
*Source:* Oliver Goldsmith

"I was an assistant coach . . ."
*Source:* Insert from Speechwriter's Newsletter. (Lawrence Ragan Communications, Inc., Chicago, Ill., Undated).

"It often happens . . ."
*Source:* Insert from Speechwriter's Newsletter. (Lawrence Ragan Communications, Inc., Chicago, Ill., Undated).

**Chapter 4**    "You can map out a fight plan. . . "
*Source:* Insert from Speechwriter's Newsletter. (Lawrence Ragan Communications, Inc., Chicago, Ill., October 5, 1990).

**Chapter 5**   "Surround yourself with . . ."
*Source:* Insert from Speechwriter's Newsletter. (Lawrence Ragan Communications, Inc., Chicago, Ill., February 8, 1991).

"The same day I have a disappointment . . ."
*Source:* Insert from Speechwriter's Newsletter. (Lawrence Ragan Communications, Inc., Chicago, Ill., Undated).

"The better a man is . . ."
*Source:* Insert from Speechwriter's Newsletter. (Lawrence Ragan Communications, Inc., Chicago, Ill., March 1, 1991).

**Chapter 6**   "Time is fixed income . . ."
*Source:* Jacob M. Braude, Lifetime Speakers' Encyclopedia (Prentice Hall, Inc., Englewood Cliffs, N.J., 1962, vol. 2, 815).

"Whether these are the best of times . . ."
*Source:* Insert from Speechwriter's Newsletter. (Lawrence Ragan Communications, Inc., Chicago, Ill., Undated).

**Chapter 7**   "Technical training is important but . . ."
*Source:* Jacob M. Braude, Lifetime Speakers' Encyclopedia (Prentice Hall, Inc., Englewood Cliffs, N.J., 1962, vol. 1, 393).

**Chapter 8**   "The best man for the job is often a woman."
*Source:* Anonymous

**Chapter 9**   "I know that you believe you understand . . ."
*Source:* Anonymous

"I wish I had done a better job of communicating . . ."
*Source:* Insert from Speechwriter's Newsletter. (Lawrence Ragan Communications, Inc., Chicago, Ill., November 2, 1990).

**Chapter 10**   "Real leaders are ordinary people . . ."
*Source:* Jacob M. Braude, Lifetime Speakers' Encyclopedia (Prentice Hall, Inc., Englewood Cliffs, N.J., 1962, vol. 1, 423).

"Be willing to make decisions. . . ."
*Source:* Insert from Speechwriter's Newsletter. (Lawrence Ragan Communications, Inc., Chicago, Ill., Undated).

"You can lead an organization . . ."
*Source:* Insert from Speechwriter's Newsletter. (Lawrence Ragan Communications, Inc., Chicago, Ill., August 10, 1990).

**Chapter 11**    "The only way to motivate an employee . . ."
*Source:* Frederick R. Herzberg, "Does Money Really Motivate?" Copyright © 1970 by Frederick R. Herzberg, Case Western University.

**Chapter 12**    "The privilege of encouragement . . ."
*Source:* Anonymous

**Chapter 13**    "Indifference is probably the severest criticism . . ."
*Source:* Jacob M. Braude, Lifetime Speakers' Encyclopedia (Prentice Hall, Inc., Englewood Cliffs, N.J., 1962, vol. 1, 152).

"I never gave them hell. I just . . ."
*Source:* Insert from Speechwriter's Newsletter. (Lawrence Ragan Communications, Inc., Chicago, Ill., July 1, 1990).

"If criticism had any real power . . ."
*Source:* Insert from Speechwriter's Newsletter. (Lawrence Ragan Communications, Inc., Chicago, Ill., Undated).

**Chapter 14**    "In so complex a thing . . ."
*Source:* George Eliot

"All generalizations are dangerous . . ."
*Source:* Insert from Speechwriter's Newsletter. (Lawrence Ragan Communications, Inc., Chicago, Ill., Undated).

**Chapter 15**    "I use not only all the brains I have . . ."
*Source:* Anonymous

**Chapter 16**    "As a rule . . . the person who . . ."
*Source:* Insert from Speechwriter's Newsletter.

(Lawrence Ragan Communications, Inc., Chicago, Ill., Undated).

"All decisions should be made . . ."
*Source:* Robert Townsend, *Up the Organization,* (New York: Fawcett World Library, 1970), 27.

"If I had to run up in one word . . ."
*Source:* Insert from Speechwriter's Newsletter. (Lawrence Ragan Communications, Inc., Chicago, Ill., February 8, 1991).

"Information is the lifeblood . . ."
*Source:* Insert from Speechwriter's Newsletter. (Lawrence Ragan Communications, Inc., Chicago, Ill., Undated).

**Chapter 17**  "Have no fear of change as such . . ."
*Source:* Robert Moses

"Progress occurs when . . ."
*Source:* Insert from Speechwriter's Newsletter. (Lawrence Ragan Communications, Inc., Chicago, Ill., Undated).

"People who are part of the team . . ."
*Source:* Insert from Speechwriter's Newsletter. (Lawrence Ragan Communications, Inc., Chicago, Ill., Undated).

**Chapter 18**  "I have made this letter rather long . . ."
*Source:* Blaise Pascal

"I had heard you were a very great man . . ."
*Source:* Insert from Speechwriter's Newsletter. (Lawrence Ragan Communications, Inc., Chicago, Ill., Undated).

"This is something up with . . ."
*Source:* Winston Churchill (attributed)

**Chapter 19**  "Meetings: Where you go to learn . . ."
*Source:* Anonymous

**Chapter 20**  "A budget is a means of . . ."
*Source:* Anonymous

**Chapter 21**  "Quality never costs as much money as it saves."
*Source:* Anonymous

"We are not at our best . . ."
*Source:* John W. Gardner, "Thoughts on the Business Life." *Forbes* (January 17, 1983), 126.

**Chapter 22**  "There's a way to do it better—find it."
*Source:* Thomas A. Edison

**Chapter 23**  "The person who sees a career . . ."
*Source:* Insert from Speechwriter's Newsletter. (Lawrence Ragan Communications, Inc., Chicago, Ill., June 1, 1990).

**Chapter 24**  "Laws should be like . . ."
*Source:* Clarence Darrow

"Ignorance of the law . . ."
*Source:* D.H. Weiss. *Fair, Square, and Legal.* (New York: AMACOM, A Division of American Management Association, 1991), xv.

**Chapter 25**  "What we got here is failure to communicate."
*Source:* Movie—"Cool Hand Luke"

**Chapter 26**  "If you don't have them . . ."
*Source:* Robert Townsend, *Up the Organization* (New York: Fawcett World Library, 1970), 77.

# Index

*Note:* Page numbers in *Italics* indicate material found in tables, figures, or exhibits.

# About the Authors

**RICHARD L. PHILLIPS**, BA, is an experienced correctional manager who has worked in juvenile and adult corrections at both the state and federal levels. His 30 years of correctional experience includes field management assignments in minimum, medium, and high security felony facilities as well as in an urban detention setting, an agency regional office, and a headquarters administrative post. He is a private correctional consultant who specializes in providing management support services to a variety of corrections-related organizations and individuals. He has served as an accreditation auditor for the American Correctional Association (ACA), chaired or been a member of several ACA committees, and is an author or contributing editor of various correctional publications for ACA and other correctional organizations. He holds a bachelor's degree in sociology from Northern Illinois University.

**CHARLES R. McCONNELL**, BS, MBA, has been an industrial engineer, management consultant and educator, and human resource executive in a variety of settings, including manufacturing, trade associations, and health care. He is the author of 8 previous books and nearly 170 articles, and is the editor of 6 collections and a quarterly professional journal. He holds a master's degree in business administration from the State University of New York at Buffalo and has served as adjunct faculty at several colleges.